MR. JUSTICE MILLER
AND THE SUPREME COURT

MR. JUSTICE MILLER

MR. JUSTICE MILLER
AND THE SUPREME COURT
1862-1890

By Charles Fairman

NEW YORK

RUSSELL & RUSSELL

PREFACE

THIS BOOK is the product of studies in judicial biography extending now over ten years. The choice of Mr. Justice Miller from among the outstanding figures in the history of the Supreme Court was dictated by rather obvious considerations. The life and times of Marshall have always attracted interest, and lately the chief justiceship of Taney has received attention. Treatment of the period following the Civil War, however, tends to become less adequate just when the matters dealt with become more involved. The forces of nationalism released by that struggle produced a variety of new constitutional issues. The Fourteenth Amendment was to be construed; the commerce clause had to be applied to an expanding system of transportation and business; corporate management and municipal issues of railroad-aid bonds raised legal issues of tremendous economic magnitude. The resulting press of litigation and the tendency to extend the scope of federal justice gave critical importance to the organization and jurisdiction of the courts of the United States. In the consideration of all these problems Justice Miller took a conspicuous part. Around his towering figure the landmarks of an epoch in the history of the Supreme Court have been grouped. The book is less a biography than a study of a distinct period in the annals of the Court.

The character of an essay such as this is governed in no small measure by the resources available to the author. The justice's opinions in the law reports must always be an important element, though it should be borne in mind that an opinion for the Court expresses a collective judgment. The study will take color from such other materials as are at hand. The novel feature of the present book is a collection of letters written by Justice Miller. They cover virtually his entire

judicial career, and present a more intimate view of the Court than anything heretofore put in print. Other collections of correspondence have been used, as well as unpublished biographical sketches and diaries, the newspapers, and the little-worked files of the older law journals.

My first acknowledgment is to Mrs. Lida M. Touzalin, Justice Miller's daughter, and to Mrs. Coker Clarkson, his granddaughter, for permission to use the Judge's letters. Without this material the book would not have been written. Mrs. Clarkson has also added greatly to my understanding of the more personal aspects of her grandfather's life.

About the Harvard Law School there cluster numerous obligations which it is a pleasure to recall. My tenure of the Brandeis Research Fellowship during two years made possible the writing of the book, while its publication has been supported by the Law School Publication Fund. To Professor Thomas Reed Powell and Professor Felix Frankfurter, as he then was, I offer my sincere thanks for constant encouragement and stimulation in the execution of the work. Mr. Powell read the entire manuscript prior to its final revision and suggested improvements in both form and substance by which I have greatly profited. To Professor Edwin Merrick Dodd and Dean James M. Landis I am also indebted for their comments upon the work. I have had the privilege of drawing upon the recollections of Professor Roscoe Pound, who knew Justice Miller personally; of Professor Samuel Williston, who was secretary to Mr. Justice Gray; and of Professor Eugene Wambaugh, for impressions of the Eighth Federal Circuit at the close of Judge Miller's career. In a number of ways I have had the friendly help of Professor Erwin N. Griswold. And finally I would record my appreciation of the unfailing helpfulness and good will of Professor Eldon R. James, Librarian of the Harvard Law School, and the members of his staff. It will perhaps be enough to say that their courtesy has proved as great as the richness of the Library itself.

In the quest for fresh material I have laid tribute upon the kindness of several gentlemen. To James C. Davis, Esq., of Des Moines, Iowa, I owe my thanks for the opportunity to consult his father's unpublished collection, "Keokuk Biographical and Historical," containing an autobiographical sketch by Miller and other relevant items. Mr. Davis appeared before Judge Miller both on the circuit and in the Supreme Court, and contributed generously in reminiscence. Thomas D. Tinsley, Esq., of Ashland, Kentucky, placed at my disposal the Journal of the Barbourville Debating Society, in which Miller's name figures most prominently. J. Spalding Flannery, Esq., of Washington, D. C., kindly gave me access to the "Recollections" of William A. Maury, sometime Assistant Attorney General, and other materials which had belonged to Maury. Now and again reference is made to the papers of Mr. Justice Bradley. For the very great privilege of using this material while preparing a life of Judge Bradley I am indebted to the late Charles Bradley, his son, and Charles B. Bradley, Esq., his grandson. John Stokes Adams, Esq., of Philadelphia, whose father was Miller's lifelong friend, gave me the benefit of his recollections. In learning something of Judge Henry C. Caldwell, Miller's associate on the circuit, I have had the assistance of Caldwell Martin, Esq., of Denver, Colorado. Mrs. Charles F. Norton, Librarian of Transylvania College, was kind enough to supply information concerning Miller's course in the medical school. Members of the staff of the Supreme Court — particularly the late marshal, Frank Key Green, and his successor, Thomas E. Waggaman, Esq. — gave me repeated proofs of their courteous consideration.

Among the libraries whose manuscripts I have been permitted to consult mention should be made of the archives division of the University of Texas, where I was accorded particular facilities for using the diary of William Pitt Ballinger, Justice Miller's brother-in-law; the Missouri Historical Society, for the use of the letters of Judge Samuel Treat; the Maine Historical Society, where the papers of Justice Clifford have been deposited; and the Manuscript Division of the

Library of Congress, where among others the papers of Chief Justice Chase, Thomas Ewing, Philip Phillips, and J. C. B. Davis were examined. The archives of the Historical Department of Iowa contain some items which proved of value.

For permission to use without citation material which I had incorporated in earlier articles I am indebted to the editors of the *Harvard Law Review*, the *Iowa Law Review*, the *Political Science Quarterly*, and the *Mississippi Valley Historical Review*. Quotations from *The Autobiography of a Pennsylvanian*, by S. W. Pennypacker, are made by permission of the John C. Winston Company, Publishers.

My wife has not merely prepared the manuscript in its various revisions, but has endured the wearisome excursions after material and the tedious copying from files which the research has involved.

C. F.

STANFORD UNIVERSITY
July 1939

CONTENTS

CONTENTS

ILLUSTRATIONS

I

THE COUNTRY DOCTOR

THE AMERICAN SYSTEM of constitutional limitations calls for a peculiar type of judicial statesmanship. It may or may not be wise to make the courts a point of final reference on questions of governmental policy; but where the system prevails the public must be more than ordinarily concerned with the judicial process. The mode of proceeding and the form in which the results of judicial action are cast are so specialized that it is difficult to discern just how far the judge is performing the function of the statesman. Generally the fiction is maintained that the court is but discovering the judgment which the Constitution itself pronounces upon the case at hand. Or resort may be had to such obscurant phrases as "the spirit of our free institutions," "fundamental conceptions lying at the basis of the social compact," or "the general principles of jurisprudence." Yet the element of deliberate choice and purpose is very considerable, as may be seen from observing the adjustments which result from the impact of a dominant personality among the justices.

Our particular concern is with the life of Samuel Freeman Miller, who in fifteen years bridged the gap which separated a country doctor in the Kentucky hills from a place on the Supreme Court at Washington. There he sat from 1862 to 1890, "beyond question," as Chief Justice Chase declared, "the dominant personality [then] upon the bench, whose mental force and individuality [were] felt by the Court more than any other." [1] In his day he enjoyed a marked preëminence in the determination of constitutional questions, his opinions being regarded as second only to those of Marshall. In later years he often recalled with pride that he had "been

---

[1] Recollection of Henry Strong, in *Annals of Iowa*, 3 ser. 1 (1894), 247.

[*3*]

the organ of the Court in that class of cases as often as any one who ever sat on that bench." [2] Today he ranks among the half-dozen most outstanding figures in that branch of our law.

There are no lengthy family annals to preface the story of Miller's life. In 1812 two brothers of Pennsylvania-German stock, Frederick and Jacob Miller, emigrated from the vicinity of Reading to Richmond, in the bluegrass region of Kentucky. There in 1815 Frederick was married to Patsy, one of the thirteen children of Samuel Freeman. The paterfamilias had come from North Carolina prior to 1782 and settled on what is locally known as Poosey Ridge, where, an old resident explained, "nobody was rich and nobody poor; there were very few slaves." At Richmond, on April 5, 1816, Samuel Freeman Miller was born, the first of their eight children. The most that can be learned of the home influence lies half hidden in a cryptic passage in a letter in which Miller was speaking of his mother:

I think you know how much I value her, how dearly I loved, and how much of the success which has attended my life I attribute to her example, her instruction, and the qualities I have inherited from her. . . . Owing to my father's habits I was at a very early age taken into her confidence as a substitute, and the care of my younger sisters and my brother were a joint affair. . . .[3]

The boy was brought up on the farm, and had his schooling at the academy in Richmond. He is said to have stood at the head of his class, and to have been particularly strong in grammar and mathematics.[4] But the school days may be

[2] Manuscript autobiographical sketch, p. 26. Miller dictated this account in June 1882, in response to a request from C. F. Davis, Esq., of Keokuk. It was preserved by the latter in volume v of his collection of manuscript sketches, "Keokuk Biographical and Historical." For access to this material I am indebted to James C. Davis, Esq., of Des Moines, Iowa.

[3] Letter of October 24, 1872. Unless otherwise indicated, Miller's letters cited herein were written to his brother-in-law, William Pitt Ballinger of Galveston, Texas. The collection was placed in my hands for use in writing this book by Mrs. Coker Clarkson of Scarborough, New York, granddaughter of Justice Miller.

[4] Interview published in the New York *World*, December 12, 1886.

passed over lightly: for better or worse, Miller's mind bore no marks of the trammels of formal education. He had no predilection for manual labor; in later life he used to say that his motto was "Never walk when you can ride, never sit when you can lie down"; that it was fortunate he was born poor, as otherwise he would never have worked. Of course this was whimsical exaggeration: certainly from his youth he was bent upon making his resources in character and intellect count for the most in achievement.

On leaving school he became a clerk in the drugstore of Dr. Leverill, a relative of his mother, and then, as he later wrote, "at the age of eighteen began the study of medicine, and after several years study which included two courses of lectures in the medical department of Transylvania University at Lexington, received the diploma of Doctor of Medicine in 1838." [5] The college records show that he matriculated in the autumn of 1835, naming Dr. H. S. Venable (a prominent physician at Richmond) as his preceptor. He did not attend the following year, but returned as a second-year student in 1837, his residence then being recorded as "Barberville." In February 1838 he submitted his "inaugural dissertation" — a manuscript of twenty-three pages on *cholera infantum* — and on March 9 was "examined and received" for the degree.[6] Transylvania, then hailed as the "focus of medical science in the West," [7] attracted some 260 medical students, half of whom came from outside Kentucky and some even from states as remote as New Hampshire and Louisiana, but the course was largely empirical and included such subjects as phrenology. Miller's mind was too critical not to be aware how limited were the attainments of medical practitioners in his day. In 1871, a quarter-century after he had abandoned the profession, he expressed the opinion that if Southern doctors

[5] Autobiographical sketch, p. 13.
[6] For this information I am indebted to Mrs. Charles F. Norton, Librarian of Transylvania College.
[7] Robert Wickliffe, Jr., *An Address Delivered on the Occasion of Laying the Corner Stone of the New Medical Hall of Transylvania University, July, 1839* (Lexington, Ky., 1839), p. 28.

had kept pace with the march of their science, "they have changed very much since I was one of their number." [8]

Between his first and second years at medical school Miller took up his residence at Barbourville, in the hills of southeastern Kentucky, on the turnpike leading down from Cumberland Gap into the bluegrass country. The town was the seat of Knox County, the center of a self-contained community which produced livestock, sugar, grain, some cotton, tobacco, and whisky.[9] To a relatively high degree the goods consumed were made in the home. In Miller's day Barbourville never had as many as two hundred inhabitants. The population of the county was about seven thousand, of whom less than a tenth were slaves.[10] In politics the county was overwhelmingly Whig.[11] Thanks to the intellectual vigor of its citizens, Barbourville was later described, somewhat expansively, as having been "the Athens of the Kentucky Highlands from the early days until the railroad penetrated that country." [12] Today the primitive folk of the surrounding mountains have become a depressed class, living in the "land of do without." [13]

Barbourville is set on the east bank of the Cumberland River at the mouth of Richland Creek, a locality well known to early travelers and near the site of the first cabin erected in Kentucky. Settlers moving west from Virginia and the Carolinas found their access barred by the parallel highlands of the Cumberland and Pine mountains. The road crossed the first range at the Cumberland Gap and then, descending, came upon the Cumberland River at a point where its course, turning north, breaks through the Pine Mountain range and opens a route into Kentucky. Down this rugged valley the turnpike wound its way past the village of Barbourville.

[8] Letter of April 9, 1871.
[9] Sixth Census (1840), pp. 278–279.
[10] Seventh Census (1850), pp. 611, 612.
[11] In the election of 1836, Knox County gave 309 votes to Harrison, ninety-five to Van Buren (*Niles Register*, LI, 212, December 3, 1836).
[12] *Green Bag*, IX (1897), 310.
[13] *New York Times*, April 25, 1937, ii, 12:5.

Thus Miller lived beside one of the great paths along which emigration flowed into the Ohio Valley. Richmond, his boyhood home, was ninety-five miles to the northwest along the same road. Once a week a rider carried the mail between the two towns.[14]

On May 27, 1837, Miller participated in the organization of the Barbourville Debating Society, and thereafter was the foremost participant in its encounters. Every Saturday, "at early candle light," a dozen or so of the young men of the town would meet at the courthouse and debate some question of current interest. When winter set in the society disbanded, but reappeared in 1838 and 1839. Here Miller discovered his ability for effective public address and developed those tastes which caused him to turn from medicine to the law. As the journal of the society[15] shows, he was an enthusiastic Whig, an advocate of a constitutional revision which would put slavery in Kentucky in the course of extinction.

Miller's chief rival in the debates was Green Adams, later a state judge and member of Congress from 1847 to 1849 and from 1859 to 1861. Another of the debaters was Joseph Eve, later a judge and member of the legislature; in 1841 he was appointed chargé d'affaires to Texas. A young lawyer named Silas Woodson was another member of the club; he was later to be elected governor of Missouri.[16] The log cabin which he and Miller shared as an office is still standing. Apparently it was from Woodson's books that Miller did his first surreptitious reading in the law. Among the boys who came to hear the speaking was William Pitt Ballinger, whose sister became Miller's wife; in 1843 he moved to Texas and, return-

[14] *Report of the Committee on Post Offices and Post Roads, June 9, 1834,* p. 141; Senate Document 422, 23 Cong., 1 Sess.

[15] This journal is still in existence, and for an opportunity to use it the author is indebted to Thomas D. Tinsley, Esq., of Ashland, Kentucky. On an occasion when the Knox County Court House was being reconditioned Mr. Tinsley found the journal lying in a pile of debris, and preserved it.

[16] On April 4, 1864, when Montana was about to be organized as a territory, Miller recommended Woodson to President Lincoln for chief justice of the Territory (Paul M. Angle, *New Letters and Papers of Lincoln,* Boston and New York: Houghton Mifflin Co., 1930, p. 347). But a different selection was made.

ing from the Mexican War, was admitted to the bar. He became one of the most respected lawyers of the Southwest, and in 1874 was appointed to the Supreme Court of Texas — an office which he promptly declined. His name was seriously considered by President Hayes in connection with the vacancy on the Supreme Bench in 1877. Other members of the Debating Society went to the state legislature. It was not a bad showing for a village in the backwoods.

In the club's order of business the roll call would be followed by a declamation and an essay. But the minutes frequently relate that there was no declaimer, and that the essayist offered an excuse which was accepted by the house. Evidently such *ex parte* performances were less relished than the joined issue of debate. Two members had previously been detailed on each side of the question. A general discussion ensued, in which guests were invited to join. A vote would then be taken on the merits of the question. The last item of business was the choice of the topic for the next debate, and the naming of participants.

For the most part the questions for debate were the current political issues:

> Is it constitutional and expedient for the United States in their federative capacity to make internal improvements?

The vote on the merits was nine in the affirmative to four for strict construction.

> Would it be politick to admit Texas as a member of this confederacy. Provided she establishes her independence?

The count showed five expansionists to eleven in the negative. Three months later the same question was reargued, resulting in a draw, five to five. Miller seems to have been vehemently opposed to annexation, probably because of its relation to slavery. In 1839 the Texas question came up again, and Miller carried off a victory of six votes against three.

> Would it be politick and constitutional in Congress to grant a charter for a national Bank?

[*8*]

On the merits the vote stood in the affirmative, twelve to one.

> Would it be more expedient and right to appropriate the surplus revenue received by the State of Ky. from the Genl. government to internal improvement than education?

The house divided three for improvements to two for education. Later a similar question was argued:

> Is education of more importance to the people of Kentucky than Internal improvements?

Miller spoke three times for education, and carried his point by five to three. A year later the question was reargued, and Miller spoke twice for improvements. Improvements carried, four to three.

> Are Railroads of more publick utility than Canals?

Miller joined with the majority in an affirmative decision, six to two.

> Would it be politick for the Legislature of Kentucky to grant a Bank charter to the Charleston & Ohio Railroad Company?

The vote was in the affirmative, nine to five.

> Should the Goverment [*sic*] admit the emigration [*sic*] of foreigners into the Country with the privilege of enjoying all the rights of citizenship?

In the general debate on this proposition Miller spoke in the affirmative against Green Adams. The vote was eight affirmative, three negative.

> Should foreign immigration to this country be prohibited by law?

The house divided evenly, Miller voting in the negative.

On October 28, 1837, Dr. U. S. Williams read "an instructive essay upon the Science of Phrenology," which was followed by debate on the question:

> Have the acts of Andrew Jackson been of more benefit than injury to the United States?

Miller argued that they had, but when the vote was taken, assumed the Whig position and joined in a vote of censure, six to three. Throughout his life he continued to hold a poor opinion of Jackson.

On April 14, 1838, Miller proposed as the next topic:

> Should Henry Clay be the candidate run by the Whigs for President in preference to Wm. H. Harrison?

This was debated on April 28, when the meeting must have taken on the aspect of a monologue by Miller. First he read an essay; then, being the only one of the appointed debaters present, he spoke in favor of Clay's candidacy; next, general discussion being in order, he again took the floor. Two speeches in the negative were heard, and the vote was taken; the result showed six for Clay and four for Harrison. Miller then proposed the question for the next meeting — the admission of Texas; Joseph Eve, the future chargé to that republic, was appointed to take the affirmative. On Miller's motion the house was adjourned.

The first question selected when the society was reorganized in the spring of 1839 was:

> Would it be to the interest of the United States to declare war against Great Brittain [sic] if she refuses to give possession of the disputed territory?

As usual, Green Adams and Miller opposed one another, Miller being on the negative side. The vote was four for war to three for peace.

> Would it be politick in the Genl Govt to wholly exterminate the Seminole Indians, if they continue their depredations upon the citizens of the United States?

Three members thought it would; Miller and four others thought not. He was subsequently, as spokesman for the Supreme Court, to uphold the exclusive power of the federal government to protect "these remnants of a race once powerful." [17]

[17] United States v. Kagama, 118 U. S. 375 (1886). Also United States v. Holliday, 3 Wallace 407 (1866).

No doubt it was Andrew Jackson's energetic portrayal of the role of president which turned the attention of the house to questions of patronage and executive power. On April 13, 1839, Miller suggested as a topic:

> Should federal officers be prohibited from using means to secure [?] elections?

The vote was in the negative, four to two, Miller being absent. Twice there was debate on the question:

> Should the patronage of the president of the U.S. be curtailed?

The vote was two yeas and seven nays, and later six yeas and five nays; Miller thought the patronage should not be curtailed. He evidently favored a single presidential term of six years, for he proposed that subject and argued in the affirmative, but the society voted in the negative, nine to three. A later debate on the same question ended in a negative vote of seven to one.

On September 9, 1837, the debate was on the question:

> Has the President the power under the Constitution to turn out of office any individual Commissioned by and with the advice and consent of the senate?

The vote was in the negative, five against three. Ninety years later, in the Myers Case,[18] the Supreme Court of the United States had to pass upon the very same question, and answered in the affirmative by a six to three decision. Perhaps it would have been just as well if we could have had the eight honest men of Barbourville to decide the controversy for us. At any rate the Myers decision was very much criticized, and in 1935, in *Humphrey* v. *United States*,[19] a unanimous Court overruled the dictum of the earlier case and held that the president alone could not remove a federal trade commissioner. Thus, so far as members of administrative tribunals are concerned, the Court has put itself squarely behind Dr. Miller's debating society.

[18] 272 U. S. 52 (1926).
[19] 295 U. S. 602.

Who should be allowed to vote was a matter of anxious solicitude a century ago, and one debate was held on the question:

> Should the right of suffrage be restricted by a property qualification?

Miller was strongly opposed to such restriction, and so were his fellows, who voted unanimously in the negative. This was the era of the omnicompetent citizen, and the entries in the journal show that these men of the Kentucky hills were concerned with various aspects of egalitarian philosophy. Were all persons endowed with the same intellectual capacity? Miller and a majority of the society thought that they were not. Was the mind of man more capacious than that of woman? Should women be equally educated with men? Has wealth more influence than talent? Miller voted that it did not, and believed as he voted. He never rendered homage to financial power, and held in contempt those who claimed precedence in right of wealth. His whole life was oriented by his confidence in his own mental powers. In later years he fully realized that he had become a great judge — great not in legal earning but in statesmanship. He had made more constitutional law than most of the founding fathers. And with this realization there came a certain impatience with all inconsequence, a touch of wolfishness toward those who proved tedious or prolix. It was on Miller's motion that the society voted to limit the length of speeches; yet he did not hesitate to take the floor himself more often than any other member.

> Will wealth enable a man to pass through the world with greater honor to himself than education?

Miller argued that it would not, and the society agreed in a vote of seven to two. Years later, after he had vindicated his faith in the efficacy of well-directed intellectual effort, he assured young lawyers that in America it could be predicted with almost perfect assurance that a practitioner of adequate training, if he proved studious, diligent, and of unquestioned integrity, would find that all the things he desired would be added unto him.[20]

Is civil fame more desirable than Military?

The house was evenly divided.

These backwoodsmen of Kentucky did not share the opinion that the Negro was naturally and providentially destined to servitude, and their interest was enlisted in the fight to maintain the right of petition for those opposed to slavery:

> Should congress refuse the reception of abolition documents as contended by the Southern delegation?

Miller argued in the negative against Green Adams. In the general discussion the society was addressed by Robert Wickliffe, Jr., a Lexington lawyer who had been east and studied under the renowned Justice Story. The vote was two yeas, twelve nays.

> Is it a greater crime to drive the Indians from their land than to keep the negroes in Bondage?

The vote was three in the affirmative, six in the negative.

> Should any laws exist regulating the rate of interest?

The vote was for *laissez-faire*, seven to two.

> Should imprisonment for debt be abolished?

The house thought that it should, voting eight to two.

> Is there a moral justification for capital punishment?

The house always voted yes, but Miller thought not, and said so each of the five times the subject was debated. This suggests an interesting aspect of his character. His physical courage was unquestionable, as he once showed by undergoing a very painful operation without any anesthetic, and on the bench his imperious ways became proverbial; yet at heart he was exceedingly tender and sympathetic. One major reason

[20] "The Study and Practice of the Law," 2 *Chicago Legal News* 82 (1869).

which drove him from the practice of medicine was that he could not endure to see his patients suffer in cases he could not cure. When on the circuit bench it became his duty to impose the sentence of death he was frank to say that his own mind did not approve that penalty,[21] and on the Supreme Court there was one class of case which he would approach with hair-splitting nicety: he was glad to find even the narrowest constitutional ground to save the life of a murderer. So singular a departure from his ordinary mode of constitutional construction is to be explained only on the basis of that deep aversion to the taking of human life which he expressed so often in debate.

Only occasionally would the discussion turn to a bootless topic — the merits of Washington versus those of Columbus, of Napoleon versus Hannibal. Once the question was a religious one:

> Apart from Revelation and Human Tradition have we any evidence of the existence of Deity?

Miller argued that there was no other evidence, and so voted. The house divided three yeas, two nays. This would indicate that Miller was something of a free thinker, which is probably the case. In later years he was prominent in the Unitarian Church, whose latitudinarian tenets were congenial to his highly critical habits of thought.[22]

This record affords no little insight into the background of a great judge, and incidentally into the political views of those Kentuckians among whom he lived. The vital questions of the day were questions of public policy; their solution was sought not in books, but in original thinking and public discussion. As an academy of learning the Barbourville debat-

---

[21] United States v. Gleason, 1 Woolworth 128, Fed. Case No. 15,216 (1867).

[22] On moving to Keokuk, Iowa, Miller became one of the founders of the Unitarian Church there, and drew up its articles of incorporation in 1853 (Charles N. Gregory, *Samuel Freeman Miller*, Iowa City: State Historical Society of Iowa, 1907, p. 59). He was vice-president of the National Conference of the denomination in 1878, 1880, and 1882, and president in 1884, 1886, and 1889. He was described as a "Unitarian of the Channing school" (*Christian Register*, vol. LXIX, 1890, p. 677).

ing society had its limitations; but its graduates seem to have emerged with self-reliant habits of thought, convincing modes of utterance, and a flair for statecraft. The political tenets which the society inculcated included loyalty to the federal union, a liberal interpretation of the Constitution, the efficacy of democratic institutions, and the ability of the common man to work them. The journal is an authentic representation of the political philosophy of the American frontier.

Later, when he had become a justice of the Supreme Court, Miller used to refer to the Debating Society as marking a stage in his development. It had drawn the mind of a country doctor in a mountain hamlet into the current of national thought and afforded him a means of relating himself to the great public questions of the day. No wonder he found this outlet far more satisfying than the practice of medical pseudo-science. "About the year 1845," as Miller later wrote of himself, "he decided to change his profession, and after two years study of the law, was admitted to the bar in the same town where he was busily engaged as a medical practitioner." [23]

In 1842 Miller had been married to Lucy L. Ballinger, daughter of a locally prominent family which had come from North Carolina.[24] The Ballingers and their relations did business in writs and warrants.[25] There were already two children

[23] Autobiographical sketch, p. 15. It appears that he was admitted to the bar of the Circuit Court of Knox County, March 22, 1847, on motion of Silas Woodson (Order Book G of that court, p. 350).

[24] The marriage license was issued on October 8, 1842, by the bride's brother, William Pitt Ballinger, the deputy clerk of the Knox County Court. Her father, James F. Ballinger, was "present and consenting." J. F. Ballinger was then clerk of the court. The marriage was performed on November 8 by William T. Hopper, a Baptist minister of the locality (*Lexington* [Ky.] *Leader*, August 30, 1936).

[25] Of Miller's father-in-law it is recorded that "he was no doubt the best Clerk in Kentucky — Knew the form of every judgt & order known to common Law & Equity Practice — . . . He was the counsellor and transacted the business of many of the country people in the mountains who had the very greatest confidence in him. . . . His familiarity with Shakespeare led to his being given that as a nickname — Scott's novels & poetry very familiar to him — knew English history — read the newspapers & exceedingly well informed on the history of the day." These are recollections which the son, William Pitt Ballinger, set down in his diary on August 11, 1875 — the day following J. F. Ballinger's death (Ballinger Diary, Library of the University of Texas).

in Miller's family when he was overtaken by the belated desire to turn to the law, and those in whom he confided felt
assured that no good would come of it.[26]

Even before he began his new studies Miller had been enrolled in one of the most ancient of Anglo-Saxon institutions
for training in public affairs: in April 1844 he was sworn a
justice of the peace, and took his seat as a member of the
County Court.[27] This gave scope for statecraft of a low order
— caring for paupers, settling with toll-gate keepers, laying
out new roads. He was elected president of the court in 1846,
and resigned his commission as justice in August 1847.

Miller was an active emancipationist [28] and aspired to a
seat in the Kentucky constitutional convention of 1849. In
this, however, he deferred to the claims of his friend Silas
Woodson, on the condition that the latter stand openly in
favor of gradual emancipation.[29] But the election of delegates
registered the triumph of the slave interests. As the Louisville
Examiner explained in its *post mortem*, August 11, 1849:

Appeals were made by the newspaper organs of both of the
old political parties to oppose the emancipation ticket. Indeed,
opposition to that ticket was made a test of orthodoxy in both
political parties. — Both parties feared the effect of the mad dog

[26] As Miller recalled in an interview published in the New York *World*,
December 12, 1886. B. F. Gue's *History of Iowa* (New York, Century History
Co., 1903), IV, 192, states that Miller studied law with "Judge Ballinger."
Probably this was Judge Franklin Ballinger, a kinsman of Mrs. Miller, and a
member of the Debating Society.

[27] As appears from the record books of the Knox County Court.

[28] In the records of the clerk's office at Barbourville there is a chattel mortgage of a Negro girl, Hannah, about thirteen years old, executed by Peter
Vannoy to secure a debt of $92.72 to Miller, under date of January 8, 1848.
There seems to be no record of a discharge. (*Lexington* [Ky.] *Leader*, August
30, 1936). Whatever may have been the circumstances of this transaction, it
supports no inference that Miller condoned slavery.

Charles Noble Gregory, in his sketch of Miller's life, says that he brought
slaves with him from Kentucky, and freed them (*Samuel Freeman Miller*, p. 64).
His father-in-law, when he followed Miller to Iowa, disposed of his slaves, most
of whom were old, to masters of their own choosing. The only one fit for freedom was a young carpenter worth $2500, whom he took to Iowa and freed.
The total value of his slaves is said to have been $6000 (*Gate City*, Keokuk,
July 16, 1856).

[29] As recalled by Justice Harlan, whose boyhood was spent close to these
scenes, in 3 *Central Law Journal* 333 (1890).

cry of abolitionism throughout the State, and the leaders of both for weeks before the election cautioned and besought their friends not to show any respect for emancipation. The people were told, what was true, namely, that emancipation would inevitably fail at the present time, as the most ardent Emancipationists had not the remotest expectation of carrying the State. This view of the present prospects of the Emancipationists had a powerful influence every where, and deterred thousands from voting emancipation tickets, and is perhaps the most forcible reason for the seeming ill success of our friends throughout the State.

When Miller, whose antipathy to slavery went back to a day in his childhood when he had seen his Negro "mammy" flogged, became satisfied that slavery "would never be voluntarily abolished in a Slave state, he decided to leave Kentucky and in the autumn of 1849 first saw Keokuk in a general tour of the North-West. He determined to make that place his future home, and arrived there on the 7th day of May, 1850, with his family." [30]

[30] Autobiographical sketch, p. 15.

II

THE WESTERN LAWYER

MILLER'S CHOICE for his new home is not surprising. Iowa was an attractive country, then being filled up by New Englanders and men from Ohio and Indiana, "interspersed," as Miller recalled complacently, "with the vigor of the people of Kentucky and Missouri." [1] Keokuk, "the Gate City," was in the southeasternmost part of the state, at the foot of the first rapids of the Mississippi and at the head of deep-water navigation. Its population at the time was about thirty-one hundred, of whom only forty-two were Negroes. Many of its people had come from Kentucky, and it had the flavor of a Southern town. Prior acquaintance with Kentucky statutes on the part of many of the newcomers resulted in their being largely adopted in Iowa, and the practice of the law in Keokuk retained many of the informal characteristics of Kentucky justice.

When Miller walked across the gangplank on that May morning the future stretched before him as fresh and unspoiled as the ground to which he stepped, then covered with a late snow. He supposed himself unknown to any human being in the place. In this he was mistaken, for shortly he encountered "Bill" Clark, the city's first mayor, an old schoolmate who with his brothers had emigrated from Richmond, Kentucky. Through this friendship it was brought about that Miller, as he himself later recalled,

formed an advantageous partnership with Lewis R. Reeves, who was perhaps the ablest lawyer of the Keokuk bar then in active practice and who having a large real estate interest in the half breed tract,[2] desired a law partner who would attend to the gen-

---

[1] *Annals of Iowa*, 3 ser. VII (1906), 368.
[2] On the half-breed lands, see Haight *v.* City of Keokuk, 4 Iowa 199, 209 (1856), a case where Miller appeared as counsel, and Webster *v.* Reid, 11 Howard 437 (1850).

eral business of the firm, and aid him in the litigation which then involved all half breed lands. The connection proved in every way a fortunate one for Mr. Miller, who at once found himself engaged in a large and remunerative practice, and took a front rank among the lawyers of the State. The friendship and confidence between Mr. Reeves and himself was unreserved, and uninterrupted until the death of Mr. Reeves in 1854, when the latter gave the strongest evidence of this in making Mr. Miller one of his executors of a will which left them a very large discretion in the control of his property for many years of the expected minority of his only child.

Not long after the death of Mr. Reeves, Mr. Miller also lost his wife by consumption, leaving him three young children, all girls.

In about two and a half years after this, he and Mrs. Reeves united their fortunes in marriage,[3]

or, as it was said at the time, "the old firm of Reeves and Miller was renewed under a different contract."

After their wedding Miller and his wife went on a trip to Texas, where for a fortnight they were cordially entertained in the home of William Pitt Ballinger, the brother of Miller's first wife. Miller's affection for Ballinger survived political differences, war, and long separation, and remained the closest friendship of his life. Ballinger's regard for Miller was recorded in this diary entry of April 18, 1857: "I like him better & feel more obligation towds him that almost any person living." Mrs. Miller was described in an earlier entry as "rather a handsome woman with a fine figure, and high animal spirits — likes to dance, ride, & take active exercises — Is a woman of cool, practical business sense — I infer is an excellent housekeeper & domestic manager. Is sprightly & exhibits good sense in conversation — I think her warm-hearted — sincere and candid." Other characteristics noted were impulsiveness and a craving for admiration. "He will be rendered occasionally uncomfortable by her want of discretion & a little

[3] Autobiographical sketch, pp. 18–21. From the gravestones in the Keokuk cemetery it appears that Miller's first wife was born March 5, 1827, and died November 12, 1854. The second Mrs. Miller was born December 4, 1828, and died December 1, 1900. The minor child of Reeves, to whom Miller refers, was a daughter, Alice, born February 17, 1850, who died December 4, 1855.

oppressed at times by her exacting." "On the whole I like her very much and believe she will make him a good wife." [4]

The law partnership of Reeves and Miller was thus described in the professional advertisement inserted in the weekly issue of the local paper:

L. R. Reeves.   S. F. Miller.

Reeves & Miller
Attorneys at Law
Keokuk, Iowa.
Office adjoining the Court Room.

We have full memorandums of all the Conveyances or Records in Lee county, procured at great expense, and are prepared to investigate titles and give opinions as to their validity. The Profession can have the use of our records for a stipulated compensation. We also attend regularly the courts of Van Buren and Jefferson counties, and have arrangements for collections in other counties in the interior of the State.[5]

Among their brothers at the local bar was John Walker Rankin, who became Miller's partner sometime after Reeve's death. Rankin was a graduate of Washington College (later Washington and Jefferson) in Pennsylvania, and had come to Keokuk in 1848. There he had been associated in turn with lawyers whose names are gratefully remembered in the annals of Iowa: Charles Mason, Iowa's first chief justice;[6] Samuel R. Curtis,[7] and James M. Love, for many years United

---

[4] Ballinger Diary.

[5] *Des Moines Valley Whig*, Keokuk, December 9, 1852.

[6] Mason graduated from the United States Military Academy in 1829, standing No. 1 in a class where Robert E. Lee was No. 2. He resigned in 1831, became an editorial writer on the New York *Evening Post*, and studied law. On the organization of the Supreme Court of Iowa Territory in 1838 he was appointed chief justice. He left the bench in 1847, after Iowa became a state. His first opinion, In the matter of Ralph, 1 Morris 1 (1839), held that where a master permitted his slave to become a resident in free territory he could not thereafter exercise ownership over him in the territory.

[7] Like Mason, Curtis was a graduate of the Military Academy, being of the class of 1831. He resigned and studied law, practicing at Zanesville, Ohio. He served as adjutant general of Ohio and colonel of the Third Ohio Infantry during the Mexican War. In Iowa he was one of the foremost of the Republican leaders. During the Civil War he rose from colonel to major general, the last promotion being in recognition of his victory at Pea Ridge. He died in 1866.

States district judge in Iowa.[8] Reeves's death in 1854 had left Miller without a partner, and the appointment of Love to the bench shortly afterwards placed Rankin in the same predicament. They joined forces under the title of Rankin and Miller,[9] a partnership which continued until 1862 when Miller was appointed to the Supreme Court. The new associate is described as "warm hearted, generous, unassuming; no man of his influence in the State had more friends or fewer enemies. In politics he was ultra Republican." [10] Another comment was: "Rankin was wonderfully endowed by nature. He seemed to know the law by intuition. He was kindhearted to a fault." [11] This appraisal came from George W. McCrary, who read law in Rankin and Miller's office and in 1862 took Miller's place in the firm.

It is scarcely necessary to recall McCrary's subsequent career as member of Congress, Secretary of War in the Hayes cabinet, and United States circuit judge. Another student in the office was John Bruce, who went off to the wars and emerged a brevet brigadier general, and was later appointed United States district judge for Alabama. But this does not exhaust the list of Keokuk's great and near great during Miller's years at the bar. On his arrival in 1850 he found on the bench of the local district court one George H. Williams, who was later to be Attorney General in Grant's cabinet at a moment when both he and Miller supremely wanted the chief justiceship. Williams moved to Oregon in 1853 when he was appointed chief justice of the Supreme Court of the territory,

[8] Appointed by President Pierce in 1856. He died at Keokuk in 1891, the eldest in commission of all the district judges. He is spoken of as a profound lawyer and a gifted scholar, charming in manner and of "a modesty of demeanor almost shrinking" (E. H. Stiles, *Recollections and Sketches of Notable Lawyers and Public Men of Early Iowa*, Des Moines: Homestead Publishing Co., 1916, p. 163).

[9] Later there was a third partner, T. F. Enster. He left Keokuk in the spring of 1862 and died at Natchez, Mississippi, shortly after. ("The Keokuk Bar of 1860," a series of articles beginning January 28, 1885, in the *Gate City*, Keokuk.)

[10] MS. of the late C. F. Davis, in his collection of biographical and autobiographical sketches, "Keokuk Biographical and Historical," vol. v.

[11] Same collection, autobiographical sketch by George W. McCrary.

and entered the national scene in 1865 as senator from Oregon. Here too lived another member of the Grant cabinet, W. W. Belknap, subsequently to be drummed out of the public service in disgrace. And here came John W. Noble, recently from Yale and the Cincinnati Law School, to practice in 1856. He distinguished himself in the army and later at the bar, and served as Secretary of the Interior in the Harrison cabinet — the fourth of the future ministers who lived in Keokuk in the 1850's. But our business is with Miller, not with his professional associates: their names are passed in review only to recall that at Keokuk, just as at Barbourville, he lived his life in a stimulating community and among men who were on the make.

There can be no mistake as to Miller's standing among the Iowa lawyers of his day. In a communication in 1856 he speaks of "some three hundred cases in which I am engaged" awaiting trial at the next term of court. Turning through the Iowa Reports one sees that throughout the period between 1851 and 1862 Miller, or the firm of which he was a member, was continually appearing before the state supreme court. His name figures in over seventy of the reported cases, in a majority of which he was successful.[12] (This fact, however, is of no great importance, since the determination of causes is something more than a trial of skill in advocacy.)

Years afterward one of his juniors at the bar gave this account of Miller as a lawyer:

I was impressed by his mental vigor and originality, and by his terseness of expression, whether in written pleadings or oral arguments. I had come from an Eastern law college where I had been taught to practice most strictly upon the *stare decisis* theory of the law, and to yield unquestionably [*sic*] to the weight of authority, which meant the doctrine of the majority as applied to court opinions, departing only far enough to admit that where the numbers were nearly equal, the judgments of Chief Justice Shaw,

---

[12] Miller's legal papers are spoken of as models of clarity, and when he became a judge he had no patience with counsel who were clumsy at their craft. I was anxious, therefore, to examine the records and briefs in some of the cases he argued before the Supreme Court of Iowa, but the search brought no reward for disturbing the dust of years.

and such as he, were entitled to special consideration. Miller's method, however, was to cite few cases, but to impress the court which the reason of the law. As already stated his terseness in pleading particularly impressed me. A page of legal cap written in an open hand would have been for him a long declaration or answer. One of his bills in Chancery was a marvel of condensed statement and yet I do not recall a successful attack upon his practice in this regard, by demurrer or by a motion for a more specific statement. He grasped at once the theory of the code of practice then and still in vogue here, and in this respect his court papers were an education to the younger bar. He was almost invincible in argument in the higher courts, so that we younger men were inclined to feel that he appeared before the Judges *auctoritate doctissimi*, who treated his utterances as *responsa prudentum*, and that our learning was not fully appreciated.[13]

The remark that Miller grasped at once the theory of the Iowa code of practice will bear some elaboration. In 1848 the New York legislature adopted a Code of Civil Procedure, one of the first fruits of David Dudley Field's labors to reform the law. This lead was followed within a few years by Massachusetts and by most of the western states. In Iowa the cumbrous system of common-law pleading was swept away in 1851 when the legislature adopted a code covering both substantive law and procedure. Thus it was Miller's good fortune that in less than a year after his arrival it became the law of Iowa that "all technical forms of action and of pleadings are hereby abolished." "The courts and the lawyers," he later recalled, "with few exceptions, conformed to the change in the proper spirit, and the result is that fewer practice cases are reported in the forty-eight volumes of Iowa Reports than in any equal number of such volumes in the United States." In New York, however, the reform encountered "the hostility of a profession which shrinks from innovation as from a plague." In 1878, delivering the annual address before the state bar association, Miller recalled that New York had been the pioneer in the introduction of the code system:

[13] Henry Strong, in *Annals of Iowa*, 3 ser. 1 (1894), 255. Strong had practiced in partnership with John W. Noble.

Here it met its first and fiercest opposition. . . .

I take the liberty of saying also, that the principal source of the contests over the Code of Procedure was the hostility of the lawyers and those who then occupied the bench. All of these had been bred as lawyers under a system of pleading very technical, very difficult to understand, which constituted of itself a branch of learning supposed to be very abstruse and very valuable. It was one of the titles to reputation and success in the profession, that a man was a good special pleader. To find, as many of these erroneously supposed, all this learning of a lifetime rendered useless, was more than human nature could bear with composure.

To see the tyro in the profession, made by this change in the law of pleading, as capable of preparing a good declaration, a good plea, or a good bill in chancery, as the patriarch of the bar, to see his blunders remedied by the simple process of amending the pleading, instead of gratifying his adversary by being turned out of court as a tribute to that adversary's learning, was very provoking.[14]

It was a characteristic of Miller's mind to be impatient of mere form and routine and to be content with no rule which did not commend itself to his reason. It is significant that this tendency was confirmed by the practice at the Iowa bar.

The most satisfactory portrayal of Miller as a lawyer is to be found in his somewhat intimate address to the Iowa bar association in 1879,[15] remarks filled with that paternal sort of admonition which is often the most revealing form of autobiography. He was speaking on the subject of professional training, in which he found the lawyers of the Northwest inferior to their eastern brethren — a condition due in part to the necessity which drove the former from school at an early age. One recalls that this had been notably true in his own

[14] *New York State Bar Association Reports*, II (1879), 31, 47, 49. Mr. Charles Warren discusses the era of the codes in his *History of the American Bar* (Boston: Little, Brown and Co., 1911), chap. XIX. He recalls the language of Justice Grier, speaking for the federal Supreme Court in 1859, apropos of the Iowa code of procedure and similar "experiments" in reforming the common law: "This system, matured by the wisdom of ages, founded on principles of truth and sound reason, has been ruthlessly abolished in many of our States, who have rashly substituted in its place the suggestions of sciolists, who invent new codes and systems of pleading to order" (McFaul v. Ramsey, 20 Howard 523, 525).

[15] 20 *Albany Law Journal* 25 (1879); 13 *Western Jurist* 241 (1879).

case, and sees between the lines that he is describing the methods by which he himself had triumphed in spite of initial disadvantage.

The *practice* of the law is an art. There is no question that, like painting or sculpture, there is necessary to its perfect attainment a certain native genius for its pursuit. But this does not mean, as in those arts, imagination, taste, a delicate sense of beauty in form or color. In the law a much more useful, and a much more common quality, is the native foundation of success. It is a sound judgment, a clear head, a strong development of the reasoning faculty, a capacity to reduce all propositions to the test of sound logic, without regard to the syllogisms of Aristotle or Whately, and independent of rhetoric as a science or an embellishment.

But this natural faculty, like all other gifts of nature, is susceptible of vast improvement in its use by cultivation, by polish, and, above all, by training.

I confine myself, for the present, to the latter. And by this training I mean the exercise of the faculties in the best mode possible, of presenting your case to the tribunal which must decide it; I mean the restraint which use enables you to impose on an exuberant imagination, the caution which experience teaches, of careful statement and safe movements, the courage which familiarity inspires in battling for the right, and, above all, the skill which is acquired by constant observation, practice and correction in setting forth your case in the strongest light, and the most inviting aspect.

He illustrates his point by holding up as a model Benjamin R. Curtis, "the first *lawyer* of America, of the past or of the present time." And the virtues which he thinks particularly worth imitation by Western lawyers are unceasing mental discipline, careful preparation for trial, systematic organization of oral argument, and brevity.

Passing to cultural attainments outside the profession, Miller recognized that the superiority of Eastern lawyers in this respect was attributable to the proximity of good schools and libraries. "I am not advocating a collegiate course as a prerequisite to the study of law, or admission to the bar. Least of all do I attach the importance which so many classical scholars do to proficiency in Greek and Latin languages."

(Such Latin as Miller knew he had picked up for himself after he began to study law.)[16] But it was within the reach of all to acquire some knowledge of natural science, some mastery of world history, and some acquaintance with the great names in the profession. Most of all he commended a study of Milton and Pope, Addison and Steele, and others who wrote when "the perfection of style in the English tongue was attained."

And now, gentlemen, if I have dealt plainly with you it is because the love I have borne the bar of this State makes it worth while that I should do so. . . . Here in agricultural Iowa, where every case presents an honest contest of law or fact, where there are no great cities to foster shysters, nor great wealth to tempt or mislead the lawyer, where in his village office, with ample time and a well-selected, if small, library,[17] the attorney, who is at the same time counsellor and barrister, traces in each case the principles involved in their original sources, imbibes their spirit, discovers their philosophy, and assures himself of their application to his case. It is here that we must look for the continuation of the race of great lawyers. It is here that the learning is sound, the principles pure, the practice established. It is from some western prairie town rather than some metropolis that future Marshalls and Mansfields shall arise and give new impulse and add new honor to the profession of the law.

While attending strictly to his professional duties, Miller interested himself in projects for building plank roads and railroads,[18] and, like a true follower of Henry Clay, joined in resolutions "reiterating the wishes heretofore so often and so emphatically expressed in favor of an appropriation by Congress of land for the construction of these works." He was active in the Whig organization, beating the bushes in

[16] Interview in the New York *World*, December 12, 1886.

[17] The modest resources which had been available when Miller was at the bar may be inferred from the following entry in the Iowa Reports in 1856: "Note by the Court. — We desire to say to the profession, both for this and other causes, that our access to books is very limited. We cannot, therefore, in this case, determine the correctness of the citations of many of the cases in the note in 1 Smith's Leading Cases, but we give them, that others, having better opportunities, may examine." (Cooper *v.* Sunderland, 3 Clarke 114, 140.)

[18] *Valley Whig & Keokuk Register*, October 24, 1850; *Des Moines Valley Whig*, Keokuk, January 29, 1852, June 24, 1852.

an unsuccessful effort to carry the state for General Scott in 1852.[19]

The movement to repeal the Missouri Compromise in 1854 filled him with alarm, and elicited the following letter to his brother-in-law in the South:

My Dear Will,

I feel for the first time in my life that there is real danger that you and I shall live to be citizens of different *nations*. Whenever there is such danger ahead, one of the best safeguards is to be found in a full knowledge by all parties concerned of its nature and extent. Hence in 1820 and in 1850 when danger was threatened over the slavery question safety was brought about by compromise and concession growing out of the full conviction of the necessity of so doing to avoid danger. But in the pending effort to repeal the Missouri Compromise, the real danger is concealed. The whole scheme has been broached since the meeting of Congress. The members of Congress are more obedient to party drill than ever they were, the people less so. For several years past the death of all the old party leaders, the decay of old party questions and the introduction of new ones have weakened the hold of party ties upon the people. *In the calculation of Douglas* [sic], *Pierce, and Cass that they can carry the party with them in the North they will be deceived.* The passage of the Nebraska Bill as it came from the Senate will arouse a fury in the North which will abolish party ties and create a new organization of party on territorial bases fatal to the Union as I fear.

An abolitionist has been my abhorrence all my life. So has been a proslavery disunionist such as Calhoun & Jeff Davis. If it were a question of the introduction or passage of the Missouri Compromise for the first time the North would perhaps submit to it. But all sensible men know that the pretense that it was repealed by the acts of 1850 is false, and *all both sensible and foolish* feel this to be an aggressive step in favour of extending and propagating slavery by violating plighted faith and honorable compromises. The men who are at the head of this measure in the North have no such hold on the affections of the people as

[19] *Des Moines Valley Whig*, April 22, May 20, July 22, October 14, 1852. Lee County, where Keokuk lies, returned Scott 1379, Pierce 1708, Hale 201. The returns for the state were Scott 15,895 and Pierce 17,823, while Hale, the Free-Soil candidate, polled only 1612 (*ibid.*, November 4 and December 16, 1852).

to enable them to still the demon they have raised. They really dont know the danger they have invoked. The action of members of Congress and State Legislatures are [*sic*] no index of popular feeling on the subject.

I have written above more than I have ever said on the subject to any one. I eschew politics steadily. I was solicited to address a public meeting in the subject and declined. I shall firmly discountenance all agitation on the subject; But I say to you now, that the repeal by the national Legislature of the Missouri Compromise act will be but the beginning of the end. I doubt if another fugitive slave will ever be returned after such an act shall have become law.[20]

Miller was an original Republican, and in the canvass of 1856 took such part as his professional engagements would allow. In the Republican county convention he reviewed the action of recent Democratic administrations on the subject of slavery, and moved resolutions on the outrage to Sumner and "the late murders by armed ruffians in Kansas." [21] A fortnight later he was chosen president of the first Republican organization in Keokuk, and in a speech described the party as one "of national and patriotic aims, in which good men were combining, without hope of office or pecuniary benefit." [22] That summer he was nominated for the state senate, under circumstances described in a statement which he addressed to the voters. It is worth quoting at length because it is the best expression of Miller's political views and foreshadows some of the opinions he was later to express on the bench:

To The Voters of Lee and Van Buren Counties:
My Fellow-Citizens:

Just on the eve of the August election I find myself, very unexpectedly and very much against my wishes, a candidate for State Senator. It had been urged upon me repeatedly to permit my name to be used for this purpose up to the time of the nomination made by the Republican committees of the two counties, and I had peremtorily refused. I also told the members of the committee from Lee county, when they started for Farmington, not

---

[20] Letter of March 19, 1854.
[21] *Gate City*, Keokuk, May 31, 1856.
[22] *Gate City*, June 17.

to use my name, for I could not possibly run the race. The reason why I refused to become a candidate was this: that I could not properly canvass the District without causing immense injury to the affairs of others, committed to my care as a lawyer. It is near a year since we have had a term of the court at Keokuk, and there are on the docket now, for trial at our next term, commencing on the first Monday of September, some three hundred cases in which I am engaged for one side or the other. The ordinary office business of our firm demands the continual attention of one man. My partner, Mr. Rankin, is absent in the East and will not be home before the election, and with all the preparations for trial of these causes on my hands, besides the usual business of the office, it was impossible for me to canvass the two counties. If, however, I were to refuse now to accept the nomination it would be equivalent to leaving my political friends without any candidate for Senator, as it is too late to take measures to get out another with any hope of success. I have therefore concluded to accept the nomination, and have offered the foregoing remarks by way of apology for failing to canvass the two counties in person. I am compelled, then, in this manner to address you, my fellow-citizens, in order to apprise you of my sentiments upon the political questions which are agitating the country.

My political action heretofore has been in general accord with the Whig party. That party no longer has an existence, or if it has, there is no representative of it in this field for any office in regard to which you and I are called upon to vote. In speaking of it then as a party which has passed into history, I may be permitted to say that I believe that in the true honesty of its purposes, in the soundness of its principles, and in the brilliant constellation of talent which guided its course, it has never had an equal in this or any other country, and its members who yet survive find themselves enjoying those honors which are usually paid alone to the dead. The questions which gave vitality to the Whig party, and which constituted the battle ground between it and the old Democratic party, having been either adjusted or passed away in the rapid progress of the country, or having become of such minor importance as no longer to attract public attention in any sensible degree, I find myself, in common with all my fellow-citizens of both the old political parties, compelled to act in reference to a new, a vastly important, and overshadowing issue, thrust upon us in a manner that admits of no evasion and requiring at our hands a conscientious solution.

You will understand at once that I speak of the Slavery question. Upon the subject of Slavery I have no *unfounded* prejudices. I was raised and lived in its midst until 30 years of age, and have had ample opportunity of knowing its workings and observing its influences. The result of this is, a conviction that both to the white man and the black it is full of evil. The institution of African Slavery as it exists in the United States, is in my judgment the most stupendous wrong, and the most prolific source of human misery, both to the master and the slave, that the sun shines upon in his daily circuit around the globe. The last vote I ever gave in Kentucky was given for a candidate for delegate to amend the Constitution, who was pledged to vote for a system of gradual emancipation, and when that hopelessly failed I determined to leave the State.

But while thus opposed to Slavery, I recognize, in the fullest sense of the term, the exclusive right of the States within which it exists to deal with it for themselves. Slavery is the creature alone of local statutory law, and to the States where those laws exist, belongs the responsibility for its continuance, and the sole right to provide for its removal.

But while the nation was reposing itself upon the satisfactory settlement of the Slavery question after the agitation which resulted in the Compromise measures of 1850, the men who had obtained control of the old Democratic party, with the Democratic administration at their head, without any necessity or reason for so doing, which has ever been shown, except personal aggrandizement, commenced a series of measures for the extension of Slavery into regions where by law it did not previously exist. This statement I make advisedly and on due reflection, but can only allude, without amplification, to some of the evidences of its truth.[23]

He goes on to discuss the attempt to impose slavery upon the people of Kansas, his analysis and point of view being identical with what one finds in contemporary speeches by Lincoln. Speaking of the local violence which was accompanying this effort, Miller continued:

When a portion of this Government becomes the scene of fraternal bloodshed by armed bodies of citizens of the Union, one against another, and this is continued for a period of nearly a year, and no prospect is seen now of relief or redress; when organ-

[23] *Gate City,* July 17.

ized bodies of men in one State close up such a great avenue of travel, trade and commerce as the Missouri River by force of arms; when the peaceable citizens of this Union are told that they cannot be permitted to travel over the soil of that State, nor on any terms to take up their residence in Kansas; and when we are repeatedly told by all the mouthpieces of the Democratic party, that resistance to this state of things will lead to a dissolution of the Union, I am justified in saying that the question involved in these matters overrides all others, and requires you and me to lose sight of minor matters, and shape our political action with reference to that question.

In common, then, with the great mass of the old Whig party, and with all those of every party who agree with us in sentiment, and have the nerve to emancipate themselves from old party domination, I have assisted in forming the great Republican party.

That party, as well as myself, is opposed to the Repeal of the Missouri Compromise; opposed to the extension of Slavery into Free Territory, and will never consent that acts of conquest, achieved by armed invasion, shall impose upon a free people, who are entitled to the protection of the laws of this Union, the institution of Slavery against their will, and with that institution a set of laws more odious than those which govern the serfs of Russia.

A word as to two charges — the common staple of declamation against the Republican party, and I close. We are called Abolitionists.

Intelligent men who make this charge are guilty of deliberate falsehood, but there are those perhaps who think it is true.

The Abolitionists are a distinct party, originating in the northeast part of the Union some twenty years ago. Their avowed purpose as a party was to *abolish* Slavery every where in the United States, and hence their name of Abolitionists. They have kept up their organization and their purpose to the present hour, and have now in the field as their candidates for President and Vice-President, Gerrit Smith and Fred. Douglass. They denounce the Constitution of the United States as "a compact with hell," and seek a dissolution of the Union. They are the counterpart of the present Democratic party, the latter seeking to extend Slavery every where, and the former to abolish it every where, and they are equally regardless of the most sacred constitutional and legal compacts and compromises. While the Republican party, saying to both these ultra sectional factions, Hold off, reposes upon the Union as it is, and makes the federal Constitution the basis of its eternal duration. The true Abolitionists hate us worse than they do the Democrats, because we intend to preserve the Union at all hazards, while they recognise in the action of the Democratic party the ultimate success of their own wishes.

We are called disunionists. This charge comes with ill grace from the party which includes within its bosom all the followers of J. C. Calhoun in his nullification doctrine, all the States rights men of Georgia who openly defied the laws of the Union as decided by the Supreme Court in the case of the Cherokee Indians, all the men who composed the Nashville seceding convention, and all who at any time have threatened to dissolve the Union, and whose Cabinet officer, possessing more influence than all the others put together, is Jeff. Davis, the notorious Mississippi secessionist.

In contrast with these I venture the assertion, that no prominent man acting with the Republican party, ever made the declaration that in any event would he or his party favor a dissolution of the Union.

And now even in this exciting contest, the result of which is so momentous, we intend to stand by the Union at all hazards. If we are defeated we will submit to the rule of the majority; if we succeed we shall endeavor to see if the laws of this great Government cannot be enforced, if a factious minority endeavor to carry out their disunion threats.

We are for the Union, for the whole Union, and have so declared in every public or private declaration of our principles; and if the Union must be dissolved, the Republican party, wraping itself in the mantle of the principles of the Declaration of Independence and of the Constitution, will fall like Caesar at the base of its pillar of eternal truth, clinging to the wreck so long as a fragment of the great temple remains.

The outcome of the election was that Miller was defeated; considering the voting habits of the district, it was just as he had expected.

In July 1860 Ballinger came north to see his parents, then living on a farm near Keokuk, and spent some time with his brother-in-law. In his diary he wrote:

Miller has a very fine house & lives in good style. . . .[24]
After dinner [on July 14] went over into Illinois to witness a Republican meeting & hear Mr Miller who was chief speaker.

[24] July 10.

It was not well attended — Miller md. a sensible & I shd think pretty effective speech — Bruce a lawyer from Keokuk [trained in Miller's office] & old Dr Winter [Mrs. Miller's father, a Baptist minister from Pennsylvania] made speeches also.

Miller and Ballinger were by that time far removed in politics. The latter held the view that

if the hand of Providence be visible in any thing in this world it is in the American slavery — necessary, I believe, in the first place to the development of this country — 'elevating' to the African race & promising their redemption hereafter.[25]

I think the Republican party dangerous & unconstitutional and I think experience has demonstrated the necessity for further guards against sectional majorities — But I believe they are to be sought peacefully & within the Union & that the disruption of the Union without such efforts is treason to humanity.[26]

To leaf through the Keokuk papers during the presidential campaign of 1860 is to catch a feeling of the pulsing life of the Northwest in Lincoln's day. Miller was a member of the State Central Committee, and leader of the host at Keokuk. There were barbecues and basket meetings, with oratory spouting from all the grandstands in every picnic grove; torchlight processions, with Wide-Awakes on foot and Wide-Awakes on horseback, and a boy's brigade called the "Lincoln Rangers." One reads of a train of 170 wagons lumbering in from one locality; another delegation coupled its wagons together and came behind twenty yoke of oxen. The summons ran throughout the countryside, to "all good Republicans and the rest of mankind, with their wives, children and sweethearts, and baskets and stores." Republican young ladies presented a campaign flag to their Wide-Awake beaux, while their sisters of the opposite persuasion went about wearing blue scarves embossed in gilt letters to proclaim their uncompromising alternatives: "A Democrat or no Husband." The many German emigrants in the locality were attracted to the

[25] Diary, June 21, 1860.
[26] From a long memorandum in Ballinger's diary, written at the close of 1860.

rallies, where they would be found grouped about the stand where Edmund Jaeger recounted in their own tongue the reasons why they were all going to vote for Lincoln.

The big moment for the Republicans of Lee County came at the "Grand Outpouring" on October 10, with Miller in charge. For days the *Gate City* had been working up enthusiasm. Advertisements of the distinguished speakers invited to be present suggested that all the heavy artillery west of the Alleghenies was to be let loose on Keokuk at a single moment: Tom Corwin, Carl Schurz, Frank Blair, Caleb B. Smith, Cassius M. Clay, John Sherman, Owen Lovejoy, Orville H. Browning, Lyman Trumbull, Dick Yates, B. Gratz Brown, and others of smaller caliber. Though the event hardly came up to these representations, it was nonetheless "the grandest public day Keokuk had ever seen." Twenty-five thousand were on the ground. Ferry boats operating as fast as the wind would permit toiled until three in the afternoon to bring over the crowds from Illinois, while others were turned back. There were twenty-six companies of Wide-Awakes from all the near-by towns. At the speakers' stand Miller presided and introduced the orators of the day — men who were soon to have an important relation to his own personal fortunes. For there were James W. Grimes, United States Senator from Iowa, and John A. Kasson, who was to be first assistant postmaster general under Lincoln, friends who were to aid in procuring his appointment to the Court. And with them on the stand sat Orville Browning [27] from Quincy, Lincoln's friend who was to seek a judgeship

[27] Browning's diary records the following:

"Wednesday Oct 10 1860 Bright, fine Autumn day, but windy. About 10 A M went with Frank Marsh in a buggy to Hamilton on my way to Keokuk to attend Republican meeting. The wind was high, and difficult to cross the River, but landed on the other side before 12.

"Dined at Sam Millers — then went to woods up the River where the stands were erected for speaking. The wind blew almost a gale, but I spoke to a very large crowd for about two hours. . . . From 20,000 to 30,000 persons at the meeting. Brilliant wide awake procession at night

"Thursday Oct 11, 1860 Stayed all night at Sam Millers last night."

(*The Diary of Orville Hickman Browning*, I, 431; Collections of the Illinois State Historical Library, vol. xx, 1925.)

at the same time as Miller, only to lose to Lincoln's other friend, Judge David Davis of Bloomington.

Along with the irrationalities there was solid talk about homestead legislation and free labor and federal aid for internal improvements. The Republican newspaper ran an editorial entitled "Capitalists Own the Soil and the Laborers," concluding that "the Democracy can't stand it to see [the] territories occupied by 'small fisted farmers,' who cultivate their own 'dirty acres.' Not they; they go in for gentlemen owning the soil and the laborers who cultivate it." [28] Miller's partner, Rankin, published a letter to point out that

the great principle of a homestead addresses itself directly to the laboring men of America. The first object after marriage is to secure a lot and house, or a farm which the occupant can call his own, which he can *own*, even when panics or reverses afflict the country. In the present political canvass for the Presidency, this principle grows in importance. There is a determination among the laboring masses that our broad prairies shall not be given up to speculation and peculation; but that the Government shall divide out amongst honest men, toiling men, among bones and muscles, with their upright minds to animate them, our vast, unappropriated domain.

He went on to argue that if elected Lincoln would favor the use of the public lands to redress inequalities of opportunity.[29]

In the result, Iowa went Republican by a comfortable margin, while on the local front Keokuk returns gave Lincoln 858, Douglas 705, Breckenridge 6, Bell 43. Lee County went to Douglas by fourteen votes.

On the morrow of the victory Miller wrote:

My Dear Bro.

The election is over and the result is ascertained beyond any resonable doubt. Mr Lincoln is fairly elected President for four years from the 4th March next. However much we may have differed in our wishes in reference to this event before its occurrence I feel sure that we will agree in the desire that he may have

[28] *Gate City*, Keokuk, September 29, 1860.
[29] *Gate City*, August 25, 1860.

a fair trial in the administration of the government and that that trial may result in satisfying the country, both North and South, that no just cause exists for revolution. My confidence in the real conservatism of Mr Lincoln is strong, and my hope is that in this he will be vigorously supported both by the mass of the republican party and the better portion of all parties at the South. It is however undeniable that a class of men high in the confidence of the Southern people have for many years desired a dissolution of the present union, and a separate Southern Confederacy.

That these men will renew and continue the slavery agitation, and that they will seize the occasion of Mr Lincolns election, to influence to its utmost, the discontent of the South is certain. The Republicans have conscientiously exercised their right and elected a President in the mode pointed out by the Constitution. A man against whose fair character the well known skill of democratic detraction, has failed to urge any serious fault. It remains then for the South alone to determine this question.

For myself, I am hopeful that if disunion is determined on by any respectable portion of the South, the States which concur in that design, will, instead of foolish invective and gasconading preparations for war, appoint their commissioners duly authorised, and treat like sensible men of the basis on which two nations shall be established. It is true we cannot permit a single State to set up for herself in our midst, but if enough join in the movement to make it creditable let the thing be done decently and in order.[30]

The moderation of the last paragraph is remarkable. Greeley's *Tribune* of November 9 had said much the same thing.

Miller was now one of the outstanding leaders in the state, and the course of political development seemed to call him to some public employment. His oft-repeated remarks about his unwillingness to become a candidate should not be taken to mean that he was indifferent to holding an *important* office, or that he supposed that by political foreordination the office would go seeking out the man. To be war governor of Iowa, for instance — that would be something really worth his while. Governor Samuel J. Kirkwood had been elected in 1859, and through his manager, Elijah Sells, had done what

[30] Letter of November 11, 1860.

was needful to secure a renomination in 1861. But as Sells recalled later,

at the convention there were other candidates, and one of the most prominent was Hon. Samuel F. Miller of Keokuk, a warm personal friend, who appealed to me earnestly for help; he was extravagant in his estimate of my influence; he said to me, "you can nominate me if you will; you were for Kirkwood before, you ought to be for me now." I said that for him it was hopeless, that Kirkwood would be nominated on the first ballot, that votes enough were pledged to him to secure it; that I was unconditionally for Kirkwood; that I had been working for him in good faith from the beginning and could not and would not stultify myself.[31]

When the convention met an informal ballot was taken, giving Kirkwood 272½, Miller 31, with 70½ votes being cast for others. The official ballot which followed gave Kirkwood 310½ and Miller 19, with 44½ votes going to others.[32]

This defeat did not prevent Miller from rendering valuable service in putting Iowa on a war footing. A special session of the legislature in May 1861 voted bonds to create a War and Defense Fund. But it made no appropriation for immediate needs, and the bonds did not find a ready market. Miller and others gave their own notes to raise the funds necessary to pay and arm the troops.[33] On another occasion the officer in charge of the state forces in southeastern Iowa received a warning that fifteen hundred of the enemy were about to come on a raid from Missouri for the purpose of stealing horses and supplies preparatory to going south to join the rebel army. Believing Keokuk to be their objective, he hastened there, only to find no troops available. He called on Miller, who immediately organized a committee of safety. A consignment of arms was commandeered and the several towns threatened were made ready to resist attack.[34] In the

[31] John M. Davis, "Elijah Sells," in *Annals of Iowa*, 3 ser. II (1896), 518, 525.
[32] D. E. Clark, *Samuel Jordan Kirkwood* (Iowa City: State Historical Society of Iowa, 1917), pp. 197, 422n.
[33] Clark, *Kirkwood*, p. 207; Pollock, "The Iowa War Loan of 1861," *Iowa Journal of History and Politics* (1917), xv, 496.
[34] Recollection of General Cyrus Bussey, in the Washington *Evening Star* at the time of Miller's death; quoted in the *Gate City*, October 18, 1890.

summer of 1862 he joined in the call of the State Central Committee to all loyal citizens to support the Administration in a vigorous prosecution of the war, and presided at a meeting which pledged that Lee County would supply all calls by volunteers without need of resort to the draft.[35]

But ours is not the story of any village Hampden. Its scene now shifts to the nation's capital.

NOTE. The reader may mark the omission from the foregoing account of various particulars which Mr. Burton J. Hendrick sets out in his description of Miller as a lawyer, *The Bulwark of the Republic* (Boston: Little, Brown and Company, 1937), pages 380–384. I am compelled entirely to dissent from that account, many of whose details I have been unable to substantiate. Mr. Hendrick's distinction as a biographer and the popularity which his book has enjoyed make it proper that I should not ignore his comments. While the anecdote concerning John J. Crittenden is probably founded in fact, to say that Crittenden "sent" Miller from Kentucky to the West thirty years before 1862 is quite wrong chronologically, and magnifies into a cause what I think was at most a mere incident in Miller's life.

The description of Miller while at the Iowa bar, "circuit riding from county court to county court, frequently amid rain and snow, and camping in the open," encounters many objections. The county court was not a court of general jurisdiction, but merely a court of probate with a variety of governmental duties, such as supervision of roads and bridges, which were transferred in 1860 to a county board of supervisors (Iowa Code of 1851, c. 15; Code of 1860, c. 22). There was at that time no tribunal known as the circuit court. The court of general jurisdiction was styled the district court. Without citing the numerous statutes on the subject enacted between 1850 and 1862, it will suffice to say that when Miller came to Iowa five such courts had been created, and that the number was thereafter increased. It was set at eleven by the constitution of 1857. In 1850 the first district, in which Miller practiced, included five counties. After 1853 it comprised only four: Lee, Des Moines, Louisa, and Henry. This was a relatively small segment of the state, lying along the Mississippi River in the southeastern corner of Iowa. The district court held terms in every county. When one takes note of the dates set for the various terms, and of the intervening distances, it seems most improbable that Miller ever had to camp on his way to appear at court. The district court for Lee County sat at Keokuk and also at Fort Madison, twenty-five miles distant. Reeves and Miller advertised that they also attended the court for Van Buren County, which was in the second district. The district court for Van Buren County sat at Keosauqua, fifty miles from Keokuk. To reach the district court for Jefferson County involved a somewhat longer journey.

Mr. Hendrick goes on to say that "Miller frequently crossed the Mississippi into Illinois, and here, at country taverns and in courtrooms, he met now and then another legal luminary. That Abraham Lincoln and the Keokuk attorney should find much in common was inevitable." The suggestion is even ventured that Lincoln borrowed freely from Miller's "perpetual flow of stories." This is irreconcilable with the evidence of John A. Kasson of Iowa, First Assistant Postmaster General under Lincoln, that when he called on the Presi-

[35] *Daily Hawk-Eye*, Burlington, July 3, 1862; *Gate City*, August 15, 1862.

dent to urge Miller's appointment to the Supreme Court in 1862, he found that Lincoln did not know who Miller was (*Annals of Iowa*, 3 ser. 1, 1894, p. 252). It is well known that Lincoln followed the Eighth Illinois Circuit, presided over by his friend Judge David Davis, whom he was later to appoint to the United States Supreme Court. This circuit lay along the eastern edge of Illinois. (See the map in F. T. Hill's *Lincoln the Lawyer*, New York: Century Company, 1912, p. 169.) That Miller would have left an extensive practice in Iowa to follow a circuit court through the eastern part of Illinois is most improbable. Nor has it been shown that Lincoln and Miller met elsewhere at the bar. Miller's name does not appear in the published record of Lincoln's day-by-day activities (B. P. Thomas, *Lincoln, 1847–1853*, Springfield, 1936; P. M. Angle, *Lincoln, 1854–1861*, Springfield, 1933; published by the Abraham Lincoln Association). Miller's letters do not refer to Lincoln or to Justice Davis as persons with whom he had been acquainted prior to 1862.

For the assertion that Lincoln understood that Miller's nomination "would arouse unfavorable comment," no evidence has been adduced.

The incident recounted by Mr. Hendrick on page 384 occurred, not on the bench of the Supreme Court, but in the federal circuit court at Saint Louis (New York *Sun*, September 26, 1892; 25 *Chicago Legal News* 52, 1892).

III

A NEW JUSTICE ON THE SUPREME COURT

A FEW DAYS after the regular session of Congress had convened in December 1861, Senator Hale of New Hampshire, sometime Free-Soil candidate for the presidency, rose to introduce a resolution:

That the Committee on the Judiciary be instructed to inquire into the expediency and propriety of abolishing the present Supreme Court of the United States, and establishing, instead thereof, another Supreme Court, in pursuance of the provisions of the Constitution, which, in the opinion of Congress, will meet the requirements of the Constitution.[1]

The Senator went on to sketch the beneficent results which his proposal sought to accomplish:

I know, Sir, that a great many people, in their hearts, read the clause of the Constitution relative to the judiciary in this way: that the judicial power of the United States shall be vested in the Supreme Court. That is the way it is commonly read and understood; but that is not the way it reads in the book. The Constitution says:

"The judicial power of the United States shall be vested in one Supreme Court" —

It limits Congress from creating more than one — "and in such inferior courts as the Congress may, from time to time, ordain and establish."

The supreme judicial court and the inferior courts, in whom the judicial power is vested, are all grouped together and qualified to be such as Congress shall from time to time establish. I do not like, sir, to say unpleasant things of anybody, anywhere, but sometimes I have to do so and I feel the necessity now. I undertake to say that the Supreme Court of the United States, as at present established, has utterly failed. It is bankrupt in everything that was intended by the creation of such a tribunal. It has lost public confidence; it does not enjoy public respect, and

[1] *Congressional Globe*, 37 Cong., 2 Sess., p. 26; December 9, 1861.

it ought not. . . . The Supreme Court has been a part of the machinery of the old Democratic party, just as much as the Baltimore conventions were; and the result is that it stands to-day before the community wanting in public confidence.

Such being the case, I ask Congress to look this thing right in the face, right in the eye, and march up to their duty and establish a Supreme Court as the Constitution requires them to do "from time to time"; yes, sir, "from time to time." . . . My idea is that the time has come; that this is one of the very times the framers of the Constitution contemplated. One of those times was at the adoption of the Federal Constitution, and the other time has now arrived.

I know how this court has been filled. I know how it has been filled in my own circuit. A man was imposed upon us against all but the unanimous voice of the people.[2] What was he put there for? . . . The reason assigned on this floor . . . was that, upon the questions that were elucidated and brought out in the Dred Scott decision, he was known to sympathize with the men who were for forcing those doctrines upon the country. This court have not been careful to study and find out and declare the law; but they have been careful to declare what was agreeable to the party in power, and have declared it. The party which was then in power has gone out of power, and it seems to me it is not incumbent on us, now that they have abandoned the ground, to hold up and maintain what they have built up as the citadel of their power in our midst, to wit, the present Supreme Court of the United States.

The proposal was one of those root-and-branch propositions which caused anti-slavery leaders to be distinguished rather for candor than for moderation. Only a few of the Senator's colleagues were prepared to go so far. And aside from the obvious speciousness of his construction of the Constitution, there was little reason why they should display such haste to reap the fruits of victory. There were already three vacancies, through the deaths of Justices Daniel and McLean and the resignation of Justice Campbell. Chief Justice Taney was almost eighty-five, older than any other justice who had sat upon the bench before. Of the four others who had joined in the detested Dred Scott decision, the youngest was then

[2] Justice Clifford of Maine, appointed by President Buchanan on December 9, 1857, to take the seat Justice Curtis had resigned on September 1.

sixty-nine. The Republican leaders could well afford to exercise restraint.

President Lincoln took his time in placing his own appointees upon the Court he had so often criticized. In his
annual message he had drawn attention to the three vacancies
and explained why he had forborne to make any nominations:

> I have been unwilling to throw all the appointments north-
> ward, thus disabling myself from doing justice to the South on
> the return of peace; although I may remark that to transfer to
> the North one which has heretofore been in the South would not,
> with reference to territory and population, be unjust.
> During the long and brilliant judicial career of Judge McLean
> his circuit grew into an empire — altogether too large for any one
> judge to give the courts therein more than a nominal attendance.

The President pointed to the necessity for amending the
Judiciary Act. The country had been divided into nine
circuits, in each of which one of the Supreme Court justices,
when not sitting in Washington, was required to hold circuit
court. But as new states were admitted it had been impossible
to make the services of the justices stretch so far, with the
result that Wisconsin, Minnesota, Iowa, Kansas, California,
and Oregon, as well as Florida and Texas, had never been
brought within any of the nine circuits.

> Nor [continued the President's message] can this well be reme-
> died without a change in the system, because the adding of new
> judges to the Supreme Court, enough for the accommodation of
> all parts of the country with circuit courts, would create a court
> altogether too numerous for a judicial body of any sort. And the
> evil, if it be one, will increase as new States come into the Union.
> Circuit courts are useful or they are not useful. If useful, no
> State should be denied them; if not useful, no State should have
> them. Let them be provided for all or abolished for all.

The President went on to suggest three possible courses:

> Let the Supreme Court be of convenient number in every event;
> then, first, let the whole country be divided into circuits of con-
> venient size, the Supreme judges to serve in a number of them
> corresponding to their own number, and independent circuit
> judges be provided for all the rest; or, secondly, let the Supreme

judges be relieved from circuit duties and circuit judges provided for all the circuits; or, thirdly, dispense with circuit courts
altogether, leaving the judicial functions wholly to the district
courts and an independent Supreme Court.

In these views the President was thirty years ahead of his
time — or, more exactly, the persistence of traditional thinking in Congress caused it to postpone for a generation a
reform already needed. Without considering any of the President's suggestions, the legislature set out once more to group
the states (other than California and Oregon) so that they
would fall into nine circuits.

It will be evident at once that the pattern finally to be
adopted for the new division would determine which of the
many aspirants for appointment to the Court would be
geographically available. The first, second, third, and fourth
of the existing circuits, embracing the north and middle
Atlantic states, presented no problem. The South was, at the
moment, unconcerned as to how Congress might legislate for
an area in arms which no justice had visited since Judge
Catron's escape from his Confederate neighbors in Tennessee.
The question was simply how three circuits were to be carved
out of the West, where no possible scheme of grouping could
take advantage of the wealth of talent. And while senators
and congressmen talked geography, everyone was thinking of
personalities. At last one member blurted out, "I fear too
many mantles for Supreme Court judges have already been
cut out, and made up. If it were not for that, there would be
little trouble in arranging the States in compact circuits." [3]

In Ohio, where the late Justice McLean had lived, there
was Noah H. Swayne. He had lost no time in registering his
claim. On April 4, 1861, he wrote to Chase, his professional
friend, and now Secretary of the Treasury, to say:

Intelligence of the death of Judge McLean reached here this
morning. My friends will name me to the President as one of
those from whom a selection is to be made to fill the vacancy upon
the Bench of the Supreme Court, thus created. If you can deem

[3] *Congressional Globe*, 37 Cong., 2 Sess., p. 2564; June 4, 1862.

it proper to give me your friendly support you will lay me under a lasting obligation.[4]

From Indiana came Caleb B. Smith, then Secretary of the Interior in Lincoln's cabinet.[5] He was destined to receive only the consolation prize of a district judgeship. The President's own state offered an embarrassment of riches: there was his personal friend Orville H. Browning, temporarily occupying Stephen A. Douglas' seat in the Senate; Judge David Davis, who had managed Lincoln's campaign, could not be ignored; and finally there was Judge Drummond of the federal district court, whose name was being urged by the Illinois bar.[6] The senator from Wisconsin, James R. Doolittle, was displaying an active interest in the drawing of the circuits. And then of course there was Iowa to be heard from.

Miller had no false modesty. Conscious of his ability, and never doubting the soundness of his principles, he longed for an opportunity to wield public power. Personal ambition and zeal for the common good found in him a happy combination. The formula used to attain his objective seems to have been the same that Forrest gave as the secret of his success in battle: "To get there fustest with the mostest men." The senators and representatives from Iowa and the congressional allies they enlisted, the state bar, the Governor and the legislature, all went into action, and presently the candidate himself went on to Washington to see that nothing was left undone. The maneuver had two stages. It was first essential to

[4] Chase Papers, Library of Congress.

[5] *The Diary of Edward Bates 1859–1866*, edited by Howard K. Beale (Washington: Government Printing Office, 1933), p. 244. The Attorney General made this entry for March 26, 1862: "To day, at my office — and tonight at my house, again had long talk, with Judge S.[wayne] about the filling of the va[ca]nt seats on the Sup[rem]e. bench. He thinks that a very strenuous effort is making to get C. B. Smith appointed, and that the effort is almost crowned with success — That there is a bill pending to gerrymander the Circuits to suit — so as to give Smith a circuit without interferring [sic] with Browning — nobody it [I] think objects to Browning — He is a proper man — *Note* I have warned the Prest to be on his guard."

[6] Thomas Drummond had been appointed district judge in 1850. Lincoln had tried cases before him. President Grant appointed him circuit judge when that office was created in 1869.

cause the four trans-Mississippi states, Missouri, Iowa, Kansas, and Minnesota, to be grouped in the ninth circuit. This involved resisting all the other circuit-makers who sought to occupy this territory. It was an effort of six months' duration. The second and much the simpler part of the undertaking was to convince the President that Miller was a proper appointee. This was finally accomplished in four days.

On January 24, 1862, while the new judiciary legislation was under discussion, the Senate consented to the appointment of Swayne of Ohio as successor to the late Justice McLean. President Lincoln is said first to have offered the place to Aaron F. Perry of the firm of Taft and Perry — a leader at the Cincinnati bar and a stanch Republican.[7] Some appointment had been necessary to give assistance to a Court reduced to six, of whom Taney and Catron were in precarious health.[8] Before the bill came to a final vote, Justice Swayne had started on his circuit, where he created so favorable an impression that the bars of neighboring states were eager to be grouped with Ohio. This suggested various permutations and combinations which made the game of the Iowans seem now won, now lost.

As the bill [9] emerged from the Senate Committee on the Judiciary, Trumbull of Illinois in charge, the division was made as follows: Kentucky went with Ohio in the seventh; Indiana, Michigan, Wisconsin, and Minnesota in the eighth; while Iowa was bracketed with Illinois, Missouri, and Kansas in the ninth.[10] This would have placed Miller in competition with the several candidates from Illinois. Senator Grimes of Iowa endeavored to secure an amendment to bring together the four states beyond the river. In this and subse-

[7] Biographical Directory of the American Congress (Washington: Government Printing Office, 1928), p. 1403.

[8] Charles Warren, The Supreme Court in United States History (Boston: Little, Brown and Company, new ed. 1926), II, 378.

[9] S. No. 89. As introduced by Senator Sherman of Ohio, it would have had Ohio, Indiana, and Michigan compose the seventh circuit, and Illinois, Wisconsin, Minnesota, Iowa, and Kansas the ninth. The committee reported it with amendments.

[10] Congressional Globe, 37 Cong., 2 Sess., p. 187; January 6, 1862.

quent debates each legislator argued that he should have what he wanted because his state was developing so rapidly and its people were so phenomenally litigious. Senator Grimes made the point that his proposal brought together four states which had similar codes of practice not found elsewhere. The Iowan's amendment was defeated and the bill passed as it had come from committee, and went to the House.[11]

It was fortunate for Miller that one of the representatives from Iowa, James F. Wilson, was a member of the House Judiciary Committee, since he was thereby enabled to get control of the Senate bill. It emerged from his committee with amendments proposed, restoring the arrangement the Iowans desired. Wilson had had four months to prepare the way and to think up new, if not more convincing, reasons why Iowa should have what it wanted. Not only did the four western states have similar procedure, but they were "all more or less affected by the old Spanish and French grants"; they traded together along the Mississippi and Missouri rivers; territories presently to be admitted as states could conveniently be added to this circuit; and finally the Iowa troops were very brave in battle.[12]

During the debate one member from Indiana declared that he wanted an appointment from his state if it should be separated from Ohio, but that he preferred that it should be united in order that it might enjoy the services of Justice Swayne. Later on it will appear that Justice Swayne earned less golden opinions, so it is important to a fair judgment to note how great was his popularity as disclosed in the congressional debate. The member from Indiana said: "I have before me a petition signed by almost all the leading members of the bar of Indiana who practice in the Federal courts, requesting that Indiana and Ohio shall be retained in the same circuit, in order that they may have the judicial services of that pure, able, and learned jurist, Judge Swayne." [13]

---

[11] *Congressional Globe*, 37 Cong., 2 Sess., p. 469; January 24, 1862.
[12] *Congressional Globe*, 37 Cong., 2 Sess., pp. 2561ff.; June 6, 1862.
[13] *Congressional Globe*, 37 Cong., 2 Sess., p. 2665; June 11, 1862.

The House passed the bill with the amendments Wilson desired, leaving Indiana united to Illinois and Wisconsin.

Back in the Senate the Judiciary Committee reported adversely to the House amendments, requesting at the same time to be discharged from further consideration of the petitions of the Indiana bar, as well as of a resolution wherein the Iowa legislature had urged that the state be placed in a circuit lying west of the river.[14] The senators from Indiana insisted on an amendment restoring Justice Swayne to their state. The senators from Ohio and Michigan were agreed with them in desiring to be together. Said Senator Wright of Indiana:

> The judge of that circuit is willing to take a population of four million and a half, or his representatives here are. Why not allow us, then, to be together in one circuit? We have a judge there that we are satisfied with. I presented the other day the petition of members of the bar from every county in my State, desiring Judge Swayne to be their judge.[15]

They were allowed what they desired, and in that shape the measure went to conference.

Of the conference committee, only two members had a direct interest in the measure: Senator Wright of Indiana and Representative Wilson of Iowa. The latter obtained unanimous consent to have one circuit west of the Mississippi. And the gentleman from Indiana succeeded in forcing Michigan into an unwelcome union with Wisconsin and Illinois in order that Indiana might share Judge Swayne with Ohio.

When the conference report was presented, the senators from Michigan cried out against the unnatural cruelty which would sever those ties of kindred affection which had always bound their people to those of Ohio.[16] Moreover, Michigan had a large amount of admiralty business, and they were con-

---

[14] *Congressional Globe*, 37 Cong., 2 Sess., p. 2914; June 25, 1862. The joint resolution of the Iowa legislature had been adopted March 10, 1862 (*Acts and Resolutions* of the Ninth General Assembly, p. 245; Joint Resolution No. 9).

[15] *Congressional Globe*, 37 Cong., 2 Sess., p. 3090; July 3, 1862.

[16] *Congressional Globe*, 37 Cong., 2 Sess., p. 3276; July 12, 1862.

vinced that Justice Swayne (whose practice had been at Columbus) was particularly strong in that branch of law. They had put their heads together with that of Senator Doolittle of Wisconsin, and had worked out a substitute which would leave Michigan with Ohio and Indiana, and join Wisconsin with Iowa and Minnesota. Senator Doolittle secured the floor and enlarged upon the theme. "Laying aside all questions about who is going to be judge or anything of that kind, and coming right down honestly to the business transactions of the people," there was no doubt that Wisconsin, Iowa, and Minnesota should be one circuit. After this final struggle the conference report was adopted by a vote of twenty-four to twelve in the Senate, and without division in the House. This left Indiana grouped with Ohio, Michigan with Illinois and Wisconsin, and the four northwestern states together. On July 15 the bill became a law.

Miller's name had already been presented to President Lincoln. It seems that Governor Kirkwood was in Washington while the matter was pending, and that Senator Harlan of Iowa had invited him to go, along with the representatives from that state, to call upon the President and urge Miller's appointment. The story goes that they found him at his writing desk, his legs twined in a grapevine twist. The Senator and the Governor said that they were very anxious that he should make the appointment, whereupon Lincoln untangled himself, reached for pen and paper, and asked whom they wished to be appointed, and to what place. Harlan replied that they wanted Mr. Miller of Iowa to be appointed to the Supreme Court. " 'Well, well,' replied the President, replacing his pen and pushing back his paper, 'that is a very important position, and I will have to give it serious consideration. I had supposed you wanted me to make some one a Brigadier General for you.' " [17] Miller also

[17] Henry W. Lathrop, in *Iowa Historical Record*, VII (1891), 16. Lathrop was not present, but he was well acquainted with Kirkwood, whose biography he wrote. Some time previously Governor Kirkwood had been urging the President to appoint more brigadier generals from Iowa (S. H. M. Byers, *Iowa in War Times*, Des Moines: W. D. Condit and Company, 1888, p. 88).

worked through John A. Kasson, who left this recollection of the matter:

When, at his request, I called on President Lincoln to ascertain the cause of delay in his nomination, I found that his reputation as a lawyer had not then even extended so far as Springfield, Illinois, for the President asked me if he was the same man who had some years before made a frontier race for Congress from the southern district of Iowa, and had trouble about the Mormon vote.[18]

The President was thinking of another Keokuk lawyer, Daniel F. Miller, who resembled Sam Miller only in name. D. F. Miller had figured in an election contest over a seat in the Thirty-first Congress; a new election was ordered, which he won. He was something of a character, looking and dressing like Andrew Jackson, whose picture was always hanging in his law office.[19] He lived to preside over a meeting of the Keokuk bar called to adopt resolutions on the death of Justice Miller in 1890.[20]

When in 1879 Justice Miller addressed the Iowa bar association, bringing back his laurels that they might share them, he recalled that at the time of his appointment he was "comparatively unknown as a lawyer outside the borders of Iowa," and continued:

It was, therefore, due, in an unusual degree, to the heartiness and unanimity with which the bar of my own State recommended my appointment that the application was successful. It was a time of great political excitement and I have always felt peculiarly gratified that members of the bar who were zealous democrats vied with those of the republican party, of which I had, since its first organization, been an active supporter, in the sincerity and vigor of their recommendations. I do not recall that any lawyer

[18] *Annals of Iowa*, 3 ser. 1 (1894), 252.
[19] Biographical sketch and photograph in C. F. Davis, "Keokuk Biographical and Historical" (MS.), v, 97ff. In 1860 D. F. Miller had pushed himself forward as an independent candidate for a vacancy of the Iowa Supreme Court, against George G. Wright, one of the most distinguished of Iowa judges. Sam Miller had come out strongly for Wright, notably in a long letter in the Keokuk *Gate City* for October 10, 1860.
[20] *Gate City*, Keokuk, October 19, 1890.

in the State, of either political party, who was applied to for the use of his name, declined to give it.[21]

In response to an inquiry from the widow of Senator Grimes he wrote some further details of how his nomination was brought about:

My appointment was known to depend upon such an arrangement of the Judicial circuits by a bill then pending in Congress, as would include Iowa in a circuit entirely west of the Mississippi river. To this end all three of the gentlemen named [Senators Grimes and Harlan and Representative Wilson] contributed their best efforts, but Mr. Wilson, being on the Judiciary committee of the House, to which the bill was referred, was especially efficient. As soon as the bill was passed as they desired, Mr. Grimes drew up in his own handwriting a recommendation of my name for one of the two places then vacant on the Bench of the Supreme Court, to be laid before the President. This he signed, and assisted by Mr. Harlan, the other Iowa Senator, procured twenty-eight of the thirty-two senators then in Congress to sign it also, the latter number being all that was left of that body after the secession of the Confederate senators. Mr. Wilson circulated a similar recommendation in the House of Representatives, and it received the signatures of over one hundred and twenty members, which was probably three fourths of those in attendance.

I do not know or remember who presented these petitions to the President, but he afterwards said in my presence that no such recommendations for office had ever been made to him.[22]

On the night of July 16 President Lincoln sent the nomination to the Senate, where, in Miller's words, it was "confirmed in half an hour without reference to committee, a courtesy usually reserved for persons who have been members of that body." [23]

The *New York Times* was quick enough to catch this news in time for the issue of July 17. The *Tribune* recorded the event on July 18, in a despatch on the judicial reorganization,

---

[21] 20 *Albany Law Journal* 25 (1879).
[22] *Iowa Historical Record*, VII (1891), 88.
[23] Autobiographical sketch, p. 24. He says there were 126 names on the petition from the House of Representatives.

noting that the ninth circuit would be presided over by "Jus. Daniel F. Miller." [24] The *Tribune* added: "Mr. Miller's name is printed *Samuel* in the despatches, but we presume it is Daniel F. Miller, the first Whig Member of Congress ever chosen from Iowa." As to the appointment for the eighth circuit, the despatch mentioned Senator Browning and "Judge Daniel Davis" of Illinois as candidates. Elsewhere on the same page, however, the *Tribune* was more accurately advised as to just what the country had drawn in the way of a new justice, for it mentioned the support Miller had received on the part of members of Congress, and continued:

The Iowa, Minnesota, Kansas, Nebraska, and Colorado delegations here, and Frank Blair of Missouri, were among those who favored his appointment. The other Missourians here preferred Judge Brodhead of the State. Judge Miller is a Kentuckian by birth. He fought the battle of emancipation with Cassius M. Clay, and is a thorough Republican. He is 46 years of age, reputed the best lawyer in his State, and possesses great physical vigor. He was formerly the law partner of Col. Rankin of Keokuk, now commanding a regiment from Iowa. No appointment was made in the other new circuit, comprising the State of Illinois, Wisconsin, and Michigan. This is regarded as virtually the defeat of Senator Browning's aspirations to a seat on the bench. No appointment can now be made until the next session.

The *Chicago Tribune* reported the appointment on July 21, adding that "Judge Miller is a lawyer of a high order of talent, and has for many years occupied a prominent position in the Republican party of Iowa."

Back home the *Gate City* announced the good news to its readers on July 18, adding an appreciative review of the attainments of their fellow townsman. It said that "at the present time he has probably a more extensive practice than any other Lawyer in Iowa," and continued:

Mr. Miller has been distinguished for his mental energy and power, for his capacity for business and for intense and protracted labor in the pursuits of his profession, and for strong

[24] The same notice appeared in the Cincinnati *Daily Commercial* of July 22, and the Springfield *Daily Illinois State Journal* of July 24.

practical common sense and clear legal comprehension. These qualities have given him a power, influence and success in business, and with Judges and jurors above all competitors in his field.

His mind has a constitutional adaptation to the Law, while his earnest convictions, strong common sense and clear comprehension of the very spirit and marrow of the matter, prevents his being overwhelmed by the dust of antiquated precedents or entangled by the cobweb filaments of more modern technicalities.

He is in the very prime of life, in possession of a remarkably fine constitution and in the healthy enjoyment of all his mental and bodily powers. He is the model the *beau ideal* of a Western Lawyer and a Western Judge, and his advent to the Bench cannot fail to create a sensation even in that fossilized circle of venerable antiquities which constitutes the Bench of the Supreme Court of the United States.

There is no reason to suppose that Miller would have dissented from this contemporary characterization of the Court, or from the prophecy as to the part he was going to play in its redemption. Toward the most venerable of the "antiquities" he had entertained the same sentiments as virtually every other Republican of the time — as he himself later explained somewhat as follows:

When I came to Washington, I had never looked upon the face of Judge Taney, but I knew of him. I remembered that he had attempted to throttle the Bank of the United States, and I hated him for it. I remembered that he took his seat upon the Bench, as I believed, in reward for what he had done in that connection, and I hated him for that. He had been the chief Spokesman of the Court in the Dred Scott case, and I hated him for that. But from my first acquaintance with him, I realized that these feelings toward him were but the suggestions of the worst elements of our nature; for before the first term of my service in the Court had passed, I more than liked him; I loved him. And after all that has been said of that great, good man, I stand always ready to say that conscience was his guide and sense of duty his principle.[25]

[25] Miller's words as recollected by Henry E. Davis, and recalled by him in the *Proceedings of the Bench and Bar of the Supreme Court of the United States in Memoriam Samuel F. Miller*, p. 17.

A NEW JUSTICE

Whatever his own sentiments toward his brethren might be, and however they might clash over the decision of controversies, Miller always strove to maintain good personal relations within the Court. And it is due to his first graceful act of this sort that we are able to record Taney's initial reaction to his new colleague. As soon as he was commissioned, Miller requested Attorney General Bates to present him to the Chief Justice, as the latter recalled in a letter to Justice Clifford:

I saw Judge Miller our new brother a few days ago. He called as he was good enough to say to pay his respects to me & to ask me to administer the oaths of office — which I did — It was the first time I had seen him, & his appearance & manner made a very favorable impression on me — I learned from him & Mr. Bates who introduced him, that the appointment of Mr. Browning to the vacant circuit, although probable was not certain. He has it seems two competitors both of whom are pressed by strong friends — One of them is Drummond the District Judge. I do not recollect the name of the other candidate — It seems that the claims of the rival candidates has [sic] been regarded as strong enough to produce some hesitation on the part of the President — [26]

This initial kindliness between men of utterly divergent views survived the ordeal of the conference room, for a year later, when the Court rose, the Chief Justice took leave of his colleague with words such as these:

My brother Miller, I am an old and broken man. I may not be here when you return. I cannot let you go without expressing to you my great gratification that you have come among us. At the beginning of the term I feared that the unhappy condition of the country would cause collisions among us. On the other hand, this has proved one of the pleasantest terms I have ever attended. I owe it greatly to your courtesy. Your learning, zeal, and powers of mind assure me that you will maintain and advance the high traditions of the Court. I predict for you a career of great usefulness and honor.[27]

[26] Written from Washington, August 2, 1862; Clifford Papers, Maine Historical Society.

[27] J. M. Woolworth, in remarks before the United States Circuit Court for Nebraska on the occasion of Miller's death. Printed in an addendum to the

The other appointment to the Court, which lay between Browning, Drummond, and Davis, after remaining in suspense until October 17, finally went to Davis.[28] The President's original inclination to favor Browning seems to have been overcome through the intervention of Leonard Swett in Davis' behalf. Swett had traveled up and down the famous eighth Illinois circuit, where Judge Davis held court, and where Lincoln had found a zest in life never known while he lived at home and attended to office business. And Swett had been a companion of those fabulous nights when the elect gathered in Davis' room to hear Lincoln talk — of which H. C. Whitney's *Life on the Circuit with Lincoln* [29] preserved only a little of the quality and flavor. The efforts exerted are illustrated by the following letter from Swett to Judge Samuel Treat of the federal district court at Saint Louis. Treat was an influential War Democrat who had opposed the repeal of the Missouri Compromise and had supported Douglas' presidential candidacy in 1856 and 1860.

Bloomington Jan 31 1862

Hon Samuel Treat
    St Louis Mo.

Dear Sir,

I take the liberty of addressing you a note in behalf of our mutual friend Hon David Davis. As one of his friends, I am desirous that the President should appoint him Judge of the U S. Supreme Court for the new district. I have been giving the matter some attention, and am quite positive the choice, in the mind of the President, lies between Judge Davis & Hon O H. Browning.

Proceedings quoted above, at p. 61. Woolworth was a close friend of Justice Miller, and his recreation of Taney's remarks may be taken as a faithful recollection of what Miller had told him.

[28] Friends of Davis had been active in his behalf from the moment Justice McLean died in 1861. When Davis heard that Judge Drummond might be appointed, thus creating a vacancy as federal district judge, he said he "would prefer it to the Supreme Judgeship because I know I could discharge the duties of the one satisfactorily, but am diffident about the other" (Letter to Ward H. Lamon, April 14, 1861, quoted by H. E. Pratt in "David Davis 1815–1886," *Publication Thirty-seven of the Illinois State Historical Library*, 1930, p. 171).

[29] (Boston: Estes and Lauriat, 1892).

It seems to me that the legal men of the district should be consulted, and I have no doubt the President would pay great regard to their opinions.

The Convention [30] now in session at Springfield, in this State, have very generally, irrespective of party, recommended Judge Davis.

If the bar of St Louis, would do the same thing, I believe, it would decide the matter in favor [of] Judge Davis.

If you think proper to move in this matter, & will get such a recommendation, I should think it a great favor; or if you prefer it, I will come there & do what I can myself.

I would be glad to hear from you upon this subject.

> Yours Truly
> Leonard Swett [31]

On the letter is an endorsement in Judge Treat's handwriting:

He came here, and with the co-operation of friends, the desire & recommendation of the Mo. Bar was had, also large recommendations from Ills.

Judge Davis was appointed.

President Lincoln asked us to get up and forward the recommendations.[32]

In enlisting support for Davis at Saint Louis Swett supposed, of course, that Missouri would be placed in the same circuit with Illinois.

When after the new circuits were created the President made no motion to fill the remaining vacancy, Swett determined to make a personal appeal, under circumstances which he recalled as follows:

I was then living at Bloomington, and met Judge Davis every day. As months elapsed we used to get word from Washington in reference to the condition of things; finally, one day the word came that Lincoln had said, "I do not know what I may do when

---

[30] The constitutional convention of 1862.

[31] Samuel Treat Collection, Missouri Historical Society.

[32] In a letter to the President on November 24, 1862, Treat wrote: "Permit me to express my great gratification at the service done the country in appointing Judge Davis to the U. S. Supreme Bench — a gratification felt alike by the Bar and loyal people here, as well as by the Bar and people of Illinois." The same sentiment was expressed in the course of another letter to the President on December 13, 1862. (Letters in the Samuel Treat Collection.)

the time comes, but there has never been a day when if I had to act I should not have appointed Browning." Judge Davis, General Orme, and myself held a consultation in my law-office at Bloomington. We decided that the remark was too Lincolnian to be mistaken and no man but he could have put the situation so quaintly. We decided also that the appointment was gone, and sat there glum over the situation. I finally broke the silence, saying in substance, "The appointment is gone and I am going to pack my carpet-sack for Washington." "No, you are not," said Davis. "Yes, I am," was my reply. "Lincoln is being swept off his feet by the influence of these Senators, and I will have the luxury of one more talk with him before he acts."

I did go home, and two days thereafter, in the morning about seven o'clock — for I knew Mr. Lincoln's habits well — was at the White House and spent most of the forenoon with him. I tried to impress upon him that he had been brought into prominence by the Circuit Court lawyers of the old eighth Circuit, headed by Judge Davis. "If," I said, "Judge Davis, with his tact and force, had not lived, and all other things had been as they were, I believe you would not now be sitting where you are." He replied gravely, "Yes, that is so." "Now it is a common law of mankind," said I, "that one raised into prominence is expected to recognize the force that lifts him, or, if from a pinch, the force that lets him out. . . . Here is Judge Davis, whom you know to be in every respect qualified for this position, and you ought in justice to yourself and public expectation to give him this place." We had an earnest pleasant forenoon, and I thought I had the best of the argument, and I think he thought so too.

I left him and went to Willard's Hotel to think over the interview, and there a new thought struck me. I therefore wrote a letter to Mr. Lincoln and returned to the White House. Getting in, I read it to him and left it with him. It was in substance, that he might think if he gave Davis this place the latter when he got to Washington would not give him any peace until he gave me a place equally good; that I recognized the fact that he could not give this place to Davis, which would be charged to the Bloomington faction in our State politics, and then give me anything I would have and be just to the party there; that this appointment, if made, should kill "two birds with one stone"; that I would accept it as one-half for me and one-half for the Judge; and that thereafter, if I or any of my friends ever troubled him, he could draw that letter as a plea in bar on that subject. As I read it Lincoln said, "If you mean that among friends as it reads I will take it and make the appointment." He at once did as he said.[33]

It may be an interesting, though ordinarily a futile, field of speculation to imagine what would have been the course of constitutional adjudication if some other among the rivals for a judicial appointment had received the preference. When a vacancy occurs several candidates appear, each praised by his friends in superlative terms. One is taken, and his name is perpetuated in the record of the collective labors of the Court. The others are often so lost to fame as to leave the historian wondering what sort of men they were. In so far as they may all have been children of their time, quite possibly one seated on the bench of justice would have acted much as another. The impact of social needs might have produced the same consequences from the Court however constituted. The influence of mind on mind in the conference room may deflect initial tendencies — as when Joseph Story comes on, pink-cheeked and thirty-two, as the disciple of Jefferson, and lives to utter dire prophecies on those who would not follow where Marshall had led.[34] Admit all this, and yet the personal element in constitutional interpretation remains very great.

In the case of Orville H. Browning we have more than mere conjecture as to what his course on the bench would have been, for his diary is rich in information.[35] Browning had come of a gentle Kentucky family, and was the advocate of a mild "border state" policy which would avoid extreme

[33] Letter of August 29, 1887, to William H. Herndon. It appears in chapter XVII of Herndon's *Lincoln* (Chicago, 1889), edited by Paul M. Angle, with an introduction and notes, under the title, *Herndon's Life of Lincoln* (New York: A. & C. Boni, 1930).

[34] *Cf.* Jefferson's advice to President Madison the year before Story was appointed: "It will be difficult to find a character of firmness enough to preserve his independence on the same bench with Marshall" (*The Works of Thomas Jefferson*, Federal Edition, 1905, XI, 139).

[35] *The Diary of Orville Hickman Browning*, being volumes XX (1925) and XXII (1933) of the Collections of the Illinois State Historical Library. There are excellent introductions by Professors T. C. Pease and J. G. Randall, respectively. It is to be noted that there is no mention of his being under consideration for a judgeship.

measures such as confiscation or general emancipation. While the reorganization of the circuits was before Congress, he made himself the head and front of the opposition to the bill "to confiscate the property of rebels" then being pushed by his colleague Trumbull and other radical Republicans.[36] For this reason it seems likely that Swett was mistaken in supposing that it was senatorial influence which was impelling Lincoln to appoint Browning. On the legal-tender bill the diary records this judgment: "I cannot believe that Congress has power to make any thing but gold and silver a tender in payment of debts, and if it had I believe it would injure the credit of the Country to do so, and I shall therefore feel constrained to vote against the bill." [37] In which connection it may be recalled that the act was at first held invalid, and later upheld by a bare majority of the Court.[38] By the November elections in 1862 he had ceased to be a vocal supporter of the President's policies, and the Emancipation Proclamation brought him to despair. For the rest of the war Browning's relation to the government was that of a lawyer-politician who used his *entrée* at Washington to intercede for clients whose objectives were not always meritorious. As a member of Johnson's cabinet in the early period of reconstruction he was completely out of sympathy with developments in national politics. It seems fair to suppose that if Lincoln's choice had finally fallen on Browning rather than Davis the relations between the Court and Congress would have been even more strained.

When Miller took his place on the bench at the December term of court in 1862 he doubtless felt as did Lord Birkenhead when promoted to the woolsack: "I approach the discharge of the high duties that await me in a spirit of anxious solicitude; but not, believe me, in one of morbid self-distrust." [39] He had already undertaken to master the new field

[36] Confiscation Act of July 17, 1862; 12 Statutes at Large 589.
[37] Entry for February 12, 1862; vol. I, p. 529.
[38] Hepburn v. Griswold, 8 Wallace 603 (1870); Knox v. Lee, 12 Wallace 457 (1871). Justice Davis was on the side holding the act constitutional.
[39] 10 *Canadian Bar Review* 71 (1932).

of federal jurisprudence, starting with 2 Dallas and working down to 1 Black.[40] To many lawyers in practice such a concentrated effort would have seemed quite formidable, but Miller took it in his stride. For, as he wrote in 1866, "You know I was about thirty when I commenced reading law, and from that time to this, say twenty years, few men of my acquaintance, have given as many hours to study, to hard intellectual labour as I have." [41]

He felt no undue diffidence in the presence of his elder colleagues, though he did not, as is sometimes stated, proclaim his advent by immediately launching a lone dissent.[42]

His presence in the Court did, indeed, invite interesting reflections. At the time when the Chief Justice was appointed, Miller had been in his first year at medical school. To the right and left of the Chief sat Wayne and Catron, the other survivors of the six whom Andrew Jackson had elevated to the bench.[43] In length of service the one was a year senior, the other a year junior to Taney. To the right and left again sat Judges Nelson and Grier. They had come on in 1845 and 1846 respectively — the years when Miller had just begun to study law. Justice Clifford, whose commission bore the date of December 9, 1857, was the newest of those who belonged to the old dispensation. He had been attorney general of Maine when Miller was working for an apothecary, and attorney general of the United States when Miller was admitted to the Kentucky bar.

This was the threshold of one of those periods — of which there have been several in the history of the Court — when in

[40] J. M. Woolworth, in *Proceedings . . . in Memoriam*, p. 61.
[41] Letter of July 2, 1866.
[42] Owing to the fact that the cases in 2 Black are not reported in chronological order, the opinion by Justice Miller first recorded is his dissent in Calais Steamboat Co. *v.* Scudder, 2 Black 372, 393. This was decided January 19, 1863. Prior to that he had spoken for the Court in Russell *v.* Ely, 2 Black 575, on December 15, 1862, and Lindsey *v.* Hawes, 2 Black 554, decided January 5, 1863.
[43] Justice Catron was nominated by President Jackson on March 3, 1837, and his nomination confirmed by the Senate on March 8, after Van Buren's inauguration.

a comparatively short time a majority of the personnel is renewed. For on March 3 following Congress established a tenth circuit, comprising California and Oregon, and increased the membership of the Court to ten. Promptly thereupon Lincoln appointed Stephen J. Field, the chief justice of California and a War Democrat. It was desirable, no doubt, that there be on the Court someone familiar with the land and mining law of California; but not the poorest reason for the statute was that it assured that questions of the power of government to suppress rebellion would not come before a Court too hopelessly weighted on the side of the old-line Democratic view of public policy. Following Taney's death, Salmon P. Chase came on the bench as chief justice in December 1864. This made five Lincoln appointees in a Court of ten; on Judge Catron's death on May 30, 1865, they became a majority.

This renewal of the Court brought Miller into a more influential position among its members. By 1870 he was reflecting that his life was like the Norway Maelstrom: yearly the course of events swept him more and more into the center of things.

I have never as you know been an idle man. But as I find here year after year not only an increased docket, but an increasing demand upon me *personally* in view of my special position in the court, and of the grave and doubtful questions which I am called on to decide, and as I feel the increasing responsibility attached to *my opinions* and actions, certainly the current requires greater labor to keep in the safe way and the circle *seems* to be narrowing as each year seems to grow shorter, until I too must go down to the last resting place of all men.

I have been striving to keep the court in what seems to me the wise course. I have earnestly worked to make it a court of law, and of justice. I hope not altogether without success. There is not much talent in it. There is much prejudice, or rather preoccupation. There is much political feeling of which perhaps I have my share. A good man can do much good in the court. I hope I have done some good and not much ill.[44]

<hr>

[44] Letter of February 10, 1870.

JUSTICE WAYNE

JUSTICE CATRON

JUSTICE GRIER

JUSTICE CLIFFORD

Some quantitative notion of the amount of Miller's judicial labors may be gathered from the accompanying table. The writer is fully conscious of the delusive exactness of such data. The enumeration deals with opinions, not cases. It is often a mere matter of convenience whether several contemporary controversies involving the same question of law are grouped together in one inclusive opinion, or are treated separately. No note is taken of cases determined without any opinion being filed, as was sometimes done, particularly where the Court stood evenly divided. And there is, of course, no way of representing the magnitude of the controversy or the significance of the decision in the life of the nation. This being noted, a few observations are warranted. First, the enormous increase in the work of the Court during Miller's service. One consequence of the social revolution which accompanied the Civil War was a tendency, illustrated by the Fourteenth Amendment and by legislation expanding the jurisdiction of the federal courts, to nationalize rights and to make the federal judiciary a haven of refuge for all corporations chartered under national law and for itinerant state corporations. Nationalist though he was in many respects, Miller saw in this tendency a menace to the vigor of the federal system, and struggled against it. More clearly, too, than almost any other man of his time he foresaw that the antiquated judicial machinery must break down under the new load. But his efforts in this regard were so important that they demand a separate chapter.

Again, Miller is spoken of as a great dissenter, and the figures afford some idea of the truth of this impression. It will be seen how the ratio of disagreement falls off, which may in part be attributed to Miller's influence over his brethren. But it is also true that in later years he tended to remain silent where dissent seemed futile. In 1871 he recorded that "I have grown more averse to dissents." [45]

Finally, it will be observed that Miller was assigned about twice his normal share of opinions in cases where the Consti-

45 Letter of May 1, 1871.

DECISIONS OF THE SUPREME COURT, 1862–1890

(Figures in italics refer to cases where the Federal Constitution was construed)

	DECISIONS OF THE COURT				WHERE MILLER WROTE THE OPINION			
Years and Reports	No. of Decisions	Miller for the prevailing opinion	Miller concurs	Miller dissents	No. of prevailing opinions by Miller	Dissents where M. wrote Court's opinion	Miller wrote concurring opinion	Miller wrote dissenting opinion
1862–66 2 Bl.–3 Wall.	240 *18*	227 *15*	1 *0*	12 *3* 5%	34 *4*	4 *1*	1 *0*	1 *1*
1866–70 4 Wall.–10 Wall. 308	507 *56*	476 *46*	3 *1*	28 *9* 5.5%	67 *12*	6 *5*	1 *0*	12 *3*
1870–74 10 Wall. 308–20 Wall. 375	672 *66*	641 *58*	4 *1*	27 *7* 4%	91 *15*	19 *8*	1 *0*	7 *3*
1874–78 20 Wall. 375–97 U. S. 360	858 *65*	827 *62*	0 *0*	31 *3* 3.6%	94 *14*	14 *1*	0 *0*	10 *2*
1878–82 97 U. S. 361–105 U. S.	852 *60*	824 *57*	1 *1*	27 *2* 3.2%	109 *13*	8 *2*	1 *1*	15 *2*
1882–86 106 U. S.–118 U. S. 541	1079 *94*	1058 *91*	2 *2*	19 *1* 1.8%	100 *19*	12 *6*	1 *1*	10 *0*
1886–90 118 U. S. 541–136 U. S.	1125* *119*	1102 *114*	1 *1*	16 *4* 1.4%	121 *18*	15 *8*	2 *2*	7 *3*
Totals	5333* *478*	5155 *443*	12 *6*	160 *29* 3%	616 *95*	78 *31*	7 *4*	66 *14*

* Including 6 decisions announced as "by a divided court."

NOTE: – While it is quite possible that I have made some small error in the count, the result is sufficiently accurate for the present purpose. Moreover, there is a fair margin for disagreement as to whether a decision involved a construction of the Constitution

tution was to be construed.[46] For this was the branch of law where his preëminence was undisputed. It was a period when the Court's jurisdiction also extended to a mass of chancery and common-law cases which now, more appropriately, receive final determination elsewhere. In many of these Miller was aware that his background was less adequate than that of some of his brethren. As a discriminating friend exclaimed after Miller was gone, "if his mind had been enriched in his young manhood with all the treasures of legal lore under the guidance . . . of the great lawyers of his time, who can measure the power, weight, and authority he would have wielded in the wide domain of jurisprudence?" [47] Great questions of public right, on the other hand, called rather for judgment than learning. Indeed, "learning" in such forms as Blackstone's obfuscated political science or the black letters of constitutional antiquities, in a judge of servile mind, might have been a positive detriment. Miller's distinction lay in the muscularity of his thinking and in his grasp of political values.

Justice Miller was not long on the Court before certain notable characteristics became apparent. They are to be marked throughout his work. "Authorities" were more or less persuasive according to their inherent reason and the character of their source.[48] Thus he would note that a principle

[46] The assignment of cases among the justices is a prerogative of the chief justice, except where he is dissenting, when the senior justice among the majority makes the assignment. Marshall, of course, kept the best cases for himself. William A. Maury, in his unpublished "Recollections" (p. 19), throws in this interesting aside: "By the way, speaking of harmony in the Court, Judge Campbell told me on the authority of Judge McLean that Judge Story made a good deal of trouble and unpleasantness in the Court by the way in which he reached out for the particular cases that he desired to write opinions in." For permission to use Maury's Recollections I am indebted to J. Spalding Flannery, Esq., of Washington, D. C.

[47] James H. Embry, in Proceedings . . . in Memoriam, p. 22. Embry came from Madison County, Kentucky, where Miller was born.

[48] Miller gave an interesting address on "The Use and Value of Authorities" to the Law Department of the University of Pennsylvania, October 1, 1888. It is printed in 121 Pa. St. xix; in 23 American Law Review 165 (1889); and as an appendix to Gregory, Samuel Freeman Miller, pp. 123ff. There is also a letter by Miller on the "Weight of Authorities" in 16 Virginia Law Journal 582 (1886).

had been stated "by Chancellor Kent, with his usual force and clearness";[49] by "Judge McLean, . . . with his usual ability";[50] "by Chief Justice Robertson, whose reputation as a jurist entitles his views to the highest consideration";[51] by "the Supreme Court of Massachusetts — a court whose opinions are always entitled to great consideration";[52] or by some other "court of high character." In a lecture to law students he pays his devoirs to the "recent writers of books" — "mainly at the instance of law publishers" — who are producing so-called treatises which generally prove to be "but ill-considered extracts from the decisions of the courts"; and asserts that "this field of literary labor has been overworked" and that the profession "is tired of the endless production of books not needed and of little value." He reminds them that the fact that the opinion of some commissioner or referee gets into print does not make it an "authority," and goes on to say, "It has often been my fortune to listen to able counsel citing the decision of some very inferior judge or judicial officer as if it were entitled to control the action of the court which he addressed, and the observation has been forced from me, 'Tell me what *you* think about this, for I esteem your opinion of much more value than that of the authority cited.' "[53]

With all due respect for Justice Story, Miller retained his independence of judgment, and in an early case on the circuit where the *Equity Jurisprudence* had been cited as authoritative, Miller put it aside with the remark: "I have been much pressed by counsel . . . with the argument of the distinguished jurist just named. . . . But it is evident that the author is there stating not what the rule is, but what he thinks it should be. And I cannot say that I am very strongly impressed by the reasoning with which he supports the abstract propriety of his opinion."[54] In a case on mining law — in

[49] Savings Bank v. Creswell, 100 U. S. 630, 642 (1879).
[50] Gelpcke v. Dubuque, 1 Wallace 175, 213 (1864).
[51] Campbell v. Holt, 115 U. S. 620, 624 (1885).
[52] Buck v. Colbath, 3 Wallace 334, 341 (1865).
[53] "The Use and Value of Authorities," *supra*, note 48.
[54] Ross v. Union Pacific Ry. Co., 1 Woolworth 26, 43, Fed. Case No. 12,080 (1863).

which Miller himself was quite competent — he refers generously to "Brother Field, whose learning on that subject is
equal, perhaps, to that of any judge of the United States
courts, and whose diligence and precision are equal to his
learning," and to "my Brother Hallett whose experience is
greater than mine in this matter." [55]

In his self-reliance Miller could be "entirely satisfied" with
a decision which, as he remarked, took the profession by surprise and went contrary to the opinion of Chancellor Kent
and of the Supreme Court of Massachusetts.[56] In *Woodruff*
v. *Parham*,[57] after exhibiting cogent reasons of policy why the
Constitution should be given a certain construction, seem-
ingly at variance with the opinions of Chief Justices Marshall
and Taney, he adds complacently: "If we examine for a
moment the results of the opposite doctrine, we shall be well
satisfied with the wisdom of the Constitution as thus construed" — by himself.

Justice Miller always sought to make the law square with
justice: "This is the honest and fair view of the subject, and
we think it conflicts with no rule of law"; [58] "this is just and
is sound policy"; [59] "if this is not due process of law, it ought
to be"; [60] "as I have had no opportunity to examine the
authorities cited in the opinion, I can do no more than protest against the doctrine." [61] He disliked all tergiversation.
When the Court concluded it had gone astray, Miller said so
frankly, disapproving an earlier opinion he himself had delivered.[62] He was too candid to acquiesce when the Court

[55] Stevens *v.* Williams, 1 McCrary 480, 487, 488, Fed. Case No. 13,413 (1879).
Hallett was the district judge for Colorado. His opinions will be found in
all the casebooks on mining law.
[56] Buck *v.* Colbath, 3 Wallace 334, 341 (1865).
[57] 8 Wallace 123 (1868).
[58] Pettigrew *v.* United States, 97 U. S. 385, 389 (1878).
[59] Iron Silver Mining Co. *v.* Campbell, 135 U. S. 286, 301 (1890).
[60] Davidson *v.* New Orleans, 96 U. S. 97, 100 (1878).
[61] Dissenting in Trustees *v.* Greenough, 105 U. S. 527, 538 (1881).
[62] Union Pacific R. R. *v.* McShane, 22 Wallace 444 (1875), overruling Kansas
Pacific Ry. *v.* Prescott, 16 Wallace 603 (1873). The federal government had
granted lands subject to a contingent right of preëmption. Held, in the later
case, that the state might tax the land. The Court has not always been so
downright in getting rid of bad precedents in this field.

reached a result he approved by resorting to a distinction which he deemed invalid.[63] And in a variety of other ways he was constantly recognizing the fact that judges, like other mortals, are subject to limitations.[64]

Justice Miller had no reticence in allowing his personal sentiments to appear in his opinions. Thus, for example, he shows his antipathy for the "gambling stockbroker of Wall Street" who "buys at twenty-five per cent of their value" municipal bonds of doubtful validity, and regrets that the decision of the majority will facilitate the operations of "rich corporations . . . or rich men, making contracts with the legislatures . . . with such appliances as it is known they do use" in effecting their antisocial ends.[65] Elsewhere he speaks of a decision of his brethren as arrived at by "a stretch of fancy, only to be indulged in railroad bond cases." [66] Miller felt a deep revulsion for what Professor Parrington later

[63] Compare Thorington v. Smith, 8 Wallace 1 (1868), with Hanauer v. Woodruff, 15 Wallace 449 (1872); also United States v. Dashiel, 4 Wallace 182 (1866), with United States v. Thomas, 15 Wallace 337 (1872). The two cases last cited were suits on official bonds, and raised the question whether the liability was absolute, or only such as the law imposed on the officer. The earlier case was that of an army paymaster who had been robbed without any want of vigilance on his part. Defendant was held liable. The later case was that of a surveyor of customs at Nashville, whose funds had been seized by the Confederate authorities. Here the majority held that overruling necessity was a sufficient discharge, intimating that the earlier case had been wrongly decided, but not overruling it. When this hard case was distinguished for the benefit of one who had delivered the money of the United States into the hands of its enemies, Miller protested vigorously. Compare also United States v. Klein, 13 Wallace 128, 148 (1872), with United States v. Anderson, 9 Wallace 56 (1870), and United States v. Padelford, 9 Wallace 531 (1870).

[64] E.g., Bartlett v. Russell, 4 Dillon 267, 268, Fed. Case No. 1080 (1877): "I have given this case all the consideration I shall have time to give it, and, although there are conflicting authorities on the subject, I have arrived at a conclusion satisfactory to myself, and will proceed to announce it." American Middlings Purifier Co. v. Christian, 4 Dillon 448, 453, Fed. Case No. 307 (1877): "It is possible, in a court like ours, where we are all of one opinion and at one time, that something may have escaped our attention; but two of the best patent lawyers of the court [Clifford and Strong, JJ.] dissented from the opinion and judgment of the court [in Cochrane v. Deener, 94 U. S. 780 (1877)]. . . . The fact . . . shows that their objections must have been carefully considered in court, and rebuts any suggestion that there was any hasty or ill-advised action in the matter."

[65] Gelpcke v. Dubuque, 1 Wallace 175, 214 (1864).
[66] Meyer v. Muscatine, 1 Wallace 384, 397 (1864).

dubbed "the great American barbecue" — the spectacle of government providing a feast of grants, franchises, and tax exemptions for fat exploiters of the natural and social resources. In the greater freedom of private correspondence he wrote:

I have met with but few things of a character affecting the public good of the whole country that has shaken my faith in human nature as much as the united, vigorous, and selfish effort of the capitalists, — the class of men who as a distinct class are but recently known in this country — I mean those who live solely by interest and dividends. Prior to the late war they were not numerous. They had no interest separate from the balance of the community, because they could lend their money safely and at high rates of interest. But one of the effects of the war was greatly to reduce the rate of interest by reason of the great increase in the quantity of the circulating medium. Another was by the creation of a national funded debt, exempt from taxation to provide a means for the investment of surplus capital. This resource for investment was quadrupled by the bonds issued by the States by municipal corporations, and by Rail Road companies. The result has been the gradual formation of a new kind of wealth in this country, the income of which is the coupons of interest and stock dividends, and of a class whose only interest or stake in the country is the ownership of these bonds and stocks. They engage in no commerce, no trade, no manufactures, no agriculture. They *produce nothing*.[67]

Justice Miller's accession to the bench came at a period of transition in the nation as it was a season of renewal in the Court. It so fell out that they went on simultaneously. The exertions of Lincoln's administration to preserve the Union involved what many regarded as heroic measures, so that for years a collision between the Court and the popular branches of the government seemed an imminent possibility. Throughout the tense period of war and reconstruction, when bitter partisans often invited the Court to adventure into the realm of political controversy, Miller urged the wisdom of judicial self-restraint. He thought that the Court ought not to invent constitutional limitations even when it saw that for the

[67] Letter of April 28, 1878.

moment political power was being exercised recklessly. Presently Republican appointees, educated by the times to broad national views, became dominant in the Court and for a generation gave expression to the impulses emerging from the war. In applying the fundamental law to the problems of this expanding society, Justice Miller played the most conspicuous part.

IV

THE COURT AND THE CIVIL WAR

CHIEF JUSTICE TANEY was at war with the Administration within a few weeks after Lincoln's call for volunteers. Seeking to release on writ of habeas corpus a Southern sympathizer detained by the military authorities at Fort McHenry,[1] he found his order set at nought by an officer acting under direction of the President. It is necessary to a fair understanding of the case that the circumstances be set out at some length.

Troops responding to the President's call were hastening south to the defense of Washington. The line of railroad communication lay through Baltimore, many of whose citizens were opposed to the war and anxious to prevent the passage of troops. In a letter of April 18 the Secretary of War, at the President's direction, drew the attention of the Governor of Maryland to the danger that "unlawful combinations of misguided citizens" would make an attempt to prevent troop movements, concluding that "it would be as agreeable to the President as it would be to yourself that it should be prevented or overcome by the loyal authorities and citizens of Maryland rather than averted by any other means." [2] On the next day a mob fell upon the Sixth Massachusetts Militia as it passed through Baltimore, causing a number of casualties, some fatal. The regiment went on to Washington, leaving behind its baggage and a considerable number of missing. That night the mayor sent an appeal to the President not to permit any more units to come through the city:

The people are exasperated to the highest degree by the passage of troops and the citizens are universally decided in the opinion

---

[1] *Ex parte* Merryman, Taney's Decisions 246/ Fed. Case No. 9487 (1861).
[2] *The War of the Rebellion: Official Records*, 2 ser. 1, 564.

that no more should be ordered to come. . . . Under these circumstances it is my solemn duty to inform you that it is not possible for more soldiers to pass through Baltimore unless they fight their way at every step.

To this the Governor appended his endorsement. That night the board of police commissioners met and unanimously reached the conclusion, as they later reported to the legislature,

that, as good citizens, it was their duty to the city, and to the State of Maryland, to adopt any measures whatsoever that might be necessary at such a juncture to prevent the immediate arrival in the city of further bodies of troops from the Eastern or Northern States, though the object of the latter might be solely to pass through the city.

It was decided that the most feasible method was to disable some of the railroad bridges, and the mayor stated that the Governor concurred in this view. "This was accordingly done. . . . Subsequently . . . further and greater damage was done to other structures on the roads by parties in the country and others, but this was without the sanction or authority of the board." [3]

That the Administration was acting with great self-restraint is reflected in Attorney General Bates's entry in his diary touching the cabinet meeting of April 23:

The People of Maryland and Virginia are in a ferment, a furore, regardless of law and common sense.

In Maryland there is not even a pretence of state authority, for their overt acts of treason.

In Virginia it is a mere pretence. . . .

Yet both in Maryland and Virginia, they are in open arms against us, and by violence and terror, they have silenced every friend of the Government.

They think and in fact find it perfectly safe to defy the Government, And why? Because we hurt nobody. *They* cut off *our* mails; we furnish theirs gratis. *They* block our communications. *We* are careful to preserve theirs — *They* assail and obstruct our troops in their lawful and honest march to the defense of this

---

[3] *Official Records*, 1 ser. II, 7ff.; 2 ser. I, 564ff.

CHIEF JUSTICE CHASE

CHIEF JUSTICE TANEY

Capitol [*sic*] while *we* as yet have done nothing to resist or retort the outrage.

They every day are winding their toils around us, while *we* make no bold effort to cut the cord that is soon to bind us in pitiable impotence — . . .

But I am asked, under present embarrassing circumstances, what can we do?

I answer. . . .

4. Baltimore having wantonly cut off her main line of R.R. to the North, we can easily cut her off from the rest. And I see nothing to hinder us from closing the mouth of the Patapsco.[4]

Bates was a representative of the "border states" and one of the moderates in Lincoln's cabinet.

On April 27 the President issued an order to the Commanding General to the effect that "if at any point on or in the vicinity of any military line which is now or which shall be used between the city of Philadelphia and the city of Washington you find resistance which renders it necessary to suspend the writ of habeas corpus for the public safety, you personally or through the officer in command at the point where the resistance occurs are authorized to suspend the writ." [5]

On May 25, 1861, two officers of the First Pennsylvania Volunteers appeared at Fort McHenry, at Baltimore, with a prisoner, John Merryman, whom they had arrested early that morning at his home north of the city. They made a certificate to the effect that Merryman was

first lieutenant of a secession company who have in their possession arms belonging to the United States Government for the purpose of using the same against the Government. The prisoner acknowledged being lieutenant of said company. . . . It can also be proven that the prisoner had been drilling with his company and has uttered and advanced secession doctrines. . . .

The officers making the arrest belonged to, and acted under orders originating in, a military department other than the Department of Annapolis, into which they now brought the

[4] *Diary of Edward Bates*, p. 185.
[5] *Official Records*, 2 ser. II, 19.

prisoner. This was the first that General Cadwalader, commanding the Department of Annapolis, knew of Merryman's arrest. He directed the officers making the arrest to furnish more specific charges and specifications, together with the names of witnesses and the nature of the testimony they could give — intending to forward the record to the Headquarters of the Army for instructions.[6]

On the day of his arrest the prisoner, through counsel, petitioned the Chief Justice for a writ of habeas corpus. As Taney relates in his subsequent opinion,

The petition was presented to me, at Washington under the impression that I would order the prisoner to be brought before me there, but as he was confined in Fort McHenry, in the city of Baltimore, which is in my circuit, I resolved to hear it in the latter city, as obedience to the writ, under such circumstances, would not withdraw General Cadwalader, who had him in charge, from the limits of his military command.[7]

Thereupon the Chief Justice, acting under the statute authorizing any justice of the Supreme Court or district judge to grant writs of habeas corpus,[8] ordered that a writ be directed to General Cadwalader returnable the next day, May 27, at the circuit court room in Baltimore. The General at once reported the foregoing events to the Headquarters of the Army, and was presently informed that he was to hold all persons implicated in treasonable practices unless satisfied the arrest was made without sufficient evidence; that in return to any writ of habeas corpus he was respectfully to decline for the time to produce the prisoners, "but will say that when the present unhappy difficulties are at an end you will duly respond to the writs in question." [9]

Before these instructions were received General Cadwalader had responded to the writ. He sent one of his officers to appear before the Chief Justice with a letter reciting the circumstances of the arrest and concluding:

[6] *Official Records*, 2 ser. 1, 574ff.
[7] *Ex parte* Merryman, Taney's Decisions 246, 254, Fed. Case No. 9487 (1861).
[8] Judiciary Act of 1789, section 14; 1 Statutes at Large 82.
[9] *Official Records*, 2 ser. 1, 576.

[The undersigned] has further to inform you that he is duly authorized by the President of the United States in such cases to suspend the writ of habeas corpus for the public safety. This is a high and delicate trust and it has been enjoined upon him that it should be executed with judgment and discretion but he is nevertheless also instructed that in times of civil strife errors if any should be on the side of safety to the country. He most respectfully submits for your consideration that those who should co-operate in the present trying and painful position in which our country is placed should not by reason of any unnecessary want of confidence in each other increase our embarrassments. He therefore respectfully requests that you will postpone further action upon this case until he can receive instructions from the President of the United States when you shall hear further from him.[10]

For this failure to comply the Chief Justice ordered that an attachment issue against General Cadwalader for contempt. Whereupon the marshal went to Fort McHenry, but on sending in his name was informed that "there was no answer to his card" — which he duly reported to the Chief Justice. Taney observed that the power refusing obedience was far superior to any posse the marshal could summon, and held that the marshal was excused from doing more.

The opinion which Taney later filed holds that the President, under the Constitution, cannot suspend or authorize the suspension of the privilege of the writ of habeas corpus; that a military officer has no right to arrest and detain a person not subject to the articles of war, except in aid of the judicial authority and subject to its control; and that if the military authority makes an arrest, it is its duty immediately to deliver the prisoner to the civil authority, to be dealt with according to law. The Chief Justice was clear that Merryman was entitled to be set at liberty. The opinion concludes that a copy of the proceedings will be transmitted to the President; "it will then remain for that high officer, in fulfilment of his constitutional obligation to 'take care that the laws be faithfully executed,' to determine what measures he

[10] Taney's Decisions 246, 250, Fed. Case No. 9487; *Official Records*, 2 ser. 1, 576.

will take to cause the civil process of the United States to be respected and enforced."

It has become something of an article of liberal faith to regard this opinion as a great classic of liberty. And the case, of course, offers all the requisites for fine writing about the history of the great writ and the glorious example of an independent judge asserting the law in the face of arbitrary executive power. But judicial self-assertion may be a vice or a virtue, according to circumstance. It was the Chief Justice's contention that a citizen detained on a charge of hostile operations must immediately be surrendered to the civil authorities. This means that Merryman could not be brought to trial until a grand jury had indicted. Conviction would have required the unanimous verdict of a jury chosen in a district so hostile to the national government that troops could pass only by fighting their way through a mob. And the trial would have been in the circuit court before Taney as Circuit Justice and the district judge. Of the former it may be said that he had no sympathy for the prosecution of the war. In a letter to Franklin Pierce he observes that the

paroxysm of passion into which the country has suddenly been thrown appears to me to amount almost to delirium. I hope that it is too violent to last long, and that calmer and more sober thoughts will soon take its place; and the North, as well as the South, will see that a peaceful separation, with free institutions in each section, is far better than the union of all the present states under a military government, and a reign of terror preceded too by a civil war with all its horrors, and which end as it may will prove ruinous to the victors as well as the vanquished.[11]

This is not quoted as being discreditable, but simply as disclosing the emotions with which Taney approached the question of the constitutional powers of the president. Inevitably the Constitution was going to give a very different answer to one who was convinced that the Union was not worth a war and its consequences, from what it was going to mean, for

[11] Letter of June 12, 1861, in Pierce Manuscripts, Library of Congress; quoted by Carl B. Swisher in his *Roger B. Taney* (New York: The Macmillan Co., 1935), p. 554.

example, to Miller, who, whatever his initial moderation, had come to believe with all his heart that the war was justified.

How Taney himself had understood the law at a time when his thinking was not distorted by emotional pressure we learn from his opinion in *Luther* v. *Borden*.[12] During Dorr's Rebellion in Rhode Island, the legislature of the established government had enacted that "martial law" should be exercised. Under color of this authority some militiamen entered the house of the plaintiff Luther to arrest him as an adherent to the rebellion. The plaintiff later moved to Massachusetts and, diversity of citizenship being thus established, sued in trespass in the federal court. In the Supreme Court the case went off on the view that it was for the political branches of the national government to decide which of the rival state governments to recognize; that the President had recognized the old government, and that a good defense had been set up by invoking its declaration of martial law. It will be recalled that this was long before the adoption of the Fourteenth Amendment, when there were relatively few federal grounds on which state action could be held *ultra vires*. But in his opinion Taney made it clear that if the question had been one on which the federal court should form an independent judgment, he would have regarded the acts of the defendants as justified on general principle:

Unquestionably, a State may use its military power to put down an armed insurrection, too strong to be controlled by the civil authority. The power is essential to the existence of every government, essential to the preservation of order and free institutions, and is as necessary to the States of this Union as to any other government. The State itself must determine what degree of force the crisis demands. And if the government of Rhode Island deemed the armed opposition so formidable, and so ramified through the State, as to require the use of its military force and the declaration of martial law, we see no ground upon which this court can question its authority. It was a state of war; and the established government resorted to the rights and usages

[12] 7 Howard 1 (1849).

of war to maintain itself, and to overcome the unlawful opposition. And in that state of things the officers engaged in its military service might lawfully arrest any one, who, from the information before them, they had reasonable grounds to believe was engaged in the insurrection; and might order a house to be forcibly entered and searched, when there were reasonable grounds for supposing he might be there concealed. Without the power to do this, martial law and the military array of the government would be mere parade, and rather encourage attack than repel it.[13]

How much more fittingly this describes the situation at Baltimore in 1861 even than that in Rhode Island in 1842 scarcely needs argument.

Since, however, the Constitution specifically provides that "the privilege of the writ of habeas corpus shall not be suspended, unless when in cases of rebellion or invasion the public safety may require it," one may think that the Chief Justice stood on firm ground. The President referred the legal question to the Attorney General, who rendered an opinion, the gist of which lies in these sentences:

If by the phrase "the suspension of the privilege of the writ of habeas corpus" we must understand a repeal of all power to issue the writ, then I freely admit that none but Congress can do it. But if we are at liberty to understand the phrase to mean that in case of a great and dangerous rebellion like the present the public safety requires the arrest and confinement of persons implicated in that rebellion, I as freely declare the opinion that the President has lawful power to suspend the privilege of persons arrested under such circumstances; for he is especially charged by the Constitution with the "public safety," and he is the sole judge of the emergency which requires his prompt action.

[13] Justice Woodbury wrote an interesting opinion dissenting on this question of justification. He dwelt (1) on the want of power under the Rhode Island charter to enact such a statute, and (2) on the provisions of the federal constitution which, he thought, left no war power to the states. When it has wanted to do so, the Supreme Court has discovered inherent limits on state power quite independently of the text of the Constitution.

One bent upon finding harmony in Taney's two pronouncements might, of course, make the point that in Rhode Island it was the legislature which unleashed the extraordinary power, whereas Merryman was detained at a time when Congress had not yet granted authority to suspend the privilege of the writ of habeas corpus. But it is doubtful if this is the reason why Taney's reaction to the two cases was so different.

This power in the President is no part of his ordinary duty in time of peace; it is temporary and exceptional, and was intended only to meet a pressing emergency when the judiciary is found to be too weak to insure the public safety; when (in the language of the act of Congress) [14] there are "combinations too powerful to be suppressed by the ordinary course of judicial proceedings or by the powers vested in the marshals." Then and not till then has he the lawful authority to call to his aid the military power of the nation and with that power suppress the insurrection.[15]

The day before this opinion was rendered President Lincoln had sent his message to the special session of Congress, in which he stated that in some cases it had been deemed necessary to arrest and detain without resort to the ordinary processes of law. This authority had been exercised very sparingly.

Nevertheless, the legality and propriety of what has been done under it are questioned, and the attention of the country has been called to the proposition that one who is sworn to "take care that the laws be faithfully executed" should not himself violate them. Of course some consideration was given to the questions of power and propriety before this matter was acted upon. The whole of the laws which were required to be faithfully executed were being resisted and failing of execution in nearly one-third of the States. . . . Are all the laws *but one* to go unexecuted, and the Government itself go to pieces lest that one be violated?

He did not, however, admit that he had acted unconstitutionally.

In talking about the suspension of the privilege of the writ of habeas corpus we really have to do with two different situations.[16] There is the case where, in time of rebellion or invasion, it is desired that the government have authority

---

[14] To provide for calling forth the militia to execute the laws of the union, suppress insurrections, and repel invasions (Act of February 28, 1795; 1 Statutes at Large 424).

[15] 10 Opinions of the Attorney General 74 (1861).

[16] I have discussed most of the legal problems raised in this chapter in *The Law of Martial Rule* (Chicago: Callaghan and Company, 1930).

to hold persons temporarily without having to appear in court and justify on grounds recognized by the ordinary law. This seems to be the situation to which the constitutional provision addresses itself, and the Chief Justice was doubtless right in holding that it was for Congress to determine when the public safety requires such a course. But there is a different sort of suspension of the writ which comes with war and exists without the necessity of proclamation, as in the immediate vicinity of hostilities. This difference was brought out fully in a subsequent decision of the Supreme Court of Wisconsin,[17] and by a number of perfectly hard-headed lawyers such as Joel Parker who came forward to uphold the President's action.[18] Parker asked, what if Justice Catron were to issue writs of habeas corpus in similar cases in his circuit, which lay in the western theater of operations?

The degree of control the courts should attempt to exert over military authorities under circumstances differing in degree from the very scene of hostilities is difficult to determine. The question came before the Supreme Court in the Milligan Case,[19] presently to be discussed, which was decided after the close of the war. In May 1861 Maryland was scarcely less hostile than Tennessee and Virginia. From its geographical position it was more important in the defense of the capital than were those states. It would have been perfectly possible for the Chief Justice, without renouncing generally the exercise of jurisdiction, to have held his hand for the time being. That he did otherwise was not because of the compulsion of any constitutional provision.

It was not until 1863, when the Prize Cases[20] came on to be decided, that a question of war power reached the Supreme Court. On April 19, 1861, President Lincoln had proclaimed a blockade of the coasts of the states then in rebellion, and on April 27 this was extended to North Carolina and Virginia.

[17] *In re* Kemp, 16 Wis. 359 (1863), discussed below.
[18] Parker's article in *North American Review*, XCIII (1861), 471, is one of the best discussions of the Merryman Case.
[19] 4 Wallace 2 (1866).
[20] 2 Black 635.

Agreeably to the Administration's theory that the Confederate Government was not to be recognized as a belligerent, the blockade was spoken of as a measure to put down insurrection, and the existence of a state of war was not expressly declared. Congress was called in special session for July 4, and on July 13 a statute was enacted authorizing the president to close and blockade ports of entry. Had there been power to make captures prior to this enactment?

If the power to take as prize was to be upheld, it would have to be on the footing that a war then existed — a proposition which for diplomatic reasons the government had not conceded at the time. Mr. Evarts, of counsel for the government, began by submitting that

at the time of the capture, there existed in the United States a civil war, waged against the National Government, . . . by a great population occupying an extensive region of country. This civil war had already carried into complete revolt whole States, and had organized the forms of a separate and independent government, which was conducting open military hostilities, with all the outward circumstances of public war. . . . War is, emphatically, a question of actualities.

Argument was heard for twelve days between February 10 and 25, after the cases had been advanced on the motion of the Attorney General. It would be a serious blow to the Administration if judgment went for the claimants, and, while the new appointees were expected to support the right of capture, serious doubts were entertained as to the views of the older judges. Some encouragement, however, was derived from the fact that after Richard Henry Dana's argument for the government Justice Grier had patted him on the shoulder and assured him that all his doubts were now cleared.[21]

A decision was reached on March 10, 1863. A bare majority, consisting of Justices Grier, Wayne, Swayne, Miller, and Davis, upheld the exercise of war power. Chief Justice Taney

[21] C. F. Adams, *Richard Henry Dana* (Boston and New York: Houghton, Mifflin and Company, 1891); II, 270.

and Justices Nelson, Catron, and Clifford dissented. The opinion by Judge Grier followed the line which Evarts had invited the Court to take. An insurrection might or might not culminate in an organized rebellion. A civil war was not solemnly declared: it became such by its accidents — the number, power, and organization of those who carried it on. Not being proclaimed, its existence was a fact of which the court would take notice. "This greatest of civil wars . . . sprung forth suddenly from the parent brain, a Minerva in the full panoply of war. The President was bound to meet it in the shape it presented itself, without waiting for Congress to baptize it with a name." The Queen's proclamation of neutrality — which Secretary Seward had so much deplored — was cited as illustrative of the universal awareness that in fact a condition of war existed when the captures were made.

It will be evident that materials were not lacking to construct a dissenting opinion. The essence of Judge Nelson's opinion may be compressed in a few sentences. The government had shown that there was a war, and in a material sense a war of most extensive dimensions; but this was irrelevant to the legal question, was it war within the meaning of the Constitution? War could be declared only by Congress, and however extensive an insurrection might become, it was not competent for the President on his own authority to exercise belligerent rights.

It would be a mistake, it is submitted, to regard either view as the "right" answer. Whichever is adopted involves obvious dangers. That of the prevailing opinion lies couched in these words: "Whether the President . . . has met with such armed hostile resistance, and a civil war of such alarming proportions as will compel him to accord to them the character of belligerents, is a question to be decided *by him*, and this court must be governed by the decisions and acts of the political power of the government to which this power was intrusted." In more recent times, on occasions of industrial strife, this doctrine has been carried into state law to give the semblance of legal respectability to the vicious practice of declaring that labor disorders have become a "war." [22] The dissenting opinion, on the other hand, involved too strict a version of executive power to satisfy the public needs of 1861, and perhaps of future emergencies. Which of two possible views a judge would choose depended upon his evaluation of competing considerations.

We can now know the drift of the extra-judicial thoughts of both the justices who wrote opinions. Three days after Bull Run Grier wrote to Judge Clifford:

> The result of this great battle will make a *long war* of this. We must conquer this rebellion or declare our republican government a failure, if it should cost 100,000 men & 1000 millions of money.[23]

The outbreak of hostilities evoked quite different sentiments from Judge Nelson. On April 19 he had written Judge Clifford:

> Telegraph just announcing Virginia is out — and forces south mustering —
> I disbelieve yet as to war — Necessity will compel a peaceful separation.
> Too late in the age for men to fight without any useful purpose — everybody agrees the Union can't be saved by this means.[24]

Nor did the course of events serve to mollify his apprehension. On September 22, 1862, the President issued his preliminary proclamation to the effect that on January 1 following he would declare free all persons held as slaves in states which should at that time be in rebellion. Three days later Judge Nelson wrote:

> *Proclamations* and *orders* thicken upon us from Washington. The plunge of emancipation is taken in one, and military de-

[22] The Supreme Court had occasion to state more clearly the limits on the power of a governor, in Sterling *v.* Constantin, 287 U. S. 378 (1932). But the practice seems not to have been materially altered since this decision.

[23] Letter of July 24, 1861; Clifford Correspondence, Maine Historical Society. The Judge records that he has just returned from a visit with his son-in-law at Frankfort, Kentucky, and was "sorry to find he was a secessionist as insane as the others."

[24] Clifford Correspondence.

portation in the loyal States, in the other — no man can see the end — The darkness deepens — [25]

The most notorious of "Copperheads" was Clement L. Vallandigham, commander of the Sons of Liberty. As a member of Congress prior to March 1863 he had opposed every measure for the prosecution of the war and advocated a negotiated peace. In May 1863 he had been arrested at his home in Dayton and brought before a military commission at Cincinnati, charged with having uttered disloyal sentiments in a public speech, with the purpose of weakening the power of the government in suppressing the rebellion. He was found guilty and sentenced to be kept in confinement for the duration of the war. On May 19 the President commuted the sentence, directing that Vallandigham be sent beyond the lines into Southern territory, whence presently he went to Canada. To show their disapprobation, the anti-war Democrats of Ohio nominated Vallandigham for governor, and his counsel, George E. Pugh, for lieutenant governor, in the election of 1863.

Vallandigham presented a petition to the Supreme Court for a writ of certiorari to the Judge Advocate General of the Army, with a view to bringing up the proceedings of the military commission for review and revision. The case was argued on January 22, 1864, and on February 15 a unanimous Court, speaking through Justice Wayne, denied the relief sought.[26]

This case has been inaccurately spoken of as arising on habeas corpus to test the legality of a trial of a civilian by military commission at a place removed from the theater of active operations. And inasmuch as Milligan's Case,[27] decided after the close of the war, held a similar military trial to have been illegal, it has been suggested that the judgment on Vallandigham's petition was based upon a technical and

[25] Letter of September 25, 1862; Clifford Correspondence.
[26] *Ex parte* Vallandigham, 1 Wallace 243 (1864). Nelson, J., concurred in the result. The answer of Judge Advocate General Holt appears in *Official Records*, 2 ser. VI, 620, more fully than in Wallace's report.
[27] 4 Wallace 2 (1866).

unsubstantial ground. This calls for an examination of the particulars of the case.

Vallandigham had been arrested on May 5, and brought before the military commission on the 6th. On the 9th, while the sentence was in the hands of the authority convening the commission, Vallandigham appeared by counsel before the United States Circuit Court at Cincinnati and applied for a writ of habeas corpus to be directed to General Burnside, commanding the Department of the Ohio. The Circuit Court was then being held by District Judge Leavitt alone, Justice Swayne not being present. The court declined to grant the writ except upon a sufficient showing, and directed that the General be notified. The hearing was set for May 11. General Burnside sent a respectful though somewhat oratorical response to the court, and arranged to be represented by counsel, consisting of Aaron F. Perry and the United States District Attorney. After lengthy argument for and against the application, the writ was denied.[28] The judgment held, first, that the case was governed by a precedent which the court had established at the October term, 1862, Justice Swayne presiding. In the unreported case of Bethuel W. Rupert, Justice Swayne had delivered a lengthy oral opinion holding "that this court would not grant the writ of habeas corpus, where it appeared that the detention or imprisonment was under military authority." In the absence of his senior, the district judge did not feel at liberty to disregard a decision in which they had concurred. But as counsel for the applicant had been allowed to argue the case generally, the court went on to state its reasons for holding that under the circumstances a case for judicial interference had not been made out. The court added that if its view of the law had led it to a different conclusion, it was certain that its order would not have been obeyed.

This judgment was rendered on May 16, 1863. On May 19 the President commuted the sentence, and on May 25 Vallandigham was taken under flag of truce to the Confederate

28 *Ex parte* Vallandigham, Fed. Case No. 16,816 (1863).

lines.[29] This disposition of the case left no ground for seeking a review by the Supreme Court of the judgment denying the writ of habeas corpus. Counsel then adopted the course of applying directly to the Court for a writ of certiorari to be directed to the Judge Advocate General to send up the proceedings of the military commission.

It must be obvious that in denying this petition the Court was deciding a perfectly clear case. The Constitution defines the extent of the judicial power of the United States, and declares that it shall be vested in one Supreme Court, and in such inferior courts as the Congress may, from time to time, ordain and establish. It goes on to limit the original jurisdiction of the Supreme Court (to cases affecting ambassadors, etc., and those in which a state shall be a party), and continues that in all other cases before mentioned the Court shall have appellate jurisdiction, with such exceptions and under such regulations as Congress shall make. The writ of certiorari — and for that matter the writ of habeas corpus and other writs — may be issued by the Court only in the exercise of its jurisdiction under the Constitution and the laws. A military commission is no part of the judicial establishment, and the Supreme Court was devoid of authority to call up its proceedings for review as though it had been an inferior court.

Several months after his case was decided in the Supreme Court, Vallandigham reappeared in Ohio and threw himself into the campaign of 1864. But he was unharmed by "King Lincoln" and his "minions." Indeed the course of political and military events was such that he became more of a liability to his friends than he was to the Administration.

After a good deal of debate, Congress on March 3, 1863, passed an act relating to habeas corpus and regulating judicial proceedings in certain cases.[30] The statute begins by enacting "that, during the present rebellion, the President of the United States, whenever, in his judgment, the public safety may require it, is authorized to suspend the privilege of the

[29] *Official Records*, 2 ser. v, 705.
[30] 12 Statutes at Large 755.

JUSTICE SWAYNE

JUSTICE MILLER

JUSTICE DAVIS

JUSTICE FIELD

writ of habeas corpus in any case throughout the United States, or any part thereof." The language is susceptible of interpretation as recognizing a power already possessed, though it seems rather to concede a power to which legislative assent was requisite. The opinion has already been suggested that while the substantive power referred to in the Constitution rests in Congress, this is not incompatible with the existence in the president of power to take such measures as seem reasonably necessary to suppress insurrection, repel invasion, or to execute the law. This would appear to flow from specific grants, such as that to command the armed forces, and from the general principles of our Constitution — and it is in harmony with the principles of the common law.[31]

The Act of March 3 went on to provide for the discharge by the federal courts of political prisoners, in states where the administration of the laws was unimpaired, if a grand jury should subsequently have met and terminated its session without finding an indictment. There were other provisions in the nature of a bill of indemnity, which were subsequently to receive a generous interpretation by Justice Miller.

Prior to this enactment there had been many detentions, and applications for habeas corpus were presented in a number of state and federal courts. One of the most instructive of these was *In re Kemp*,[32] in the Supreme Court of Wisconsin. The petitioner had been arrested on order of the Governor of Wisconsin for violent interference with the draft,[33] and was held by the commander of the Department of the North West. The return consisted of the documents in the case and a copy of the President's proclamation of September 25, 1862, declaring the privilege of the writ of habeas corpus suspended in certain cases. The court held that this was not a justification, but denied as futile a motion for an

[31] *Cf.* Sir Frederick Pollock, *The Law of Torts* (London: Stevens and Sons, 13th ed. 1929), p. 127.
[32] 16 Wis. 359 (1863).
[33] These anti-draft riots had repercussions which reached the Administration (*Diary of Edward Bates*, p. 280).

attachment. Each judge rendered an opinion, and that by Chief Justice Dixon is particularly candid and luminous.

He began by regretting that Congress had not exercised its undoubted power to withdraw altogether from the jurisdiction of state courts all cases arising under the Constitution and laws of the United States. He continued:

I think the President has no power, in the sense of the ninth section of the first article of the constitution of the United States, to suspend the privilege of the writ of *habeas corpus*. It is, in my judgment, a legislative and not an executive act; and the power is vested in congress. Upon this question it seems to me that the reasoning of Chief Justice Taney in *Ex parte Merriman*, is unanswerable. And in saying this, I accept, as just, the strictures of Professor Parker, in the article referred to,[34] upon the decision there made. I agree that there is a plain distinction between the suspension of the writ in the sense of the clause of the constitution, and the right of a military commander to refuse obedience, when justified by the exigencies of war, or the *ipso facto* suspension which takes place wherever martial law actually exists, which the chief justice seems to have overlooked. But this kind of suspension, which comes with war and exists without proclamation or other act, is limited to the necessities of war. . . .

Does martial law prevail at the present time in the state of Wisconsin? . . . The precise limits of the jurisdiction of the military commander, in cases arising near the scene of strife, may be a question for discussion, to be determined according to circumstances; but over remote districts, and those not immediately connected with the operations of the contending armies, all courts and writers concur in saying that martial law cannot be extended. . . .

. . . In stating my convictions of the law, I desire to add that they are given without the slightest disrespect to the President, who has, in all his actions, been governed by the highest motives of patriotism, public honor, and fidelity to the constitution and laws. Penned at the gloomiest period of our public misfortunes . . . the proclamation in question is not a welcome subject of criticism. . . . If, under these circumstances of national and executive embarrassment, the President has transcended his lawful authority, he has committed an unintentional error, which he will be the first to repair, and the last to vindicate. My duty, how-

[34] In the *North American Review* for October 1861, already cited.

ever, compels me to judge his acts, not by his intentions, but by the constitution and the laws, giving a fair and reasonable scope to all the powers which they confer upon him.

The Kemp Case was decided on January 13, 1863, and shortly thereafter Secretary of War Stanton conceived the idea of carrying an appeal to the Supreme Court. Attorney General Bates

advised urgently against it, urging that a decision of the Court pronouncing the arbitrary arrests illegal would "do more to paralyze the Executive . . . than the worst defeat our armies have yet sustained," and that such an adverse decision was to be anticipated, in view of the "antecedents and present proclivities" of a majority of the Court, taken in connection with the expressed opinion of certain of its members.[35]

Cases multiplied where the courts held that the President's proclamation based on his own authority was no answer to a writ of habeas corpus. The upshot was that on September 15, 1863, a new proclamation was issued, reciting the provisions of the Act of March 3, and declaring that the privilege of the writ was suspended pursuant to its terms.[36] Bates's diary records the Cabinet discussion of the matter:

Sep. 14. — A 11. a.m. C.[abinet] C.[ouncil] (by special call) to consider the difficulties arising out of the frequent and increasing issue of writs of Hab: corp: for soldiers and military prisoners. At first there seemed to be very various opinions. The Prest. was greatly moved — more angry than I ever saw him — declared that it was a formed plan of the democratic copperheads, deliberately acted out to defeat the Govt., and aid the enemy. That no honest man did or could believe that the State Judges have any such power, &c.[37]

[35] From James G. Randall, *Constitutional Problems under Lincoln* (New York: D. Appleton and Company, 1926), p. 132, quoting a letter of January 31, 1863, from Bates to Stanton, marked "Confidential." It is in the Stanton Papers, No. 52,223, in the Library of Congress.

[36] 13 Statutes at Large 734. Vallandigham's petition for habeas corpus in the Circuit Court had been brought after the Act of Congress of March 3, but prior to the President's proclamation thereunder. It was common ground in the argument that the authority there attempted to be exercised did not flow from that statute.

[37] In Tarble's Case, 13 Wallace 397 (1872), it was held that a state judge has no jurisdiction to issue a writ of habeas corpus for the discharge of a

Some (e.g. M. Blair [Postmaster General]) suggested that a *case be made*, before a Federal Judge, so that we might have a *legal* judgment on our side.

I objected that *no judicial* officer had power to take a prisoner or soldier, out of the hand of the Prest. by Hab: Corp: and proposed that we act purely upon the defensive — i.e. inform the judge who issued the writ, of the cause of imprisonment, refuse to deliver the body, and retain possession, by force, if need be. And in case of attempt to punish the officer, for contempt, protect him, by force if need be.

I resisted the idea, held out by some, of vengeance, or penal justice, by imprisoning the judge who issued the writ.

Sep 15. Again C.[abinet] C.[ouncil] met, and, after some consultation, the result was that an order was to be issued to refuse obedance [*sic*] to the writ, and protect the officer refusing — Also to issue proclamation suspending the privilege of the writ of Hab Corp: *in such cases*, under the act of Congress of Mar. 3. 1863.[38]

It will not be supposed that the justices of the Supreme Court were personally indifferent to these stirring events. Years later, in the relaxation of post-prandial discourse, Justice Miller fell into reminiscence, of which the following memorandum was recorded:

The Justice said that during the war the most strenuous efforts were made to use the Court in such a way as to embarrass the Government in its conduct of operations by endeavoring to get decisions upon such questions as the right of Mr. Seward to confine obnoxious persons in the forts, the right of Mr. Stanton to confiscate the property of citizens in the rebellious states, etc. One lawyer from Mississippi spent about two years in endeavoring, in various ways to get a decision upon some case of this kind. Once upon an application to advance a *habeas corpus* case the court seemed inclined to take the action. The Justice took occasion to see a friend of Justice Nelson and tell him that it would depend on how Nelson voted as to whether the case should be advanced upon the list, and since it was a matter simply of the methods and administration of the business of the court, it did not seem improper to talk to him about its effect on public affairs. Nelson

---

person held under the authority, or claim or color of authority, of the United States. Chief Justice Chase dissented.

[38] At p. 306.

afterward voted against the advancement. The Justice did more to prevent interference by the court than perhaps any other member of it.[39]

Justice Swayne was likewise concerned lest the Administration be crippled by the Court. After the argument in the Prize Cases was concluded he called on the Attorney General to say that Mr. Eames, who had been placed in charge of the conduct of the argument for the government, had "made himself very obnoxious to the Court."

Mr. Bates's reaction was:

This is all very unjust, not to say c[r]uel, and shews a degree of passion and prejudice not very creditable to that high court — I am afraid that the feeling may endanger the *Prize cases.*

Of course, this conversation was private and *confidential*, between Judge S. and me. His *motive* was kind to me, and his object to warn me to *get rid of Mr. E.* in Govt. cases, because his presence was offensive to the Court.[40]

Chief Justice Taney was also concerned with the progress of war cases, but with somewhat different thoughts in mind. Dr. Swisher has traced the story in his recent biography.[41] By the use of military power the secession of Maryland was nipped in the bud, disloyal persons were imprisoned, and presently the atmosphere became as uncongenial to Southern sympathizers as it had formerly been to Unionists. Indictments for treason were found against some sixty persons, including Merryman, growing out of the destruction of the railroad bridges and other acts. The accused, the tables now being turned, did not stand on their constitutional right to

[39] S. W. Pennypacker, *The Autobiography of a Pennsylvanian* (Philadelphia: The John C. Winston Company, 1918), p. 130. On October 1, 1888, Justice Miller had delivered the opening address to the law class of the University of Pennsylvania. (He spoke on "The Use and Value of Authorities," as quoted in an earlier chapter.) A dinner was tendered to him by the law faculty, at which Pennypacker was present. He wrote the memorandum of the Judge's conversation immediately after.

[40] *Diary of Edward Bates*, p. 281. The report of the Prize Cases in 17 L. Ed. 459 sets out some of the arguments at considerable length, but not that of Mr. Eames.

[41] Carl B. Swisher, *Roger B. Taney* (New York: The Macmillan Co., 1935), pp. 557ff.

a speedy trial, and Justice Taney and District Judge Giles did what they could to stall the prosecution. Taney found himself too ill to hold terms of the circuit court, and wrote the district judge not to try the cases alone, pointing out that if two judges sat they could certify a question to the Supreme Court, whereas if a single judge sat there would be no review of a conviction. Dr. Swisher gives the substance of a letter Taney wrote to Justice Nelson on May 8, 1864, pointing out the prevalence of military authority in Maryland, and saying that under the circumstances a fair and impartial trial could not be had. His conclusion was that if the district attorney pressed the cases, he would simply refuse to take them up. In the end they never came to trial. Taney's exercise of judicial discretion was humane, and doubtless served the ends of justice. It is quoted here in no captious spirit. But his insistence that the circumstances of May 1861 were no reason for staying the course of proceedings for a single moment, followed by his unwillingness to let indictments be tried for years following, furnishes an interesting contrast.

The incidents narrated above teach one that far-reaching judgments on vital public questions may be secreted in decisions on jurisdiction or procedure or in the exercise of judicial discretion, quite as truly as in decisions on points of substantive law.[42]

The most important of the cases on executive power in time of war did not reach the Court until after hostilities were ended.[43] On October 5, 1864, Lambdin P. Milligan was arrested at his home in Indiana. Presently he was tried before a military commission at Indianapolis, and found guilty of

[42] *Cf.* United States *v.* Armour, 142 Fed. 808 (1906), where the Roosevelt administration's prosecution of the meat packers under the Anti-Trust Act was brought to a complete stop by the decision of a single district judge, holding that the individual defendants were immune from prosecution. As the law then stood, no appeal lay at the suit of the government in criminal cases, so that every criminal statute was at the mercy of any court of first instance. This grave responsibility was pressed upon the district judge in the Armour Case, but his conclusion was that "the parties are entitled to the best judgment of the court upon the questions involved."

[43] *Ex parte* Milligan, 4 Wallace 2 (1866).

conspiracy to overthrow the government, giving aid and comfort to rebels, inciting insurrection, "disloyal practices," and violation of the laws of war. Milligan was a major general in the Order of the Sons of Liberty, and other members of that Copperhead organization were tried jointly with him. He and two of his co-defendants were sentenced to be hanged. Habeas corpus proceedings were then brought and carried to the Supreme Court, which on April 3, 1866, held that the prisoners must be discharged.

These Indiana treason trials are a part of the political and military history of the time. The extent of the disaffection among the people of Ohio, Indiana, and Illinois in 1863 and 1864 was a matter of great concern in political circles both North and South. The Sons of Liberty and related orders were known to have enrolled considerable numbers in an organization in which fraternal, political, and military features were combined. Morgan's raid into Indiana and Ohio in July 1863, just after the Vallandigham trial, and during the state election contest in Ohio, was a bid to those who wished to bring the war to an end. But the raid ended in defeat and capture [44] and demonstrated that the Copperheads could not bring their courage to the sticking point.

In the summer of 1864, however, Confederate commissioners in Canada placed a good deal of money in the hands of leaders of the order, and July 20, August 16, and August 29 were successively fixed as the date for an armed uprising. The scheme was to overpower the guards of the various prisoner camps at Chicago, Springfield, Rock Island, Indianapolis, Cincinnati, and elsewhere and to take over the state governments. The date last set was chosen with an eye to the assembling of the Democratic National Convention at Chicago, which was thought to afford a good opportunity for bringing together the participants. But the government was

[44] Among those taken prisoner was a young Tennessean named Horace H. Lurton. Subsequently, when almost at the point of death in a Union prisoner camp, Lurton was released by President Lincoln in response to an appeal by the boy's mother. He was later appointed to the Supreme Court by President Taft.

aware of the plans, and took measures which completely disheartened the conspirators.

Under date of October 8 the Judge Advocate General submitted to the Secretary of War a report on the ramifications of the organization,[45] which created something of a sensation in the presidential canvass. There was a contest on in Indiana, where Governor Morton was running for reëlection against Joseph E. McDonald. McDonald was a man of high character, of undoubted loyalty to the Union, and in cordial personal relations with Morton. He had won an overwhelming nomination in the Democratic State Convention over his anti-war rival, Milligan. Undoubtedly McDonald was going to receive the Copperhead vote, while Morton was losing nothing politically by the revelations of the plot. Such was the position when in October General Hovey, commanding the District of Indiana, on orders from Washington, caused Milligan and others to be arrested. It seems that General Carrington, who had collected the evidence against the accused, wished to have them tried in the federal court, but that Secretary Stanton and Governor Morton thought that trial by military commission would have a more salutary effect in discouraging further plots.[46]

It should be remembered that this was no case where an overzealous officer accused a civilian of some nebulous offense. Vallandigham's trial had been initiated by a fidgety general, and Lincoln had resorted to a practical joke as a way out of the embarrassment thrust upon him by a subordinate whom he was unwilling to repudiate. But the evidence of attempted treason lay heavy on Milligan. In his petition for habeas corpus he made no allegation of innocence, and as the Chief Justice pointed out, his guilt was admitted on the record.

McDonald was now retained as counsel for Milligan. Early in 1865 he went to Washington to appeal to the President not to approve the sentence of the commission. Lincoln went

---

[45] *Official Records*, 2 ser. VII, 930ff.

[46] W. D. Foulke, *Life of Oliver P. Morton* (Indianapolis and Kansas City: The Bowen Merrill Company, 1899), I, 419.

over the record and suggested certain errors and imperfections. " 'You may go home, Mr. McDonald,' he said, with a pleased expression, 'and I'll send for you when the papers get back; but I apprehend and hope there will be such a jubilee over yonder,' he added, pointing to the hills of Virginia just across the river, 'we shall none of us want any more killing done.' " [47] Justice Davis, who was urging the President "that the various military trials in the Northern and Border States, where the courts were free and untrammelled, were unconstitutional and wrong," records that Lincoln told McDonald that he would not allow the prisoner to be hanged, but added, "I'll keep them in prison awhile to keep them from killing the Government." [48] But when the record finally came up for action, Lincoln had just been assassinated, and Johnson approved the sentence. May 19, 1865, was the date set for the execution.[49]

On May 10 petitions for writs of habeas corpus were filed in the United States Circuit Court at Indianapolis. The privilege of the writ had been suspended pursuant to the Act of March 3, 1863; but that Act had further provided that if a grand jury had met and failed to return an indictment, a prisoner might apply to be discharged from military custody.[50] Justice Davis was in favor of granting the petition, while the district judge opposed. On certificate of division of opinion the case went up to the Supreme Court.

In the meantime Justice Davis had a talk with Governor Morton in which he pressed upon him the view that the trial by commission could not be sustained, and urged him to use his influence to secure a pardon.[51] President Johnson, after

---

[47] McDonald's account, in *Herndon's Lincoln*, chap. xix.

[48] Davis to Herndon, on September 10, 1866, in *Herndon's Lincoln*, chap. xix.

[49] *Official Records*, 2 ser. viii, 543ff.

[50] Apparently the reason no indictments were found was that no attention had been paid to the Act of March 3. After the prisoners had sought habeas corpus, indictments were asked for and returned. In 1867 nolle prosequis were entered (*The Milligan Case*, edited by Samuel Klaus, New York: Alfred A. Knopf, 1929, p. 45).

[51] Foulke, *Morton*, 1, 428.

considerable hesitation, at the last moment commuted the sentences to life imprisonment at hard labor.[52]

In the Supreme Court argument was heard from March 5 to March 13, 1866. Attorney General Speed, Henry Stanbery, and Ben Butler appeared for the government, while for the petitioners McDonald was supported by David Dudley Field and J. S. Black. James A. Garfield made his maiden effort on the same side, not only contributing an excellent argument, but also serving to lift the curse of disloyalty from the advocacy of an unpopular cause. Though the war was over, the case had a present importance for the effect it might have on the system of military government set up in the Southern states.

On March 25, it being Sunday, Orville H. Browning went to church as was his habit, and was rewarded by the following information which he set down in his diary:

Judge Grier went with me. He told me that the Supreme court, in the Habeas Corpus case from Indiana, to try the legality of military commissions, had unanimously decided in favor of the Habeas Corpus, and against the Commissions — the only difference being that some of the Judges desired to confine the decision to the legality of the Commission which tried the case in question, but that the majority extended it to all military commissions for the trial of persons not in the Military or Naval Service.[53]

On April 3, 1866, the decision of the Court was announced as Judge Grier had indicated, but no opinions were delivered until December 17, when the Court reconvened.[54]

In holding that under the circumstances the Executive was without power to try Milligan it was unnecessary to consider whether it lay within the powers of Congress to grant such authority. Five of the justices, however, wished to go

---

[52] *Offical Records*, 2 ser., vii, 637.

[53] *Diary of Orville Hickman Browning*, ii, 67.

[54] Milligan later brought an action against General Hovey, by whose order he had been tried, and the members of the military commission (Milligan *v.* Hovey, Fed. Case No. 9605, 1871). He was successful, but a statute of limitations (the Act of March 3, 1863) barred recovery for the greater part of his imprisonment, and the damages given were only nominal.

further and declare that trial by military commission, except where hostilities had effectually closed the courts and deposed the civil administration, would have been invalid even if Congress had authorized it. Possibly they wished the nation's great sanguinary episode to close on a note of constitutional restraint, thus discouraging arbitrary measures of reconstruction. This was suggested by Judge Davis, who went on to discuss the case on the broadest constitutional grounds, so as not only to cover the case of martial rule under presidential authority, but also the hypothetical situation where Congress might attempt to authorize such rule. He recalled that Indiana had not been the scene of hostilities. The federal courts were open, and held "by judges commissioned during the Rebellion" (thinking, doubtless, of the judges of whom the Administration had been justly apprehensive).

If, in foreign invasion or civil war, the courts are actually closed, and it is impossible to administer criminal justice according to law, *then*, on the theatre of actual military operations, where war really prevails, . . . [the military power] is allowed to govern by martial rule until the laws can have their free course. As necessity creates the rule, so it limits its duration. . . . Martial rule can never exist where the courts are open, and in the proper and unobstructed exercise of their jurisdiction. It is also limited to the locality of actual war.[55]

Chief Justice Chase, for himself and his brothers Wayne, Swayne, and Miller, filed a concurring opinion. They were with the majority in holding that under the Act of March 3 the petitioners were entitled to be discharged.

But the opinion which has just been read goes further; and as we understand it, asserts not only that the Military Commission held in Indiana was not authorized by Congress, but that it was not in the power of Congress to authorize it; from which it may be thought to follow, that Congress had no power to indemnify the officers who composed the commission against liability in civil courts for acting as members of it.
We cannot agree to this. . . .

[55] 4 Wallace at 127.

We by no means assert that Congress can establish and apply the laws of war where no war has been declared or exists.

Where peace exists the laws of peace must prevail. What we do maintain is, that when the nation is involved in war, and some portions of the country are invaded, and all are exposed to invasion, it is within the power of Congress to determine to what states or districts such great and imminent public danger exists as justifies the authorization of military tribunals for the trial of crimes and offenses against the discipline or security of the army or against the public safety.[56]

The fact of the courts being closed or open as the test of the legality of trial by military tribunal is familiar in English constitutional history, going back even before the struggle with the Stuarts. On this point, Justice Davis' opinion was a paraphrase of familiar British authorities. It is significant, however, that more recently the test has been abandoned by the courts of South Africa and Ireland, and by the Judicial Committee of the Privy Council; [57] which suggests that if a like emergency arose again the Supreme Court would be apt to adopt a view more in keeping with that of the concurring minority. The present Chief Justice, in an address at the close of the World War, has implied as much:

Certainly, the test should not be a mere physical one, nor should substance be sacrificed to form. The majority recognized "a necessity to furnish a substitute for the civil authority," when overthrown, in order "to preserve the safety of the army and society." If this necessity actually exists it can not be doubted that the power of the Nation is adequate to meet it, but the rights of the citizen may not be impaired by an arbitrary legislative declaration.[58]

Mr. Warren's review of contemporary comment in the press [59] shows how resentfully the Radical Republicans perused the majority opinion. And regret was expressed that the majority had gone forward to meet the question of legis-

[56] 4 Wallace at 136, 140.

[57] Fairman, *The Law of Martial Rule*, pp. 106ff.

[58] Charles E. Hughes, *War Powers under the Constitution*, p. 12; Senate Document No. 105, 65 Cong., 1 Sess.

[59] *The Supreme Court in United States History*, chap. xxix.

lative power to establish a military government. For the time was at hand when the Court was going to find itself in collision with the Congress over questions of military reconstruction in the South. Justice Miller, as will be seen, was aware of the dangers of vindictive action on the part of the leaders in Congress. But he deemed it the part of duty and of wisdom for the judges to refrain from pronouncements not required by the facts in hand,[60] and to provoke no needless conflict with the popular branches of the government.

Two observations should be appended to this chapter. The relations of Lincoln's administration to the judges involved some conflicts and many hairbreadth escapes. Had it not been for the new appointees to the Supreme Court things would have gone worse than they did. It should not be inferred that it was the Constitution which proved too rigid to permit an effective exercise of war power. A later Court — presided over by Chief Justice White, who himself had been a Confederate soldier — showed that this is not the case, and that adequate power was granted if the justices were willing to find it. Indeed it may well be that, so far as freedom of speech and of the press is concerned, more ballast than necessary has been thrown overboard.

Secondly, it is not the purpose of this chapter to produce a factitious spectacle of judicial conflict. It should be remembered that week after week, in time of war as in time of peace, the Court was disposing of the ordinary grist of cases with no particular uncertainty of decision. This is not a record of the causes it decided, not even of all those involving constitutional questions. Only those controversies relating to the war power have been considered. It would be a crude oversimplification to suppose that because the justices varied so greatly in their enthusiasm for the war these differences would be reflected in every decision on national power. Thus

[60] In the Milligan Case, the assertion of the minority that Congress would have had power to authorize trial by military commission was quite as much *obiter dictum* as the assertion of the majority that it would not. But it seems that the minority would have been content to confine themselves to the facts of the particular case if the majority had done so.

Justice Nelson, on the same day that he read the minority opinion in the Prize Cases, was the organ of the Court in *Bank of Commerce* v. *New York City*,[61] holding that a taxpayer was not subject, in respect of his investment in United States securities, to even non-discriminatory state taxation. The result was greatly to enhance the borrowing power of the government by giving its issues an advantage over all other investments. In most of the litigation which came before the Court, the principles to be applied seemed clear to all the justices. This is an important part of the truth, just as is the other fact — that the views of some of the justices threatened to impose a very serious clog on the power to preserve the Union.

[61] 2 Black 620 (1863).

V

THE COURT AT THE CLOSE OF THE WAR

SALMON P. CHASE resigned his commission as Secretary of the Treasury in June 1864, and was surprised to find that it was accepted. For months he had nursed his presidential candidacy while a member of the president's cabinet, and now he was under no restraint in his efforts to supplant his former chief. But Sherman's capture of Atlanta and Sheridan's success in the Valley of Virginia suddenly revived Lincoln's prestige. By the end of September Chase was in a mood to support a reëlection. And shortly thereafter an event occurred which caused him to develop even some friendliness toward the Administration. On October 12 the chief justiceship fell vacant, and Chase became an active candidate.[1] In fact the appointment was very generally regarded as an obvious one.

There was opposition and rivalry aplenty. Montgomery Blair, who had also until recently been a member of Lincoln's Cabinet, wanted the place for himself, and secured the support of Welles, and perhaps Seward.[2] But the Blairs detested Chase so heartily that no positive self-interest would have been needed to enlist their opposition. Attorney General Bates, who was just leaving the Cabinet, records that he had word from a friend who came directly from the President, that the latter, "if not overborne by others would gladly, make me Ch. J — that Chase was turning every stone, to get it, and several others were urged, and from different quarters. . . . If I get it, it is a mere gratuitous addition, to be

---

[1] The relations of Chase to the Lincoln administration are traced in D. V. Smith's *Chase and Civil War Politics* (1931), reprinted from the *Ohio Archaeological and Historical Quarterly* for July and October 1930.

[2] *Diary of Gideon Welles* (Boston and New York: Houghton Mifflin Company, 1911), II, 181–182.

held only for a little while, and as a crowning and retiring honor." [3]

William M. Evarts was urged upon the President, having the endorsement of the judges of the New York Court of Appeals [4] and of Governor Andrew of Massachusetts. E. R. Hoar and Richard Henry Dana, Jr., went to Washington to manage the candidacy, and tried to enlist Senator Sumner, but found him "entirely in the interest of Chase." Evarts was attracted to what he described as "a place of great political importance over and above its simple judicial authority." He felt no duty to defer to Chase, explaining later that he had doubted "the special aptitude of his intellect to thread the tangled mazes of affairs which form the body of private litigation." But in a eulogy pronounced after Chase's death he said that the Chief Justice had by his "patient and laborious application" disproved these apprehensions.[5]

Henry S. Foote, in his *Casket of Reminiscences*,[6] states that Lincoln offered the Chief Justiceship to Justice Swayne; that the latter accepted; that the President was then urged to appoint Chase in consideration of his withdrawing from his candidacy for the presidency; and that Swayne released the President from his promise. It should be recalled that Foote is repeating hearsay, as he was within the Confederate States at the time. There is more weight, however, to the evidence of Welles's Diary:

Governor Dennison, Postmaster-General, called at my house this evening to have some conversation on the subject of judge. He says he is and was at the last session committed for his fellow townsman Judge Swayne, who was at the time recommended by all on the bench; that he had called on the President at that time

[3] *Diary of Edward Bates*, p. 427; entry for November 22, 1864.

[4] Sherman Evarts, in *Great American Lawyers*, edited by William Draper Lewis (Philadelphia: The John C. Winston Company, 1907–09), VII, 241.

[5] Sherman Evarts, *Arguments and Speeches of William Maxwell Evarts* (New York: The Macmillan Co., 1919), III, 80. Evarts' candidacy for the chief justiceship is traced by Brainerd Dyer, who has consulted the correspondence, in his *Public Career of William M. Evarts* (Berkeley: University of California Press, 1933), pp. 155ff.

[6] Published as a book in 1874 (Washington: Chronicle Publishing Company), after having appeared in the *Washington Chronicle*. Pages 413ff.

in behalf of Swayne, and the President then remarked that that seemed a settled question in which all agreed. Governor D. is now a little embarrassed, for he feels particularly friendly to Blair.[7]

As to Foote's assertion that Chase received the chief justice-ship as compensation for withdrawing his presidential candi-dacy, it will be remembered that Chase had given up the idea of forcing Lincoln to retire from the presidential contest some weeks prior to Taney's death; but this alone does not disprove the bargain, since it had been evident for some time that the chief justiceship would presently fall vacant. It is inconsistent with other evidence to suppose that Lincoln felt he had com-mitted himself to the elevation of Swayne; and it seems im-probable that any of the justices, except possibly Davis, would have urged Swayne's appointment.

It is clear that Judge Swayne's friends were active in seek-ing his promotion, as shown by the following letter written by Rutherford B. Hayes, on December 12, 1864:

I am very glad Governor Chase is Chief Justice. I had almost given up his appointment. I received letters from Swayne's friends urging me to write in his behalf. I heard nothing of the kind from friends of Governor Chase. I suppose they felt safe. I replied to Perry [8] and others that I was for Governor Chase.[9]

That Swayne was not in a position to maintain his candidacy against Chase's claims is evident. It will be recalled that he had enlisted the Secretary's support for his own appointment as Justice McLean's successor; he had also written most ap-provingly of Chase's great accomplishments in the Treasury.[10] And the party leaders in his own state, Ohio, threw their support decisively behind Chase: one promised to get

---

[7] *Diary of Gideon Welles,* II, 182; entry for November 26.

[8] Probably Aaron F. Perry, previously mentioned as said to have been offered the appointment as associate justice which went to Swayne.

[9] *Diary and Letters of Rutherford Birchard Hayes* (Columbus: The Ohio State Archaeological and Historical Society, 1922–26), II, 547.

[10] In a letter on November 4, 1863, Swayne wrote to Chase to regard his achievements as "the works of a kind providence," and adjured him: "Instead of a *great author,* consider yourself only *an instrument* and deport yourself accordingly" (Chase Papers).

35,000 votes for the Administration if Chase received the appointment.[11]

Orville Browning was one of the Conservatives who opposed the former Secretary. The morning after Taney's death he called on Secretary Fessenden, Chase's successor at the Treasury. In his diary he recorded their conversation:

After despatching my business I asked Mr Fessenden if his friends, without his participation, would procure him to be appointed Chief Justice, he would accept the place. He replied that it would be vain to make an effort in his behalf, and that he could not consent that any steps should be taken by his friends looking to such a result, for he knew that the place was designed for Mr Chase, and that the appointment would be tendered to him, and accepted by him — that when Mr Chase resigned as Secretary of the Treasury, and Tod, of Ohio, was nominated to the vacancy he, Fessenden, as Chairman of the Finance Committee of the Senate called on the President to induce him to withdraw Tod's nomination and reinstate Mr Chase — that the President refused to do so, and showed a determination not to take him back into the cabinet, but remarked that he had great respect for Mr Chase, and that if the Chief Justiceship of the Supreme Court was now vacant he would appoint him to that place — that previously when it was thought the Chief Justice was near his end, he had made up his mind, in the event of his death to appoint Mr Chase, and that he had not changed his mind, and would appoint him now if the place was vacant. Mr Fessenden added that he had communicated this conversation to Mr Chase as his friend — that he was satisfied Mr. Chase would accept, and that he could not now, honorably, consent that any movement should be made in his behalf.

I did not further press the subject, tho I was entirely sincere in my offer. Judge Curtis of Massachusetts was my first choice, but I knew there was no hope of his appointment, and I, therefore, sincerely desired the appointment of Mr Fessenden knowing him to be a good lawyer, and a thoroughly upright man.[12]

That Browning wrote to Thomas Ewing the elder appears from a reply in Ewing's Letterbook:

[11] D. V. Smith, *Chase and Civil War Politics*, p. 159 and note.
[12] *The Diary of Orville Hickman Browning*, I, 686; entry for October 13, 1864.

Lancaster Ohio Oct 24/64

My Dear Sir,

I suppose myself quite powerless in the matter, but am willing to do all I can to prevent Chase being made C Justice. His appointment would not be esteemed a compliment by the Ohio Bar. But in casting about among those who have Executive favor I think we lack material for the office. Stanton is not highly qualified though I would very much prefer him to Chase. I presume the appointment will not be made till we have had time to confer about it. . . .

I am very truly
Yours

Hon O H Browning   T Ewing.[13]

Presently Ewing came to Washington and took the matter up directly:

No 12 N A Street
Washington Dec 3, 1864

To the President

I write to express to you the opinion that Chase would not be acceptable to the Bar of Ohio as Chief Justice of the Supreme Court. He has no considerable reputation as a lawyer. He is a politician rather than a lawyer & unless he changes his nature always will be even if made Chief Justice. I am unwilling to see the Chief Justice of the U S intriguing & trading for the Presidency.

I am very truly
Yours
T. Ewing [14]

That Chase was a statesman of very great ability was generally admitted. It was urged against him that he had long been away from practice at the bar, but this seemed more than offset by his experience in public affairs. Lincoln had taken the measure of his Secretary's greatness even if the latter could not reciprocate; and he was too big to withhold the appointment because of the shabby treatment he had suffered. He believed that Chase would sustain what had been done in regard to emancipation and the legal tender, but was very

---

[13] Thomas Ewing, Letterbook, 1864–1868, p. 20; Library of Congress.
[14] Ewing Letterbook, p. 72.

mistrustful whether he would ever overcome his obsession about the presidency. With a total want of enthusiasm — he was quoted as saying that "he would rather have swallowed his buckhorn chair" [15] — Lincoln made the appointment, on December 6, 1864.

In the eight years of his chief justiceship Chase displayed abilities which fulfilled the high hopes of his admirers — and he also justified the apprehensions of the president who appointed him.

We have an interesting sketch of Chase and his brothers as seen through the eyes of the crier of the Court.[16] The Chief Justice

was dignity personified. . . . No matter how long, dull and prosy an attorney might be . . . , the chief justice never displayed any impatience. . . . In presiding he always leaned forward over his desk, never resting himself as some of the justices frequently did, by lolling back in the great armchairs. He seldom asked questions of the attorneys, but when he did it was only to make more clear some statement. He made copious notes. He was ever prompt in opening the session of the court, and, as a rule, was equally prompt in closing at the hour appointed.

The senior associate justice when Chase came to the bench was James M. Wayne of Georgia, the sole survivor of those who sat with Marshall. Wayne was born in 1790, the son of a former officer in the British army. He had been educated in the North, graduating from Princeton in 1808, and later studying law with Judge Chauncey at New Haven. He had served as mayor of Savannah, as judge of the superior court, and as a Jacksonian Democrat in Congress, when appointed to the Court. He adhered to Jackson's sentiment, "The federal union: it must be preserved"; when the war broke he remained on the Court, and took the view favorable to executive power in both the Prize Cases and *Ex parte Milligan*. To the state of his birth he became an alien enemy, and his

[15] *Diary of Gideon Welles*, II, 196.
[16] W. H. Smith, "Supreme Court and its Justices in Days Following the Civil War," *Sunday Star*, Washington, April 22, 1923.

property was confiscated — though as a matter of fact it was not sold, but turned over to the Justice's son, the Adjutant General of Georgia.[17] In appearance he is described as having

a high and prominent forehead, a large nose and mouth, and, notwithstanding his great age, a heavy head of hair which he always kept brushed with the greatest care. He always paid close attention to the arguments of attorneys, frequently making copious notes. He seldom interrupted an argument by asking a question, and when he did so it was in the most courteous manner. In fact, he was courteous with every one.[18]

Next toward the right of the bench sat Judge Grier, a salty old gentleman with a touch of uncouthness. "During a sitting of the court it was the habit of Justice Grier to sit with his eyes closed, and the thought was often expressed by members of the bar and attendants in the lobby that the aged justice was dozing, but such was not the case." This is confirmed by an anecdote William A. Maury tells of his senior, Philip Phillips. "On one occasion Judge Grier complimented Mr. Phillips on an argument he had made. 'But,' said Mr. Phillips, 'I thought you were asleep, Judge.' 'Oh,' said the Judge, partly excusing himself, 'you see, Phillips, when I have seen where you go in, I know where you are coming out; but with some of these fellows I have to keep awake and watch them all the time.' "[19]

Justices Swayne and Davis occupied the two seats at the extreme right of the Chief Justice and in personal appearance were much alike. They were each more than six feet in height and otherwise large physically. They both loved candy, and it was no unusual thing for one or the other of them to send a page out for a dime's worth of the old-fashioned stick candy and the two to munch it while listening to the argument.[20] They frequently grew tired

[17] Warren Grice, *The Georgia Bench and Bar* (Macon: The J. W. Burke Co., 1931), I, 316.
[18] W. H. Smith, *supra*, note 16.
[19] Maury's Recollections (MS.), p. 56.
[20] The *Daily Iowa State Register*, a Republican newspaper published at Des Moines, in its issue for March 26, 1872, carried a short article in which a visitor to the Supreme Court was quoted as having observed one justice eating an apple, and another molasses candy, on the bench.

of sitting and would stand for a time, leaning against one of the heavy pillars back of the seats of the court.

. . . In all dealings with the attorneys they were extremely courteous and seldom interrupted by questions. They were great companions off the bench and nearly always arrived at the Capitol together. It was a rare occasion when they did not leave together.[21]

On the immediate left of the Chief Justice sat Judge Nelson, a man destined to spend almost half a century in judicial office. Before coming to the federal bench he had been in turn circuit judge, associate, and then chief justice of the Supreme Court of New York. "Justice Nelson was the quiet member of the court. He always sat well back in his chair, paying close attention but rarely making a note or asking a question." [22]

One of the merits claimed for Justice Nelson by his admirers was that during the stress of war and reconstruction he maintained a serenity of mind more successfully than any of his brethren. Thus in an obituary note published in 1874 the *Central Law Journal*, after praising his judicial temperament, patience, and freedom from partisan bias or hasty views, added, "We have good authority for the statement, that in the heat and ardor which sometimes attend the discussions of the conference room, one member was never known to lose his evenness of temper." [23] But what some regarded as mental equipoise seemed to others to be a constant leaning away from the measures of the dominant political party.

Nathan Clifford was, in avoirdupois, the largest one of the justices. His mouth was of a rather peculiar shape, as if he were ready to dispute with some one. When the lobby was approximately empty he would sit leaning back in his chair, looking as if he were taking little interest in the proceedings. But let the

[21] W. H. Smith, *supra*, note 16.

[22] *Ibid.*

[23] 1:2 (1874). Reference may also be made to a letter written by Nelson in 1873, explaining a decision in prize — The Circassian, 2 Wallace 135 (1864) — where he alone denied the right to capture. "The truth is," he wrote, "that the feeling of the country was deep and strong against England, and the judges, as individual citizens, were no exceptions to this feeling" (8 *Albany Law Journal* 410, 1873).

lobby fill up and then would come a marked change. Leaning forward, he would fire a question at the attorney who was speaking, and, hardly waiting for an answer, would shoot at him another, and then turn toward the lobby with a broad smile, as if to say, "Did you see how I got him?"

As long as the lobby remained full this by-play would go on, but when the lobby emptied Clifford would sink back in his seat as if no longer interested in what was going on.

. . . In disposition he was always kindly and courteous to every one.[24]

We may tarry long enough for a thumbnail sketch of Justice Clifford. Early years spent close to the grudging soil in an isolated New England village — a struggle for an education in the "Academy" while teaching district school — learning the function of each writ by apprenticeship to a local practitioner — it was a background calculated to develop self-restraint and a certain rigidity of mind. Ambition pointed the way successively to the Maine legislature, the Democratic National Convention of 1832, the attorney-generalship of the state, and two terms in Congress. In 1846 Polk appointed Clifford to be Attorney General, knowing little about him, but being assured of his "political orthodoxy" and that "his attainments as a lawyer were respectable." [25] On December 13, after less than two months in office, Clifford appeared at the White House to present his resignation. A little kindly inquiry elicited the reason: the Supreme Court was about to convene, and the law officer of the government was in a funk.[26] Some encouragement from Polk, and a successful appearance before the Court, overcame the desire to flee. Next came his appointment as commissioner and then minister to Mexico at the conclusion of the war, bringing bigger affairs and a wider horizon than residence in the town of Newfield had afforded; then private practice at Portland, unsuccessful efforts to

---

[24] W. H. Smith, *supra*, note 16.

[25] P. G. Clifford, *Nathan Clifford, Democrat* (New York and London: G. P. Putnam's Sons, 1922), pp. 139, 141.

[26] *The Diary of James K. Polk*, edited by M. M. Quaife (Chicago: A. C. McClurg Co., 1910), entry for December 13, 1846.

reach the Senate, and finally, when Justice Curtis resigned, a seat on the Supreme Court. President Buchanan had known Clifford from their days in Polk's cabinet, and, after some hesitation, decided to give the nomination to one of whose views he was so well assured.[27]

The appointment aroused considerable opposition, and unflattering contrasts were drawn between Clifford and such predecessors from the First Circuit as Story and Curtis. Clifford now had more self-confidence, however, and was not so astounded at his own temerity as on the occasion of his appointment as Attorney General. Still, his first circuit court at Boston was going to try his measure before the truly great — giants such as Judge Curtis (now at the bar), Rufus Choate,

[27] That President Buchanan reposed confidence in Justice Clifford's Democracy is indicated by the following letter, preserved among the Clifford Papers:

"*Private*

"Washington 16 July 1858

"My dear Sir,

"Some person sent me the speech of Mr [George F] Shepley at the late Maine Convention, *marked*, & I must say it is a most extraordinary production for a Democrat, a Lawyer & a U. S. District Attorney. In former times we used to hear of Bank Democrats; but a Squatter Sovereignty Democrat is still more absurd. At the date of the Kansas Nebraska Bill many Democrats contended that under the Constitution Slavery was a local institution & the master could not hold his slave as property in the Territories although I was of a different opinion. Hence the provision in the Bill was 'subject to the Constitution of the United States' & facilities were offered by it to bring the question before the Supreme Court. That Tribunal has decided the question; & it is now Revolutionary to attempt to defeat their decision by squatter sovereignty. I can not longer recognise Mr Shepley as a sound Democrat & I am unwilling that he should continue to hold the office of District Attorney. I see that the Republicans of Maine have adopted his doctrine & its effect will be the same with that of rank Free Soilism. I wish to proceed prudently in this matter & I desire to know from you who will be a fit successor for Mr Shepley. I know you will recommend none but a sound lawyer & a sound Cincinnati Platform Democrat.

"I expect to set out on Monday for Bedford Springs Pa where I shall be glad to hear from you.

"Your friend
"Very respectfully
"Hon: Nathan Clifford."   "James Buchanan"

In fact, Shepley was allowed to retain his office to the end of Buchanan's administration. During the Civil War he was closely associated in the military exploits of Ben Butler at New Orleans. When the office of federal circuit judge was created in 1869, President Grant appointed Shepley to that office in the First Circuit.

and Sidney Bartlett. He was relieved to discover his own capacity: "No question has been presented that will give me much trouble." [28]

It should be added that he was a magistrate of the most absolute integrity and great personal dignity; that he grew in his office so as to live down the charge that he was no better than a nonentity; and that he deserved Justice Miller's words of appreciation: "I have not met in a long life of public service, a more conscientious and industrious man in the discharge of all his official duties." [29] The *American Law Review*, whose successive editors were among the most accomplished lawyers at the Boston bar, in reviewing Justice Clifford's circuit court reports, said that they were "characterized by much learning, conscientious and painstaking labor, and a due regard for precedents," and fully sustained the high reputation enjoyed by the work of his predecessors;[30] and again, "his reputation as a judge has been steadily rising since the day of his appointment. On many branches of the law his authority is generally recognized, especially in maritime questions; and his patience, good temper, and courtesy on the bench and to all the bar has won for him a large share of personal esteem and regard." [31]

Resuming our survey of the bench, on Judge Clifford's left sat his brother Miller. Contrast could hardly be greater, in political outlook or in personality. Where the one suffered from stiffness and frugality of the emotions, the other had an engaging ease and naturalness of manner. As the crier of the Court recalled,

with the employees of the Court Justice Miller was the most popular, in this respect ranking with Justices Swayne and Davis. . . . He always had a kindly smile and greeting for all the employees . . . and never failed to thank any of them for a service. The pages fairly adored him and would spring with alacrity when he signalled for one of them.

[28] Clifford, *Nathan Clifford*, p. 274.
[29] Miller to Justice Clifford's son, November 9, 1885; Clifford Papers.
[30] 5:118 (1870).
[31] 12:796 (1878).

Justice Field . . . was decidedly the "fidgety" member and was disposed to be faultfinding with the attachés, and rarely failed to complain of some neglect on the part of the pages. A full lobby always affected him but in a different manner from the way it acted on Justice Clifford. With an empty lobby he usually sat back in his chair with an appearance of listening to the argument of the attorney, but let the lobby fill up and a change would come. He was sure to grow nervous and fidgety. Seizing a pad and pencil, he would make out a list of books and send a page to the library. On the return of the page with arms full of books, Mr. Field would seize upon them, turn the pages rapidly, and frequently with considerable noise throw the books on the floor, and then make another long list.[32]

The casual visitor to the present Supreme Court has a superficial awareness of the smooth efficiency with which case after case is called and argued. It may never occur to him that the swift-flowing spectacle is produced only by the combined operation of a highly developed internal economy, carefully drafted legislation restricting the intake of cases, and a rigid insistence on the rules of court. At the time of which we have been speaking it was quite different. The tempo was leisurely, though there were fewer of the great oratorical field days than when Wirt and Webster and Pinkney appeared before Marshall's Court. Time was not so precious but that Jeremiah Black could pause in his argument long enough to deposit a wad of tobacco in his cavernous jaws, or reach for the silver snuff box which was still a part of the fixtures of the Court. Whereas today each side must compress its oral argument into an hour or less, then two counsel on a side were allowed two hours each. In cases of importance special leave would be granted so that, as has been seen, the debate might go on for days. A flood of litigation was coming on which could never be handled by these methods, as Justice Miller foresaw. But the pressure was not yet felt.

Some short mention of a few of the leading advocates of that day may help to recreate the atmosphere of the court

[32] W. H. Smith, *supra*, note 16.

room where Chase presided. And in this we may draw on a number of candid characterizations from Justice Miller's pen. The ability and attainments of counsel will be reflected in the work of the Court, so that complete understanding of what falls from the bench involves some consideration of the adequacy of presentation at the bar.

One of the most colorful of the habitués of the court room was Jeremiah S. Black of Pennsylvania. He had been chief justice of that state, and then Attorney General in the Buchanan administration, where he had rendered the much-derided opinion giving a narrow construction to the power of the president in the event of an attempted secession.[33] Buchanan had nominated him to be an associate justice in February 1860, but through the general disintegration of the Democratic party the nomination failed of confirmation by the narrow vote of twenty-five to twenty-six. Black was a state-rights dogmatist, and had he been confirmed he would doubtless have set out on a judicial crusade against President Lincoln and all his works. Justice Miller's opinion of him was recorded as follows:

Black, as a man, was simply abominable, but there was no one who appeared before the court to whom it was so agreeable to listen. In hearing him you felt that you did not care a damn whether he was talking about his case or about any other case, but there was a wealth of illustration, a knowledge of the Bible and of Shakespeare wrought into his arguments which made you feel that you would like him to go on forever. . . .

He never was a sound lawyer. When he first came down to Washington, he had only been in the habit of getting ten and fifteen dollar fees, but he soon found that he could get almost any sum and he afterwards charged enormous fees.

Toward the latter part of the time he used to argue for the listeners and pay less attention to the law and would maneuver so as to postpone his cases until there were hearers. We humored him, more or less, in the matter.[34]

---

[33] Opinion of November 20, 1860, 9 Opinions of the Attorney General 516.
[34] From the memorandum taken down by S. W. Pennypacker after hearing Judge Miller's conversation at table (Pennypacker, *The Autobiography of a Pennsylvanian*, p. 131).

In the argument of the Milligan Case, Black was followed by the notorious Ben Butler, who went whacking about the subject with characteristic indifference to the rational issues. Here is a fair sample:

> He [Black] told you, with rotund voice and very great earnestness, . . . that "there were dangers which might threaten the life of the nation, and in that case it would be the duty of the nation, and it would be its right, to defend itself." He classed those dangers thus: first, rebellion; second, foreign invasion; third, corruption of civil administration.
> . . . But, may it please your Honors, there is a fourth, a greater, a more imminent, a more perilous danger, from which this country came nearer ruin than by any other, in regard to which the gentleman had some unfortunate experience which he forgot to mention. That danger is *imbecility of administration*; such an Administration as should say "there is no constitutional right in a State to go out of the Union, but there is no power in the Constitution to coerce a State or her people, if she choose to go out." It is in getting rid of that danger, unenumerated by my learned friend, that we have had to use military power. . . .[35]

Browning was in the court room at the time, and pronounced a proper judgment on Butler: "his manner pompous, and his matter paltry. He is a weak man — a humbug." [36]

A bright adornment of the bar was James M. Carlisle, of whom Judge Miller wrote: "He is a true noble, honest, interesting man. . . . At once the most accomplished lawyer and cultivated warm hearted gentleman in Washington." [37] He had a knack for dashing off some pungent verse as he sat waiting for his case to be called, and the readiest of wits in argument. "These flashes . . . not infrequently acted like volatile salt on the flagging attention of the judges in the midst of some sleep-compelling argument." Carlisle's swarthy complexion and black hair coupled with the circumstance that he moved in Latin society and derived considerable prac-

[35] *Argument of Benjamin F. Butler* . . . (separately printed, Lowell, Mass., 1866), p. 13.
[36] *Diary of Orville Hickman Browning*, II, 65.
[37] Letter of July 30, 1869.

JEREMIAH SULLIVAN BLACK

JOHN ARCHIBALD CAMPBELL

DAVID DUDLEY FIELD

MATTHEW HALE CARPENTER

tice from that source created the illusion that he was a distinguished Spanish gentleman.[38]

A contemporary was Reverdy Johnson, sometimes called "the trimmer" because of the catholicity he had shown in political doctrine. He had been Taney's junior when *Brown* v. *Maryland* [39] was argued before Marshall's Court in 1827; he had been on the successful side in the Dred Scott Case,[40] and lived to make winning arguments against the test oath and other features of Radical reconstruction. He had a vehement style of address said to have been cultivated in imitation of the great William Pinkney; his friend Badger [41] once explained banteringly in his presence that "you have a very fair idea of Johnson's oratory if you have ever heard a militia general haranguing his troops on a windy day." [42]

After the test oath of unbroken loyalty to the Union was declared unconstitutional in 1867, John A. Campbell of Alabama returned to the bar of the Court where until 1861 he had been a judge. He had sought to avert the war, and then to restore peace, and now, beginning anew, he was to do the best legal work of his life in arguing great and novel constitutional issues. Miller mentions him in correspondence with the comment, "I esteem him very highly and look upon him as a man of honor and an unfortunate one." [43] Campbell was a philosophical and "scientific" lawyer, which explains how it was that on so many questions his mind ran along congenially with that of Justice Bradley, before whom he appeared on the circuit as well as in the Supreme Court.

[38] Maury's Recollections (MS.), pp. 14ff., 117ff.

[39] 12 Wheaton 419 (1827).

[40] "It was his forcible presentation of the Southern view of our Constitution in respect to the relations of Slavery to the Territories and of the Territories to Slavery, that contributed more than any thing else to bring about the decision that was made in that cause" (George Ticknor Curtis in *Memorial Proceedings by the Bar of the Supreme Court*, 1876, 92 U. S. x).

[41] George E. Badger of North Carolina. He was a distinguished lawyer who had been nominated to the Supreme Court in the closing days of Fillmore's administration, but the Senate, for political reasons, had postponed consideration by a vote of twenty-six to twenty-five. When Pierce came in John A. Campbell was nominated and confirmed.

[42] Maury's Recollections (MS.), p. 10.

[43] Letter of February 10, 1870.

Often associated with Judge Campbell was Philip Phillips, one of the great counselors of his day, whose name seems, undeservedly, to have been writ in water. He was born in Charleston, South Carolina, in 1807, the son of a German Jew. After an adequate education he was admitted to the bar, attended the Nullification Convention as an active Unionist, and then in 1835 removed to Mobile, Alabama, to participate in the growth of that new state. In 1853, very much against his will, he was nominated as the Democratic candidate for Congress, and carried the election. He declined to accept renomination and, having sacrificed a practice worth eight thousand dollars a year, opened an office in Washington. He wrote a series of articles urging the organization of a Court of Claims, which, being published in the *National Intelligencer* and reprinted in pamphlet form, did much to bring about that beneficent legislation. He did not believe that the election of Lincoln was an adequate reason for leaving the Union. His wife, however, was an ardent secessionist, and in August 1861 their home was searched and its inmates held prisoners. In an unpublished autobiographical sketch he writes:

During my confinement I was visited one night by Mr. Edwin M. Stanton, afterwards so celebrated as Secretary of War. He was a friend, and at that time a *stronger sympathizer with the South* than I was. It appears that subsequent events carried him over to the other side. His motives I have no right to question. I am indebted to him for his zeal in aiding the liberation of my family.[44]

Like his friend Justice Campbell, he went South with a heavy heart. At the close of the war he returned to Washington, but being unable to subscribe to the test oath, he returned to New Orleans. Judge Campbell encouraged him not to give up, saying that the bar of the Supreme Court was his proper theater of action. When the Test Oath Cases had been decided he went North. Professional advance was slow. His natural clients, the Southern people, were too impoverished

[44] "A Summary of the Principle Events of My Life" (MS., written in June 1876), p. 44; Phillips Papers, Library of Congress.

to pay fees, and believed moreover that to accomplish anything at Washington, even before the courts, political influence was requisite. Presently, however, he was able to record that "for the last few years my docket in the Supreme Court has numbered some fifty cases. This is a greater number, the Clerk informs me, than any lawyer has ever had." [45] To a correspondent he wrote in 1874, "in nearly all the cases from the south I am employed on one side or the other." [46] In those days it was more of an undertaking for counsel to come to Washington to appear before the Court than it is today, and at the urging of Chief Justice Waite, Phillips made arrangements with local counsel throughout the South to take over their cases on appeal to the Supreme Court. [47] He performed a most useful service to the Court and to the profession by publishing, in 1872, a book on *The Statutory Jurisdiction and Practice of the Supreme Court of the United States*. With the tremendous increase in the volume of litigation in the federal courts which marked the close of the war, the Supreme Court had had to check the looseness of practice which had been tolerated in Taney's day, [48] and to this end Phillips' manual was an aid greatly appreciated.

Everyone about the court was familiar with the tall figure and cold gray eyes of David Dudley Field, eldest of a phenomenal family. His brother, Justice Field, had read law in his New York office. That D. D. Field was among the greatest masters of the profession none will deny. His fight for the codification of substantive and procedural law is one of the most memorable events in American legal history. His devotion of his talents to the services of "Jubilee Jim" Fiske, Jay Gould, and "Boss" Tweed is also memorable, as anyone who recalls Nast's cartoons or Charles Francis Adams' *Chapters of Erie* well knows. We need not seek to strike a balance

[45] "Summary," p. 70.
[46] Letter of December 7, 1874, Letterbook, 1874–75, p. 84; Library of Congress.
[47] *E.g.*, letter to W. P. Ballinger, September 13, 1877, Letterbook, 1877–78, p. 144.
[48] *Cf. The Diary of Edward Bates*, p. 356.

here. Field himself did in his old age, when he had taken to writing verse, and his conclusion was

> Mistakes too often, but successes more,
> And consciousness of duty done.[49]

Certainly both columns of the account were long. Among his successes were the Milligan and Test Oath cases, and a host of other great causes argued before the Supreme Court.

Matthew Hale Carpenter was another of the advocates who appeared throughout the reconstruction litigation and later. He had been appointed to West Point, but the discipline was uncongenial to his irregular character, and after reading law with Rufus Choate he moved west. He represented Wisconsin in the Senate after 1869, a seat in Congress in those days making no demands incompatible with an active practice before the Supreme Court. He argued many of the celebrated political causes of the day, not always on the side congenial to his own party's program. Both as an advocate in the courts and as a member of the Senate, where he sought effective federal control of interstate commerce, Carpenter won the enmity of the railroad interests. Judge Miller, who was his friend, recorded this frank appraisal:

Washington Feby 27. 1881

My Dear Brother.

I am just from the funeral of Matt. Carpenter as he is familiarly called by all classes from the President down to the boy who made his fires. He was one of the most remarkable men whom I have known in public or private life, and I have known him intimately for nearly twenty years.

He was beyond any one whom I have known — in fact he is the only man whom I recall, to whom I would apply the old fashioned phrase — "a man of genius." Take his will, his manner, his command of language and his skill in argument. I think he is the foremost *orator* of his day. As a lawyer he stood in the front rank deservedly. This was founded on all the elements which go to make up a great lawyer. In addition to his eloquence his logic was close, his judgment sound and his perception of the legal

[49] "Lines Written on My Eighty-seventh Birthday," 26 *American Law Review* 255 (1892).

principles involved in a case both quick and accurate. With all this he spent as much labor on the case which he argued as if he had just entered the profession. As a senator he was laborious, attentive, careful; a ready successful debater and popular with his fellow Senators. He was not a statesman, but he was a sound constitutional lawyer. He was the only man I have ever known, who while fitted with learning, and brilliant with genius never omitted ample and careful preparation, whether before the courts, or in the Senate, or on the stump.[50]

But with all these qualities, I might say advantages he has left no impress of himself upon the history of his country or upon its thought. He was never a man of principle, in the sense of having fixed rules of conduct, or set purposes in life. He was only great for the occasion, and was as ready to lend all his talent, his knowledge, and his eloquent [?] power to one purpose almost as another. He was not a man of profound convictions in any moral sense, nor of any vigorous or self-sacrificing friendships, though every body's friend.

He wanted some fixed purpose or aim. He sadly wanted dignity of demeanor, or sense of reverence or respect for himself, or for position in himself or in others. He delighted in the dress and swagger of the bar room. In his loftiest flight of eloquence, or closest train of logic, if a funny or ridiculous illustration struck him he would have it out then without regard to its fitness. He had the finest private library both legal and miscellaneous, of any man west of the Allegheny Mountains and he was familiar with its contents.

His death at the age of fifty six is the result of intemperance in the proper sense of that word. He was intemperate in work, in reading, in writing [?], in his application to his profession, and to his senatorial duties.

He was intemperate in eating, in drinking and in that other pleasure which exhausts the vital forces more than eating or drinking. Though I never saw him drunk or seriously affected by liquor. He was always fearing consumption but died of Brights disease, and might have lived to be an old man before he would have died of consumption. He was a singular man in another respect. He made large sums of money by his profession yet was always poor, but to his credit be it said he was never embarrassed by debt and left life insurance policies to his family

---

[50] The qualities noted in this paragraph are precisely those which Justice Bradley mentioned in an appreciation of Carpenter, quoted by J. B. Cassoday in *Reports of the Wisconsin State Bar Association*, VII (1907), 155, 191.

of about $75,000. He lived well, entertained elaborately, and left his family, a wife and two children pretty well provided. He was a remarkable man and I have given you this sketch of his character because no man of my day has better deserved such an analysis of his mind, his habits, his career —

When Chase ascended the bench James Speed of Kentucky had just been appointed Attorney General. He continued in the Johnson administration, but proved to be in sympathy with the Radicals who favored a rigorous military reconstruction of the South as against the milder measures the President was trying to carry out. When in February 1866, Johnson vetoed the Freedmen's Bureau bill establishing military jurisdiction over parts of the country containing freedmen or refugees, Speed expressed his disagreement, and from then on relations grew strained until finally he resigned. He had appeared for the government in the Milligan Case, in which Browning pronounced his argument "a feeble uninteresting, uninstructive harangue." [51] Justice Miller referred to him in a letter to Ballinger written March 4, 1866, in these terms:

It is well known that he did not approve the veto measure, and I presume he stands in other respects on a feebler footing than any other member of the cabinet. One reason for this *inter nos* is that the session of the Court has developed his utter want of ability as a lawyer — He is certainly one of the feeblest men who has addressed the Court this term.

A few days later, while the elder Thomas Ewing was visiting in Washington, he sent this word of advice to President Johnson:

Among the multiplicity of things of which we spoke last night I forgot to mention the Atto-General — It is of the utmost importance that you have a stronger man in that place — it is due to yourself and also to the Court, for Mr. Speed is not a competent legal adviser especially on the present critical condition of affairs — and I know that the Court does not rely on him — I believe he is loyal and you ought not to turn him adrift but make him District Judge some-where, say in Mississippi. Henry Stanberry

[51] *The Diary of Orville Hickman Browning,* II, 66.

of Kentucky [52] has been named to you for Attorney it is sufficient for me to say of him that he stands with the head of the Bar in the West — "if not first, in the *very first line*." [53]

This letter of recommendation from Stanbery's old senior was written just after the conclusion of argument in the Milligan Case, where Stanbery had been the only strong lawyer on the government side. On April 16 President Johnson sent Stanbery's name to the Senate — not for the attorney-generalship, which Speed still occupied, but to be associate justice, vice Justice Catron deceased. Johnson's enemies in the Senate, however, were not disposed to permit him to make any appointment to the Court, so the nomination was not acted upon, while a bill was introduced and hurried to enactment, providing that no vacancy as associate justice should be filled until the Court had been reduced to seven members; the circuits were rearranged on the basis of the then actual membership of nine judges.[54] This put a quietus on Stanbery's nomination to the Court, and on the day the bill was approved the President nominated him to be Attorney General in place of Speed, who had just resigned. Stanbery held office until March 12, 1868, when he resigned to serve as chief counsel for the President in the impeachment proceedings. At the close of that trial he was renominated to be Attorney General (the place had been filled *ad interim*), but the Senate refused to confirm.[55] Thereupon William M. Evarts, who had also been of counsel in the trial of the impeachment, was appointed, and served to the close of Johnson's term.

Stanbery made a very proper law officer. Thoroughly able as counsel, dignified and impressive in argument, always a

[52] A slip of the pen. Speed came from Kentucky, and Stanbery was from Cincinnati, Ohio. His name was often incorrectly spelled with a double *r*, or a *u*.

[53] Copy of letter of March 15, 1866, in the Ewing Papers, vol. XVIII, Library of Congress. On being admitted to the Ohio bar in 1824 Stanbery had been taken into Mr. Ewing's office.

[54] Act of July 23, 1866, 14 Statutes at Large 209.

[55] "The Senate has been guilty of the littleness of rejecting him in revenge for his defence of the President" (*The Diary of Orville Hickman Browning*, II, 201, June 5, 1868).

gentleman, inspiring confidence by his good sense and probity, he was well qualified to stand at a focal point at a time of perversity and intemperance. He was personally in favor of moderation in the treatment of the South. But he argued the test oath case *Ex parte Garland*, and successfully opposed efforts to prevent the execution of the Reconstruction Acts by the device of an injunction against the President or the Secretary of War.[56] Having advised, however, that the legislation was invalid, he declined to appear in their defense in McCardle's Case.[57]

President Grant's first appointee as Attorney General was Ebenezer R. Hoar of Massachusetts. Judge Miller characterized him as "an able lawyer but no statesman. An honest man, a little rude sometimes, and thoroughly radical. Son of the Hoar who was not permitted to land in Charleston so many years ago, a fact which he does not forget."[58] During Hoar's tenure of the attorney-generalship the President had occasion to appoint eight new circuit judges as well as to fill two vacancies on the Supreme Court, and the excellence of these appointments — a notable thing for the Grant administration — was largely due to Hoar's advice.[59] He himself had been nominated for the first vacancy on the Court, but a combination of objections united enough opposition in the Senate to prevent confirmation. In part this sprang from resentment engendered by his fight for good circuit judges. "What could you expect for a man who had snubbed seventy Senators?" said Hoar's friend, Senator Cameron of Pennsylvania.[60]

The members of the bar in active practice before the Court

[56] Mississippi *v.* Johnson, 4 Wallace 475 (1867); Georgia *v.* Stanton, 6 Wallace 50 (1867).

[57] Warren, *The Supreme Court in United States History*, II, 465.

[58] Letter of July 30, 1869.

[59] "There is no service which I have been able to render to the country which I look back upon with such entire satisfaction, as upon the share which I have had in filling the judicial positions. . . . If better appointments could have been made . . . it must have been from information not accessible to me." (Hoar to Justice Bradley, June 20, 1870; Bradley Papers, in private hands.)

[60] *Proceedings of the Massachusetts Historical Society*, 2 ser. IX, 304.

were less numerous than at present, making possible a spirit of comradeship, and the bench was less insulated from the bar. Most of the justices would reserve rooms in some hotel — usually the National or the Metropolitan — to avoid the expense of a house. (The judicial salary was then $6000.) Sometimes two or three arranged to have their meals together, a fashion which had been in vogue in ante-bellum life at the capital. There was a good deal of dining and calling back and forth between judges and counsel, and the standard of propriety in the discussion of pending cases was lax to a degree which the Court today would consider shocking.

Two premature disclosures of impending decisions are historic. When the Dred Scott Case was under consideration Justice Catron wrote in confidence to President-elect Buchanan, informing him of the position of affairs and urging him to use his influence upon Judge Grier. Subsequently Grier, with the concurrence of Taney and Wayne, informed Buchanan what the result would be.[61] Mr. Warren points out that at the time it was not unusual for a member of the Court to impart the outcome of a pending case, and that so long as the seal of secrecy was imposed the practice was not regarded as improper.[62] It is also a familiar fact that Chief Justice Chase informed the Secretary of the Treasury, Boutwell, how the legal-tender question would be decided "about two weeks in advance of the delivery of the opinion" in *Hepburn* v. *Griswold*.[63] These instances are sometimes spoken of as though they were unique. Examples involving only private rights are found in Philip Phillips' professional letterbook:

Washington April 28.70

Confidential
Dear Sir —
    As you are so anxious to hear about Morris' case [64] I may say that a little bird has whispered that we will soon have a favor-

---

[61] *Works of James Buchanan* (Philadelphia and London: J. B. Lippincott Company, 1908–11), x, 106–108n.
[62] *The Supreme Court in United States History*, II, 295.
[63] George S. Boutwell, *Reminiscences of Sixty Years* (New York: McClure, Phillips and Company, 1902), II, 209.
[64] *Ex parte* Morris, 9 Wallace 605 (1870).

able decision[.] I argued the case on last Friday at considerable length — having given the case the best consideration I was capable of[.] I sent you the brief and believe you will find that the decision which will be rendered on Saturday merely clothes the brief in judicial language —

On April 30 Justice Swayne delivered the judgment as indicated.

In another instance:

Washington May 6. 72

Gentln
The Court adjourned today without delivering opinion in the Insurance case.[65]

I will say to you *in confidence* that I have reason to say that it is all right. There is a little difficulty — but th[at] will be overcome, and we will get the judgment in Nov.[66]

On November 18 judgment was rendered in favor of Phillips' clients, Justice Clifford dissenting.

Throughout the pages that follow justices will be quoted as making statements which would now be considered improper, and it must be borne in mind that a great evolution has taken place in this regard.

[65] Phoenix Ins. Co. *v.* Hamilton, 14 Wallace 504 (1872).
[66] Phillips Letterbook, 1871–72, p. 441.

VI

JUSTICE MILLER ON RECONSTRUCTION

A CONSTITUTION not written in contemplation of an attempt at secession did not, of course, speak very directly to the question of what would be the legal position after an attempt in arms had been repelled. Now that the issue was raised in a variety of cases, the justices had to find answers by resort to general reasoning and conceptions of public policy. But events did not wait upon the course of litigation; in its main outlines, reconstruction was the work of political forces operating without judicial restraint. President Johnson had sought a prompt restoration of the Southern states to their normal relation in the Union on the basis of their acceptance of the abolition of slavery. In Congress, however, the Radical wing of the Republican party was in full control. It declared the governments organized under the President's authority to be provisional only; divided the ten states into five military districts in which administration, including the trial of offenders, was vested in the commanding general; and sought to force the granting of Negro suffrage by requiring the ratification of the Fourteenth Amendment as a condition to the admission of Senators and Representatives to Congress. These measures were all enacted over President Johnson's veto.[1] Congress endeavored to take the control of the army away from the President, and when the latter asserted his authority by removing Secretary of War Stanton from office, the House voted charges of impeachment. But here the designs of the Radicals fell through, for in the Senate the Republican lines broke just enough to prevent a vote of conviction. In the meantime attempts were

[1] Act of March 2, 1867, 14 Statutes at Large 428; of March 23, 1867, 15:2; of July 19, 1867, 15:14.

made to bring the constitutionality of the reconstruction acts before the Court; but when an adverse decision was about to be rendered Congress passed an act to take away the Court's jurisdiction. The party was in mad career, ready to crash into any barrier before it. It is not too much to say that for a time judicial review of legislation was *de facto* suspended; the power remained in theory only because it was not exercised.

Of all the justices on the Court, Miller was least out of sympathy with the course of Congressional reconstruction.[2] In voting to sustain the Radical legislation, he did not for a moment think that it was wise. But after pondering all the elements in the ugly situation, he reasoned that the war had released great irrational forces which would have to spend themselves; and that, there being no express constitutional provisions to be vindicated, the Court would do well not to challenge Congress on the issues of reconstruction. We have the expression of his personal views in his letters to his brother-in-law in the South; they appear most significantly when set out in chronological order, along with an account of the Judge's judicial opinions.

The correspondence between Miller and Ballinger, broken off by hostilities, was resumed in June 1865, and at once turned to an exchange of political views. On August 31, 1865, Miller wrote:

Our views of the conduct to be pursued by the government towards the great body of the people engaged in this rebellion do not differ much if any.

I think that towards them, clemency, liberality, forgiveness, and a restoration to their civil rights as soon as they *abandon their former leaders* and evince a sincere intention to yield slavery, and give a true and loyal support to the federal government is the proper course.

But there is [*sic*] between us some differences on fundamental propositions, which would be likely to affect in many ways the details of any system of reconstruction or temporary government of the revolted states.

[2] So far as one can judge from his action on the Court, Justice Swayne took much the same position.

As I take you to be one of the fairest representatives of a large class of men in the south, namely those who are sick of the rebellion, and yet desire a reunion on terms as pleasing to the rebels as can be obtained, and as I take myself to be a member of the dominant party, and yet not one of its most ultra or one concurring in all that the leading men of that class desire, it may not be without benefit to point out those radical differences.

The first of these differences of which I speak, relates to the view which we now take of the *philosophy* of the rebellion if I may so state it.

You claim that this rebellion and the war which it originated was a necessity, growing out of conflict of opinion in regard to the limits of federal and state authority, and having direct reference to differences between the majorities in the northern and southern States.

And you affirm that which is a true and necessary accompaniment of that proposition, namely, that such differences can only be settled by war.

And you draw the further inference from this proposition that there is no personal guilt on the part of those who have participated however prominently in the rebellion.

In order to show the pernicious fruits to be expected from this doctrine, I will add that it seems to me to be a necessary corollary from it that whenever in our future history it shall again happen that on some point of practical value, the governing majority shall differ with any considerable minority, north or south, that minority may resort to arms to maintain their views, without incurring personal guilt, or meriting other punishment than, that which may result from possible failure.

This doctrine contains a standing invitation to revolution, and can be tolerated by no government which expects to be or claims to be any thing more than a temporary arrangement of convenience.

The practice of it is fully exemplified in the history of Mexico, and the South American Republics. It is more disastrous in its consequences than the doctrine of secession, for that recognises at least the right to enforce obedience to state laws, and the guilt of resistance to state sovereignty.

But apart from the consequences of such a doctrine, there exists in our form of government no such *necessity* for resort to arms to support real or imaginary rights, for the Supreme Court is and has always been regarded as the final and just arbiter of these differences. I will not as I am situated, comment further on this proposition. But I will add that seventy years of government, during which many and fierce conflicts over the rights of federal and state governments, and of resistance by large masses of men to the authority of the former, show that all these differences may be adjusted without resort to arms. Nay further they convince me, after looking at the tariff agitation, and its result, nullification, that no question of less force and power than the slavery question, ever could have produced armed rebellion against federal authority, of any serious extent.

Now with these views, I cannot regard the men who participated in this rebellion, as having incurred no personal guilt. They violated a well known existing law, whose penalty is death. This heavy penalty is imposed because of the awful consequences usually attendant upon treason. Have any of those consequences been wanting to heighten the guilt of this treason? I forbear to comment, further than to say, that if any thing were needed before to show that treason is a crime which merits the severest punishment which men are allowed to inflict, it has been furnished by the misery and horror incapable of description which have attended this rebellion!

It is proper however here to say that I concede at once that this guilt does not necessarily involve the same degradation of character, which, assassination or theft, or forgery do. In fact while you yourself were undoubtedly guilty of treason, it did not in the least affect my estimate of your character for honor, & truthfulness, nor diminish my affection for you. But I cannot the less deny, that you were guilty of a crime, and if there was no one else but you, in whose person the law might be vindicated, it would be the judgment of my *reason*, that in some way you should be punished; or that if you had been the most eminent in guilt of all the rebels, that you should suffer the highest punishment which the law provides for all.

And this brings me naturally to a second important matter on which we differ; namely that you think it would be right to pardon at once *all* the leaders of the rebellion as well as the masses, and restore them to all their civil rights, trusting to the effect of this generous treatment in securing their future support of the government.

Punishment both in law and in philosophy is justified only on account of tending to prevent future crimes, and not as a gratification of resentment for the crime actually committed. Hence just that extent of punishment, which is calculated to produce this effect is justifiable, and no more. This principle which lies at the foundation of all penal codes, is eminently applicable as a guide in cases of suppressed rebellion.

In its application to the penalty of death as regards the guilty in this rebellion I would limit it to half dozen of the most *prominent* and most *wicked* for among these are in my opinion many who have been governed alone by a selfish and wicked personal ambition.

But the great question of policy is as to the course to be pursued in other matters, toward other influential leaders in the great crime of the age.

It is my profound conviction that to restore these men at once to the condition in which they would again become the leaders in legislation, and in shaping the political action of the rebellious states, is to prolong indefinitely the struggle which led to war, and which would occasion its early renewal.

Very few of these men were governed by any better motive than an ambition to become the leaders of a southern aristocracy. Many of them may have believed that a separation from the north and the independence of the cotton states would largely promote the interest of the class — not numerous — to which they belonged. Few of them in my judgment gave themselves any trouble, or consideration, about their constitutional obligations to the Union.

Upon these men failure has wrought no change, other than some slight insight into the power of the government. Any occasion of weakness in that government, as a foreign war, an imbecile or treacherous President, would be seized by them as affording a prospect of more successful result in another effort. Their constant effort would be as it has been for many years past, to stir up strife between northern and southern interests, and the materials left by the war are unfortunately at hand to enable them to do this with success.

The duty which these men owe to the people whom they have misled to ruin, is obvious. It is either to leave the country, and by this relieving the administration from the fear of their influence, leave it at liberty to act generously towards all others, or otherwise to come forward actively as the advocates of any policy which the government, showing as it has done no vindictive disposition, may deem necessary for the pacification of the country. Very few of them I apprehend will be found equal to either of these courses.

The consequence is that in my opinion the government should not pardon these men until they have shown by a proper course of conduct their loyal disposition. By thus keeping them in a condition where they can exercise no *legitimate* influence on popular opinion, where they can hold no office, and by depriving them of all their property by confiscation in cases where they show a sullen or an evil tendency, I would cripple their influence in all possible ways.

The number of men to be thus treated is not large. From twenty five to fifty in each state, steadily branded as the objects of suspicion, and holding their lives and property at the mercy of the government, they would soon either leave it, or become engaged in active efforts to prove their devotion to it.

In short I believe in the policy of committing the political power of the rebellious states to other hands, than those which have caused this rebellion. I do not believe in the necessity or policy of a *speedy* reconstruction. And such I believe is the *growing* sentiment in the north.

And in this perhaps I differ with you more widely than in the propositions I have discussed, but the weather which is warmer here, than it has been this summer, is too hot for a discussion of this branch of the subject.[3]

Subsequent letters show a constant diminution in personal feeling and an increasing apprehension of the outcome of Radical politics. On January 11, 1866, Miller wrote:

The discussion on reconstruction is just opened in both houses, and promises to be able, and somewhat bitter. As far as I can form an opinion the President will not break with the majority in Congress if he can avoid it. That is he will make every concession consistent with any due regard to his personal dignity, and his own convictions of his duty. I believe he will assent to almost any means of securing the civil rights of the negro, short of imposing negro suffrage on the states in rebellion against their will. There is also a large body of influential republicans who are determined that the civil rights of the negro must be rendered safe, before the members from those states are permitted to take part in the legislation of Congress; but who are quite anxious to prevent a rupture with the President. I hope much from them and him. There are however three other classes of men, who desire this rupture and whose powers of mischief are very great.

The most potent of these are certain ultra negro suffrage impracticables, who have no faith in the President giving any aid to their policy, and who desire to precipitate a rupture while they

[3] Written at Keokuk, August 31, 1865.

are yet as they suppose themselves to be, the leaders of the majority. The next most mischievous class is composed of certain men who are republicans, but are anxious to signalise themselves as special friends of the President and his policy, in order that they may monopolise the executive patronage. These while claiming to speak for the President and thus making him as far as they can, responsible for their utterances, really know but little more of his views than I do. The third class are those who were elected distinctly as democrats, and whose only hope of a return of their party to power, is in the break up of the great party which has suppressed to the rebellion, against their wishes and efforts. The prospect ahead is not cheering. One thing however I think is clear. There is no hope for southern members being admitted into this Congress, unless some security is given against the manifest intent thus far shown by every southern state, to refuse to place the negro on an equality with the white man in all his civil rights. The power to make laws which are to operate on the black man and not on the white, will be taken from those states, before the present Congress will admit their delegations. This may be relied on.

The laws proposed by Mississippi, Alabama, South Carolina, &c do but change the form of the slavery. As it *was*, the individual slave belonged to, and laboured for the individual white man. As it is *proposed to be*, the whole body of the negro race in each state, must belong to and labour for the whole body of the white people of that state, under compulsion of law.

The pretence is that the negro wont work without he is compelled to do so, and this pretence is made in a country and by the white people, where the negro has done all the work for four generations, and where the white man makes a boast of the fact that *he* will *not* labour.

Argument in the Milligan Case had been closed on March 13, 1866. On the next day the Court heard *Ex parte Garland* [4] argued at the bar, and from March 15 to March 20 it gave its attention to *Cummings* v. *Missouri*. [5] Garland's Case raised the question of the constitutionality of the Act of Congress of January 24, 1865, providing that no person should be allowed to practice in a federal court until he had

---

[4] 4 Wallace 333 (1867).
[5] 4 Wallace 277 (1867). *Cf.* T. S. Barclay, "The Test Oath for the Clergy in Missouri," *Missouri Historical Review*, XVIII, 345ff. (1924).

subscribed to the so-called "iron-clad" oath that he had never voluntarily borne arms against the United States, nor voluntarily given aid, counsel, or encouragement to persons in armed hostility thereto, and so forth. The Cummings Case involved a similar oath prescribed by the Missouri Constitution of 1865 as a qualification for holding public office, practicing as an attorney, and performing the offices of a clergyman. When the cases were decided ten months later a bare majority of the Court, speaking through Justice Field, held both requirements to be unconstitutional. Justice Miller filed a dissent in which three of his colleagues concurred.

Augustus H. Garland had been admitted to practice in the Supreme Court at the December term, 1860. Subsequently he had served as a member of the Confederate Congress. In July 1865 he was pardoned, and thereupon moved for leave to practice notwithstanding the statutory requirement of an oath. He appeared *pro se*, and was supported by Reverdy Johnson (on whose motion he had first been admitted to practice before the Court) and by Matt Carpenter. The Attorney General opposed. Cummings was a Catholic priest who had been convicted of acting in that character without having taken the Missouri test oath. He was represented by Reverdy Johnson, David Dudley Field, and Montgomery Blair. G. P. Strong and Senator Henderson of Missouri appeared for the State.

The Court reached no conclusion during that term, and Justice Miller, knowing that his brother-in-law was deeply interested in the outcome, wrote him in a letter of July 31, 1866:

Private (In reference to your practice in the Sup. Court, I can only say that up to the present time, no person has been permitted to appear formally in the court without taking the oath.

You are aware that the validity of the act, and the effect of a pardon on its requirements were twice elaborately argued during last term. No decision was made.[6]

[6] The Lawyers' Edition of the Supreme Court Reports records that argument was heard on March 14 and December 15, 1866. It should be December 15 and 22, 1865, and March 14, 1866.

A similar oath was required by the new Constitution of Missouri, and a case from the Sup Court of that State was also argued before our Court on the ground of its conflict with the federal Constitution. As to the probability of the final decision, I can only say that while no vote was taken on either case, it was apparent that the court was nearly equally divided. There was [sic] four in favor of supporting the oath and four against it. Of the future vote of those eight if they all be present I am reasonably sure they will be as they then indicated. But there was one Judge, who said that if a vote was taken he should sustain the congressional oath, but should hold the Missouri oath which is almost identical void as in conflict with the federal Constitution!! He made an earnest effort to have the vote taken on the latter proposition, but insisted on postponement of the former.

What a Judge will do next winter who could come to such conclusions and who could desire such action as he desired of course no man can tell now from any thing he then said. This is of course strictly confidential)

He added that there would be no difficulty in preparing briefs and having some qualified attorney to sign them, and that pending cases could be continued if both parties consented.

Other justices were making similar disclosures in confidence. Orville Browning had been informed for months. Within a week after argument in the Cummings Case had closed he had been told by Judge Grier "that a majority of the Court viz: Justices Wayne, Nelson, himself, Clifford and Field decided against the Missouri test oath in the Supreme Court, but that Chief Justice Chase and Justices Swayne, Miller & Davis were for sustaining these oaths. He said the decisions would be announced before the adjournment of the present Term, but that the opinions would not be delivered until next Term." [7] And on April 7 he had further information to record: "Judge Field told me that on Tuesday when the Judges met, Miller made a personal appeal to have the test oath case from Missouri postponed till next term, and

[7] *Diary of Orville Hickman Browning*, II, 67.

that Grier in the kindness of his heart consented, but was afterwards very sorry for it." [8]

This is confirmed by a letter which Miller wrote to the Chief Justice on June 5, which shows that it was Field who wished to decide the Missouri case and postpone the other. By that date Miller was out in his circuit, where he had heard that Reverdy Johnson had told some Missouri politicians that he had it from one of the justices that the test oath would be declared unconstitutional. Miller appealed to the Chief Justice:

I call your attention to the statement of Mr. Johnson in the enclosed slip. Whatever may be our guesses at the individual conclusions of the members of the Court, it is certainly false that the Court ever decided the case, or ever took a vote upon it. Not only so but there are several members of the Court, who have never so far as I know *expressed* any opinion on the subject.

A very animated political contest is now going on in the state of Missouri, between the radicals and their opponents; the latter including every returned rebel in the state. This contest is looked upon by both parties as settling the future of the state for years to come, not only in its political relations, but as affecting the personal safety of the respective parties.

In this contest the stringent character of the oath prescribed by the Missouri constitution, which was before us in the case referred to by Mr. Johnson, is made a strong point in the attack upon the radicals; and the assertion that the Supreme Court of the United States has decided it to be in conflict with the Constitution of the United States is telling with fatal effect on the radicals.

Undoubtedly this was the purpose aimed at by the motion of Judge Field, that we should decide this case, and postpone the Congressional Oath case. This move you will remember was defeated by my appeal to the Court not to decide this case if they passed the other, which succeeded by the good feeling and sense of justice of our brother Grier.

Now shall this falsehood be permitted to work successfully its injurious effects or shall it be contradicted? The Honorable Mr. Hogan [9] is asserting the same thing everywhere in public

---

[8] *Ibid.*, II, 69.

[9] John Hogan, Democratic member of Congress from Missouri, running for reëlection. He was defeated.

speeches, and so is Gen'l Blair. It was certainly a violation of judicial propriety for any judge to state what Mr. Johnson says he knows, and I do not believe any judge said it, because it is false.

But it seems to me that while we may well feel restrained from from stating what *did* take place, there is nothing wrong, but a manifest propriety in contradicting the assertion that the Court has decided an important case, or an important principle when it has done no such thing. I think if any of the radicals of reputable standing should ask me, I should feel bound to contradict the statement, but I believe they are afraid to do so, lest the story of Johnson and Hogan might be confirmed.

I write this in private confidence, to learn your views of the matter, and also to suggest that such a confidential communication between yourself and Senator Henderson, or Brown, or Gen'l Loan,[10] as would at least enable them to claim as boldly as Hogan and Johnson assert, might do a great deal of good without committing any impropriety; if you concur with me in this matter.[11]

The matter came to Judge Field's attention, as Dr. Swisher shows in his biography. On June 30 Field wired to the Chief Justice:

Have read with amazement Reverdy Johnson's letter to Hogan on the Missouri case. Does it require any notice from judge. Please answer.

He despatched a letter in elaboration:

I received a day or two since the correspondence between Mr. Hogan of the House of Representatives, and Reverdy Johnson in relation to the supposed action of the Supreme Court in the Missouri test oath cases. I read the letter of Mr. Johnson with amazement, both as to the strange character of his statements, and the singular indelicacy of giving them publicity, even if they were in fact true. As we are aware no decision was reached in the cases — the only vote taken being on the question of the postponement of their consideration until the next term. As announced by you on the last day of the session they were held over under advisement. Mr. Johnson has evidently confounded the action of the Court in the military commission cases with the

[10] Benjamin F. Loan, then member of Congress and Radical candidate for reëlection. He was successful.

[11] In the Chase Papers, quoted by Swisher, *Stephen J. Field*, p. 142.

supposed views of some of the judges in the Missouri cases. The conduct of Johnson is indefensible — more, it merits some rebuke. How foolish he would appear if the decision of the Court should be different from what he supposes it will be, or if a re-argument should be ordered. I suppose he got what he knows on the subject from Judge Nelson with whom he was very intimate — mingled up known with other matters. I do not regret that I was never intimate with him.

The proposed amendments to the Constitution, prepared by the committee on reconstruction, and passed by Congress appear to me to be just what we need. I think all members of the Union party can unite cordially in their support. If the President withholds his approval he will sever all connection with the Union party. Two things are certain — the American people do not intend to give up all that they have gained by the war — and they do intend that loyal men shall govern the country.[12]

In his haste to charge Judge Nelson with indiscretion Field does not appear in a very favorable light. For we know that he had been confiding in Browning, which suggests that he would have done as much for his brother, who was Reverdy Johnson's associate in the case. It is true, however, that Nelson had been talking about what had gone on in conference.[13]

Shortly after the December term opened the Court decided the Garland Case in conference, as Miller hastened to inform his brother-in-law:

Confidential
Today in consultation the court decided the congressional oath exacted of Attorneys to be void. The vote was 5 to 4. I was of the minority and am to write the dissenting opinion. I have felt bound by my clear convictions of law thus to vote and I am not sorry that the result is adverse to my opinion, on your account and generally because I think the requirement unnecessarily harsh at present. The opinions may not be read for two weeks yet and you will regard this as strictly confidential, but I know the personal interest you feel in the matter and desire you to have the good news at your earliest chance.[14]

[12] Chase Papers, quoted by Swisher, p. 145.
[13] *Diary of Orville Hickman Browning*, II, 69.
[14] Letter of December 8, 1866.

Opinions were rendered on January 14, 1867, Justice Field speaking for the Court. It would perhaps not have been evident at a glance just what provision in the federal Constitution forbade the people of Missouri from writing the challenged requirement into their Constitution. Counsel had invited the Court to regard it as a bill of attainder, a judgment pronounced without judicial proceedings; also as an *ex post facto* law, in that it imposed an additional punishment for the crime of treason. Once the requirement was looked upon as a punishment, the conclusion was reached easily enough. And the Garland Case, of course, went off in the same way, with the additional reasoning that the pardon relieved the petitioner from all penalties, and that this alone would have supported the judgment in his case.

Judge Miller's dissenting opinion for the two cases ran on wholly different lines. He begins by dwelling upon the "extremely delicate power of this court" to declare legislation unconstitutional: "the incompatibility of the act with the Constitution should be so clear as to leave little reason for doubt, before we pronounce it invalid." He took the legislation as what it purported to be, a statement of the qualifications requisite to acting as an attorney in the courts:

The right to practise law in the courts as a profession, is a privilege granted by law, under such limitations or conditions in each state or government as the law-making power may prescribe. . . .

I venture to affirm, that if all the members of the legal profession in the states lately in insurrection had possessed the qualification of a loyal and faithful allegiance to the government, we should have been spared the horrors of that Rebellion. If, then, this qualification be so essential in a lawyer, it cannot be denied that the statute under consideration was eminently calculated to secure that result.[15]

He argued that this should be viewed as a not unreasonable regulation of a public calling, and was in no proper sense a punishment, and asked,

[15] 4 Wallace at 384, 386.

Where, then, is this *ex post facto* law which tries and punishes a man for a crime committed before it was passed? It can only be found in those elastic rules of construction which cramp the powers of the Federal government when they are to be exercised in certain directions, and enlarge them when they are to be exercised in others. No more striking example of this could be given than the cases before us, in one of which the Constitution of the United States is held to confer no power on Congress to prevent traitors practicing in her courts, while in the other it is held to confer power on this court to nullify a provision of the Constitution of the State of Missouri, relating to a qualification required of ministers of religion.[16]

In October 1865 and again in July 1867 Ballinger visited his brother-in-law at Keokuk, and noted some of his impressions in his diary. On the later occasion he wrote:

Miller is enjoying his vacation — and takes life philosophically — I don't [know] any one who seems to have a truer contentment. His health is fine — They have a good pair of horses & drive out every evening.[17]

Something of Miller's warm yet rugged nature is reflected in this note of October 1865:

Miller is as much like a brother as I could desire. I believe he is sincerely attached to me. I love him most warmly and de-·votedly. I don't know that I have known any man of more real strength of character & ability — or who lives more faithfully to discharge his sense of duty. He acts from principle rather than from sensibility, & is often rather rough & stern towds others — I think perhaps he prides himself somewhat on his frankness and plain speaking. I hardly know any one of [in] whose acts I should repose more explicit confidence, tho' the manner may sometimes be harsh.[18]

As an example of Justice Miller's plain speaking may be cited the following letter to his former partner. Rankin had expressed approval of the Radical Republicans in their fight

[16] 4 Wallace at 392.
[17] Ballinger Diary.
[18] In a later diary entry Ballinger wrote: "There is no one in the world I respect more highly than Miller or outside of my own direct family am more attached to."

against President Johnson. On February 4, 1867 — exactly one year before the House of Representatives voted articles of impeachment — Miller wrote from Washington:

My Dear Rankin:

I received your letter on Saturday morning, three days since. I laid it aside, and read it over carefully on yesterday (Sunday) again.

The impression it first made upon me, is not removed or much modified by a second perusal. It bears the marks certainly of your usual haste in letter writing, but as it is a second letter on the same subject, I must consider it to express your matured convictions. If I understand it, you would, if you had the power, impeach and remove the President, would abolish or reconstitute the Supreme Court, begging pardon of the Constitution for any infraction of that instrument this action would require. In other words you would overturn deliberately two of the great primary departments of the government, by the third, because their action does not conform to the wishes of that department, in which wishes you concur.

Mr. Hamilton in the Federalist says, that he concurs with the maxim of Montesquieu, that there can be no liberty where the power of judging, is not kept separate from the executive and legislative powers. I know of no prominent statesman of our country, who has not considered the independence of the judiciary, and the separation of the executive, legislative and judicial departments, an essential to a free government.

You however propose to prostrate the judicial and executive branches of the government, at the feet of the legislative or at the behest of a temporary popular majority. If the Supreme Court is to be reconstructed for what reason is it to be done? Not for any crimes or misdemeanors of the judges, because for this the individual members of the Court can be impeached; and the dominant party in Congress have a sufficient majority in both branches to carry such an impeachment beyond doubt, if any such ground can be proved. And they have the will to do so.

But if reconstructed at all, it is simply because a majority of the Court have the misfortune to be compelled to construe the Constitution, and in doing this their judgment differs from that of the majority in Congress, and from yours.

And so, whatever may be finally charged against the President, he will be impeached, if at all, because like the Supreme Court he stands in the way of certain political purposes of the majority in Congress. If the President were willing now, to heartily co-operate with Stevens, Sumner, Boutwell & Co., no one for a moment supposes that any attempt would be made to impeach him. Mr. Boutwell who is perhaps the ablest member of the Judiciary Committee, declared last summer, that the President must be removed, because what the radical majority wants to do cannot be accomplished while he remains. Now in all this I understand you to concur, and to be impatient at the delay of your representatives, in Congress, in putting it into execution.

Of course I know that such is the feeling of many persons. Such persons here who are leaders and know what they are after, are working for the election of Genl Butler to the next Presidency. I am not surprised that there are such persons. My surprise is that you should be of the number, and I confess that when I see a man of your constitutional training, a sound lawyer, a moderate reasonable man in ordinary affairs, favoring these things, and deliberately putting on paper your wishes that you had the power to do all this, my confidence in the people, so far from being as implicit and unlimited as that which you express, has received a sensible shock, by the very manner in which you express yourself.

These differences however make no change in the sentiments with which I am your friend.

Sam F. Miller [19]

Miller's letters make clear his disapproval of the course of legislation which, as a judge, he was to refuse to strike down. On April 24, 1867, he wrote:

How is reconstruction going in Texas? Will the state adopt the programme laid down by Congress? It is in my opinion as necessary for the north as it is for the south, that this should be generally adopted by the southern states.

The strain upon constitutional government, from the pace at which the majority is now going, is one which cannot be much longer continued without destroying the machine. Yet as long as there is southern resistance, there is no power in the north capable of arresting the onward course of public affairs.

Such an attempt was being made at that very moment. The Radicals had just pushed through the Reconstruction Acts of March 2 and 23. On April 12 counsel for the State of Missis-

[19] Miller sent a copy of this letter to Ballinger, by whom it was preserved.

sippi, invoking the Court's original jurisdiction in suits to which a state is party, moved for leave to file a bill for an injunction against the execution of the statutes by the President.[20] Attorney General Stanbery contended that the bill could not be received. Three days later the Chief Justice, speaking for a unanimous Court, denied leave on the ground that there was no jurisdiction to control the President in the performance of his official duties. Promptly thereafter bills were filed on behalf of the states of Georgia and Mississippi to enjoin the Secretary of War, the General of the Army, and district commanders, from carrying into execution the Reconstruction Acts.[21] This effort likewise failed. Judge Nelson for the Court pointed out that the rights alleged to be in danger were rights of sovereignty, not of person or property, and that the issue was political and beyond judicial cognizance. Relief had not been prayed in respect of the State's proprietary interest in its public buildings, treasury, etc., and as soon as the decision was announced an attempt was made to amend the bill so as to show this interest. But the motion was denied by an equally divided Court, Justices Wayne, Clifford, Nelson, and Field being in favor and the Chief Justice and Associate Justices Swayne, Miller, and Davis opposing. Mr. Warren points out that if Judge Grier had been present the motion would probably have been granted, and the constitutionality of the legislation thus brought to an issue.[22]

We turn back to the correspondence to see the drift of Miller's political thinking. On December 22, 1867, he wrote:

There seems to be no doubt that Grant will be the nominee of the convention called to meet at Chicago next May.

Many thinking men among the Republicans doubt whether even his name can secure victory. There are also many republicans who now regret the extreme policy of the reconstruction

---

[20] Mississippi v. Johnson, 4 Wallace 475 (1867).
[21] Georgia v. Stanton, Mississippi v. Stanton, 6 Wallace 50 (1867). The cases were decided on May 16, 1867, but the opinion was not delivered until February 10, 1868.
[22] Supreme Court in United States History, II, 464.

acts, in the question of suffrage. But the strict party men, — the coolest among them — feel as did Macbeth, that they have waded so far into this sea of radicalism, that it were easier, (and safer) to go over than turn back. Negro Suffrage in the North will probably be abandoned as a party platform but the experiment of reconstruction on the Congressional basis will probably be adhered to. 1st because the party cannot turn back, second because it affords the only chance for a republican party in the South.

I speak of these things with no feeling, and hardly a wish. I think the progress of Congress in invading the functions of the Executive and Judicial branches of the Government, was only less dangerous than a return to power of the democratic party, with absolute control of the rebel States, governed by exasperated rebels, and their party in the north under their control, as they always have been, even during the rebellion.

I feel more than I ever did in my life indifference to party success, and surely if it be desirable that a judge should not be a partisan, I am quite as near possessing that qualification, as any man on the bench.

And on January 19, 1868:

The political situation looks to me more gloomy than it has ever looked. I never thought a separation by success of the rebellion the worst misfortune that could occur. But in the threatened collision between the Legislative branch of the government and the Executive and judicial branches I see consequences from which the cause of free government may never recover in my day. The worst feature I now see is the passion which governs the hour in all parties and all persons who have controlling influence. In this the Supreme Court is as fully involved as the President or House of Representatives.

Within a fortnight the Court was indeed deeply involved, by having the McCardle Case brought before it. The appellant was a Mississippi editor who had been charged with disturbing the peace, inciting to insurrection, libel, and impeding reconstruction; he had been held for trial before a military commission under the authority of the Reconstruction Acts. Habeas corpus proceedings had been brought in the United States Circuit Court, which resulted in the petitioner being remanded to military custody. From this order an appeal was taken to the Supreme Court, under the recent statute of February 5, 1867.[23]

The act just cited had greatly widened the jurisdiction of the federal courts in habeas corpus by extending it, in addition to authority already conferred, to "cases where any person may be restrained of his liberty in violation of the Constitution or any treaty or law of the United States." "From the final decision of any judge, justice, or court inferior to the Circuit Court, an appeal may be taken to the Circuit Court . . . , and from the judgment of said Circuit Court to the Supreme Court." This characteristic piece of reconstruction legislation was now turned to serve the purposes of one of the unreconstructed. The first clash was over jurisdiction, D. D. Field, J. S. Black, and W. L. Sharkey appearing for the appellant, Matt Carpenter, James Hughes, and Lyman Trumbull against. Jurisdiction was resisted on the contention that, under the language quoted above, appeal lay to the Supreme Court only in cases which had come to the Circuit Court on appeal, whereas this case was brought originally in the Circuit Court. The Supreme Court did not so read the statute, and the motion to dismiss was accordingly denied.[24]

Shortly thereafter, on March 2, 3, 4, and 9, 1868, the appeal was argued on its merits — namely, the validity of so much of the Reconstruction Acts as authorized military trial of civilians. On completing his argument Carpenter wrote: "Miller's face was as the face of an angel radiant with light and joy; Davis and Field looked troubled; Nelson, Clifford and Grier dead against me. But I shook them up and rattled their dry bones." What he actually said was in part as follows:

This court has been told, not for the first time, that it is the great conservative department of the government; that if it does not keep constant vigil over the other departments, they will rush, as would the planets without the law of gravitation, into

[23] 14 Statutes at Large 385.
[24] *Ex parte* McCardle, 6 Wallace 318 (1868).

"hopeless and headlong ruin." There is nothing within the circle of human emotions, unless it be the pleasure with which a lover praises the real or imaginary charms of his mistress, at all to be compared with the delight experienced by a lawyer in glorifying a court. . . . Within proper bounds this disposition is commendable; but the bar, in a free country, often have higher duties to perform; and this adulation of the judges may be carried to excess. . . . It is our duty, when occasions require, to admonish and warn, and that, too, *whether courts will listen, or whether they will refrain.*" [25]

The McCardle Case never came to judgment on the merits. While it was under advisement Congress hastened to pass the Act of March 27, 1868,[26] repealing the provision of the Act of February 5 under which the case had been appealed. In short, the Radicals were prepared to repeal as much legislation conferring jurisdiction as might be necessary to forestall a decision adverse to the Reconstruction Acts.[27] The Court, over the protest of Justices Grier and Field, deferred until the next term the question of the effect of the repeal upon the pending case. A year later, on April 12, 1869, the statute was held to have deprived the Court of its power to determine the case, and it was accordingly dismissed. The Chief Justice did, however, observe that the repeal had not struck down any jurisdiction exercised under statutes other than that of February 5, 1868.[28]

Out of this concluding remark there blossomed *Ex parte Yerger*,[29] one more effort to have the Reconstruction Acts held unconstitutional. Edward M. Yerger had been charged with the murder of an army officer at Jackson, Mississippi, and brought before a military commission for trial.[30] At Washington on July 16, 1869, an agreement was entered into be-

[25] H. D. Ashley, in *Green Bag*, VI (1894), 441, 443.

[26] 14 Statutes at Large 44. The President, then undergoing trial on the impeachment, had vetoed the bill.

[27] Warren, *Supreme Court*, II, 473ff., gives an account of the debate in Congress.

[28] *Ex parte* McCardle, 7 Wallace 506 (1869).

[29] 8 Wallace 85 (1869).

[30] *Trial of E. M. Yerger, before a Military Commission* . . . (1869).

tween J. M. Carlisle and Philip Phillips, Yerger's counsel, and Attorney General Hoar, to suspend the military trial while habeas corpus proceedings were had in the circuit court and, if necessary, before the Supreme Court. The prisoner was brought into the custody of the circuit court, which on July 22 dismissed the writ and remanded him to the military authority.[31]

The question then was whether the Supreme Court could grant the writ of habeas corpus, aided by certiorari, to revise the decision of the circuit court. It was contended for the petitioner that this jurisdiction existed under the original Judiciary Act of 1789, and had not been affected by the legislation of 1867 — citing the Chief Justice's remarks in dismissing McCardle's Case. The·Court (Justice Miller dissenting without opinion) upheld its jurisdiction.[32] This was on October 25, 1869, and it seemed only a question of time before the question of the constitutionality of the Reconstruction Acts would finally be before the Court.

To forestall this just as a decision in the McCardle Case was prevented, Senator Trumbull introduced a bill declaring that the validity of the Reconstruction Acts was a political question and forbidding the Supreme Court to entertain jurisdiction in any case growing out of their execution. Even more hostile legislation was proposed. But Attorney General Hoar took steps to avoid such an incident. He made an agreement with Yerger's counsel whereby the *status quo* was to be preserved until the State of Mississippi was declared to be reconstructed, when the prisoner would be surrendered by the military authority to the State. This relieved the pressure behind Trumbull's bill. By Act of February 23, 1870, Mississippi was readmitted to representation in Congress, and on March 11 Phillips moved that the petition be dismissed, its object having been fulfilled by the transfer of the prisoner to

[31] *Trial of E. M. Yerger*, pp. 120ff.
[32] *Ex parte Yerger*, 8 Wallace 85 (1869). *Cf.* Philip Phillips, *The Statutory Jurisdiction and Practice of the Supreme Court of the United States* (Washington, 1872). The author was counsel in the case.

the civil authorities. In the correspondence of Phillips and Carlisle with the petitioner's local counsel the whole situation is made clear and one sees how a collision at long last was avoided.[33]

In cases not so big with public consequences the Court was left free to work out solutions which seemed just and consistent with public policy. The question at once arose how far effect would be given to acts performed and transactions

[33] On January 14 they wrote:

"We have to say in reply to yours 29' ult that we do not doubt that the Govt will fairly carry out the agreement. We have been acting on the ground that our duty to our client was not inconsistant with such a course as would prevent a collision between congress and the court. If we press the motion we presume the Bill to take away the jurisdiction which now seems quietly to sleep will also be pressed. We presume Virginia will be admitted today. If so Mississippi will be admitted as soon as her representatives appear — on this we will claim that the prisoner be turned over to state authorities — Should our careful expectation on this head be disappointed then we would immediately apply to the Court — If Hoar is not confirmed [as Associate Justice] it is probable that some one supposed to represent the South will be nominated.

"If Hoar is confirmed — will he take part in the decision of the case? As Atty Genl he may claim to have acted entirely in an official capacity uninfluenced by those considerations which apply to a private suit.

"The question of moving at once is a very doubtful one — You are as well posted as we are and we therefore will conform to your judgment in the matter. Write then at once and advise us when the State will be here.

"We have recd a letter from Mr. E. M. Y. Assure him we will do every thing in our power for him and advise him to acquire if possible the good will of his custodians by strict compliance with all their regulations"

On February 23:

"We had this morning an interview with the Attorney Genl in reference to Mr. Yerger — He said to us 'be quiet wait until the excitement is over in the Senate where Davis is hammering over the senators credentials you will find that orders have been sent down to turn the prisoner over to the state authorities, but we shall furnish a guard to see that he does not escape.' I have jotted down as near as may be the words used — We have no doubt it is all right — Let us hear from you if any order has been executed."

And finally on March 12:

"Yours 1" inst recd — on yesterday (Friday) we called up the case for Habeas Corpus, stating to the Court that we had authentic information that Mr. Yerger had been delivered up by the military to the Civil authorities of the State and as the object of the petition was thus accomplished we moved to dismiss the same. The Court ordered the dismissal to be entered as with the consent of the attorney General — This we believe ends our professional connection with the case. The movement has been a fortunate one as without doubt it has saved the life of the applicant."

(Phillips Letterbook, 1870–71, pp. 8, 53, 76. The letters are addressed to William Yerger of Jackson, Mississippi.)

entered into during the period of rebellion. The Chief Justice, speaking for the Court in *Texas* v. *White*,[34] had said generally that statutes enacted by the Southern states would be regarded as valid in so far as they related to the peace and good order of the community, but would be deemed void where passed in furtherance of the rebellion. That suit had been brought to recover to the state bonds alienated for the purchase of supplies during the war, without conforming to certain restrictions on alienation imposed by an ante-bellum statute. Whether the entity known as the State of Texas could maintain a suit at a time when its government was vested in a military commander carrying on reconstruction was the initial issue. The holding of the Court was that Texas had never ceased to be a state and that it had a standing in the Court, though Justices Grier, Swayne, and Miller, dissenting, thought that the Court was bound by the action of Congress to regard Texas as not then being a state within the meaning of the Constitution. On the merits the Court held the contract to be invalid, as one made in aid of the rebellion, and decreed the restitution of the bonds.

On his circuit in the spring of 1868 Justice Miller, sitting with District Judge Caldwell in the Circuit Court for Arkansas, had heard a case involving the validity of a note to repay in money where the consideration was Arkansas war bonds. The District Judge was clear that the note was void, but Miller preferred not to make a ruling "because I did not wish to feel committed in that Court for Judge C. would have yielded to me at once if I had wished it." [35] So the question was sent up on a certificate of division of opinion. The leading case on this subject is *Thorington* v. *Smith*,[36] in which the Court enforced a contract made in the usual course of business, wherein Confederate currency was named as the consideration. Miller shrank from any decision which might serve as a signpost to future rebellion, and assented to the

[34] 7 Wallace 700 (1869).
[35] Letter of May 21, 1869.
[36] 8 Wallace 1 (1869).

judgment "with much reluctance" and solely on the ground that such a principle was necessary "to prevent the grossest injustice in reference to transactions of millions of people." [37] It was later held that Arkansas war bonds were an illegal consideration, being distinguished from Confederate money on the ground that they were not a forced currency though in fact used as a circulating medium,[38] and here Miller interposed a specially concurring opinion, saying that he did not think the instant case differed in principle from the case of currency, so that while he did not agree to the distinction he was content to see the doctrine of the earlier case limited. Judge Miller was candid and intellectually honest.

After the termination of hostilities, cases involving the war power still cropped up. In *Miller* v. *United States* [39] Justice Miller was with the majority in holding that in confiscating the property of rebels Congress was acting *jure belli* and was not limited by the bill of rights. And in another confiscation case [40] he rejected the doctrine, "long inculcated, that the Federal Government, however strong in a conflict with a foreign foe, lies manacled by the Constitution and helpless at the feet of a domestic enemy." Field and Clifford, dissenting, had argued that the Confiscation Act should be strictly construed. Not so Miller, who would construe the Act by "reasonable and sound rules . . . , and not by a system, . . . so captious, so narrow, so difficult to understand or to execute, as to amount to a nullification of the statute."

The same Act of Congress of March 3, 1863, which authorized the suspension of the writ of habeas corpus, also purported to make an order of the President during the rebellion a defense to any action, and further provided that any suit or prosecution for acts done during the rebellion under color of authority must be commenced within two years. Whether Congress could go so far as wholly to take away the right of

[37] As he relates in Hanauer *v.* Woodruff, 15 Wallace 439, 449 (1873).
[38] Hanauer *v.* Woodruff, cited.
[39] 11 Wallace 268 (1870).
[40] Tyler *v.* Defrees, 11 Wallace 331 (1870).

action for such a wrong was never brought before the Court; but Justice Miller did, on circuit [41] and then as spokesman for the Court,[42] uphold the statute of limitation in cases of spoliation by a military officer in the loyal state of Missouri, holding that the time bar applied also to suits brought in a state court.

It is a common belief that where environmental conditions have given a certain bent to a judge's mind, all cases relevant thereto will be sent down the same groove. This theory of judicial decision is subject to substantial qualification, and for this the case of *Dow* v. *Johnson* [43] will serve as an example. During the occupation of New Orleans some of General Butler's subordinates were alleged to have plundered a house and taken certain silverware — the silver spoons famous in post-bellum politics. General Neal Dow was sued in the New Orleans court, and judgment was given by default. The plaintiff later sued on that judgment in the Circuit Court for Maine, where Dow resided. The Supreme Court held that the officer was not liable to an action in the local courts for injuries resulting from his acts. What is striking is that the opinion was rendered by Justice Field, while Justice Miller is bracketed with Justice Clifford in dissenting. To find Miller and Clifford standing together in a war case is remarkable in itself. Then, in arguing that the soldier was bound to appear before the civil court, Miller recounts the episode of General Jackson's being fined for contempt of the District Court at New Orleans in 1815, and concludes: "I confess I have always been taught to believe that Judge Hall was right in imposing the fine, and that General Jackson earned the brightest page in his history by paying it, and gracefully submitting to the civil power." The very form of expression is striking, for in no other recorded opinion, it is believed, did Miller's self-reliant mind ever take refuge in any opinion he

[41] Clark *v.* Dick, Fed. Case 2818 (1870).
[42] Mitchell *v.* Clark, 110 U. S. 633 (1884). Field, J., dissenting, held that the seizure could not be a defense in a suit between private parties.
[43] 100 U. S. 158 (1879).

had been "taught to believe." This is not a close discussion of the points of the case, and it is needless to inquire whether any of the judges took positions inconsistent with their other opinions. It is cited merely as an illustration of the truth that deep-seated sympathies will not wholly explain judicial conduct.[44]

[44] Evidently Justice Miller became reconciled to the doctrine of Dow *v.* Johnson, for in Freeland *v.* Williams, 131 U. S. 405 (1889), he cites it with approval and goes on to hold that where the courts of West Virginia had persisted in rendering judgments against Confederates for alleged torts committed under military authority in accordance with the usages of war, it was competent for a constitutional convention virtually to recall such decisions by forbidding the seizure or sale of property under final process to give effect to judgments thus erroneously rendered. Justice Harlan dissented.

VII

THE LEGAL TENDER CASES

WITH what undeviating pertinacity Justice Miller supported the Legal Tender Act of 1862 until that measure was finally declared to be constitutional is well known. This result was accomplished in 1871 only by overruling a judgment of unconstitutionality rendered in 1870. The fact that this was made possible only by the participation of Justices Strong and Bradley, who came on the bench after the first decision, has focused attention upon their responsibility for the outcome. But as important a factor was the dauntless will of Justice Miller. He referred to himself, as we shall see, as the "leader in marshalling my forces, and keeping up their courage," which was certainly no exaggeration. Whether praise or censure be visited upon the new majority, no one was more completely committed to the action than Justice Miller.

To the close of 1861 the war was financed chiefly by loans from bankers.[1] Specie was thus received into the subtreasury, but as disbursements were made it flowed out again and eventually back into the vaults of the banks. Unwarranted optimism as to the duration of hostilities and a reluctance to call for a great increase in taxation led Secretary Chase to rely largely on borrowing for war expenses. Unfavorable developments in December arrested the return of specie to the banks, with the result that they were forced to suspend payment on December 30. Thereafter, of course, the Treasury was unable to redeem its notes in coin. A sharp increase in taxation, accompanied by an issue of long-term bonds, might perhaps have sufficed to meet the crisis. Within the House Committee

[1] W. C. Mitchell, *A History of the Greenbacks* (Chicago: University of Chicago Press, 1903).

on Ways and Means, however, the initiative was seized to propose an issue of fiat money. Secretary Chase reluctantly fell in with the plan, and pronounced it to be "indispensably necessary" in the emergency.[2] Both on grounds of constitutionality and of economics, public men had since the founding of the federal government entertained scruples against making paper money a legal tender. Nevertheless, Congress gave its consent to what was represented as an unavoidable expedient. The Act of February 25, 1862, authorized the issue of $150,000,000 in treasury notes. This money was receivable in payment of all dues to the United States except duties on imports; was payable for all debts of the United States except interest upon bonds and notes; and otherwise was made "a legal tender in payment of all debts, public and private, within the United States."[3] Other issues of like amount were authorized by the Acts of July 11, 1862, and March 3, 1863.

That much of the dislocation and injustice which resulted from this greenback episode might have been avoided if the Government had had better technical advice seems very likely. But the Civil War was carried on by volunteers, in administration not less than in the field.

It strikes one as a curious fact that a case involving the constitutionality of the Legal Tender Act did not come before the Supreme Court on its merits until several years after the war was over. This was, indeed, a fortuitous reprieve. A controversy involving the question might, of course, have been brought for review either from an inferior court of the United States or from the highest court of a state. That the issue was not presented in a case coming up on writ of error to a state court is explained by the holding of the Supreme Court in *Roosevelt* v. *Meyer* [4] in 1863. Roosevelt held a mortgage in discharge of which Meyer made a tender of greenbacks. The creditor refused to accept other than gold coin, and it was agreed that suit be brought by the debtor to

---

[2] *Congressional Globe*, 37 Cong., 2 Sess., p. 618.
[3] 12 Statutes at Large 345.
[4] 1 Wallace 512.

obtain a decision on the issue. The defendant relied on various constitutional provisions to establish the invalidity of the Act. The Court of Appeals of New York gave judgment for the plaintiff, to which a writ of error was sued out. The defendant in error moved to dismiss for want of jurisdiction. Argument was heard on December 21, 1863, whereupon the motion was granted. Justice Nelson dissented.

The jurisdictional point is quite simple and, particularly since the Court later held that it had been wrongly decided, it is worth stating. The original Judiciary Act of 1789 had, in general, left the vindication of rights claimed under the Constitution and laws of the United States to the state courts, providing however that if the decision there should be against the claim of federal right, the judgment might then be re-examined in the Supreme Court. Writ of error was to be granted [1] "where is drawn in question the validity of a . . . statute of . . . the United States, and the decision is against [its] validity"; or . . . [3] "where is drawn in question the construction of any clause of the constitution . . . or statute of . . . the United States, and the decision is against the title, right, privilege or exemption specially set up or claimed by either party." The Court, apparently fastening its attention on the first of these clauses, held that, since the right claimed by the debtor under the Legal Tender Act had been upheld, there was no jurisdiction to review the judgment. But it is evident that, the defendant having set up constitutional objections to defeat this claim, the case was one where the construction of the Constitution had been drawn in question and the decision was against the right claimed thereunder by the defendant. There was jurisdiction, therefore, under clause 3 above. The motion to dismiss was granted on the day it was argued, and the result announced by Justice Wayne in few words. Thus the question could not have been examined elaborately. But one would suppose that the Court was letter perfect in its familiarity with Section 25 of the Judiciary Act, and the fact that Justice Nelson dissented shows that there must have been some serious consideration.

The composition of the Court at that time gives no encouragement to the idea that the justices were adopting an unwarrantably narrow view of their jurisdiction in order to spare the Legal Tender Act from the ordeal of scrutiny. For they should have taken jurisdiction, and then might have upheld the Act had they seen fit to do so.

The result of this case gave the profession to understand that so long as the state court upheld the right claimed by debtors to pay their debts in greenbacks, no review could be had in the Supreme Court. In *Trebilcock* v. *Wilson*,[5] decided in January 1872, Justice Field announced for the Court that *Roosevelt* v. *Meyer* had been wrongly decided, and jurisdiction was entertained in a similar case.

It was not until June 1865, when the Court of Appeals of Kentucky rendered its decision in *Griswold* v. *Hepburn*,[6] that the highest court of any state gave judgment holding the Legal Tender Act unconstitutional. Earlier decisions had gone the other way. As Justice Miller observed, "fifteen state courts, being all but one that has passed upon the question, have expressed their belief in the constitutionality of these laws." [7] He did not enumerate the instances which went to make up this impressive body of authority, but doubtless he had reference to the following. The New York Court of Appeals had upheld the Act in 1863, after a very elaborate examination in *Meyer* v. *Roosevelt* and *Metropolitan Bank* v. *Van Dyck*.[8] It was followed by the courts of California,[9] Iowa,[10] New Hampshire,[11] and Wisconsin [12] in 1864, and by Pennsylvania,[13] Michigan,[14] Indiana,[15] and Nevada [16] in 1865. The Supreme Court of Vermont [17] in 1866 and that of Massachusetts [18] in 1867 said that they would not treat the ques-

---

[5] 12 Wallace 687.
[6] 2 Duvall 20.
[7] 8 Wallace at 638.
[8] 27 N. Y. 400.
[9] Lick v. Faulkner, 25 Cal. 404.
[10] Hintrager v. Bates, 18 Iowa 174.
[11] George v. Concord, 45 N. H. 434.
[12] Breitenbach v. Turner, 18 Wis. 140.
[13] Shollenberger v. Brinton, 52 Pa. St. 9.
[14] Van Husan v. Kanouse, 13 Mich. 303.
[15] Thayer v. Hedges, 23 Ind. 141.   [16] Maynard v. Newman, 1 Nev. 271.
[17] Carpenter v. Northfield Bank, 39 Vt. 46.
[18] Essex Company v. Pacific Mills, 14 Allen 389.

tion as open, but would await the final determination in the Supreme Court of the United States. The Supreme Court of Missouri [19] assumed the constitutionality of the law without argument, while the Illinois court gave effect to the Act without being required to pass directly upon the question.[20] To make up Justice Miller's count of fifteen one must throw in a decision of the Supreme Court of Tennessee [21] in 1867 and one by that of South Carolina [22] in 1869.

This remarkable concurrence of judicial opinion merits closer scrutiny. That judges sitting under military supervision in South Carolina should have upheld an Act of Congress does not strain one's credulity. The same may be said of the reconstructed court in Tennessee. The Illinois court was composed of one Republican judge; one Democrat appointed by a Republican governor and thrice elected thereafter in a Republican district; and another Democrat who had held office under John Quincy Adams and been removed by Jackson, and who had bitterly opposed the Kansas-Nebraska Act. Taking the twelve other courts that upheld the legal tender law, and the Kentucky court which decided against it, one has sixty-odd judges. Of these it appears that every Democrat held the Act invalid, and every Republican but one held it constitutional.[23]

The first issue of greenbacks were still crisp and new when the legal tender question came before the Supreme Court of Indiana — [24] a court of four Democrats who, as contemporary events showed, were politically-minded to a high degree. The

---

[19] Appel v. Woltmann, 38 Mo. 194 (1866).

[20] E.g., in Whetstone v. Colley, 36 Ill. 328 (1865), where it was common ground that the Act was valid, the question being whether it applied to a promissory note which was payable "in gold." The Illinois Court held that it did, thus going beyond what the Supreme Court later held in Bronson v. Rodes, 7 Wallace 229 (1869), and Trebilcock v. Wilson, 12 Wallace 687 (1872).

[21] Johnson v. Ivey, 4 Coldwell 608.

[22] O'Neil v. McKewn, 1 S. C. 147.

[23] Included in this generalization are a very few judges on whom it has not been possible positively to fasten a party label, without more extensive inquiry than the point warrants. In these cases a highly probable affiliation is assumed to have been the true one.

[24] Reynolds v. Bank of the State, 18 Ind. 467 (1862).

spokesman argued that the Act was unconstitutional; adjured the federal Supreme Court to rise up and do its duty; and then concluded, tamely enough, that "in the case at bar, our decision is but that of a *nisi prius* Court, and we had better err in acquiescing in than declaring null the action of Congress." One judge dissented: that is, he agreed in opinion with his brethren and would have given judgment accordingly. The question came before the same bench two years later.[25] The court argued at length that the Act was invalid, invoking what was certainly the most eminent authority quoted on either side of the question:

Historically considered, we find that the Almighty, and his Prophets and Apostles, were for a specie basis; that gold and silver were the theme of their constant eulogy. *Abraham*, the patriarch, 1875 years before Christ, being about 3740 years ago, purchased of *Ephron*, among the sons of *Heth*, the field in which was the cave of *Machpelah*, shaded by a delightful grove, for the burial place of his dead; and he paid for it "400 sheckles of silver, current money with the merchant." Gen. 23, 16. So *Solomon*, the wisest of men, seems to have had a decided preference for a hard money currency. . . . Again, the prophet *Jeremiah*, one of the "greater prophets," says, chap. 32, verses 9 and 10: "And I bought the field of *Hanameel*, my uncle's son, that was in *Anothoth*, and weighed him the money, even 17 sheckles of silver, and I subscribed the evidence and sealed it, and took witnesses, and weighed the money in the balances."

The conclusion of the court was that the Act was invalid; but that, *pro forma*, it would give judgment the other way, suggesting that by petition for rehearing the case be kept open until the Supreme Court should have passed upon the legal tender question.

That autumn the people of Indiana went to the polls. A new and wholly Republican court was elected. When the case came on for rehearing, the power of Congress was emphatically affirmed.[26]

[25] Thayer *v.* Hedges, 22 Ind. 282 (1864).
[26] Thayer *v.* Hedges, 23 Ind. 141 (1865).

The deliberations of the Court of Appeals in New York were carried on in quite a different intellectual atmosphere. Opinions were delivered *seriatim*, and give evidence of candor and serious consideration. Six judges upheld the statute; Chief Judge Denio and Judge Selden dissented. The Chief Judge concluded with the assertion that, if his sense of duty had allowed him to decide the case as he would wish the law temporarily to be, he would have been with the majority. Judge Selden, concurring with him, was a Republican and formerly lieutenant governor. Judge Denio was a Democrat who had voted for Lincoln and supported the government throughout the war.

In the Pennsylvania court, Judges Strong, Read, and Agnew upheld the power of Congress, while Chief Justice Woodward and Judge Thompson, Democrats, dissented. Strong was later to write the opinion for the Supreme Court of the United States when it reversed itself and upheld the Legal Tender Act. Judge Read had been nominated for the Supreme Court in the last days of Tyler's administration, but the Senate took no action. Chief Justice Woodward had recently been unsuccessful as Democratic candidate for governor; he sat in Congress from 1867 to 1871. President Polk had nominated him to be an associate justice of the Supreme Court in 1845, but he too failed of confirmation. Thereupon Judge Grier was appointed in his stead. When Lincoln was elected Woodward wrote to Jeremiah S. Black:

I cannot condemn the South for withdrawing from the Union. I believe they have been loyal to the Union formed by the Constitution — secession is not disloyalty to that, for that no longer exists. The North has extinguished it. — And if they do go out, don't let a blow be struck against them by the present administration. Dissuade them if you can, but if you can't let them go in peace. I wish Pennsylvania could go with them. . . .[27]

In his dissent in the Pennsylvania legal tender case Judge Woodward expressed the view that Congress had paid less

[27] W. N. Brigance, *Jeremiah Sullivan Black* (Philadelphia: The University of Pennsylvania Press, 1934), p. 79.

respect to the obligations of good faith than "a community of felons would find themselves compelled to do." [28] If Judge Read had received the place that went to Grier, apparently the Supreme Court would never have held the Legal Tender Act unconstitutional. If Judge Woodward had received the place, the Republicans when they came to office would have had a different Constitution to live by. When one recalls such narrow escapes as the Prize Cases, where Justice Grier's vote was decisive, one is led to speculate what the party in power would have done if they had found so hostile a judge as Woodward on the bench instead of Grier.

The Supreme Court of Missouri is counted among those which upheld the Legal Tender Act, and indeed it is not surprising that this was so. It will be recalled that when the Republicans in that state had finally subdued their opponents, they called the Constitutional Convention of 1865 to consolidate their position. This was the convention which adopted the test oath that came before the Court in *Cummings* v. *Missouri*. One of the acts of this body was to promulgate an ordinance ousting every judge in the state, and authorizing the governor to fill all the vacancies by appointment. When the justices of the old Supreme Court declined to give place to the new appointees, they were forcibly removed from the bench by a militia general and police officers.[29] The new court upheld the constitutionality of the legal tender legislation.

Kentucky was another border state where sentiment was divided, half slave and half free. Throughout the war the relations between the governor and the Union commander had been strained. In the election of 1864 the military party struck from the ballot the name of the Democratic candidate for judge of the Court of Appeals. By a surprise move the Democrats substituted the name of the venerable George Robertson, and carried the election. In the court of four

[28] Shollenberger *v.* Brinton, 52 Pa. St. 9, 39 (1866).
[29] 4 *American Law Register* n.s. 705 (1865).

there was only one "Unconditional Unionist" judge. It was over his dissent that *Griswold* v. *Hepburn* was decided. If the military commander had only seen to it that a Republican was chosen at the election of 1864, the Legal Tender Act would evidently not have been held invalid.

It was also quite possible, of course, to raise the legal tender issue in a case brought up from some court in the federal system, such as a circuit court or the Court of Claims. In fact this was done. But these cases too came up long after the war had been won. It is pertinent to recall that such interests as the railroads, which might ordinarily be expected to support litigation, were more than ready to acquiesce in a statute which was so advantageous to themselves as borrowers. All told, it was great good fortune for Lincoln's administration that its currency system was not put in jeopardy while hostilities were going on.

The first legal tender cases to come up after *Roosevelt* v. *Meyer* went off on points of statutory construction. In *Bronson* v. *Rodes* [30] there was a contract made in 1851 to pay $1400 "in gold and silver coin, lawful money of the United States." At the time this was entered into there was no other legal tender than gold and silver coin. The opinion by the Chief Justice announced that it was the appropriate function of courts to enforce contracts according to the intent of the parties. The provision for specie must have been inserted advisedly, to preclude payment in a medium of fluctuating value. It amounted to a contract for bullion. In his view it was not necessary to pass on the question of constitutionality. Even if a contract to pay coin was a contract to pay money merely, still the Act of 1862 had not demonetized gold but had in fact required that customs duties be paid in coin. The statute was not intended to forbid the performance of contracts expressly calling for specie payments. It looked as if the Court was going to rob the Act of much of its effect by the device of strict construction. Justices Davis and Swayne appended short concurring opinions to say that they com-

[30] 7 Wallace 229 (1869).

mitted themselves only to the result reached in the instant case.

Justice Miller dissented. Of course the parties intended that payment be "in gold and silver coin, lawful money of the United States": that was the only medium there was at the time. But so too did those who contracted for the payment of money generally. The express stipulation was made, he thought, not in reference to a possible change in legislation, but to preclude an attempt to pay in state bank notes. Whatever the parties had intended, Judge Miller had no doubt what Congress intended when it passed the Act. The entire country in the settlement of contracts for incalculable millions of dollars had acted upon the understanding that Congress had overridden the intent of the parties.

In *Butler* v. *Horwitz*,[31] decided a fortnight later, there was an annual rent payable in gold. The Chief Justice took occasion to elaborate on his theory of election by the parties. The Act of 1862 recognized two kinds of lawful money, gold and paper. When the obligation called specifically for gold, it was solvable only by a tender of coin; "while the absence of any express stipulation, as to description, in contracts for payment in money, generally warrants the opposite inference of an understanding between the parties that such contracts may be satisfied . . . by the tender of any lawful money." Miller dissented for the reasons given in *Bronson* v. *Rodes*.

By the terms of the Constitution the states are forbidden to coin money, emit bills of credit, or make anything but gold and silver coin a tender in payment of debts. The federal government is placed under no such express prohibitions, but its power in the premises must be found in the grants of power to coin money and regulate the value thereof and of foreign coin; to borrow money on the credit of the United States; or in the general grant of power to make all laws which shall be necessary and proper for carrying into execution the powers thereinbefore granted. In a draft submitted to the Constitutional Convention by its committee on detail there

[31] 7 Wallace 258 (1869).

had been a clause granting power to "emit bills on the credit of the United States" and it was voted to strike out these words. But this was not a vote to forbid the issue of notes, since it was concurred in by several members who had made it clear that they were opposed to an absolute prohibition.

Through a long practical construction it became settled that the power to borrow included a power to emit treasury notes, and this was recognized emphatically by the Court in the case of *Veazie Bank* v. *Fenno* [32] in 1869. By its issues of greenbacks, and then by the national bank notes which were a feature of the national banking system created in 1863, Congress had provided a national currency. To make this action effective it was necessary to drive the state bank notes out of existence. This was done by laying a 10 per cent tax. In upholding this exaction in the Veazie Bank Case, the Chief Justice said:

It is settled by the uniform practice of the government and by repeated decisions, that Congress may constitutionally authorize the emission of bills of credit. It is not important here, to decide whether the quality of legal tender, in payment of debts, can be constitutionally imparted to these bills; it is enough to say, that there can be no question of the power of the government to emit them; . . . to fit them for use by those who see fit to use them in all the transactions of commerce; . . . to make them a currency, uniform in value and description, and convenient and useful for circulation.[33]

Thus when the Court came to grips with the constitutionality of the Legal Tender Acts it had already conceded a power to issue notes and establish a currency system. This helped considerably toward the contention that to impose the quality of legal tender on treasury notes was a proper aid to the borrowing power. It could also be argued that the legal tender law was a necessary and proper means to the accomplishment of other powers of Congress, particularly the power to wage war. While some went so far as to argue that the

[32] 8 Wallace 533.   [33] At p. 548.

grant of power to coin money included the power to print paper, this clause was invoked rather by the other side to show that a power to give the quality of legal tender to anything other than coin could not be implied.[34]

The legal tender case brought up from the Court of Appeals of Kentucky — *Hepburn* v. *Griswold* [35] — was heard at the December term, 1867, and was continued for reargument with leave to the Attorney General to be heard on the part of the government. It was decided at conference on November 27, 1869. On that date the Court consisted of eight members, and there was a division of five to three, adverse to the constitutionality of the Act. Chief Justice Chase and Justices Nelson, Grier, Clifford, and Field — all the Democrats of the Court [36] — were opposed by Swayne, Miller, and Davis, all Republicans. On February 7, 1870, the prevailing and dissenting opinions were delivered.

This was the case of a promissory note made in 1860, in discharge of which greenbacks of corresponding face value had been paid into court. The Chief Justice, speaking for the majority, had no doubt that the contract must be construed as one solvable only in coin, though this had not been expressly stipulated.

[34] "If the Constitution says expressly that Congress shall have power to make metallic legal tender, how can it be taken to say by implication that Congress shall have power to make paper legal tender?" (O. W. Holmes, Jr., in a note to Kent's *Commentaries*, 12th ed., 1873, vol. I, p. 254n.) He had expressed the same view in 1870 in a letter to the editors of the *American Law Review* (4:768). This point had not been made in Hepburn v. Griswold; but in Knox v. Lee Justice Field restated it clearly, and the majority went to some effort to overthrow it. Holmes recorded the episode with pardonable pride in 7 *American Law Review* 146 (1872).

In 1887 James Bradley Thayer met Holmes's point in his article on "Legal Tender" in 1 *Harvard Law Review* 73 (1887); see his *Legal Essays* (Boston: The Boston Book Company, 1908), p. 6ff. He showed that a power to coin money is not synonymous with a power to make legal tender. After rebutting arguments against his contention, Professor Thayer went on to give affirmative reasons to support the power to make paper money a legal tender. In later years Justice Holmes thought that Thayer had had the better of the argument.

[35] 8 Wallace 603 (1870).

[36] It seems not inaccurate to apply this characterization to Chase in 1869. Party regularity had always rested lightly upon him, and he regarded himself as an independent Democrat. He was a leading contender for the Democratic presidential nomination in 1868.

Contracts for the payment of money, made before the Act of 1862, had reference to coined money, and could not be discharged, unless by consent, otherwise than by tender of the sum due in coin. Every such contract, therefore, was, in legal import, a contract for the payment of coin.

Here, it will be noted, the Chief Justice threw over the theory of election by the parties which he had elaborated in *Bronson* v. *Rodes* and *Butler* v. *Horwitz*. Contracts to pay specie and those to pay dollars were now said to be indistinguishable — which is what Miller had said in his earlier dissent. That the Act of 1862 applied to preëxisting debts could not be doubted.[37] So the question of constitutionality had to be met. If upheld, it must be because the Act was "necessary and proper for carrying into execution" some substantive power of Congress. As to the meaning of these words the gloss of Chief Justice Marshall in *McCulloch* v. *Maryland* was accepted: "Let the end be legitimate, let it be within the scope of the Constitution, and all means which are appropriate, which are plainly adapted to that end, which are not prohibited but consistent with the letter and spirit of the Constitution, are constitutional." Here the former Secretary of the Treasury, now Chief Justice, argues that the means must be "plainly adapted," "really calculated," and then embarks on a little essay on money which culminates in the conclusion that the imposition of the quality of legal tender upon greenbacks had been unwise and was not plainly adapted to aid the war power. He returns to Marshall's language and extracts further argumentative material. The means must be consistent with the letter and spirit of the Constitution. Chase then invokes the spirit of the Constitution, and finds that it establishes justice, and since the Legal Tender Act works injustice it is obnoxious to this spirit. And finally it contravenes the letter, since the exercise of an alleged power to make paper notes a legal tender has the effect of depriving the creditor of some of the value of his debt, whereas the Fifth Amend-

---

[37] Justice Grier alone thought otherwise on this point. It is impossible to support his position.

ment declares that no person shall be deprived of property without due process of law.

To a superficial reading this may seem persuasive. But the opinion was, in fact, most unsatisfactory. That a very cogent line of reasoning might have been adopted is evident when one examines the dissenting opinions later prepared in *Knox v. Lee*.[38] Had it been decided that there was a total want of power to make anything but gold and silver coin a legal tender, that would have gone to the root of the matter. It would have disposed equally of preëxisting and subsequent contracts. The Chief Justice, however, chose to debate the point whether Congress had acted wisely in declaring that creditors under existing contracts must accept greenbacks at their nominal value. His conclusion was "that whatever benefit is possible from that compulsion to some individuals or to the government, is far more than outweighed by the losses of property, the derangement of business, the fluctuations of currency and values, and the increase of prices to the people and the government, and the long train of evils which flow from the use of irredeemable paper money." But if the question had been reduced to this point, whether it was or was not wiser to make paper notes a legal tender, the decision was a matter of policy peculiarly within the province of the legislature. In telling how the war might more wisely have been financed the Chief Justice may have been talking good economics (though no economist could agree to all of his statements); but it is not good constitutional law to say that a measure is invalid because we see it worked out badly.

It was a weak effort to evoke the spirit of the Constitution to condemn the Act because it operated unjustly on preexisting obligations. For that matter, a fluctuating currency results in unfairness in contracts made after its emission. If in the light of relevant provisions of the Constitution a judge chose to say that the power to make paper a legal tender could not be implied, it was needless to go on to show that if it did exist its exercise would be fraught with evil. If on the other

---

[38] 12 Wallace 457 (1871).

hand the power was conceded, the fact that it worked injustice was solely for the consideration of Congress. As Justice Miller replied, so too does a declaration of war, or the abolition of a tariff.

In a dissenting opinion in which Swayne and Davis concurred, Miller followed after the Chief Justice to show that in fact the Legal Tender Act had been necessary. If the drastic step had not been taken,

> the national government would have perished, and, with it, the Constitution which we are now called upon to construe with such nice and critical accuracy. . . . Certainly it seems to the best judgment that I can bring to bear upon the subject that this law was a necessity in the most stringent sense in which that word can be used.

Addressing himself to the Chief Justice's deductions from the *spirit* of the Constitution, he replied:

> The whole argument of the injustice of the law — an injustice which, if it ever existed, will be repeated by now holding it wholly void; and of its opposition to the spirit of the Constitution, is too abstract and intangible for application to courts of justice, and is, above all, dangerous as a ground on which to declare the legislation of Congress void by the decision of a court. It would authorize this court to enforce theoretical views of the genius of the government, or vague notions of the spirit of the Constitution and of abstract justice, by declaring void laws which did not square with those views. It substitutes our ideas of policy for judicial construction, an undefined code of ethics for the Constitution, and a court of justice for the National Legislature.

No other justice of that time was so reconciled to the exercise of power by the political branches of government as was Judge Miller.

The Act of Congress of April 10, 1869,[39] had made certain amendments in the judicial system of the United States. Now that Andrew Johnson no longer exercised the appointive power, the membership of the Court was expanded to nine justices. It was further provided that any Justice who had attained the age of seventy and had held his commission ten

[39] 16 Statutes at Large 44.

years might resign with salary. Justices Grier and Nelson came within the scope of this provision. The propriety of such a statute had long been evident. As early as 1864 Attorney General Bates had expressed the opinion that "Taney, Wayne, Catron and Grier, are evidently failing, being, obviously, less active in mind and body, than at the last term." [40] He added that they could not afford to resign unless Congress passed legislation granting a pension, and that while Justice Nelson walked with a firmer step, "I do not see that his *mind* stands more erect than theirs, or moves onward with a steadier gait." Judge Grier's letters throughout the 1860's show that he was failing. In 1861 he was compelled to forego his annual trout fishing for the first time in thirty years.[41] The next summer he had to give up his circuit court work,[42] a situation which became chronic.[43] In October 1866 he informed the Chief Justice that he could hardly walk, but that he needed "the exercise both of *mind* and *body* — which sitting in court would afford me." [44] And later, "I can write with difficulty, even with a pencil." [45] Justice Miller, in a letter of January 19, 1868, writes that "Brother Grier who delivered the opinion [46] . . . is getting a little muddy and may not have conveyed the idea clearly."

Yet Justice Grier was a member of the Court when *Hepburn* v. *Griswold* was taken up in conference on November 27. In fact the new law was not to go into effect until the first Monday in December. But it was believed in the Court that Grier would soon resign.[47] When the question was put

[40] *Diary of Edward Bates*, p. 358.
[41] Letter to Clifford, July 24, 1861; Clifford Papers.
[42] Letter to Clifford, August 9, 1862.
[43] 17 *Pittsburgh Legal Journal* 36 (1870).
[44] Letter of October 22, 1866; Chase Papers.
[45] Letter of April 28, 1869; Chase Papers.
[46] In League *v.* Atchison, 6 Wallace 112 (1868).
[47] Justice Miller, in "A Statement of Facts . . . ," to be discussed later. The *Legal Gazette* of Philadelphia, in its issue of August 27, 1869, stated however that it had "very strong reasons for believing" that the report that Judge Grier was about to retire was "without any sufficient warrant whatever." It went on, unwisely, to express the hope that Justices Grier and Nelson would be very deliberate about deciding to resign.

whether to affirm the judgment of the Kentucky court (holding the Legal Tender Act invalid), Justice Grier voted to reverse. This produced an equal division among the eight justices, with the result that the judgment below would be affirmed. Then *McGlynn* v. *Magraw*,[48] involving another aspect of the legal tender question, was taken up, and here Judge Grier made some remarks inconsistent with the vote he had just given. This was brought to his attention, and after some conversation his vote in *Hepburn* v. *Griswold* was changed, making a majority of five on the side of unconstitutionality. "In a week from that day every Judge on the bench authorized a committee of their number to say to [Judge Grier] that it was their unanimous opinion that he ought to resign." [49] He acted on this intimation and on January 31, 1870, he ceased to be a member of the Court.

"Under these circumstances," Justice Miller later wrote, "the minority begged hard for a delay until the bench was full. But it was denied." [50] From what has already been written, it hardly need be said that if the case were held over to be reargued after two Republicans had been added to the Court, the Act would be upheld. To reopen the question after it had once been decided would require greater hardihood. The majority were determined to go ahead. On January 29 Chase's opinion for the majority was read in conference, preparatory to a formal decision of the case on January 31, Grier's last day in office. In order to allow time for the preparation of the dissenting opinion, however, judgment was not rendered until February 7. Thus it may be said that the vote was taken in conference at a moment when the bench was full; that the opinion was accepted by the majority at a day when by law there was one vacancy; and that when the judgment of unconstitutionality was entered there were two vacancies.

[48] 8 Wallace 639 (1870).
[49] Justice Miller, in "A Statement of Facts," at p. 10. *Cf.* Charles E. Hughes, *The Supreme Court* (New York: Columbia University Press, 1928), p. 75.
[50] "A Statement of Facts," p. 8.

Whether it would have been a more proper course to postpone judgment until there could be reargument before a full bench is an issue which it is difficult to isolate from one's preference as to the final outcome of the legal tender question. Considering how long the case had been under advisement the decision cannot be said to have been reached precipitately. But the minority said by the same token that it could have been reserved a little longer. Undoubtedly Chase and his party felt that it was a race against time. If there had been a majority of five competent judges their moral position would have been stronger. For under all the circumstances, what seems more serious than the matter of a judge or two more or less is the fact that in a narrowly divided Court the majority insisted on deciding a constitutional issue when one justice did not really know what he was about.

Since January 31 press despatches had forecast that the decision would construe the Legal Tender Act as inapplicable to preëxisting debts.[51] And after it was made there was great uncertainty as to what had been held. The despatch to the *New York Tribune*[52] said that the Court decided nothing as to contracts made after the passage of the act, but that it was to be inferred that the Court as it stood when Judge Grier was a member would have held the act constitutional as to those contracts. The correspondent of the *Boston Daily Advertiser*[53] reported that "the Court, in other words, sustains the act, but declares that it is not retroactive. . . . All sorts of questions are at once raised as to the scope of Judge Chase's decision." There were some persons, in short, who regarded this as simply another legal tender case which had gone off on some point not involving the fatality of the Act. The texts of the opinions, however, appeared in the contemporary press.

The spirit in which the party in power received the decision was at once made evident. The prevailing opinion was

[51] *New York Tribune,* January 31; *Boston Advertiser,* February 7.
[52] Published in the issue of February 8.
[53] Issue of February 8.

much criticized, while Justice Miller was the object of general congratulation. On February 9 Senator Wilson of Massachusetts, a Republican leader and later vice-president, introduced a bill [54] to increase the size of the Court from nine to eleven. It was reported in the press that "the object of this measure seems to be to put the court into such shape that it cannot declare against the constitutionality of the legal-tender act." [55] "The feeling is growing among members of Congress that the Supreme Court, as now constituted, will overthrow the legal-tender act if it ever makes a decision, and there is a growing disposition to be sure of the position of additional members before they are confirmed." [56]

On February 7, at about the time of day when the decision in *Hepburn* v. *Griswold* was being announced, President Grant sent to the Senate the nominations of William Strong and Joseph P. Bradley for the two vacant places on the Court. It was by the vote of these new justices, reinforcing Miller, Swayne, and Davis, that the decision in the Hepburn Case came presently to be overruled.

Justice Strong came of a sturdy family whose roots were deep in the soil of New England. He was the eldest of eleven in a minister's family — one of those remarkable families raised on a salary of a few hundred dollars, where each son was put through college and then helped the younger brothers while teaching school. He graduated from Yale in 1828, taught in an academy while he read law, and in 1832 began to practice at Reading, Pennsylvania. In 1846 and 1848 he was elected to Congress as a Democrat, and in 1857 was made a member of the Supreme Court of Pennsylvania, from which he resigned in 1868 to take up what at once became a lucrative practice in Philadelphia. Justice Strong was a man of deep religious feeling and of simple, unaffected piety. During the Civil War he became president of a "National Association to secure certain religious amendments to the Constitution," whose purpose was to alter the Preamble so as to recog-

[54] S. No. 521.
[55] *Boston Advertiser*, February 10, 1870.   [56] *Ibid.*, February 11.

nize "the Lord Jesus Christ as the ruler of all nations, and his revealed will as the supreme law of the land." For years he was at the head of the American Tract Society and the Sunday School Union; President Grant is said first to have met him when Strong brought a delegation to present a Bible to the chief magistrate. In his eleven years on the federal Supreme Court he proved to be a very substantial member of that body, though his name is not linked with a large number of celebrated causes. He often spoke for the Court in cases arising under the Confiscation Act — matters of no present interest. In railroad litigation he consistently took a conservative view favorable to the protection of those interests. He dissented in the Granger Cases,[57] where the majority upheld state power to fix the rates charged by railroads and businesses of a like public interest. His important constitutional opinions were in *Knox* v. *Lee*,[58] where the Legal Tender Act was finally upheld; the *State Freight Tax* [59] and the *State Tax on Railway Gross Receipts*,[60] drawing a line (on a view later abandoned) between state taxation and interstate commerce; *Kohl* v. *United States*,[61] holding that the United States may exercise the right of eminent domain through its own courts; and *Strauder* v. *West Virginia* [62] and the cases following it, holding that the Negro had a constitutional right not to be discriminated against on account of color in the selection of jurors. But for the most part his lot was to write opinions in cases involving common law and equity, admiralty and patents, and the revenue laws which then formed the bulk of Supreme Court business. In a very true sense, nothing he did on the Court became him like the leaving it, for it will be seen that he resigned while in the full possession of his powers in the hope that he would create an example to be followed by others whose impaired faculties had become a detriment to the Court.

Of the other addition to the Court in 1870, Justice Bradley,

[57] Munn v. Illinois, 94 U. S. 113 (1877).
[58] 12 Wallace 457 (1871).
[59] 15 Wallace 232 (1873).
[60] 15 Wallace 284 (1873).
[61] 91 U. S. 367 (1876).
[62] 100 U. S. 303 (1880).

it is out of the question to give any adequate treatment in a paragraph. His name will appear continually, but he is entitled to a book by himself. Let it be said here simply that he was one of the most accomplished lawyers, and possessed of one of the toughest minds, in the annals of the Court. Though he illuminated virtually every branch of the law, he is particularly remembered as one who was as influential as any in striking down local impediments to the flow of a nation-wide commerce. In this he and Miller broadly agreed, though with certain differences of emphasis. In his view of the extent of the jurisdiction of the federal courts Bradley was, again, a pronounced nationalist. His participation, therefore, in vindicating the power of Congress to create a currency and impose upon it the quality of legal tender was consistent with his entire outlook.

For two years and more there had been pending in the Court two cases on appeal from the Court of Claims, in which government contractors sought to recover the difference in value between a certain sum in coin and in legal tender notes.[63] On the day after Justice Bradley took his seat, Attorney General Hoar moved that these cases be taken up, pointing out that they involved the constitutionality of the Legal Tender Act, and asking that the Court hear argument on that question. James M. Carlisle, as counsel for Latham, the appellant in one of the two cases, was present and did not intimate any reason why that question was precluded. At conference next day the Attorney General's motion was granted. But on Monday morning, before this could be announced, the Chief Justice produced a letter from Mr. Carlisle insisting that he had a right to expect that *Hepburn* v. *Griswold* had settled the law in favor of his clients. He did not contend, however, that there was any agreement of counsel or order of the Court to that effect. It was directed that the whole matter be heard in open court on March 31. At that hearing the Attorney General insisted on his motion, and

---

[63] Latham *v.* United States, Deming *v.* United States, 9 Wallace 145, 146 (1870).

Mr. Carlisle repeated his objections. The following morning it was announced that the appeals would be heard on April 11, on all the issues presented by the records — the Chief Justice and Nelson, Clifford, and Field dissenting. While Mr. Carlisle seems never to have claimed that there had been any order to the effect that his case should be governed by the Hepburn Case, he did, naturally enough, expect that such would be the outcome. The Chief Justice, however, went further and insisted that at the time the cases had been continued it had been distinctly announced from the bench, with the acquiescence of the parties, that they should abide the outcome of *Hepburn* v. *Griswold*. This was just as emphatically denied by Justice Miller. At the request of counsel the hearing set for April 11 was postponed, and on April 20 appellants moved that their cases be dismissed. To this the Attorney General objected, and Justices Miller and Bradley expressed doubt as to the right of appellants to do so. At Miller's request the Court retired, and on returning from consultation it was announced that the motion was granted.

At the conclusion of this episode Justice Miller wrote to his brother-in-law:

We have had a desperate struggle in the secret conference of the court for three weeks over two cases involving the legal tender question. The Chief Justice has resorted to all the stratagems of the lowest political trickery to prevent their being heard, and the fight has been bitter in the conference room. Finally the new judges and the minority in Hepburn v Griswold having withstood all assaults public and private, when the cases were called for argument yesterday, the Appellants dismissed their appeal. No doubt they had been paid to do it as their claims were not large and a decision in their favor hardly probable.[64]

[64] Justice Miller was mistaken in his inference that some one had purchased Latham's and Deming's claims to prevent a reargument of the legal tender question. It seems that Latham thought he "had made such arrangements as would secure a successful prosecution of the said two claims in Congress," and had induced Deming's counsel to join in asking that the appeals be dismissed (2 *Legal Gazette* 380, 1870). At the next term of court Deming came back, with new counsel, to move that his appeal be reinstated, asserting that the motion to dismiss had been without his authority. This was denied on the ground of his acquiescence by silence (Deming *v.* United States, 10 Wallace 251, 1870).

JUSTICE MILLER

The excitement has nearly used me up. It has been fearful; and my own position as leader in marshalling my forces, and keeping up their courage, against a domineering Chief, and a party in court who have been accustomed to carry everything their own way, has been such a strain on my brain and nervous system as I never wish to encounter again.[65]

The Chief Justice prepared a statement which set out his side of the controversy, and placed it on the files of the Court. Thereupon, on April 30, the five justices of the new majority subscribed to a "Statement of Facts" drawn by Judge Miller, giving in great particularity a résumé of the entire sequence of events. When he heard of this, Chase withdrew his statement; but apparently it formed the basis of the account of *Hepburn* v. *Griswold* given in J. W. Schuckers' biography, published in 1874.[66]

The rival statement remained in the possession of Judge Miller until his death. It was then secured by Judge Bradley, who had it privately printed for the use of Judge Strong and himself. On January 19, 1892, just before his death, Judge Bradley confided the original to his son, with instructions that it should not be published during the lifetime of any of the justices concerned. In 1902 it appeared in the *Miscellaneous Writings of the Late Hon. Joseph P. Bradley.*[67]

After the Court had directed that Latham's and Deming's appeals be argued on the question of constitutionality, the Washington correspondent of the *Boston Advertiser* reported:

The course of public and private discussion since the Chief Justice rendered his decision in the Kentucky case shows that there is little disposition to accept it as final and conclusive, and even if it were certain that this decision would be reaffirmed the Attorney-General thinks it best to have a rehearing before the full bench so that the decision will be the work of the court as a whole. He finds that individuals and corporations are not settling debts in accordance with the principles laid down by

---

[65] Letter of April 21, 1870.
[66] *The Life and Public Services of Salmon Portland Chase* (New York: D. Appleton and Company).
[67] Edited by Charles Bradley, Newark, 1902.

Mr. Chase, and believes that the country will not be satisfied that the questions at issue are settled until they have been passed upon by the nine judges on the bench.[68]

The same newspaper, after having digested the opinion in *Hepburn* v. *Griswold*, said editorially:

As to the scope of the actual decision of the court, we think it is much greater than its defenders admit. The amount of contracts outstanding which were created before the war, is believed to be in hundreds of millions. As we predicted when the decision was made public, payment of these in coin has been generally refused at the risk of litigation, and we believe that if the decision is maintained the resultant evil will be far greater than to allow the precedents of eight years to stand until general resumption. Upon a careful examination of the reasoning upon the case which was decided, we see nothing in it which is not just as applicable to contracts made since the passage of the act, and we think that its supporters look upon the decision as but one step towards the practical repeal of the legal-tender act in all its bearings.[69]

While the *Advertiser* conceded that it would not be a happy precedent to overrule the decision by the vote of judges appointed after it was made, it thought that allowing the Legal Tender Act to be nullified would perhaps be still more regrettable.

The fact that the new majority had held their ground in the Latham and Deming skirmish showed that they would insist on reopening the constitutional question. It was so understood in Congress, for under date of April 18 it was reported that "the judiciary committee of the Senate has concluded that further tinkering with the Supreme Court is not advisable, and today reported against the [Wilson] bill proposing to put two more judges on the bench." [70] On April 30, the last day of the term, "the Texas case of Knox against Lee, including in one of its branches the whole question of the legal tender laws, was ordered to be reargued at the next term

[68] April 11, 1870.
[69] April 22.
[70] *Boston Advertiser*, April 19, 1870.

of the court," [71] and in their "Statement of Facts" signed on April 30, the majority declared that

the decision only partially disposed of the great question to which it related, and has not been received by the profession or by the public as concluding the matter. If it is ever to be reconsidered, a thing we deem to be inevitable, the best interest of all concerned, public and private, demands that it be done at the earliest practicable moment.

In *Knox* v. *Lee*,[72] decided May 1, 1871, the question was reopened and the Legal Tender Act fully sustained, both as to prior and subsequent debts. The case had been argued elaborately, and the prevailing opinion by Judge Strong, as well as the concurring opinion by Judge Bradley and also the dissents, were all more closely reasoned than *Hepburn* v. *Griswold*. The judges now placed in the minority took it very hard. The Chief Justice and Judge Nelson had been indisposed, and when the day fixed for argument came Judge Field wrote that he also was too ill to attend and expressed the hope that the argument might be postponed until October.[73] But Judge Swayne, the senior among those in the majority, said in open court that it was high time that the case was settled and expressed a strong desire that the decision be reached during the term,[74] and this was done. Of the four dissenters, Chase, Clifford, and Field wrote opinions. That by Field ends in a characteristic vein: He is not prepared to admit that blind approval of every measure once deemed necessary to put down the rebellion is any evidence of loyalty to the country. "The only loyalty which I can admit consists in obedience to the Constitution. . . . It is only by obedience that affection and reverence can be shown to a superior having a right to command. So thought our great Master when he said to his disciples: 'If ye love me, keep my commandments.'"

[71] *Boston Advertiser*, May 2.
[72] 12 Wallace 457.
[73] Letter of April 12, 1871, to "Acting Chief Justice" Clifford; Clifford Papers.
[74] 20 Lawyers' Edition, 290–291.

One of the most interesting aspects of Justice Field is his unfailing assurance that divine Providence was on his side.

The overruling of *Hepburn* v. *Griswold* is sometimes
spoken of as though it had been very immoral, and Schuckers'
biography of Chase [75] calls it revolutionary. Certainly the
episode tended to dispel the illusion that constitutional law
is an exact science, but that is scarcely to be regretted. Should
justices who believe that governmental power has been unwarrantably crippled perpetuate the evil lest the prestige of
the Court be impaired? The Hepburn Case had involved a
preëxisting obligation, and the decision purported to deal
only with that situation. Yet the view taken by the new Court
was such that even if it had confined itself to the question
of contracts made after the act was passed, the *ratio decidendi*
could not have been logically reconciled with the holding
in the Hepburn Case. Moreover, "*stare decisis* is not, like *res
judicata*, a universal, inexorable command." [76] On this Chase
and Miller and Field were really agreed. In fact only a short
time before, when the Court had held that a state legislature
could not repeal a permanent exemption from taxation
granted by its predecessor, citing the Dartmouth College
Case, those very three Judges had united in a dissenting
opinion by Miller, saying that

> With as full respect for the authority of former decisions, as
> belongs, from teaching and habit, to judges trained in the com-
> mon law system of jurisprudence, we think that there may be
> questions touching the powers of legislative bodies, which can
> never be finally closed by the decisions of a court.[77]

From time to time thereafter cases on legal tender arose
of which only one need be cited. In *Trebilcock* v. *Wilson* [78]

[75] J. W. Schuckers, *The Life and Public Services of Salmon Portland Chase*
(New York: D. Appleton and Company, 1874).

[76] From an instructive discussion of the numerous occasions on which the
Court has reversed its position, in Justice Brandeis' dissenting opinion in
Burnet *v.* Coronado Oil and Gas Co., 285 U. S. 393, 405 (1932).

[77] Home of the Friendless *v.* Rouse, 8 Wallace 430 (1869), Washington University *v.* Rouse, 8 Wallace 439, at 444 (1869).

[78] 12 Wallace 687 (1872).

there was a note made in 1861 calling for payment "in specie."
The majority, through Justice Field, followed *Bronson* v.
Rodes and held that this could be discharged only in coin.
Justices Miller and Bradley dissented. The former reiterates
his view in the Bronson Case, while Bradley says, "In all cases
where the contract is to pay a certain sum of money of the
United States, in whatever phraseology that money may be
described (except cases specially exempted by law), I hold
that the Legal Tender Acts make the Treasury notes a legal
tender."

The extensive construction of national power for which
Miller contended in these cases has been vindicated in subsequent decisions. In *Juilliard* v. *Greenman* [79] it was held
that Congress may, in time of peace as well as in war, make
treasury notes a legal tender. Field, the sole survivor of the
minority in *Knox* v. *Lee*, was the only dissenter. And much
more recently, in *Norman* v. *Baltimore and Ohio Railroad
Company*,[80] the opinion of the Court, by Mr. Chief Justice
Hughes, repudiates Chase's contention that a contract to pay
in coin is a contract for bullion; quotes with approval the
dissenting opinions of Bradley and Miller in *Trebilcock* v.
Wilson; and adopts their view that it does not lie within the
power of private parties, by agreements *inter se*, to set at
naught the powers of Congress over the currency system.

The reader may look for some remarks directed to the question whether Grant "packed" the Court in 1870. Certainly
enough has been said to show that any lawyer acceptable to
the President and Senate must have had an outlook favorable
to upholding the Legal Tender Act. The doctrine that the
Constitution must be adequate to the preservation of the
Union, from which the constitutionality of the legal tender
law was a deduction, had become an article of faith in the
Republican party. More detailed remarks belong properly
to a study of Justice Bradley, and are reserved for another
occasion. When a complete examination of the facts of the

[79] 110 U. S. 421 (1884).   [80] 294 U. S. 240 (1935).

case is published, it will be seen that the two new justices came to the Court free from any self-reproach.

As one looks back over the conduct of the Civil War, involving as it did the assumption of powers not theretofore deduced from the Constitution, and then the period of reconstruction, when the dominant party became lost to reason, it seems remarkable that those in political authority did not have more trouble with the courts than they did. It was a windfall that President Lincoln could appoint three justices at the beginning of his term. We have seen that their friendly touch was felt in ways not revealed in the published decisions. The loyal support of some of the older justices, particularly of Judge Wayne of Georgia and Judge Grier, was an invaluable asset. But to a considerable extent the party in power was the architect of its own success. The size of the Court was increased, decreased, and increased. By the close of the war a majority of the justices were appointees of President Lincoln. In a taunting speech delivered in January 1868, Senator Garrett Davis, Democrat, of Kentucky, said that five years before

the court was composed of nine members, six of whom were eminently conservative and true to the Constitution. They were not Radicals or stuff that could be manufactured into Radicals; but Congress was preëminently radical, and determined, if possible, to make the Supreme Court radical also. A tenth judge was added to the bench, and it was the purpose of the leaders that the place should be filled with a Radical, and they so hoped even after his appointment. But the young and able lawyer summoned from the Pacific coast to become one of that great court soon proved his fealty to the Constitution, and demonstrated an amount of intellect and legal learning and official rectitude and courage worthy of the court in its best days.[81]

Chief Justice Chase was another who disappointed the hopes with which he had been placed on the Court. Before the appointment was made Secretary Welles advised the President that

[81] *Congressional Globe*, 40 Cong., 2 Sess., p. 498.

the occasion should be improved to place at the head of the court a man, not a partisan, but one who was impressed with the principles and doctrines which had brought this Administration into power; that it would conduce to the public welfare and to his own comfort to have harmony between himself and the judicial department, and that it was all-important that he should be a judge who would be a correct and faithful expositor of the principles of his administration and policy after his administration shall have closed.[82]

It was on this view that Lincoln made his selection. As George S. Boutwell later recalled the President's statement of the reasons why he had appointed Chase: ". . . we wish for a Chief Justice who will sustain what has been done in regard to emancipation and the legal tenders. We cannot ask a man what he will do, and if we should, and he should answer us, we should despise him for it. Therefore we must take a man whose opinions are known." [83]

On the matter of military arrests the President had defied Chief Justice Taney at the outset; and when state judges interfered with the draft by granting *habeas corpus*, Lincoln declared "he would send them after Vallandigham." [84] It had been suggested that the offending judges be imprisoned.[85] The Attorney General deliberately avoided a test case on the power to hold a civilian without civil trial. Like other chief executives, Lincoln found himself embarrassed by many an overzealous subordinate who was "putting weapons in the hands of the enemies of the administration by assuming arbitrary and illegal powers"; [86] yet he hesitated to revoke the action lest the subordinate " 'raise a hubbub about it.' " [87] A decision on the validity of the reconstruction legislation was precluded, first by the heroic measure of repealing a grant of jurisdiction while McCardle's Case was under advisement, and then by an arrangement between the Attorney General

---

[82] *Diary of Gideon Welles*, II, 181; November 26, 1864.
[83] *Reminiscences of Sixty Years*, II, 29.
[84] *Diary of Gideon Welles*, I, 432; September 14, 1863.
[85] *Diary of Edward Bates*, p. 307; September 14, 1863. The Attorney General resisted this idea.
[86] *Ibid.*, p. 376. [87] *Ibid.*, p. 393.

and counsel for Yerger. All told, as one reviews the course of the party then in power one is more impressed by the variety of its expedients than by the patent constitutionality of its measures.

Some of these incidents stand as precedents of unreasoning action by the political branches of the government. In others it has been argued that the reproach fell upon the judges who begrudged essential power because they disapproved of the ends toward which it was being directed. Had the Court found it possible to adopt Justice Miller's view of constitutional statesmanship, the record on both sides would have been much clearer.

VIII

THE FOURTEENTH AMENDMENT AND THE PROCESS OF JUDICIAL INCLUSION

W HEN the decision of the Slaughter-House Cases [1] made it necessary for the Court to give a construction to the Fourteenth Amendment, a cleavage developed which has persisted ever since. "Criticism of this case has never entirely ceased," said Mr. Justice Moody in 1908, "nor has it ever received universal assent by the members of this Court." [2] For the case raised for the first time that passionate issue, whether the Reconstruction Amendments had worked such an alteration in the federal system as to vest in the Supreme Court the power and duty to strike down state action which seemed unreasonable to a majority of the justices. Much of the constitutional litigation since that day has been fought over this same ground. While Justice Miller won in the first great battle, the side on which he fought, as we shall see, lost the campaign.

The facts were these. In 1869, while the reconstruction regime still prevailed in Louisiana, the legislature passed a statute "to protect the health of the City of New Orleans [and] to locate stock-landings and slaughter-houses," incorporating a slaughter-house company and giving it for twenty-five years the exclusive privilege of operating abattoirs within the city. All other butchers had to come there to land and slaughter their cattle. From a decision in the highest court of Louisiana upholding this enactment the case was brought to the Supreme Court. The contention of the plaintiffs in error was that the statute fell within the prohibition of the

[1] 16 Wallace 36 (1873).
[2] Twining v. New Jersey, 211 U. S. 78 (1908).

Thirteenth Amendment abolishing "slavery and involuntary servitude," and that it abridged the "privileges and immunities of citizens of the United States," deprived them of liberty and property without due process of law, and denied the equal protection of the law, contrary to the Fourteenth Amendment. No one would contend that the legislation was well conceived. But the question before the Court was whether the Amendments gave a remedy in the federal courts against such legislative unwisdom, rather than leaving the people of each state to find their own redress under the state constitution and through the ordinary electoral process. Judge Miller, speaking for a scant majority of the Court, adopted the restricted interpretation.

John A. Campbell, who had resigned from the Supreme Court to go South in 1861, led the argument for a control by the federal judiciary over state legislation. It was indeed a novelty that a Southern Democrat should seek to establish such a limitation upon state rights. The answer lay in the helplessness under which the once dominant class now found themselves. Campbell had described it himself in a letter he wrote to Justice Clifford in 1871:

The Southern communities will be a desolation until there is a thorough change of affairs in all the departments of the government. There is now no responsibility — and we are fast losing all of our ancient notions of what is becoming & fit in administration. The public are tolerant of corruption, maladministration, partiality in courts, worthlessness in juries, & regard government only as a means of exploitation. Indifference to anything wrong, is the common Sentiment. Hope is disappearing from the motives to exertion.

Discontent, dissatisfaction, murmurings, complaints, even insurrection would be better than the insensibility that seems to prevail — [3]

While carpetbag government continued, Southern leaders seized the opportunity to turn the Fourteenth Amendment to their own uses. "The purpose is manifest," said Judge Camp-

[3] Letter of June 25, 1871; Clifford Papers.

bell in argument, "to establish through the whole jurisdiction of the United States one people, and that every member of the Empire shall understand and appreciate the constitutional fact, that his privileges and immunities cannot be abridged by state authority." His argument was a tremendous effort to persuade the Court that it was a part of the "privileges and immunities," the "liberty and property" of the citizen to live under a system of economic *laissez faire*; that any abridgment thereof raised a federal question, and that if the Court considered the state action unreasonable it should thereupon declare it unconstitutional.

Just what this implied was pressed upon the Court by opposing counsel, one of whom, Matt Carpenter, as senator from Wisconsin, had taken a prominent part when the proposed Amendment was before Congress. They pointed out in how many respects state legislation imposed restrictions and burdens upon economic activities, and set out a prophetic list of some of the consequences which would ensue if Judge Campbell's construction of the Amendment were accepted: it would repeal all laws imposing license fees upon any particular employment, lawful under the common law; all laws regulating the mode of carrying on any lawful employment; all laws restraining the manufacture or sale of liquors; "all existing laws regulating and fixing the hours of labor, and prohibiting the employment of children, women, and men in any particular occupations or places for more than a certain number of hours per day"; and would "bring within the jurisdiction of this court all questions relating to any of these kindred subjects, and deprive the legislatures and state courts of the several states from regulating and settling their internal affairs."

The significance of Judge Miller's opinion will be more apparent if we first examine the dissent. Chief Justice Chase and Justices Swayne and Bradley all concurred in the minority opinion by Judge Field, while the two associate justices also filed opinions of their own. The minority construed the "privileges and immunities of citizens of the United States" as including "the sacred and imprescriptible rights of man." The Amendment "was intended to give practical effect to the declaration of 1776 of inalienable rights, rights which are the gift of the Creator; which the law does not confer, but only recognizes." Henceforth the Court was charged with a mission to protect these transcendental rights. Writing this sort of opinion was to Field a labor of love, for it enabled him to proclaim his own individualistic philosophy as the voice of the Constitution. Limits on the power of the British sovereign at common law — as in the Case of Monopolies,[4] holding that there could be no grant of a monopoly to manufacture playing cards — are expanded into constitutional limits on the power of a state legislature to regulate occupations. A system of free competition seems to be the end toward which the whole world has moved. Yet on closer examination it is apparent that Judge Field is simply invoking a school of economic thought which became dominant under conditions prevailing at the end of the eighteenth century. Adam Smith's *Wealth of Nations* and Turgot's decree abolishing monopolies of trades — both of 1776 — are dwelt upon. The opinion concludes with a paraphrase of Blackstone's dictum that civil liberty exists where every individual has the power to pursue his own happiness unrestrained "except by equal, just, and impartial laws." In short, any governmental action must fall if a bench of judges thought it unequal, unjust, or partial.

Miller and his colleagues of the majority felt called to no such pontifical function. Rather were they struck by the unsuspected change in the economy of the federal system if the Fourteenth Amendment were to be given the meaning contended for. In his opinion Miller points out the gravity of the occasion:

No questions so far-reaching and pervading in their consequences, so profoundly interesting to the people of this country, and so important in their bearing upon the relations of the United

4 11 Coke 84b. (1602).

States and the several states to each other, and to the citizens of the states, and of the United States, have been before this court during the official life of any of its present members.

The opinion goes on to trace the emergence of the three Reconstruction Amendments, and reaches the conclusion that

in the light of this recapitulation of events, almost too recent to be called history, but which are familiar to us all; and on the most casual examination of the language of these amendments, no one can fail to be impressed with the one pervading purpose found in them all, lying at the foundation of each, and without which none of them would have been even suggested; we mean the freedom of the slave race, the security and firm establishment of that freedom, and the protection of the newly-made freeman and citizen from the oppressions of those who had formerly exercised unlimited dominion over him. . . .

We do not say that no one else but the negro can share in this protection. . . . If . . . rights are assailed by the states which properly and necessarily fall within the protection of these articles, that protection will apply though the party interested may not be of African descent. But what we do say, and what we wish to be understood, is, that in any fair and just construction of any section or phrase of these amendments, it is necessary to look to the purpose which we have said was the pervading spirit of them all, the evil which they were designed to remedy, and the process of continued addition to the Constitution until that purpose was supposed to be accomplished, as far as constitutional law can accomplish it.

We doubt very much whether any action of a state not directed by way of discrimination against the negroes as a class, or on account of their race, will ever be held to come within the purview of this provision. It is so clearly a provision for that race and that emergency, that a strong case would be necessary for its application to any other.

Justice Miller recognized in the tendency of public thought at the time the Amendments were adopted a belief that the powers of the national government should be augmented.

But, however pervading this sentiment, and however it may have contributed to the adoption of the Amendments we have been considering, we do not see in those Amendments any purpose to destroy the main features of the general system. Under the pressure of all the excited feeling growing out of the war, our statesmen have still believed that the existence of the states with powers for domestic and local government, including the regulation of civil rights, the rights of person and of property, was essential to the working of our complex form of government, though they have thought proper to impose additional limitations on the States, and to confer additional power on that of the nation.

Construing the language of the Fourteenth Amendment in the light of this historical analysis, Miller makes a fundamental distinction between the privileges and immunities of citizens *of the United States* as such, and that larger body of rights, "whatever they may be," which must find their definition and their protection in the institutions of the several states. No rights as citizens of the United States — whatever might be their rights as citizens of Louisiana — were abridged when the butchers of New Orleans were restrained in the practice of their calling.

The narrow construction thus given to the Fourteenth Amendment seemed to rob it of its supposed significance. Justice Miller — "lest it should be said that no such privileges and immunities are to be found if those we have been considering are excluded" [5] — felt called upon to suggest some rights inherent in federal citizenship which the new Amendment might protect. There was, for example, the right to pass freely from state to state which he had enunciated for the Court in *Crandall* v. *Nevada*.[6] But this result had been reached in 1867, quite independently of the Fourteenth Amendment which was then only in the course of ratification. Another was the claim to diplomatic protection when abroad — a privilege of federal citizenship which a state could not possibly have abridged. Thus there was force to Justice Field's retort that if the new privileges and immunities clause meant no more than the majority conceded, "it was a vain and idle enactment, which accomplished nothing and most un-

[5] 16 Wallace at 79.
[6] 6 Wallace 35 (1867).

necessarily excited Congress and the people on its passage." [7]

It is significant that the Court waited until 1935 before it found a state statute which abridged the "privileges and immunities of citizens of the United States" — a provision of the Vermont income tax law giving an advantage to one who loaned money within over one who loaned without the state.[8] Perhaps after reading Mr. Justice Stone's dissent (Justices Brandeis and Cardozo concurring) one would be tempted to say that the Court waited until 1935 before it discovered a new federal privilege and immunity which thenceforth states were forbidden to abridge. Justice Stone, after recalling the close construction given to the "almost forgotten privileges and immunities clause of the Fourteenth Amendment," went on to say:

> The reason for this reluctance to enlarge the scope of the clause has been well understood since the decision of the Slaughter-House Cases. If its restraint upon state action were extended more than is needful to protect relationships between the citizen and the national government, and it did more than duplicate the protection of liberty and property secured to persons and citizens by the other provisions of the Constitution, it would enlarge judicial control of state action and multiply restrictions upon it to an extent difficult to define, but sufficient to cause serious apprehension for the rightful independence of local government. That was the issue fought out in the Slaughter-House Cases, with the decision against the enlargement.[9]

The division within the Court over the Slaughter-House Cases was not along party lines. Miller on the one hand and Swayne on the other were equally staunch Republicans. Clifford was opposed to the other Democrat, Field. Davis on the one side and Chase on the other were politically adrift, and would have welcomed a presidential nomination from either party. Justice Hunt (who had just come from the New York Court of Appeals in place of Nelson, resigned) and Justice Strong stood opposed to Justice Bradley — all Repub-

---

[7] 16 Wallace at 96.
[8] Colgate *v.* Harvey, 296 U. S. 404.
[9] 296 U. S. at 445.

·licans. It seems unlikely that Miller was impelled by a desire
to uphold the legislation of carpetbag governments, for his
correspondence shows him almost as critical of the corruption
and ignorance of Southern Republicans as he was of Democratic intransigence. While one must hesitate to attribute to
Justice Miller all of Justice Holmes's convictions about the
unwisdom of attempting, by judicial omniscience, to save
society from its own mistakes, yet it is clear that they had the
same conviction of the necessity of allowing "some play for
the joints of the machine."

When self-government was restored in Louisiana a new
constitution was adopted which vested in municipal authorities power to regulate slaughtering. At New Orleans the business was thrown open to competition, and the grantee of the
exclusive privilege contested this action as an impairment of
his contract. This gave Justice Miller, as spokesman for the
Court, an occasion to declare, what to him was a congenial
doctrine, that the police power is inalienable.

It cannot be permitted [he said] that, when the Constitution
of a State, the fundamental law of the land, has imposed upon
its legislature the duty of guarding, by suitable laws, the health
of its citizens, especially in crowded cities, and the protection of
their person and property by suppressing and preventing crime,
that the power which enables it to perform this duty can be
sold, bargained away, under any circumstances, as if it were a
mere privilege which the legislator could dispose of at his pleasure.[10]

Both decisions, therefore, leave the legislative power unimpaired.

Never after the Slaughter-House decision did Justice Miller
renew his suggestion that only discrimination against Negroes
would be found to come within the purview of the Fourteenth Amendment.[11] In December 1882 the Court heard
argument in *San Mateo County* v. *Southern Pacific Railroad*

---

[10] Butchers Union Co. *v.* Crescent City Co., 111 U. S. 746 (1884).

[11] *Cf.* Bartemeyer *v.* Iowa, 18 Wallace 129 (1874); Davidson *v.* New Orleans,
96 U. S. 97 (1878).

Co.,[12] where it was asked to hold that the discriminatory mode of assessing railroad property established by the California constitution was obnoxious to the due process and equal protection clauses. Counsel for the railroad bore down critically upon Justice Miller's prophecy in the Slaughter-House Case, thereby provoking the following colloquy:

> Mr. Justice Miller — As we decided in the Slaughter-House cases, (although the argument was the other way,) we say: "And so, if other rights are assailed by the States which properly and necessarily fall within the protection of these articles, that protection will apply, though the party interested may not be of African descent."
>
> Mr. Sanderson — I am glad to hear that, your honor.
>
> Mr. Justice Miller — I do not know that anybody in this Court — I have never heard it said in this Court or by any judge of it — that these articles were supposed to be limited to the negro race.
>
> Mr. Sanderson — But there is a notion out among the people, and our friends on the other side have cited several cases for the purpose of showing that it was the intention of this Court to give to this provision of the Constitution as restricted and limited application as possible.
>
> Mr. Justice Miller — The purport of the general discussion in the Slaughter-House cases on the subject was nothing more than the common declaration that when you come to construe any act of Congress, any statute, any constitution, any legislative decree, you must consider the thing, the evil which was to be remedied, in order to understand fully what the purpose of the remedial act was.[13]

Roscoe Conkling, arguing on the same side in the same cause, undertook to give the Court new light on the evil sought to be remedied by the framers of the Fourteenth Amendment, and in particular to show that corporations were entitled to its protection. Quoting and misquoting [14]

---

[12] 116 U. S. 138. The consideration of the case was deferred by stipulation of the parties, and it was finally dismissed in 1885.

[13] *Oral Argument on behalf of Defendant by S. W. Sanderson* (Washington, 1883), pp. 24–25.

[14] For having the insight to explore this important matter, credit is due to Mr. Howard Jay Graham. "The 'Conspiracy Theory' of the Fourteenth Amendment" (1938), 47 *Yale Law Journal* 371; 48 *ibid.* 171. The actual mis-

from the secret journal of the Joint Committee on Reconstruction, of which he had been a member, he invited the
Court to understand that those who drafted the Fourteenth
Amendment had had two separate and distinct purposes, to
protect the freedman, and also to "increase and strengthen the
safeguards of the Constitution and the laws" for all persons,
corporate as well as natural. "At the time the Fourteenth
Amendment was ratified," he said, "as the records of the two
Houses will show, individuals and joint stock companies were
appealing for congressional and administrative protection
against invidious and discriminating State and local taxes." [15]
Concluding this branch of his argument, Conkling said:

Those who devised the Fourteenth Amendment wrought in
grave sincerity. They may have builded better than they knew.
They vitalized and energized a principle, as old and as ever-
lasting as human rights. To some of them, the sunset of life may
have given mystical lore.
They builded, not for a day, but for all time; not for a few, or
for a race; but for man. They planted in the Constitution a
monumental truth, to stand four-square whatever wind might
blow.[16]

Conkling did not actually assert that the protection of
corporations was a deliberate aim of the drafters. He said
"I have sought to convince your honors" that the framers, the
Congress, and the legislatures that ratified "must have known
the meaning and force of the term 'persons.'" [17] He then
turned from "this surmise" to "the real question to be
answered":

---

quotation consisted in asserting that the committee had had before it a clause
giving Congress power to secure "to all *citizens* in every State equal protection
in the enjoyment of life, liberty and property," and had deliberately substituted
the more inclusive word "*persons.*" In fact, "*persons*" had been employed from
the beginning (*Oral Argument on behalf of Defendant by Roscoe Conkling*,
Washington, 1883, p. 18). The same misquotation appears in his Brief for
Defendant, at p. 13. The Journal has been published as Part I of Benjamin
B. Kendrick's *The Journal of the Joint Committee on Reconstruction* (New
York: Columbia University Press, 1914).
[15] *Oral Argument*, p. 25.
[16] *Ibid.*, p. 34.　　　　　　　　　　　　　　　　　[17] *Ibid.*, p. 31.

The true question, in exploring the meanings of the Fourteenth Amendment, is not, in a given case, whether the framers foresaw that particular case and acted in reference to it — the inquiry is does the case fall within the expressed intention of the amendment. All cases compassed by the letter of the language, must be included, unless obviously repugnant or foreign to its spirit and purpose.[18]

A too-ready acceptance of the inferences which Conkling's argument suggested has given rise to the theory that the framers of the Amendment were parties to an astute conspiracy to secure the adoption of a measure which, while supposedly designed to protect the Negro, would eventually become a bulwark sheltering corporations from state control. In "The 'Conspiracy Theory' of the Fourteenth Amendment," [19] an essay of exceptional importance, Mr. Howard Jay Graham has given the subject a critical examination which reaches a verdict of not proven. In the light of this study one rereads Conkling's argument with enhanced appreciation of the effectiveness of his advocacy, but with unrelieved doubt concerning the clairvoyance of the congressmen who framed the Fourteenth Amendment.

Whatever may prove to have been the ulterior motives of some members of the committee, such as Representative John A. Bingham of Ohio, one finds in Justice Miller's letters no evidence that such a design came to his attention. In a letter of February 6, 1866 — while the committee was in the midst of its labors — he incloses a newspaper clipping which sets out a draft amendment which certain Southern leaders, with the approval of President Johnson, were going to submit to the joint committee. It sketched a constitutional amendment to provide, *inter alia*, that

all persons born or naturalized in the United States and subject to the jurisdiction thereof are citizens of the United States and

---

[18] *Ibid.*, pp. 31–32. Conkling goes on to quote a well-known passage from the Dartmouth College Case, 4 Wheaton 518, 644 (1819), where Marshall, C. J., argues for an extensive construction of the contract clause.

[19] *Supra*, note 14.

of the States in which they reside; and the citizens of each State shall be entitled to all the privileges and immunities of citizens in the several States. No State shall deprive any person of life, liberty or property without due process of law, nor deny to any person within its jurisdiction the equal protection of the laws.

This, it will be noted, runs very close to the final wording of Article XIV, section 1. Other provisions denied the right of a state to secede and the right of the federal government to expel a state or to diminish its representation in Congress; secured the public debt of the United States and forbade the payment of debts incurred in aid of insurrection; and declared that if any state denied the suffrage to adult males on account of race, color, or previous condition of servitude, then its representation in Congress should be diminished accordingly. There was also a proposal for amending state constitutions to give the suffrage to every resident adult male who could read the Declaration of Independence and the Constitution and sign his name or who was owner of $250 worth of taxable property, without excluding those already eligible to vote.

Of this proposal Miller says:

I have no hesitation in saying that in the shape of an amendment it is as acceptable to me as any basis of reconstruction which I have seen offered. I am not now and have not been at any time in favour of negro suffrage as a principle or for its own sake. I am not in favour on principle of any extension of the elective franchise. I think we had better see if it will sustain itself as it is before we extend it further. . . .

I have sent you my letter to Rankin that you may know how I feel and talk to my confidential friends and to my party friends for with all its faults, and all the dangers on which I see it driving, the Republican party is the only one from which I can have any hope for the country. The democratic party of the north could not be in full power two years before Mr. Davis would be their candidate for the Presidency, and with the Southern States capable of casting their votes and the democracy as strong in the north as the republicans now are, he would be elected. It would happen thus. The moment their power was assured, the party would submit to its old leaders. Mr. Vallandigham, Pendleton, Jerry Black, J. C. Breckenridge, and that class of men, would again become its leaders. More moderate men might struggle against it but they could not prevent it.

With these views you must see that my hopes for the future are not bright. Unquestionably the republican party is going it at a killing pace. It is true also that some of its leaders are reckless, and not over honest or patriotic. But there are men and strong men among them who if they could find in the flood that is drifting them along against their will a rock or other footing on which they could make a stand would do it manfully and I hope successfully. But here is their condition.

The democratic party is utterly odious to the voting majorities every where. Mr. Johnson is now more odious than the democratic party. Any thing coming from them . . . cuts itself off from all sympathy with the dominant party. Not only so but makes it as much as a mans political existence is worth to do or say anything for them. This is just what you southern people are doing all the time. If a committee comes here they go and have a powow [sic] with Seward and Johnson, and forthwith publish it to the world, that they and the President are firm in their resistance to radicalism, that is, to the governing majority who alone can do them any good. They then call on that old political prostitute Reverdy Johnson, Saulsbury,[20] Tom Florence [21] Charles Mann, Cham[.] of Executive National Democratic Committee, &c &c all of whom are hated by all loyal men worse a thousand times than they hate many honest rebels. All this is known and published over the land and makes the majority more determined, more bitter, more exacting than ever. These men never call on moderate republicans. Sometimes for form's sake they call on Thad Stevens, Wade, or Sumner that they may report at home how hostile and offensive they are.

Of course there is a large class of men in the north who seeing these things swear that so long as it remains so, and so long as you folks cling to these political associates they can remain without political power; But there is a larger class of republicans who can overlook all this, who would be willing to incur the hazard even of a return to power of the allied democratic and rebel parties, rather than risk what we are risking, the eventual destruction of some of the best principles of our existing constitution; But who are still unwilling to trust you, I mean the Southern people, with full power over the negro, and the Union man of the South.

[20] Democratic Senator from Delaware.
[21] Thomas Birch Florence, Democratic newspaper proprietor of Washington.

I wish to call your attention to this proposition strongly because it is one which governs quite enough votes at any time to overturn the republican party and also because it is one [to] which you in your letters never allude, and which all the good men I have seen from the South shrink or belittle. We cannot in the face of the events that have occurred since the war trust the South with the power of governing the negro and Union White man without such guarantees in the federal Constitution as secure their protection. Now you will say this is unjust. Let us see. Of course I do not believe that all the stories I see in the papers about killing, beating, shooting these men are true. If you are fair minded you must admit that many of them are true. You will say that they are done by low degraded men who are found in all communities, and that your leading men disapprove of it. That is always said in reply. Show me how you disapprove of it. Show me a single white man that has been punished in a State court for murdering a negro or a Union man. Show me that any public meeting has been had to express indignation at such conduct. Show me that you or any of the best men of the South have gone ten steps out of their way to bring such men to punishment or to take any steps to prevent a recurrence of such things. Show me the first public address or meeting of Southern men in which the massacres of New Orleans or Memphis have been condemned or any general dissent shown at *home* at such conduct. You may say that there are two sides to those stories of Memphis and New Orleans. There may be two sides to the stories, but there was but one side in the party that suffered at both places, and the single truth which is undenied that not a rebel or secessionist was hurt in either case, while from thirty to fifty negroes and Union white men were shot down precludes all doubt as to who did it and why it was done.

Now as *I* feel and think, so large numbers of men who are not politicians think and feel. I am for Mr. Dixon's [22] plan of settlement. I am for your plan. I am for universal amnesty and universal suffrage, not because any of these are the best in themselves, but because we are losing what is more valuable than any of these things in the struggle which is demoralizing us worse than the war did. In my way, as I think it timely and useful I try to moderate my party friends, and work to bring about good results. But there are two parties to the settlement and your friends need quite as much working with as mine do. If I could be able to say tomorrow See here, they have hung a rebel in Texas for kill-

[22] Senator from Connecticut, supporter of Johnson's administration.

ing a negro, it would be the most effective speech that has been made since the war ended. Or if I could say see here what a former rebel said on this subject to his own comrades face to face, and then could point a public outspoken condemnation of some such conduct it would have effect. That is the place for you and your true friends to work, as holding back with a steady hand is mine. May we both do our duty where it will be most effectual. I do not believe it will be found in the concoction of terms of settlement.[23]

In August 1869, three and a half years later, Miller wrote:

It is not to be denied, that the leaders of the radical party in the gulf states since the rebellion have many of them been men of bad character, and without principle, and that still more of them have been ignorant, and unused to the exercise of political power.

It has been a sore thing to me and to most of the republican party that it is so. Yet there is this to be said. The experiment in reconstruction made under Johnson's invitation and influence, in which it was hoped that the Southern people would exhibit some self restraint, and would recognise in some shape the existence of legal rights and citizenship in the slaves freed by the war, proved precisely the reverse. Just so far as Mr. Johnson made concession, a *sine qua non* to *his* acceptance of their reformed legislation they went and not an inch further. I do verily believe today that if those States had not framed their black codes, by which negroes were substantially enslaved to the state instead of to the individual and if they could so far have restrained their fiendish hatred (which many not all of them had) for the negro, as to have forborne the Massacre of Memphis and New Orleans, the Johnson policy would have prevailed and reconstruction would have been peacefully carried out under a system which left the white man and the rebel in control of the State governments.[24]

These letters leave no doubt of the depth of Miller's feeling on the subject of equal protection for the freedman or of his strong conviction that state government should be carried on with no further restriction than was necessary to secure such protection. His great opinion in the Slaughter-House Cases was of a piece with his whole view of the public policy of reconstruction.

[23] Letter of February 6, 1866.   [24] Letter of August 29, 1869.

Those "natural rights" which, but for Justice Miller, might have become federal privileges and immunities have since been grafted to the due process clause, where they flourish in riotous profusion.[25] During his lifetime Miller resisted such a growth. In *Bartemeyer v. Iowa* [26] the state prohibition law was challenged as denying the liquor dealer his privileges and immunities, and as depriving him of his property without due process of law. The first contention was given short shrift. The second offered a more difficult issue. The defendant found substatial support in the Wynehamer Case,[27] where in 1856 the New York Court of Appeals had held that the due process clause of the state constitution forbade the legislature to make its prohibition law applicable to existing property in liquor. The true interpretation of the phrase, said Judge Comstock, is

that where rights are acquired by the citizen under the existing law, there is no power in any branch of the government to take them away. . . . When a law annihilates the value of property, and strips it of its attributes, by which alone it is distinguished as property, the owner is deprived of it according to the plainest interpretation, and certainly within the spirit of a constitutional provision intended expressly to shield private rights from the exercise of arbitrary power.[28]

Justice Miller's opinion took note of the Wynehamer decision, and observed that if Bartemeyer had owned the liquor prior to the imposition of an absolute prohibition on its sale,

[25] This development has afforded a maximum of judicial protection. For whereas the privileges and immunities clause ran only to *citizens*, the due process and equal protection clauses extend to *persons*, which has been construed to embrace corporations. Similarly the contract clause, which might have been developed to protect corporations from unreasonable rate regulation (*cf.* Gerard Henderson, "Railway Valuation and the Courts," 33 *Harvard Law Review* 902, 1031, at 907, 1920), was not available in the case of natural persons (as *Munn v. Illinois*, 94 U. S. 113, 1877), who of course had no charter on which the state legislation might be broken.

[26] 18 Wallace 129 (1874).

[27] 13 N. Y. 378 (1856). A landmark in judicial history: *cf.* E. S. Corwin, "The Doctrine of Due Process of Law before the Civil War," 24 *Harvard Law Review* 366 and 460 (1911).

[28] 13 N. Y. at 393, 398.

there would be a grave question whether the statute did not take property without due process of law. The issues were not to be lightly treated, he said, "nor are we authorized to make any advances to meet them until we are required to do so by the duties of our position." Here it was not necessary, because Bartemeyer alleged merely that the glass of liquor for the sale whereof he had been convicted had been his property since prior to the year 1860 when the prohibition law was enacted; but the legislation of 1860 was only a revision of the prohibition law of 1851, and it was not alleged that Bartemeyer had acquired the liquor prior to 1851.

If it be said that this manner of looking at the case is narrow and technical, we answer that the record affords to us on its face the strongest reason to believe that it has been prepared from the beginning, for the purpose of obtaining the opinion of this court on important constitutional questions without the actual existence of the facts on which such questions can alone arise.

The case of *Davidson* v. *New Orleans* [29] was brought to seek relief from a local assessment for the drainage of swamp land in Louisiana. It was contended that the state was taking property without due process in that the price fixed was exorbitant, that the assessment had been spread too widely to include land not benefited, and because of other objections. In affirming the judgment of the state court, Justice Miller approached anew the problem of giving content to the due process clause. He discussed the kindred phrase, "the law of the land," in Magna Charta, which admittedly was a limit only on the power of the Crown. The due process clause of the Fourteenth Amendment, he thought, should receive a broader construction so as to apply also where "the invasion of private rights is effected under the forms of state legislation." Unlike Parliament, an American legislature did not have legal power to enact that any disposition it chose to make of life, liberty, or property should be "due process." Thus a direct appropriation, as by statute purporting to give the

[29] 96 U. S. 97 (1878).

property of *A* to *B*, would fall within the prohibition. But Justice Miller never meant that the due process clause made it the duty of the Court to measure the substance of all legislation by the test of reasonableness.[30] In the fact that the Court's docket was crowded with cases where that clause was invoked he saw

abundant evidence that there exists some strange misconception of the scope of this provision as found in the XIVth Amendment. In fact, it would seem, from the character of many of the cases before us, and the arguments made in them, that the clause under consideration is looked upon as a means of bringing to the test of the decision of this court the abstract opinions of every unsuccessful litigant in a State Court of the justice of the decision against him, and of the merits of the legislation on which such a decision may be founded.

As to the type of case immediately before the Court, Justice Miller laid down the proposition

that whenever by the laws of a State, or by state authority, a tax, assessment, servitude, or other burden is imposed upon property for the public use, . . . and those laws provide for a mode of confirming or contesting the charge thus imposed, in the ordinary courts of justice, with such notice to the person, or such proceeding in regard to the property as is appropriate to the nature of the case, the judgment in such proceedings cannot be said to deprive the owner of his property without due process of law, however obnoxious it may be to other objections.

A comparison of the due process clauses of the Fifth and Fourteenth amendments showed that the latter did not cover all the ground of the federal bill of rights. But exact definition of the scope of the due process clause was said to be impossible and the attempt unwise; the elaboration of its meaning was therefore remitted to "the gradual process of judicial inclusion and exclusion."

It was good statesmanship, it is submitted, for the Court to decline to sit in review of state authorities on such questions

---

[30] This becomes more evident when one reads Justice Miller's language in the light of Justice Bradley's concurring opinion.

of detail as whether the boundaries of a drainage district had been properly drawn.[31] The minutely critical may remark that in his historical discussion Justice Miller fell into the anachronism of speaking of Parliament as an institution with which the barons were well acquainted in 1215. Miller's scholarship was homemade, and his brother Gray used to lament that a mind of such power and aptitude had never been properly grounded in the law.[32] It was rightly said that Miller was a man of wisdom rather than of knowledge, and to compare him with Gray suggests the contrast between Marshall and Story.[33]

Term after term the Court was being pressed at the bar to reconsider the renunciation it had made in the Slaughter-House decision. Persuasive reiteration found its reward — at first only in tentative concessions in the language of the opinions, finally in a complete acquiescence by a majority of the Court. The immediate objective of the forensic discussion of the due process clause was to induce the Court to strike down statutes regulating the charges of railroads and grain elevators. The next chapter will narrate how, when the roads were being constructed with very substantial aid from the public treasury, it was successfully urged that a railroad was merely a highway built under state authority, and therefore sufficiently "public" to be supported by taxation. But when the carriers proceeded to charge what the traffic would bear, and western legislatures passed laws to correct this abuse, the railroad corporations were so ungracious as to contend that their business was not "public" for purposes of rate regulation, and that a law fixing charges

[31] *Cf.* Professor Thomas Reed Powell's illuminating remarks on the zoning case, Nectow *v.* Cambridge, 277 U. S. 183 (1928), in his study of "The Supreme Court and State Police Power, 1922–1930," in 17 and 18 *Virginia Law Review,* volume 18 at p. 32 (1931).

[32] Gregory, *Samuel Freeman Miller,* p. 19. Miller had decided views on what should be the aim of education. He regretted that in the older American colleges "the student who takes the old regular Classical Course is a patrician, while the man who seeks the knowledge of *things* instead of the knowledge of *words* is a pleb" (letter of September 22, 1878). He sent his son to Cornell.

[33] 24 *American Law Review* 997 (1890).

deprived them of their property without due process of law. In *Munn* v. *Illinois* [34] and the other Granger Cases decided with it, the Court's first response to this contention was an emphatic negative.

Since Chief Justice Waite made himself the spokesman of the Court in these and most of the later cases on public regulation, Justice Miller figures merely as one of the supporting majority.

The only reference to the Granger Cases in Miller's correspondence is the following letter of September 1, 1875:

My Dear Will:

I enclose with this letter a copy of the law of the State of Minnesota regulating the fares of the railroads of that State.

Two cases [35] are pending in our court and are set for argument on the 25th of October next involving the question of the constitutionality of this law as impairing the obligation of the contract enacted by the charter of the Rail Road corporations.

I shall send by the same mail the records and briefs as far as filed in these cases.

There are no cases yet filed in our court under the Wisconsin statute or the statutes of Illinois or Iowa though it is believed there will be before the commencement of our next term. Under an order made by our court setting the Minnesota cases down specially for the third Monday of the next term all counsel having cases on the docket involving the general question are at liberty to take part in the argument of those cases.

I send you also a copy of the Wisconsin statute known as the "Potter Statute" because introduced and carried through by a gentleman of that name, who went to Canada to fight a duel with some Southern fire eater who did not appear.

The Wisconsin law was repealed or very much modified by the legislature last winter, but I do not know whether that law has been published. If you desire it and will write to Hon. Matt. H. Carpenter at Milwaukee using my name as a reference he will send you a copy of that act.

The States of Illinois and Iowa have statutes on the subject which provide for a board of commissioners whose duty it is once a year I believe or as often as they may think proper to classify

---

[34] 94 U. S. 113 (1877).

[35] Winona and St. Peter R. R. *v.* Blake, 94 U. S. 180 (1877); Southern Minnesota R. R. *v.* Coleman, 94 U. S. 181 (1877).

all the roads in the State and to determine the maximum rate of passenger and freight charges to be made by each class.

In Illinois which has perhaps the best considered statute on the subject these commissioners are charged with the duty of prosecuting violations of the statute.

Without some provision for a prosecution other than by the individual injured the law would be useless, as no man is sufficiently interested in any given case to encounter the power of the rail road company, through all the courts including ours.

In the several Granger Cases [36] argued before the Supreme Court at various times between October 1875 and January 1876, counsel flatly denied the power of a legislature to fix the charges of railroads and grain elevators.[37] Renewing con-

[36] Munn v. Illinois, 94 U. S. 113 (1877), affirming 69 Ill. 80 (1873); Chicago, B. & Q. R. R. v. Iowa, 94 U. S. 155 (1877), affirming Fed. Case No. 2666 (C. C. Iowa, 1875); Peik v. Chicago & N. W. Ry., 94 U. S. 164 (1877), affirming Piek v. Chicago & N. W. Ry., Fed. Case No. 11,138 (C. C. W. D. Wis., 1874); Chicago, M. & St. P. R. R. v. Ackley, 94 U. S. 179 (1877) — cf. The Attorney General v. Chicago and N. W. Ry., 35 Wis. 425 (1874); Winona & St. P. R. R. v. Blake, supra, affirming 19 Minn. 418 (1872); Southern Minnesota R. R. v. Coleman, supra; Stone v. Wisconsin, 94 U. S. 181 (1877), affirming 37 Wis. 204 (1875).

[37] Former Justice Benjamin R. Curtis was requested to give an opinion on the validity of the Potter Act. He advised that it was ultra vires, resting his conclusion on three grounds: that "it is not within the field of legislation, under any American Constitution, to fix and prescribe for the future, what prices shall be demanded either for commodities or for personal service, or for a union of both"; second, that it took property for public use without just compensation, in violation of the state constitution; and finally, that the statute, by diminishing the receipts of the company, impaired the obligation of contracts it had made with its creditors. Nowhere does he refer to the Fourteenth Amendment or use the phrase "due process of law" in his discussion.

In support of his first point, the limited nature of "legislative power," Judge Curtis cited Taylor v. Porter, 4 Hill 140 (1843). In that case the New York court, holding invalid a statute authorizing a private road to be laid over land without the consent of the owner, had rested its judgment on the theory that the grant of "legislative power" should be construed as being limited by principles of justice, and later had found additional support in the due process clause of the state constitution. Curtis' opinion cited the case for its exposition of "legislative power."

If Judge Curtis had seen in the Fourteenth Amendment the substantive content later given to the due process clause, he would hardly have failed to make that an additional ground for advising that the Potter Act was unconstitutional. At one point in his opinion he said: "this power to prescribe prices of commodities and service for the future, does not exist at all, or it is unlimited." Such a view is inconsistent with the result presently reached by the Court, that due process requires a "fair" return.

tentions which had been universally rejected in the courts below, it was urged: that the legislation worked a deprivation of property without due process of law; that, in the case of the railroads, it impaired the obligation of contracts embraced in the several corporate charters; and that state regulation was inconsistent with the congressional power over interstate commerce. When, after more than a year of consideration, the decision was announced, it appeared that none of these objections had received the assent of the Court. On the commerce point it was decided that, at least while the power of Congress remained dormant, state regulation would be upheld. In the cases where the contract clause had been invoked, the Court found upon examination that some reservation of power to amend or to regulate underlay every charter. In construing the due process clause, various businesses in which price-fixing was sanctioned by usage — such as ferries, inns, mills, and public wharves and warehouses — were cited as illustrative of the circumstances wherein public regulation might reasonably and constitutionally be applied. And if the legislature should abuse its power, said the Chief Justice, "the people must resort to the polls, not to the courts." [38]

Justices Field and Strong dissented throughout.

The hard saying just quoted was relieved only by an inconspicuous concession that "under some circumstances" a

---

It may seem surprising that Judge Curtis should have advised that a rate law (supposing it not to be invalid on other grounds) would, by reducing the company's revenues, impair the obligation of its contracts with its creditors. The public power to regulate would seem clearly superior to the mere expectations of mortgagees and bondholders. But he was inclined generally to give a very wide application to the contract clause. *Cf.* his dissenting opinion, when a member of the Court, in Richmond, F. & P. R. R. *v.* Louisa R. R., 13 Howard 71, 83 (1851). He gave opinions advising that the contract clause gave protection in two well-known cases where the Supreme Court subsequently held the contrary by unanimous votes (Salt Manufacturing Co. *v.* East Saginaw, 13 Wallace 373 (1872), and Boston Beer Co. *v.* Massachusetts, 97 U. S. 25 (1878)).

The opinions referred to are in the second of two books of manuscript opinions by Curtis, now in the Harvard Law Library. That on the Potter Act is at p. 444; that for the Beer Company at p. 154; that for the Salt Company at p. 166.

[38] 94 U. S. at 134.

statute regulating use or price might be so arbitrary as to amount to an unconstitutional deprivation of property.[39] In 1884 this was expanded as follows:

> As was said in that case [*Munn* v. *Illinois*], such regulations do not deprive a person of his property without due process of law. What may be done if the municipal authorities do not exercise an honest judgment, or if they fix upon a price which is manifestly unreasonable, need not now be considered, for that proposition is not presented by this record. The objection here is not to any improper prices fixed by the officers, but to their power to fix prices at all.[40]

Two years later, in the Railroad Commission Cases,[41] the language of the Court became firmer. After repeating the doctrine of *Munn* v. *Illinois*, Chief Justice Waite continued:

> From what has thus been said, it is not to be inferred that this power of limitation or regulation is itself without limit. This power to regulate is not a power to destroy, and limitation is not the equivalent of confiscation. Under pretence of regulating fares and freights, the State cannot require a railroad corporation to carry persons or property without reward; neither can it do that which in law amounts to a taking of private property for public use without just compensation, or without due process of law. What would have this effect we need not now say, because no tariff has yet been fixed by the commission, and the statute of Mississippi expressly provides "that in all trials of cases brought for a violation of any tariff of charges, as fixed by the commission, it may be shown in defense that such tariff so fixed is unjust."

In a case decided just after the Chief Justice's death in 1888, Justice Gray, upholding a statutory rate challenged by a reorganized corporation which had failed to put in evidence how much it had paid for its property at a foreclosure sale, said:

> Without any proof of the sum invested . . . the court has no means, if it would under any circumstances have the power, of

---

[39] 94 U. S. at 125.
[40] Waite, C. J., in Spring Valley Water Works *v.* Schottler, 110 U. S. 347, 354 (1884).
[41] 116 U. S. 307, 331 (1886).

determining that the rate of three cents a mile fixed by the Legislature is unreasonable. Still less does it appear that there has been any such confiscation as amounts to a taking of property without due process of law.[42]

The other members of the Court had now come so close to agreement with their brother Field that he could be made their spokesman. In *Georgia Railroad and Banking Co.* v. *Smith*,[43] Justice Field, summing up the recent cases, stated that it was common doctrine that, in the absence of inconsistent charter provision, the legislature had power to prescribe railroad rates, "subject to the limitation that the carriage is not required without reward, or upon conditions amounting to a taking of property for public use without just compensation."

It remained to be seen how this nebulous language would harden into rules for the judicial control of rate-making. In the leading case of *Chicago, Milwaukee & St. Paul Railroad Co.* v. *Minnesota*,[44] decided on March 24, 1890, the Supreme Court struck down, as a denial of due process of law, a statute which, without expressly requiring notice and hearing, directed a railroad commission finally to establish rates and (as construed by the state court)[45] directed the courts to enforce this order as conclusive. Complaints against certain of the carrier's rates had been filed with the commission, and the company had been notified and had appeared by counsel. Thereupon the commission made a finding that a lower rate was reasonable. On the carrier's refusal to comply, the commission, pursuant to the statute, applied to the state Supreme Court for a writ of mandamus. Denying all the contentions made in the return of the respondent, the court held that under the statute it had no authority to inquire into the reasonableness of the rate fixed; that the legislature might exercise its power through a commission; and that under the

---

[42] Dow v. Beidelman, 125 U. S. 680, 690 (1888).

[43] 128 U. S. 174 (1888).

[44] 134 U. S. 418. On the same day the Court decided Minneapolis Eastern Ry. v. Minnesota, 134 U. S. 467, a case arising under the same statute.

[45] 38 Minn. 281 (1888).

doctrine of the Granger Cases at judicial review was not requisite to due process of law.

On writ of error this judgment was brought before the United States Supreme Court. In his brief, counsel for the plaintiff in error asserted as his most advanced position that a legislature could not, under the Constitution, fix railway rates. To do so was inconsistent with the "natural right which belongs to every one to fix the price of his services." [46] He continued:

I find no statutes attempting to fix the compensation of existing railroads or other like property, prior to those of 1873 in Illinois, and 1874 in Wisconsin, Iowa and Minnesota, and it is most respectfully submitted, that prior to that time the history of either English or American legislation or jurisprudence furnishes no authority for the exercise of any such power by the State. That such legislation was new and theretofore unauthorized under our system of government, there can be no doubt, and that it is destructive of the rights of property and more to be feared than the insane ravings of the advocates of socialism and the commune, is manifest. Their demands are more tolerable even than those of the Legislature. They demand that the State shall first acquire our property and then operate it for their benefit, but under this system it is proposed that the State shall *take*, not acquire, the properties and then compel the owners, by mandamus, to operate them at rates wholly unremunerative and even without compensation, taking not only our property, but compelling us to render our services under the pains and penalties of punishment for contempt, if we violate the mandamus.

We object to the application of these communistic principles to our property, before the State shall have made socialistic advances so that it would be safe to subject all property to the same process. . . .[47]

We deny that it is a legislative function to adjudicate and determine what are reasonable rates. The question as to whether a given rate is reasonable and fair when challenged is for the judiciary.[48]

The Supreme Court, speaking through Justice Blatchford, reversed the judgment below. Justice Miller concurred spe-

---

[46] Brief for Plaintiff in Error, John W. Cary, Counsel, p. 18.
[47] *Ibid.*, p. 23.　　　　　　　　　　　　　　[48] *Ibid.*, p. 31.

cially, and Justice Bradley, protesting that the majority was practically overruling *Munn* v. *Illinois*, wrote a powerful dissent in which Justices Gray and Lamar joined. There has been a difference of opinion, both within the Court and among the commentators, as to the *ratio decidendi* in the case. Some have thought that Justice Blatchford rested his judgment on the narrow ground that the statute failed to require the commission to give the carrier a hearing before fixing the rate.[49] On this view, due process would be satisfied if it appeared that the administrative body had proceeded fairly and that on the evidence before it reasonable men might have arrived at the same conclusion. But the case has often been cited as establishing the broad proposition that, the Granger Cases to the contrary notwithstanding, the due process clause guarantees an independent judicial determination of the reasonableness of rates. Justice Blatchford said, in part:

> It [the statute] deprives the company of its right to a judicial investigation, by due process of law, under the forms and with the machinery provided by the wisdom of successive ages for the investigation judicially of the truth of a matter in controversy, and substitutes therefor, as an absolute finality, the action of a Railroad Commission which, in view of the powers conceded to it by the state court, cannot be regarded as clothed with judicial functions or possessing the machinery of a court of justice.[50]

The ambiguity lies in the word "judicial." One cannot be sure whether Judge Blatchford used it as meaning "by a court," or only as descriptive of a standard of orderly and rational inquiry to which administrative adjudication must conform.

"With some hesitation" Justice Miller concurred in the judgment. "Not desiring to make a dissent," he set out ten propositions as summarizing his views. He thought that the state legislature had power to establish rates between intra-

---

[49] *Cf.* John Dickinson, *Administrative Justice and the Supremacy of Law* (Cambridge: Harvard University Press, 1927), p. 191.

[50] 134 U. S. at 457. Justice Blatchford's discussion of the case, in his opinion in Budd *v.* State of New York, 143 U. S. 517, 546 (1892), leaves the meaning still in doubt.

state points, and might exercise its power through a commission. Neither the legislature nor the commission "can establish arbitrarily and without regard to justice and right a tariff . . . which is so unreasonable as to practically destroy the value of property . . . nor so exorbitant and extravagant as to be in utter disregard of the rights of the public." In such cases the ultimate remedy of the parties lay in the courts. The proper mode of seeking judicial relief was, not in suits (of which otherwise a multiplicity might be brought) between the carrier and individual shippers, but by a bill in chancery asserting the unreasonableness of the rate and asking a decree forbidding the carrier from exacting such fare as excessive, or establishing its right to collect the rate as being within the limits of just compensation for service rendered. In the instant case, where the petition for a writ of mandamus was an equivalent mode of raising the question,

I think the court has the same right and duty to inquire into the reasonableness 'of rates established by the Commission before granting such relief. . . . For the refusal of the Supreme Court of Minnesota to receive evidence on this subject, I think the case ought to be reversed on the ground that this is a denial of due process of law. . . .

This was among Justice Miller's last utterances from the bench of the Supreme Court. One wishes he had left a more satisfying discussion of a matter which has come to be of such capital importance in the working of government. But he said that the question on which the judiciary should pass in such cases was whether the rate-making authority had acted "arbitrarily and without regard to justice and right" — a test which would leave an adequate scope for effective administrative control of public utilities.

We need not trace how cases following *Chicago, Milwaukee & St. Paul Railroad Co. v. Minnesota* have built up a body of law on rate regulation. Whatever the majority meant to decide at that time, it has since been declared, on mature consideration, that where rates are challenged as confiscatory, due process means an independent judicial examination of the facts and the law.[51] The Court said it was unwilling to leave rights "at the mercy of administrative officials," particularly in view of "our multiplication of administrative agencies."

It was after Justice Miller's day that the Court discovered the broad scope of the word "liberty" as used in the Fourteenth Amendment. Even before his death that great absolute, the "liberty of contract," was being proclaimed by state courts,[52] and was yielding such results as the *Matter of Jacobs*,[53] which held invalid a statute forbidding the manufacture of cigars in tenement houses. It was unreasonable, said the New York court, to force the cigarmaker "from his home and its hallowed associations and beneficent influences," quoting Justice Field's opinions on the Fourteenth Amendment. Field's individualistic philosophy presently became the law of the land and his conservative influence was carried on by Brewer and Peckham. Then Justice Holmes was appointed to the Court and cast upon Justice Miller's position the illumination of his own philosophy. And this brings us to yesterday. Had that view prevailed the history of the country would have been appreciably different, and the Supreme Court would have escaped much of the reproach which was later cast upon it.

[51] See St. Joseph Stock Yards Co. *v.* United States, 298 U. S. 38 (1936), per Hughes, C. J., and the specially concurring opinions of Brandeis, J., and of Stone and Cardozo, JJ.
[52] Pound, "Liberty of Contract," 18 *Yale Law Journal* 454, 470ff. (1909).
[53] 98 N. Y. 98 (1885).

IX

THE MORTGAGED GENERATION

J USTICE MILLER'S earlier years on the bench came at a
period — not the first in our history — when, in their
zeal to encourage internal improvements, states and
municipalities had granted bonds and other favors with ill-
considered prodigality. In 1860 Judge Woodward, speaking
for the Supreme Court of Pennsylvania, had thus described
the situation:

We know the history of these municipal and county bonds —
how the legislature, yielding to popular excitements about railroads, authorized their issue; how grand juries, and county commissioners, and city officers, were moulded to the purposes of the
speculators; how recklessly railroad officers abused the over-
wrought confidence of the public, and what burdens of debt and
taxation have resulted to the people. A moneyed security was
created and thrown upon the market by this paroxysm of the
public mind, and the question is now, how shall the judicial mind
regard it? [1]

Taken together, the hundreds of suits on railroad aid
bonds had an economic content of a magnitude perhaps unprecedented. Though the digests arrange the cases under such
diverse rubrics as public purpose, comity between federal and
state courts, municipal corporations, and negotiable instruments, they find their unity as a phase of the great struggle between farmers and taxpayers on the one hand and railroad
promoters and investors on the other. The Supreme Court
threw its support on the side of the latter groups by a somewhat violent assertion of federal judicial power. The experience of the conference room left no doubt in Justice Miller's
mind that the entire course of decision in this matter was to

---

[1] Diamond v. Lawrence County, 37 Pa. St. 353, 358 (1860).

be explained in terms of a prepossession on the part of a majority of his brethren in favor of bondholders as against taxpayers.

Public policy, in Judge Miller's view, pointed in quite a different direction. One will recall the letter, already quoted,[2] where he says, "I have met with but few things of a character affecting the public good of the whole country that has shaken my faith in human nature as much as the united, vigorous, and selfish effort of the capitalists . . . a class whose only interest or stake in the country is the ownership of these bonds and stocks." At a time when the importunity of astute promoters was making every western county and town a fountain of negotiable securities, he thought it was the duty of the courts to give effect to the limitations upon the authority of municipal authorities. Miller knew the problem in its local context. While at the Iowa bar he had been retained to defend some bond cases and had secured admission to practice before the federal Supreme Court at December term, 1860, with a view to arguing them there.[3] Keokuk and Lee County were deeply involved in the railroad bond question, and in August 1868 Miller wrote:

I have been devoting myself this summer to two or three chancery suits submitted on the circuit, and to an effort to compromise our city debt. I am in the midst of the latter now, with some hope of success, but not sanguine. It is indispensible to any progress in our town. If I succeed I shall feel that I have conferred an immense benefit on my neighbors and fellow citizens, and have added largely to the value of my own property.[4]

But Judge Miller's candor and intellectual integrity preclude any facile assumption that he wished to twist the law because of sympathy for the tax-burdened people of Iowa, and his position in the bond litigation will be found to rest upon very substantial considerations. Even in the retrospect of sixty years the broad equities of the situation seem confused, and

[2] *Supra,* p. 67.
[3] Letter of November 11, 1860.   [4] Letter of August 27, 1868.

trustworthy generalization must emerge from a close analysis of particular instances.

We may consider first Justice Miller's attitude toward the taxing power. After presenting him as an exemplar of judicial forbearance — as in his rejection of considerations arising from "the spirit of the Constitution and of abstract justice" in his dissent in *Hepburn* v. *Griswold*, and his close construction of the due process clause — it may seem strange to come at once to his opinion in *Loan Association* v. *Topeka*,[5] expressing the bold doctrine that where a tax is laid for a purpose which the courts do not regard as "public" they may strike it down without pointing to any specific constitutional objection. The facts were that under statutory authority bonds had been issued to attract an iron works to Topeka, and an action on interest coupons had been brought in the federal court by reason of diversity of citizenship. In holding the legislation *ultra vires*, Justice Miller said:

> The theory of our governments, state and national, is opposed to the deposit of unlimited power anywhere. The executive, the legislative and the judicial branches of these governments are all of limited and defined powers.
> There are limitations on such power which grow out of the essential nature of all free governments; implied reservations of individual rights, without which the social compact could not exist, and which are respected by all governments entitled to the name.

The opinion goes on to argue that freedom from taxation for other than a public purpose is one of those "rights beyond the control of the state."

Justice Clifford, dissenting, took the positivistic position that a court had no authority to nullify legislative acts on the ground that they were "opposed to a general latent spirit supposed to pervade or underlie the constitution."

Justice Miller's expansive talk about inherent limitations on government is often cited as an expression of the doctrine of natural rights which, turned to other purposes by other

---

[5] 20 Wallace 655 (1875).

justices, has been made the instrument for subjecting social legislation to the control of judicial dogmatists. Certainly Miller believed that there were "principles of general constitutional law" from which the maxim that taxation must be for a public purpose is derivable.[6] The doctrine had recently been given classical expression in the leading case of *Lowell* v. *Boston*,[7] in the opinion of Chief Justice Dillon in *Hanson* v. *Vernon*,[8] and in Cooley's *Constitutional Limitations*.[9] It had been enunciated by the Supreme Court of Kansas in a case cited at the bar.[10] In the instant case the federal circuit court had denied recovery on two grounds: because the statute authorizing municipalities to contract debts was found obnoxious to a section of the Kansas constitution, and because aid to an iron works was not for a public purpose. In placing affirmance on the second ground, Justice Miller explained that the Supreme Court was thereby able to avoid a question of state constitutional construction "whose solution we prefer to remit to the State courts." But he was doubtless well pleased to find an opportunity to throw the authority of the Supreme Court behind the doctrine that the citizen can not be taxed to support private enterprise.

Exemption from taxation was a boon to private business only less acceptable than direct aid from the public coffers. When on second thought these favors were discontinued, beneficiaries would claim the protection of the contract clause. Justice Miller always held the view that the power to tax, like

[6] As he said in Davidson v. New Orleans, 96 U. S. 97, 105 (1877), explaining Loan Association v. Topeka. Professor Corwin explains that it was not until much later that this "constitutional waif" was "gathered under the hospitable roof of the due process clause" ("Judicial Review in Action," 74 *University of Pennsylvania Law Review* 639, 669, 1926). *Cf.* Fallbrook Irrigation District v. Bradley, 164 U. S. 112 at 155 and 158 (1896); Missouri Pacific Ry. v. Nebraska, 164 U. S. 403, 417 (1896).

[7] 111 Mass. 454 (1873).

[8] 27 Iowa 28 (1869). Overruled by Stewart v. Board of Supervisors of Peck County, 30 Iowa 9 (1870), as to the constitutionality of aid to railroads, but without denying the proposition that a tax must be for a public purpose.

[9] T. M. Cooley, *A Treatise on the Constitutional Limitations* (Boston: Little, Brown and Company, 1st ed., 1868), pp. 487ff.

[10] Leavenworth County v. Miller, 7 Kan. 479 (1871).

the police power, is inalienable, even by express grant. And for identical reasons:

This is a power which in modern political societies, is absolutely necessary to the continued existence of every such society. . . . To hold, then, that any one of the annual Legislatures can, by contract, deprive the State forever of the power of taxation, is to hold that they can destroy the government which they are appointed to serve. . . . The result of such a principle, under the growing tendency to special and partial legislation, would be, to exempt the rich from taxation, and cast all the burden of the support of government, and the payment of its debts, on those who are too poor or too honest to purchase such immunity.[11]

But this doctrine was never acceptable to a majority of the Court.

Justice Miller's dissents are strewn thickest in the reports of the cases brought to enforce railroad aid bonds. We are apt to forget how largely the financing of the railroads was a public enterprise. Whoever might have the evidences of ownership, and whoever might pocket the profits of railroad promotion, the credit on which the roads were built was raised by a mortgage upon the whole community. The chicanery by which many of these grants were stimulated was unabashed. When the temporary insanity thus induced had passed, there arose a demand for evasion which became merged with the general agrarian discontent of the seventies. In many cases the state judges upheld defenses based on constitutional limitations, want of statutory authority, and the principles of the law of municipal corporations. But the Supreme Court of the United States "set a face of flint against repudiation, even when made on legal grounds deemed solid by the State courts, by municipalities which had been deceived and defrauded."[12] And since diversity of citizenship could almost always be

---

[11] Dissenting, in Washington University v. Rouse, 8 Wallace 439, 443 (1869). He repeats this as his personal opinion while speaking for the Court in New Jersey v. Yard, 95 U. S. 104, 114 (1877); also in his *Lectures on the Constitution* (New York and Albany: Banks and Brothers, 1891), pp. 559ff.

[12] J. F. Dillon, *The Law of Municipal Bonds* (St. Louis: G. I. Jones and Company, 1876), p. 7.

shown,[13] practically all the litigation was brought in the federal courts. In hewing its way the Supreme Court, in Judge Miller's profound conviction, paid no regard to the rightful limits of its own powers and built up a body of law for the protection of bondholders which he regarded as utterly unjustifiable in its legal principles. But before examining how well founded was his criticism we may mark the scope of the conflict by borrowing the language of Judge Dillon, who knew the situation at first hand as counsel,[14] chief justice of Iowa, and federal circuit judge. His view of the law was broadly in accord with that of Justice Miller, and yet in his *Treatise on the Law of Municipal Corporations*, first published in 1872,[15] he was stating the doctrine of the Court with objectivity:

The Supreme Court has refused to follow the subsequent decisions of the state court against the validity of such bonds, in cases where the prior ruling of the state court had been in favor of the power to issue them; it has adopted liberal constructions of statutes and charters authorizing the creation of such debts; it has given no favor to defences based upon mere irregularities in the issue of the bonds or non-compliance with preliminary requirements, not going to the question of power to contract; and has

[13] Without encumbering the page with a critical note on the so-called assignee clause of the several Judiciary Acts — whose purpose has been generally to prevent the creation of diversity jurisdiction by the device of assigning a cause of action — it may be said that the federal courts were never closed to the holder of a municipal bearer bond by reason of the fact that his transferror could not have sued there. (Act of September 24, 1789, § 11; City of Lexington v. Butler, 14 Wallace 282, 293 (1872). Act of March 3, 1875, § 1; Thompson v. Perrine, 106 U. S. 589, 592 (1883). Act of August 13, 1888, § 1; Lake County Commissioners v. Dudley, 173 U. S. 243, 250 (1899).) But where the transfer was merely colorable and collusive, to create diversity of citizenship or to bring the *ad damnum* within the terms of the Act, it was the duty of the federal court to dismiss the suit. (Act of March 3, 1875, § 5; Williams v. Nottawa, 104 U. S. 209 (1881); Farmington v. Pillsbury, 114 U. S. 138 (1885); Waite v. Santa Cruz, 184 U. S. 302 (1902).) To give the federal courts jurisdiction in cases of diversity of citizenship the matter in controversy must have been in excess of $500 prior to the Act of March 3, 1887, which substituted $2000. By the Act of March 3, 1911, the jurisdictional amount was raised to $3000.

[14] He appeared for the defendant in Clapp v. County of Cedar, 5 Iowa 15 (1857).

[15] Chicago: James Cockcroft and Company.

held that the Circuit Courts of the United States were clothed with full authority, by *mandamus* or otherwise, to enforce the collection of judgments rendered on such bonds, and that this authority could not in the least be interfered with, either by the legislature or the judiciary of the states. It has upheld and protected the rights of such creditors with a firm hand, disregarding, at times, it would seem, principles which it applied in other cases, and asserting the jurisdiction and authority of the federal courts with such striking energy and vigor as apparently, if not actually, to trench upon the lawful rights of the states and the acknowledged powers of the state tribunals; yet, upon the whole, there is little doubt that its course has had the approval of the profession in general and of the public, which neither appreciates nor cares for fine distinctions, and it will be well if it shall teach municipalities the lesson that if, having the power to do so, they issue negotiable securities, they cannot escape payment if these find their way into the hands of innocent purchasers.[16]

Now to the cases, of which *Gelpcke* v. *Dubuque* [17] is the head and front. The circumstances are familiar. The Supreme Court of Iowa, overruling previous decisions by a divided court, had denied mandamus to compel a county to issue bonds in payment of a subscription to railroad stock: — first, because the legislation relied on´ had theretofore been misconstrued; and secondly, supposing erroneous statutory construction might otherwise have been left undisturbed, because there were two constitutional objections which forbade. Aid to a railroad was not a public purpose for which the citizen might be taxed, and the constitution specifically provided that "the State shall not, directly or indirectly, become a stockholder in any corporation." [18] Would the federal courts, where the same issue was presented in cases between citizens of different states, be bound by this latest exposition of the constitutional law of Iowa? No, said Justice Swayne for the Court, adopting Taney's statement that

the sound and true rule is, that if the contract, when made, was valid by the laws of the State as then expounded by all de-

[16] Section 416. The work was dedicated to Justice Miller.
[17] 1 Wallace 175 (1864).
[18] Iowa Constitution of 1846, art. 8, § 2, interpreted in Iowa *ex rel.* Burlington and Missouri R. R. *v.* County of Wapello, 13 Iowa 388 (1862).

partments of the government, and administered in its courts of justice, its validity and obligation cannot be impaired by any subsequent action of legislation, or decision of its courts altering the construction of the law.[19]

Justice Swayne went on to say:

The same principle applies where there is a change of judicial decision as to the constitutional power of the Legislature to enact the law. . . . We shall never immolate truth, justice, and the law, because a state tribunal has erected the altar and decreed the sacrifice.[20]

In an able dissenting opinion Justice Miller contended that

the Court has, in this case, taken a step in advance of anything theretofore decided by it on this subject. That advance is in the direction of a usurpation of the right, which belongs to the state courts, to decide as a finality upon the construction of state constitutions and state statutes. This invasion is made in a case where there is no pretense that the constitution, as thus construed, is any infraction of the laws or Constitution of the United States.

He conceded that, under the circumstances, the moral force of the contention of the majority was very great;

and I think, taken in connection with some fancied duty of this court to enforce contracts, over and beyond that appertaining to other courts, has given the majority a leaning towards the adoption of a rule, which in my opinion cannot be sustained either on principle or authority.

And this usurpation had been "accompanied by language as unsuited to the dispassionate dignity of this court, as it is disrespectful to another court of at least concurrent jurisdiction over the matter in question."

What this may lead to it is not possible now to foresee, nor do I wish to point out the field of judicial conflicts, which may never occur, but which if they shall occur, will weigh heavily on that court which should have yielded to the other, but did not.

[19] Ohio Life Ins. and Trust Co. *v.* Debolt, 16 Howard 416, 432 (1853).
[20] Gelpcke *v.* Dubuque, 1 Wallace 175, 206 (1864). It will be noted that the majority did not claim that the Court should exercise an independent judgment. The previous rule was to be upheld, right or wrong.

This disagreement between Miller and his brethren calls for some examination of the basis of federal judicial power. That power may be invoked, first, by reason of the matter involved. Under this head come cases arising under the Constitution, as, for example, a case where it is alleged that a state has passed a law impairing the obligation of a contract. Where such a contention has been rejected by the state court, Section 25 of the Judiciary Act granted a review by the Supreme Court of the United States. In order to give full effect to the constitutional prohibition, that Court had taken the position that it must decide for itself whether there was a contract: obviously this would often be the crux of the matter.

The Constitution also includes controversies between citizens of different states within the judicial power of the United States. And, subject to varying restrictions, Congress has given inferior federal courts original jurisdiction in such cases. By the terms of Section 34 of the Judiciary Act, "the laws of the several states" were to be "regarded as rules of decision" by the federal courts. In *Swift* v. *Tyson*,[21] Justice Story, speaking for the Court, had construed "laws" to mean statutes. "In the ordinary use of language it will hardly be contended that the decisions of courts constitute laws. They are, at most, only evidences of what the laws are, and are not themselves laws." So it was decided that while a federal court must follow the decisions of the courts of a state as to its "positive statutes" — and also in cases of land titles, etc. — it would exercise an independent judgment on "questions of a more general nature," especially of "general commercial law." At the term prior to that at which *Gelpke* v. *Dubuque* was decided, Justice Swayne had enunciated the established doctrine in declaring:

The construction given to a statute of a State by the highest judicial tribunal of such State, is regarded as a part of the statute, and is as binding upon the courts of the United States as the text.

If the highest judicial tribunal of a State adopt new views as to the proper construction of such a statute, and reverse its former decisions, this court will follow the latest settled adjudications.[22]

---

[21] 16 Peters 1 (1842).   [22] Leffingwell *v.* Warren, 2 Black 599 (1862).

But in suits to enforce municipal bonds the Supreme Court struck down defenses not only where based on the common law of the state, but also in the teeth of state decisions holding the bonds to have been invalid upon statutory grounds or by force of some general principle or some specific provision of the state constitution.

When one looks to the decisions which at various times were disregarded one is impressed by the high character of the judges who made them and also by the fact that the reasoning is cogent even if the weight of authority was heavily on the other side. In Iowa it was Justice George G. Wright whose dissent at last became triumphant in the Wapello case.[23] It is not necessary to establish his standing. Miller had strongly supported his reëlection in 1860,[24] and his colleague, Judge Dillon, later said that "the verdict of the Bar at the time and now would be that all in all Judge Wright has had no equal among the State's chief justices or judges." [25] Nor need one speak in praise of Chief Justice Dixon of Wisconsin, nor of the outstanding Michigan bench on which sat Chief Justice Campbell and Judge Cooley. Certainly the decisions which denied recovery on railroad aid bonds cannot be dismissed as the work of pliant creatures ready to make themselves the instruments of repudiating valid debts.

The doctrine of *Gelpcke* v. *Dubuque,* as Mr. Justice Holmes later remarked, was one "which it took this court a good while to explain." [26] Judge Swayne's opinion had suggested the indefensible theory that for the Supreme Court of Iowa to reverse itself amounted under the circumstances to a violation of the constitutional provision that "no State shall pass any law impairing the obligation of contracts," and Chief Justice Waite, restating the doctrine, placed it expressly on that

[23] Iowa *ex rel.* Burlington and Missouri R. R. *v.* County of Wapello, 13 Iowa 388 (1862).

[24] *Gate City,* October 10, 1860.

[25] Response to the sentiment "Early Iowa Lawyers and Judges," at the annual dinner of the Iowa Society of New York, April 28, 1906, 40 *American Law Review* 377, 381 (1906).

[26] Dissenting in Muhlker *v.* New York and Harlem R. R., 197 U. S. 544, 573 (1905).

ground.[27] In propounding this rationale for disregarding the decisions of a state court construing its own constitution and statutes the justices were unconscious of any inconsistency with the fiction of *Swift* v. *Tyson,* whereby they disregarded state decisions on common law by saying that such decisions were not themselves the law of the state but only declarations of what the law was supposed to be.[28] If the theory of the Gelpcke opinion had been tenable, it would have followed that a decision of the Iowa court holding municipal bonds invalid was itself reviewable by the Supreme Court under Section 25 of the Judiciary Act on the contention that in reversing itself the state court had denied a federal right. But counsel who tested that theory in two Iowa bond cases were turned out of court.[29] Eventually it was not only established that the contract clause had no reference to the state's judicial action,[30] but it was even denied that *Gelpcke* v. *Dubuque* and the cases following it had been rested on that ground.[31]

It may well be that the immediate result of the Gelpcke case was desirable. The magnitude of the injustice in the bond cases argued persuasively for a special rule. The consequential detriments have been less easy to assess. First-rate minds have differed in their reaction to the case.[32] Justice

[27] Douglass *v.* Pike County, 101 U. S. 677 (1880).

[28] John Chipman Gray, *The Nature and Sources of the Law* (New York: The Macmillan Company, 2nd ed., 1931), pp. 251ff.; William H. Rand, Jr., "Swift v. Tyson versus Gelpcke v. Dubuque," 8 *Harvard Law Review* 328 (1895).

[29] Railroad Co. *v.* Rock, 4 Wallace 177 (1867), per Miller, J.; Railroad Co. *v.* McClure, 10 Wallace 511 (1871), per Swayne, J. Miller, J., repeats the proposition in Knox *v.* Exchange Bank, 12 Wallace 379 (1871).

[30] New Orleans Waterworks Co. *v.* Louisiana Sugar Co., 125 U. S. 18, 30 (1888); Central Land Co. *v.* Laidley, 159 U. S. 103 (1895).

[31] Taft, C. J., in Tidal Oil Co., *v.* Flanagan, 263 U. S. 444, 452 (1924).

[32] Justice Holmes frequently criticized its doctrinal infirmities — first in a note in the twelfth edition of Kent's *Commentaries,* and later in dissenting opinions in Muhlker *v.* New York and Harlem R. R., 197 U. S. 544, 573 (1905), and Kuhn *v.* Fairmount Coal Co., 215 U. S. 349, 371 (1910). James Bradley Thayer in "The Case of *Gelpcke* v. *Dubuque,*" 4 *Harvard Law Review* 311 (1891), and John Chipman Gray, *loc cit.,* thought that the result was right. *Cf.* the interesting article by Justice J. M. Read of the Supreme Court of Pennsylvania, "The Rule in *Gelpcke* v. *Dubuque,*" 9 *American Law Review* 381, 397 (1875), in which he says, "That the Supreme Court should have adopted the principles it did, provided that these latter are not extended be-

Bradley — "in order to obviate any misapprehensions that may arise from language and expressions used in previous cases" — finally derived a more satisfying explanation from the duty of the federal courts to administer justice "unaffected by local prejudices and sectional views." [33] Justice Miller accepted this exposition,[34] and indeed he never challenged the doctrine that, on questions of common law, the federal courts were free to exercise an independent judgment.[35] But in insisting that they must recognize rights of property derived from a state statute as construed by the state court he pointed out that to hold otherwise would "introduce into the jurisprudence of the state . . . the discordant elements of a substantial right which is protected in one set of courts and denied in the other, with no superior to decide which is right"; [36] — an objection which was equally applicable to the doctrine of *Swift* v. *Tyson*.

---

yond the class of cases in which they are laid down, is not, perhaps, a subject for regret. But this is true only so long as the doctrine before us is admitted to be an anomaly; claim for it more, and hopeless, irremediable confusion in the science of the law ensues."

[33] Burgess v. Seligman, 107 U. S. 20, 33–34 (1883). Justice Bradley was inclined to support the extension of federal judicial protection.

[34] Bucher v. Cheshire R. R., 125 U. S. 555, 584 (1888). Miller, J., there remarks that the question is "an embarrassing one," that the language of the cases is not "entirely harmonious," and that it is "a subject which has not been ascertained and defined with that uniformity and precision desirable in a matter of such great importance." The instant case illustrated one of the consequences of the doctrine of Swift v. Tyson. Bucher, having sustained injuries while traveling on the railroad on Sunday, sued in the Massachusetts courts. When the Supreme Judicial Court held that the Lord's Day Act barred recovery (Bucher v. Fitchburg R. R., 131 Mass. 156 (1881)), plaintiff took a non-suit and, on the basis of diversity of citizenship, started anew in the federal courts. Justice Miller's opinion gave effect to the state statute as construed by the state court.

[35] Thus in Yates v. Milwaukee, 10 Wallace 497, 506 (1870), he said: "This [question] does not depend upon State statute or local law. The law which governs the case is the common law, on which this court has never acknowledged the right of the State courts to control our decisions, except, perhaps, in a class of cases where the State courts have established, by repeated decisions, a rule of property in regard to land titles peculiar to the State."

[36] Brine v. Insurance Co., 96 U. S. 627, 635 (1877). When in Mason v. United States, 260 U. S. 545 (1923), the Supreme Court laid down the rule that in equity cases to which Section 34 of the Judiciary Act did not apply it would follow the local statutes and decisions, it quoted with approval and followed the judgment pronounced by Miller, J., in this case.

This entire subject has been actively canvassed since Justice Miller's death. In 1893 Mr. Justice Field, repenting previous error, declared his conviction that the federal courts had no authority, save in matters specifically authorized or delegated to the United States by the Constitution, to refuse to recognize the autonomy of the state courts.[37] Justice Holmes, dissenting, protested against extensions of the doctrine of *Swift* v. *Tyson*, and pointed out that "law in the sense in which courts speak of it today does not exist without some definite authority behind it"; there was no "august corpus," no "transcendental body of law outside of any particular State but obligatory within it unless and until changed by statute," which federal courts might apply in disregard of state decisions.[38] An extensive literature grew up about the controversy.[39] Mr. Charles Warren, discovering the original draft of the Judiciary Act of 1789, challenged the historical accuracy of Story's construction of its thirty-fourth section.[40] In 1938, when a renewal of its membership permitted, the Supreme Court, in *Erie Railroad* v. *Tompkins*, not only overruled *Swift* v. *Tyson* on the point of statutory construction, but

---

However, Justice Miller's dissent in Tioga R. R. *v.* Blossburg and Corning R. R., 20 Wallace 137, 151 (1873), should be noted. In a case arising in an inferior federal court for New York, the Supreme Court bowed to the holding of the New York courts that, though a foreign corporation might be present in New York for the purpose of being sued, it was none the less "out of state" within the meaning of the Statute of Limitations. Justice Hunt, fresh from the New York Court of Appeals, was present and concurred in holding that such was the meaning of the New York decisions. But Miller, J. (Strong, J. concurring), dissented: "Nor do I believe that the courts of any State of the Union except New York, have ever held that a person doing business within the State and liable at all times to be sued and served personally with process cannot avail himself of the statute of limitations. . . . The liability to suit where process can at all times be served must in the nature of things be the test of the running of the statute."

[37] Dissenting in Baltimore and Ohio R. R. *v.* Baugh, 149 U. S. 368, 390, 401 (1893).

[38] Black and White Taxi. Co. *v.* B. and Y. Taxi. Co., 276 U. S. 518, 532 (1928); similarly in Muhlker *v.* New York and Harlem R. R. and in Kuhn *v.* Fairmont Coal Co., *supra*.

[39] Cited in the opinion of Brandeis, J., in Erie R. R. *v.* Tompkins, 304 U. S. 64 (1938).

[40] "New Light on the History of the Federal Judiciary Act of 1789," 37 *Harvard Law Review* 49 (1923).

went on to assert that the Constitution made it incumbent on federal courts to accept the voice of the highest court of a state as the authoritative expression of its law. Speaking for the Court, Mr. Justice Brandeis cited approvingly Justice Miller's dissent in *Gelpcke* v. *Dubuque*, and declared that "except in matters governed by the Federal Constitution or by Acts of Congress, the law to be applied in any case is the law of the State. And whether the law of the State shall be declared by its legislature in a statute or by its highest court in a decision is not a matter of federal concern." The case does not expressly overrule *Gelpcke* v. *Dubuque*, nor was there any occasion for the Court to address itself particularly to the situation where the state court, by reversing itself, has affected the validity of past transactions. If that specific question arose again it would doubtless provoke a mighty contest. The suggestion has been made that the Court might be induced to treat the retroactive application of the overruling state decision as a deprivation of property without due process of law [41] — a possibility which of course did not exist in 1864, and which as yet is not supported in the jurisprudence of the Court.[42]

Ten years after *Gelpcke* v. *Dubuque* was decided the Court extended the doctrine to situations where the state court had held bond issues invalid without overruling any former decision. The Supreme Court of Wisconsin, having previously affirmed the constitutionality of taxation for the purchase of

[41] Harry Shulman, "The Demise of Swift v. Tyson," 47 *Yale Law Journal* 1336, 1351 (1938). *Cf.* Robert H. Freeman, "Retroactive Operation of Decisions," 18 *Columbia Law Review* 230 (1918).

[42] See cases cited in Brinkerhoff-Faris Co. *v.* Hill, 281 U. S. 673, 680 note 7 (1930). *Cf.* Peoples Banking Co. *v.* Sterling, 300 U. S. 175, 183 (1937). In Brinkerhoff-Faris Co. *v.* Hill it was held that due process in the primary sense had been denied where the state court dismissed a suit to enjoin the collection of a tax on the ground that plaintiff had neglected to seek an administrative review, though prior to the instant case it had consistently been held that no such review existed, and the new-found remedy was, by the lapse of time, unavailable to the plaintiff. An interesting opinion by Cardozo, J., in Great Northern Ry. *v.* Sunburst Co., 287 U. S. 358, 364 (1932), holds that it is not a denial of due process for a state court, while announcing a different rule for the future, to apply its previous construction of a statute to the parties then before it. "We think the Federal constitution has no voice upon the subject."

railroad stock,[43] ruled otherwise as to a donation to a railroad.[44] Chief Justice Dixon distinguished the earlier cases and held that while the power of a municipality to become part owner of a railroad might be deduced from its power to build the road for itself, a gift to a privately owned railroad was not for such a public purpose as would support a tax. The distinction was not very satisfying, and the Chief Justice was candid enough to explain later that a majority of the judges had thought the earlier cases wrongly decided and had drawn a line which would leave them undisturbed while arresting the spread of their doctrine.[45] Judge Drummond, the federal circuit judge, thereafter took the view that *Gelpcke* v. *Dubuque* did not control inasmuch as the Wisconsin court had not overruled any precedent, and declared that the federal court "is sitting here to administer the laws of Wisconsin . . . precisely as the court of the State would apply them." [46] But the Supreme Court (Chase, Miller, and Davis dissenting) reversed the judgment of the circuit court.[47] Justice Strong declared that the federal courts need not follow the decision in the Whiting case, because "whether a use is public or private is not a question of constitutional construction. It is a question of general law. It has as much reference to the constitution of any other state as it has to the State of Wisconsin." [48] An alternative line of reasoning was said to lead to the same conclusion. Justice Strong quoted from earlier Wisconsin decisions defining a public purpose in other connections, such as the law of eminent domain; it followed that a purchaser of bonds donated to a railroad had reason to expect that the same doctrine would be applied to his situation; therefore if the state court disappointed him the federal courts should do as much for him as they had done for Gelpcke.

[43] Clark *v.* City of Janesville, 10 Wis. 136 (1859); Bushnell *v.* Beloit, 10 Wis. 195 (1859).

[44] Whiting *v.* Sheboygan & Fond du Lac R. R., 25 Wis. 167 (1870).

[45] Phillips *v.* Town of Albany, 28 Wis. 340 at 357 (1871).

[46] Olcott *v.* Fond du Lac County, Fed. Case No. 10,479 (C. C. E. D. Wis. 1870).

[47] Olcott *v.* The Supervisors, 16 Wallace 678 (1873).

[48] *Id.* at 690.

The position of the federal Supreme Court was even weaker when in *Pine Grove Township* v. *Talcott* [49] it put itself in opposition to the Supreme Court of Michigan. For when the latter court decided in the Salem Township and Bay City cases that taxation in aid of railroads was invalid and unconstitutional,[50] it did not reverse any decision, nor did counsel in the Supreme Court point to any expression on which investors had relied. The most that Justice Swayne could say on that score was that the court had not lifted its voice when the permissive legislation was passed. But he did not suggest how it might have cried out in advance of any litigation. Anyone who consulted Cooley's *Constitutional Limitations* must have gained the impression that one judge on the Michigan bench preferred the cases which denied power to tax in aid of railroads.[51] When, in the Salem Township case, the state court first passed upon the question it listened to argument for eight days and then, in a three-to-one division, held the tax invalid. The prevailing opinions ran in terms of public purpose, and the decision was not placed upon any specific constitutional limitation. Next year, in the Bay City case, the court sought to buttress its position by declaring that the due process clause and other particular provisions of the state constitution forbade taxation to support railroad construction. But when *Pine Grove Township* v. *Talcott* brought the question before the federal judiciary and presently to the Supreme Court, Justice Swayne swept all this aside. He held that the Michigan court had been in error, and proceeded to show what the state constitution really meant; chided the state judges for fabricating constitutional restraints not derivable from the text; and concluded: "It does not belong to courts to interpolate constitutional restrictions. Our duty is to apply the law, not to make it. All power may be abused where no

---

[49] 19 Wallace 666 (1874). Miller and Davis, JJ., dissented. Waite, the new Chief Justice, and Bradley, J., did not sit.

[50] People *ex rel.* Detroit and Howell R. R. *v.* Township of Salem, 20 Mich. 452 (1870); People *ex rel.* Bay City *v.* State Treasurer, 23 Mich. 499 (1871).

[51] Cooley, *Constitutional Limitations* (1st ed. 1868), pp. 213–219, with notes.

safeguards are provided. The remedy in such cases lies with the people, and not with the judiciary." [52]

In a later bond case [53] Justice Swayne, passing on a contention where his position was doubtless well taken, said: "Our duty is to execute the law, not to make it. Such an interpolation would involve the judge-made law which Bentham so earnestly denounces." Considering how much of the law of municipal bonds had been made by the Supreme Court, with Justice Swayne in the lead, this interjected censure of judicial legislation sounds naive.

One of the objectionable features of the Supreme Court's indifference to state adjudications in applying state statutes was illustrated in litigation over scrip issued by the city of Kenosha. The constitution of Wisconsin made it the duty of the legislature to restrict municipal taxing and borrowing powers so as to prevent abuse. The Kenosha charter purported to give the city *carte blanche*. The city, expressly in pursuance of this authority, issued scrip to buy railroad stock. Holding the charter provision unconstitutional, the state court upheld an injunction to prevent the collection of a tax to retire the scrip.[54] Then an action was carried up through the federal courts on scrip of the same issue, and the Supreme Court, examining the laws of Wisconsin, found a special act authorizing Kenosha to vote for a limited issue of bonds to the same railroad, and held that the scrip sued on could be upheld under this enactment.[55] Moreover, subsequent legislation recognizing the scrip issue was held in effect to cure any infirmity. Thereafter the state court pointed out that the Supreme Court of the United States had acted under a misapprehension: the authority granted by the special act had already been completely exhausted.[56] The Wisconsin court went on to decide that the subsequent legislative recognition of the scrip had not sufficed to cure the want of constitutional

[52] 19 Wallace 666, 677 (1874).
[53] Calhoun County *v.* Galbraith, 99 U. S. 214 (1879).
[54] Foster *v.* City of Kenosha, 12 Wis. 616 (1860).
[55] Campbell *v.* Kenosha, 5 Wallace 194 (1867).
[56] Fisk *v.* City of Kenosha, 26 Wis. 23 (1870).

power to issue it. But the federal Supreme Court, two months earlier, had reached the opposite conclusion, Justice Miller alone dissenting.[57]

Having determined to protect the right of the bondholder, the Court was led to go further and give him a remedy, even in the teeth of state law. In *Riggs* v. *Johnson County*,[58] in order to give effect to a judgment recovered by a foreign bondholder, the Court directed the circuit court to grant mandamus to compel county officers to levy a tax which a state court had perpetually enjoined them from issuing. Justice Miller challenged the decision of the majority on every point, and Chief Justice Chase and Justice Grier concurred in his conclusions. Then in *Butz* v. *Muscatine* [59] the Court advanced to the point of announcing that it would determine for itself the construction of a state statute — in this case one governing the bondholder's remedy — without regard to the consistent adjudications of the highest court of Iowa. A tax limit had been imposed on the city in 1852. In 1854 bonds were issued. The state code of 1860, reënacting a section of the code of 1851, provided in the title on Execution that where judgment was recovered against a municipal corporation which could not be satisfied by a levy on its property or by payment in scrip, "a tax must be levied as early as practicable." The Iowa court had held repeatedly that this section of the Code did not override the tax limit imposed by a municipal charter.[60] But the Supreme Court, per Justice Swayne, rather than "blindly following the footsteps of others," decided otherwise. Justice Miller (with whom Chief Justice Chase concurred) dissented energetically on the ground that the Court had no authority to depart from the uniform construction given to

---

[57] Kenosha v. Lamson, 9 Wallace 477 (1870).
[58] 6 Wallace 166 (1868). To the same effect was Weber v. Lee County, 6 Wallace 210 (1868), decided the same day. Miller, J., being a resident and taxpayer in Lee County, took no part in this case.
[59] 8 Wallace 575 (1869).
[60] Clark, Dodge, and Co. v. Davenport, 14 Iowa 494 (1863); Coy v. Lyons City, 17 Iowa 1 (1864); Oswald v. Thedinga, 17 Iowa 13 (1864); Porter v. Thomson, 22 Iowa 391 (1867).

a state statute, and went on to show that the two Iowa laws were perfectly consistent. He concluded:

> These frequent dissents in this class of subjects are as distasteful to me as they can be to any one else. But when I am compelled, as I was last spring, by the decisions of this court, to enter an order to commit to jail at one time over a hundred of the best citizens of Iowa, for obeying as they thought their oath of office required them to do, an injunction issued by a competent court of their own State, founded, as these gentlemen conscientiously believed, on the true interpretation of their own statute, an injunction which, in my own private judgment, they were legally bound to obey, I must be excused if, when sitting here, I give expression to convictions which my duty compels me to disregard in the circuit court.[61]

If one goes back to examine the merits of the question of statutory construction in *Butz* v. *Muscatine*, it seems pretty clear that the Iowa court and Justice Miller were right, and the majority of the Supreme Court wrong. And indeed the Court itself subsequently conceded that this had been the case.[62]

It is not surprising that a demand arose in the West for legislation to take away the jurisdiction of the federal courts in suits against municipal corporations.[63]

Looking for a moment at the substantive law, as distinguished from questions of the power of the federal courts, the leading case was *Knox County* v. *Aspinwall*,[64] which had been decided by the Supreme Court three years before Miller came on the bench. That was a suit to recover on railroad aid bonds, and the defense was the omission of the sheriff to give notice of the election at which the issue had been voted upon. The Court rested its judgment for the plaintiff on two grounds: one was that where the statute laid down some condition precedent, but invested the officers of the municipality

[61] Butz *v*. Muscatine, 8 Wallace 575, 587 (1869).

[62] Supervisors *v*. United States, 18 Wallace 71 (1873), Clifford and Swayne, JJ., dissenting.

[63] *The Nation*, New York, January 2, 1879, p. 5, cited by A. M. Hillhouse, *Municipal Bonds* (New York: Prentice-Hall, 1936), p. 166.

[64] 21 Howard 539 (1859).

with power to determine whether the condition had been complied with, their recital that it had been, made in the bonds issued by them and held by a bona fide purchaser, bound the municipality. The other and much broader ground was that if "the bonds on their face import a compliance . . . the purchaser is not bound to look further." This alternative rule amounted to imposing an unconditional liability for any bonds which the municipal officers might have issued, without regard to whether conditions precedent had been complied with. In some later cases it was applied. But the rule first stated above came to much the same thing if the Court was disposed to read all statutes as conferring power to bind the municipality by a conclusive recital of compliance.

This decision was based on the authority of an English case,[65] holding that where the directors of a joint stock company had power to borrow such sums as should be authorized by a resolution of the company, a lender had a right to presume that such a resolution had in fact been passed. Justice Miller thought that where, as in municipal borrowing, the records establishing authority were open to inspection, a different rule would govern and the lender should be bound to inform himself. He would have applied the principle which he had enunciated for the Court in *The Floyd Acceptances*,[66] where it was decided that the government was not liable on a bill of exchange which an officer had accepted without authority. Of course it was not denied that the purchaser of a municipal bond would be affected by a total absence of statutory authority to issue it.[67] But the situation constantly presented was that where the officers of the municipality were empowered to issue bonds to pay for railroad stock subject to some condition, as for instance, "no such subscription shall be made until the question has been submitted to the legal voters of said city, town, or township";[68] or until two thirds

[65] Royal British Bank *v.* Turquand, 6 Ellis and Blackburn 327 (1856).
[66] 7 Wallace 666 (1869).
[67] Anthony *v.* Jasper County, 101 U. S. 693 (1880).
[68] Town of Coloma *v.* Eaves, 92 U. S. 484 (1876).

of the resident taxpayers appearing on the last assessment roll should have filed written assent; [69] or unless the yearly interest on the bonds would be not greater than 1 per cent of the taxable property of the township.[70] In all these cases the Court took the view that the legislature could not have meant that a purchaser was bound to determine for himself whether the condition had been complied with, pointing out that that would be difficult for buyers in distant markets and thus would depress the value of the bonds; declared that *Knox County* v. *Aspinwall* governed, pointing out that its broader ground had often been followed and never overruled, but reasserting its narrower ground as undoubtedly the law; and construed the statutes as making the issuing officers the judges of whether there had been compliance with the condition.[71]

Against all this Justice Miller (Justices Field and Davis concurring) cried out:

The simplicity of the device by which this doctrine is upheld as to municipal bonds is worthy the admiration of all who wish to profit by the frauds of municipal officers.

It is, that wherever a condition or limitation is imposed upon the power of those officers in issuing bonds, they are the sole and final judges of those powers. If they decide to issue them, the law presumes that the conditions on which their powers depended existed, or that the limitation upon the exercise of the power has been complied with; and especially and particularly if they make a *false recital* of the fact on which the power depends in the paper they issue, this false recital has the effect of creating a power which had no existence without it. . . .

There is no reason, in the nature of the condition on which the power depends in these cases, why any purchaser should not take notice of its existence before he buys. The bonds in each case were issued at one time, as one act, of one date, and in payment of one subscription. All this was a matter of record in the town where it was done.

---

[69] Town of Venice *v.* Murdock, 92 U. S. 494 (1876).

[70] Marcy *v.* Township of Oswego, 92 U. S. 637 (1876); Humboldt Township *v.* Long, 92 U. S. 642 (1876).

[71] Strong, J., in Town of Coloma *v.* Eaves, *supra*. "Probably the fullest statement of the settled doctrine of this court," said Harlan, J., in Northern National Bank *v.* Porter Township, 110 U. S. 608, 616 (1884).

He shows how all the relevant facts were of public record and accessible to all.

In the matter of a power depending on these facts, in any other class of cases, it would be held that, before buying these bonds, the purchaser must look to those matters on which their validity depended. . . .

If one of two innocent persons must suffer for the unauthorized act of the township or county officers, it is clear that he who could, before parting with his money, have easily ascertained that they were unauthorized, should lose, rather than the property-holder, who might not know anything of the matter, or, if he did, had no power to prevent the wrong.[72]

Justice Bradley, specially concurring, dissented from the broader version of *Knox County* v. *Aspinwall*, but held that where the statute imposed upon a municipal officer the duty of ascertaining whether conditions precedent had been complied with, the corporation was estopped by his recital to that effect in the bonds. Of course a state legislature might provide expressly how the requisite facts should be determined,

---

[72] Dissenting in Humboldt Township v. Long, 92 U. S. 642 (1876). In the leading case of Hern v. Nichols, 1 Salkeld 289 (1701), holding that the principal was liable for the fraud of his agent committed in the course of the employment, Lord Holt had used these words: "For seeing that somebody must be the loser by this deceit, it is more reason that he that employs and puts a trust and confidence in the deceiver should be a loser, than a stranger." Distinguishing this principle in a municipal bond case, Gould v. Town of Sterling, 23 N. Y. 439, 463 (1861), the Court of Appeals of New York said: "The reason upon which this rule is founded is that given by Lord Holt in Hern v. Nichols, viz., that, where one of two innocent parties must suffer through the misconduct of another, it is reasonable that he who has employed the delinquent party, and thus held him out to the world as worthy of confidence, should be the loser. This reason can, of course, only apply to a case where the principal has himself employed the agent, and voluntarily conferred upon him power to do the act. This clearly is not such a case. The agents here were designated, not by the town, but by the legislature; and no power whatever was conferred by the town, unless the assent of the taxpayers was obtained. Any representation, therefore, by the supervisor and commissioners in respect to such assent would be a representation as to the very existence of their power. Such representations, as we have seen, are never binding upon the principal." So, where the statute made the assent of two thirds of the resident taxpayers a condition precedent to the power of the officers to issue bonds, it was held that the town was not bound by a representation that such assent had been obtained. The Supreme Court refused to follow this decision when bonds issued under the same statute were sued on in the federal courts (Town of Venice v. Murdock, *supra*, at 501).

but ordinarily it omitted to do so, thereby leaving it to the courts to decide whether to give conclusive effect to a recital. Cogent reasons could be urged in support of either view. When *Knox County* v. *Aspinwall* was decided in 1859, the Supreme Court was unembarrassed by any decision on the point by the courts of Indiana where the action arose.[73] But in later cases from states whose courts, with perfect propriety, had declared a different doctrine as the law of that state, the Supreme Court nevertheless persisted in its own view. It may seem that if municipal bonds were to be sold on any large scale, no more lenient rule would have sufficed.[74] But this

[73] In fact, when the question arose before the Supreme Court of Indiana in 1860 it cited the Aspinwall case as having settled "a principle that is entirely applicable here. . . . We might rest the case here, on the authority of that . . ." (The Evansville &c R. R. *v.* City of Evansville, 15 Ind. 395, 419, 1860).

[74] Where a bond issue was held invalid there was ordinarily no mode of recovery available to the bondholder. He had no right of action against his transferror on the ground of failure of consideration. "If the buyer desires special protection, he must take a guaranty. . . . It would be unreasonably harsh to hold all those through whose hands such instruments may have passed liable according to the principles which the plaintiffs in error insist shall be applied in this case," said Swayne, J., for the Court in Otis *v.* Cullum, 92 U. S. 447, 449 (1875) — a suit to recover the amount paid for some of the bonds held invalid in Loan Association *v.* Topeka, 20 Wallace 655 (1875).

Where corporations had purported to enter into obligations later held to have been *ultra vires*, "the courts," said Justice Miller, "have gone a long way to enable parties who have parted with property or money on the faith of such contracts, to obtain justice by recovery of the property or the money specifically, or as money had and received to plaintiff's use" (Salt Lake City *v.* Hollister, 118 U. S. 256, 263, 1886). Thus in Louisiana *v.* Wood, 102 U. S. 294 (1880), it was held that recovery could be sustained on the theory of mistake, or failure of consideration, or as for money obtained through imposition, where the city had lawful power to borrow, but had sold bonds later held invalid because antedated so as to appear to have been issued prior to the effective date of a statute requiring registration before issue. Where a city had loaned its bonds to a manufacturing company, taking a mortgage as security, and the bond issue was held invalid under the doctrine of Loan Association *v.* Topeka, the mortgagor's transferees were entitled to the net proceeds of the security. (Parkersburg *v.* Brown, 106 U. S. 487, 1883.) *Cf.* also Hitchcock *v.* Galveston, 96 U. S. 341 (1878); Chapman *v.* Douglas County Commissioners, 107 U. S. 348 (1883); Read *v.* Plattsmouth, 107 U. S. 568 (1883). But where municipal bonds had been held void because issued in excess of the constitutional limit of indebtedness, Buchanan *v.* Litchfield, 102 U. S. 278 (1880), the constitutional limit was a bar to recovery on the theory of an implied contract to repay; nor, the money (with other funds) having been applied to public works, did the lender have a lien thereon (Litchfield *v.*

consideration was not enough to justify the Court in disregarding the considered judgment of the courts of the state where the transactions took place. As Justice Miller said in the dissenting opinion just quoted:

> It is therefore clear that, so long as this doctrine is upheld, it is not in the power of the legislature to authorize these corporations to issue bonds under any special circumstances, or with any limitation in the use of the power, which may not be disregarded with impunity.
>
> It may be the wisest policy to prevent the issue of bonds altogether. But it is not for this court to dictate a policy for the states on that subject.[75]

Whether the courts should look with favor upon the issue of negotiable instruments by municipal corporations had been a matter of some discussion. In 1860 the Supreme Court of Pennsylvania had denied the quality of negotiability to municipal bonds, thereby preserving defenses against holders for value.[76] But this view was admittedly without support in other jurisdictions, and the Supreme Court declined to apply it in cases from Pennsylvania. In *County of Mercer* v. *Hackett*,[77] Justice Grier hailed this new financial invention and spoke in praise of that malleability of the common law which enabled it to adapt itself to new needs of the commercial world — though he referred with characteristic asperity to the epidemic of municipal insanity and the knavery of railroad promoters. Ten years later Justice Bradley, speaking for himself and Justices Miller, Davis, and Field, in *Nashville* v. *Ray*,[78] held that municipal corporations do not have power, without legislative authority express or clearly implied, to issue negotiable securities — adding a vigorous discussion of recent misconceptions of the limited nature of the

---

Ballou, 114 U. S. 190 (1885), per Miller, J.). In the main it was not possible to restore the parties to their original situation or its equivalent.

[75] 92 U. S. at 647.
[76] Diamond v. Lawrence County, 37 Pa. St. 353 (1860) per Woodward, J.
[77] 1 Wallace 83 (1864).
[78] 19 Wallace 468 (1874).

authority of municipal officers.[79] Justices Clifford, Swayne, and Strong dissented from this holding. Justice Miller took heart from the decision "as indicating a disposition on the part of the court to return to the old principle of holding these corporations within the just limits of their granted powers and protecting the citizen against contracts made without authority." [80]

Some of the most interesting of Justice Miller's letters are those dealing with this bond litigation. His brother-in-law had argued one of these cases on behalf of the city of Galveston in December 1877.[81] On January 13 Miller wrote:

Your case was decided against you in conference yesterday and the composition of the opinion committed to Judge Strong. When it first came up in conference the day after you left, I thought I saw that the inclination of the majority was for reversal, though the Chief Justice and Bradley announced themselves as willing to vote for affirming. During the recess, the Chief Justice changed his mind and Field, Bradley and myself alone voted for affirming. Harlan who has not returned sent his vote in this and all the other cases he had heard voting in this with the majority.

On what I consider the strongest point in your case, the limitation of the power of the city to issue the bonds or to contract the debt, no member of the court hesitates a moment except Field and myself. And the feeling which has [two words illegible] the court against all municipalities who contract any asserted obligation in them amounts to a mania. If I were a practicing lawyer today, my self respect, knowing what I do of the force of that feeling, would forbid me to argue in this court any case whatever against the validity of a contract with a county, city or town under any circumstances whatever. It is the most painful matter connected with my judicial life that I am compelled to take part in a farce whose result is invariably the same, namely to give more to those who have already, and to take away from those who have little, the little that they have.

[79] Cf. his remarks in Chisholm v. Montgomery, Fed. Case No. 2686 (1875), on "the ruinous extravagance and demoralization which have resulted from the possession of unlimited powers of expenditure and issue of bonds by municipal bodies all over the country. . . ."

[80] Letter of December 13, 1874.

[81] Hitchcock v. Galveston, 96 U. S. 341 (1878). Bradley, J., wrote a dissent in which Miller and Field concurred.

Then on February 3, the day before the judgment was rendered, he wrote again:

I am sorry to see that you are so much disappointed at the result of your case in our court. It is a result however which I readily foresaw as soon as I discovered that it was a question of a demand growing out of a contract against a municipal corporation.

Our court or a majority of it are, if not monomaniacs, as much bigots and fanatics on that subject as is the most unhesitating Mahemodan in regard to his religion. In four cases out of five the case is decided when it is seen by the pleadings that it is a suit to enforce a contract against a city, or town, or a county. If there is a written instrument its validity is a foregone conclusion.

A year later Philip Phillips appeared for the defendant in a municipal bond case,[82] on which he made the following report: "The Court yesterday decided Calhoun Cy. against us — Swayne delivered a most lame opinion. Miller, Bradley and Harlan dissented." [83] And again: "The decision by Swayne is a most slovenly one — but on the question arising out of these municipal bonds — the current has set so strong against all defenses it is impossible to resist it. There is no use to attempt the rehearing of the case." [84]

Justice Swayne led the way in these bond cases, and for that and other reasons Miller held his judicial services in low esteem. It is worth noting that the question of public aid to railroads had been fought out in the Ohio courts while Swayne was at the bar, and that in one of the cases he had appeared successfully for those seeking to enforce the bonds.[85] During the summer of 1869 Judge Swayne was to hear a railroad foreclosure suit [86] in which Miller's brother-in-law, W. P. Ballinger, represented the stockholders, with the support of

---

[82] Calhoun County v. Galbraith, 99 U. S. 214 (1879).

[83] To H. A. Barr, Oxford, Mississippi, April 15, 1879; Phillips Letterbook (1878–80), p. 177.

[84] To the same, May 21, 1879; Phillips Letterbook, p. 203.

[85] State ex rel. Smead v. Trustees of Union Township, 8 Ohio St. 394 (1858).

[86] Cowdrey v. Galveston, H. and H. R. R. This phase not reported, but for later stages, see Fed. Case 3293 (C. C. E. D. Tex. 1870), 11 Wallace 459 (1870), and 93 U. S. 352 (1876).

Jeremiah S. Black as associate counsel. Black, it will be recalled, was a distinguished Democratic lawyer-politician who had been chief justice of Pennsylvania and later Attorney General in the Buchanan cabinet. Ballinger had made inquiry what sort of person Judge Swayne was, to which Justice Miller made this reply:

I fear that in Swayne you have almost everything to fear. I do not see that I can serve you better than to take your queries in order and answer them. He *is* an extremist in upholding all negotiable bonds and especially Rail Road securities. He is not a man much affected by the justice of a case as distinguished from the principles of law which ought to govern it and his judgment is just of that kind which is much influenced by plausibilities. His judgment is not clear, nor is he very self-reliant, though not likely to show this latter trait. He will examine such a case as yours fully and thoroughly. He is much governed by authorities and is fond of the older decisions especially of the English courts. He is more familiar with the authorities than any judge on our bench, and has a just estimate of their relative value. He is capable of appreciating sound discriminations and will listen patiently and attentively to all you say, and especially to your authorities and to comments.

He dislikes Black. He has no confidence in his honesty or the truth of his statements, and Black's well known adhering to the rebellion as far as he dare go has especially embittered Swayne.[87]

Yet Swayne is timid, and Black is strong in argument and imperious, and Swayne as well as all the judges of the Sup. Court know his great powers. But after all the main hope of success must rest with you. He will give you a fair hearing. He is open to conviction.

He is very fond of the literature of the profession in which he believes himself to be remarkably well read. An appropriate allusion to some anecdote or striking event, or remark in reference to any of the great jurists of England to whom you may have occasion to refer, or any remark of yours showing that you have made yourself familiar with the history of these great names, and the general course of personal and legal history will not be lost on him. Nor will he be insensible to injustice if it be patent and

[87] Adverse judgments of this sort, passed on men of opposite political faith during the Reconstruction period, are not to be taken too seriously. Black was not loath to cast aspersions on members of the Supreme Court.

gross. He and I were alone politically last winter, and had much close consultation.[88]

After the case had been heard Ballinger expressed a favorable opinion of Swayne, to which Miller responded:

The impression which Judge Swayne seems to have made on you, is the same first impression that he makes on every one. He held a term in Indiana before the circuits were changed and he charmed every body. When I was in Washington in 1862 looking after the rearrangement of the circuit on which my own nomination depended, it became essential to make a circuit which should include Indiana and Illinois. This detached Indiana from Swayne's circuit, and one of the most formidable influences against the circuits as my friends desired them arose out of the sudden impression that Swayne had made at one term in Indiana.

Unfortunately it does not last. So much of it is found to be mere courtesy, parade of learning, Turveydropism,[89] with an absence of any real sincerity, and the presence of an ever watchful selfishness, that the impression don't last.

I say this with no personal feeling, for I think my relations with him are as close and as binding as with any member of the court, and I believe he is as frank with me as he is *capable of being* with any one.[90]

The extent to which the courts have recognized — in effect, created — rights against the public is one of the most striking aspects of American public law. One thinks at once of the contract clause as construed in the Dartmouth College Case — a doctrine against which so sane a jurist as Cooley protested.[91] More recently there has been the expansion of the words "liberty" and "property" in the Fourteenth Amend-

[88] Letter of June 17, 1869.

[89] Mr. Turveydrop, in *Bleak House*, had made a profession of "Deportment," — "showing a condescension, and a patronage, and a grace of manner, in dispensing the light of his high-shouldered presence, from which I might have supposed him (if I had not known better) to have been the benefactor" of those who ministered to his vanity. We may be sure that Miller had found particular satisfaction in reading *Bleak House*, with its report of Jarndyce *v.* Jarndyce, that "Monument of Chancery practice," in which "the flower of the Bar" and "the autumnal fruits of the Woolsack" were lavished until the estate had been consumed in costs. *Cf.* his dissenting opinion in Trustees *v.* Greenough, 105 U. S. 527, 538 (1881).

[90] Letter of August 29, 1869.

[91] *Constitutional Limitations* (8th ed., 1927), I, 567n.

ment, against which Justice Holmes struggled to the end. The favor which railroad interests enjoyed in the federal courts during the post-bellum period was a like phenomenon. Or so, at any rate, it seemed to Justice Miller, whose moral indignation sometimes carried him to heights of judicial eloquence — perhaps never more so than in his dissenting opinion in *Woodson* v. *Murdock*.[92]

The constitution of Missouri adopted in 1865 had provided: "The General Assembly shall have no power, for any purpose whatever, to release the lien held by the State upon any railroad." By a statute of 1868 the legislature had accepted $5,000,000 from the Pacific Railroad Company in commutation of a much larger claim, and released the lien by which the debt had been secured. The validity of this statute was the issue in the case. No federal question was involved, the suit being in the federal courts by reason of the parties. To construe so specific a provision of the state constitution in a case of unique importance was a work of great delicacy. But the Court (Miller and Davis dissenting) had no difficulty in holding that while the legislature might not simply release the lien, it might commute the debt. Miller, of course, was familiar with the history of the railroads in Missouri. He begins his dissenting opinion by tracing how the state had loaned them its bonds, secured by liens; how at the close of the war both the state and the roads had been impoverished; and how it had been a matter of debate whether the state should meet its own needs by forcing a sale of the roads, or on the contrary should release the roads from their obligations. "The appeal for leniency to the railroad companies had many and able advocates, and was warmly urged by them, and assisted by all the appliances which that class of corporations use with so much effect." But the answer of the people of Missouri was the adoption of the constitutional provision quoted above. From the history of the times as well as from the language adopted, Miller had no doubt of the "unmistakable determi-

---

[92] 22 Wallace 351 (1874). The plaintiff in error was Silas Woodson, governor of Missouri, Miller's friend of the Barbourville days.

nation of the Convention and the people that the companies should, in the language of the prescribed ballot, 'pay their bonds' — pay them in full — or lose their roads, their property and franchises."

But of what avail are constitutional restrictions of legislative power, or legislative restrictions of municipal power, if they are disregarded by the legislatures and municipalities?

It may be said that there remains to the people the protection of the courts. But language is at best a very imperfect instrument in the expression of thought, and the fundamental principles of government found in constitutions must necessarily be declared in terms very general, because they must be very comprehensive.

The ingenuity of casuists and linguists, the nice criticism of able counsel, the zeal which springs from a large pecuniary interest, and the appeal of injured parties against the bad faith of the legislatures who violate the constitution are easily invoked, and their influence persuasive with the courts, as they always must be.

And if language as plain as that we have been considering, a purpose so firmly held and clearly expressed is to be frittered away by construction, then courts themselves become but feeble barriers to legislative will and legislative corruption, and the interest of the people, which alone is to suffer, has but little hope from the safeguards of written constitutions.

These instruments themselves, supposed to be the peculiar pride of the American people, and the great bulwark to personal and public rights, must fall rapidly into disrepute if they are found to be efficient only for the benefit of the rich and powerful, and the absolute majority on any subject will seek to enforce their views without regard to those restrictions on legislative power which are used only to their prejudice.

X

SOME EARLY PROBLEMS OF CORPORATE RECEIVERSHIPS

THE RISE of the railroad receivership was one of the most significant developments in American law during Justice Miller's years on the bench. When a line of railroad was being constructed the requisite capital would be provided by the subscriptions of stockholders and the sale of bonds secured by a mortgage on a part or the whole of the line, or even upon rolling stock. Often, and particularly during the financial contraction which followed the panic of 1873, a company would be unable to meet maturing obligations. Bankruptcy was not a mode of escape, since railroad corporations were expressly excluded from the provisions of the Bankruptcy Act. Mortgage bondholders, representing that on a. foreclosure sale their security would prove inadequate to meet their claims, would petition a court of equity to appoint a receiver to take possession of the road and operate it pending a reorganization of its finances. It was particularly the federal courts which were thus importuned to go into the railroad business.

The liquidation of an embarrassed railroad involves the mutually antagonistic interests of mortgagees of varying seniority, unsecured creditors, materialmen and laborers, and stockholders. A receiver is described as the agent of the court, a person indifferent as between the parties. But in practice it not infrequently happens that one group procures the appointment of a friendly receiver who can be counted upon to manage the business with an eye to their particular advantage. Equity had long been familiar with receivers appointed for such modest purposes as managing the affairs of an infant and winding up the business of discordant partners. To undertake the management of a railroad for a period of indefinite duration was a momentous extension of practice. In England the Court of Chancery refused to go so far,[1] but in America the receivership became a familiar remedy during the seventies and eighties.[2] While it was the common speech of the courts to say that this extraordinary aid would be granted sparingly and with great caution,[3] the striking thing about Justice Miller was that when he expressed that sentiment he really meant it.[4] Knowing well the legal tactics by which

[1] Gardner *v.* London Chatham and Dover Ry. Co., L. R. 2 Ch. App. 201 (1867). Subsequent legislation authorized the appointment of a manager on the application of a judgment creditor (Railway Companies' Act, 1867, § 4).

[2] James L. High, in the preface to the second edition of his *Treatise on the Law of Receivers* (Chicago, 1886), said: "The law of Receivers over railways has been largely the growth of the last ten years, and it can not be said to have wholly emerged from its formative period. . . ." In reviewing the book the *American Law Review* (20:586) repeated this remark and continued: "If the learned author had gone further and assumed the role of a law reformer he could have said with justice that no department of the law has been the subject of such flagrant abuses. We have seen the spectacle of great railway lines being placed in the hands of receivers and operated by them under the protection of a Federal Circuit Court for a number of years in succession with no other apparent purpose on the part of the movers in the litigation than to hold creditors at arm's length; and lately the extraordinary spectacle has been presented of a receiver being appointed upon the petition of the railway company itself."

[3] *Cf.* the reiteration of the admonition, per Cardozo, J., in Shapiro *v.* Wilgus, 287 U. S. 348, 356 (1932).

[4] *Cf.* his opinions as circuit justice in Schenck *v.* Peay, 1 Woolworth 175, Fed. Case No. 12,450 (1868), and especially in Union Trust Co. *v.* St. Louis, I. M. & S. R. R., 4 Dillon 114, Fed. Case No. 14,402 (1877). In the latter case S. G. and G. C. Ward, agents for Baring Brothers, the mortgagees, had themselves precipitated the default by dissuading the management from borrowing to meet the interest due, and then suddenly demanding payment in full and forthwith petitioning for a receiver. In denying this relief Miller, J. (Dillon, J., concurring with him), said: "It is not necessary to impute to the Wards or their principals any other motive than that which usually governs men in moneyed transactions, viz., to make the most of their money. If having, as they do, some seven millions of dollars invested in this road, their contract gives them the right to sell it and buy it in, a court of equity must enforce that right by the foreclosure of the mortgage. And though the consequence of this may be to extinguish some thirty or forty millions of stock held by people who have done no wrong, and place in the hands of Baring Bros. & Co. a road whose future gives every promise of making that stock valuable, we must give them the benefit of the rules of chancery, in enforcing the contract which the parties have voluntarily made. . . . Unquestionably there may be a right to foreclosure without the right to appoint a receiver, or change the possession of the property. This latter depends upon the danger of ultimate

pirates of finance fought for the control of railroads, he thought that the courts should show themselves astute in dealing with this system of freebooting. He explained some aspects of the railroad receivership in a case where his brethren had held that a plaintiff could not sue a receiver without first obtaining the permission of the court by which the receiver had been appointed — thus imposing inconvenience upon plaintiffs and in effect denying a right to trial by jury.[5] It may be noted that in 1887 Justice Miller's view became the law, by an Act of Congress.[6] In his dissenting opinion Miller, J., said:

> The rapid absorption of the business of the country of every character by corporations, while productive of much good to the public, is beginning also to develop many evils, not the least of which arises from their failure to pay debts and perform the duties which by the terms of their organization they assumed. One of the most efficient remedies for the failure to pay, when it arises from inability, is to place the corporation in the hands of a receiver, that its affairs may be wound up, its debts discharged, and the remaining assets, if any there be, distributed among its stockholders. Of the beneficial results of this remedy there can be little doubt. When it is applied with despatch, and the effects of the insolvent corporation are faithfully used to meet its liabilities and its dead body is buried out of sight as soon as possible, no objection can be made to the procedure, and all courts and good citizens should contribute, as far as they may, to this desirable object.
>
> In regard, however, to a certain class of corporations, — a class whose operations are as important to the interests of the community and as intimately connected with its business and social

loss to the bondholders by permitting the property to remain in the possession of its owners until the final decree and sale, if one is to be made."

On the favorable outcome of this decision, see the remarks of Seymour D. Thompson, in his *Commentaries on the Law of Private Corporations* (7 vols., San Francisco, 1894–99), v, 5408, note 2.

[5] Barton v. Barbour, 104 U. S. 126, 137 (1881). Besides the authorities which Miller, J., cited as in accord with his view there was the judgment of Brewer, J., in St. Joseph and Denver City R. R. v. Smith, 19 Kans. 225 (1877). An emphatic expression of the contrary doctrine, upheld by the majority of the Supreme Court, was the opinion of Love, J., in the Circuit Court for Iowa, in Thompson v. Scott, 4 Dillon 508, Fed. Case No. 13,975 (1876).

[6] Act of March 3, 1887, 24 Statutes at Large 554.

habits as any other, — the appointment of receivers, as well as the power conferred on them, and the duration of their office, has made a progress which, since it is wholly the work of courts of chancery and not of legislatures, may well suggest a pause for consideration. It will not be necessary to any observing mind to say that I allude to railroad corporations. Of the fifty or more who own or have owned the many thousand miles of railway in my judicial circuit, I think I speak within limits in saying that hardly half a dozen have escaped the hands of the receiver. If these receivers had been appointed to sell the roads, collect the means of the companies, and pay their debts, it might have been well enough. But this was hardly ever done. It is never done now. It is not the purpose for which a receiver is appointed. He generally takes the property out of the hand of the owner, operates the road in his own way, with an occasional suggestion from the court, which he recognizes as a sort of partner in the business; sometimes, though very rarely, pays some money on the debts of the corporation, but quite as often adds to them, and injures prior creditors by creating a new and superior lien on the property pledged to them.[7]

Wisconsin had been added to Miller's circuit in 1863, and there he had presided over "the fiercest fight I ever saw" waged by Matt Carpenter against a group of railroad adventurers. "I was with him all the time as a judge, and he had all the right. The result was poverty to him, final success to them, and a compromise in which they bought off his opposition."[8] Ballinger was engaged in a similar struggle which Miller, from his experience, felt assured could not be won:

Keokuk. Aug 27. 1868

My Dear Will,

I was not at all surprised at your defeat in your rail road suit. I am very sorry indeed, to find your feelings so much enlisted in the suit. It amounts with me to a feeling of sympathy with you, as if you had sustained some great misfortune. This feeling has not so much relation to what is past, as what is to come.

I know *well* the men with whom you are contending, and am sure that there is nothing before you but defeat and disappointment.

---

[7] 104 U. S. at 137. [8] Letter written in the spring of 1870.

When I was appointed to the bench, these men had almost every rail road in Wisconsin, in the hands of Receivers, through the district Judge of that district.[9] They now own the whole of them. They commenced by buying up depreciated bonds, and commencing suits of foreclosure. The first proceeding was to have the roads placed in the hands of their tools as Receivers. Then the litigation might spin its length. The roads were ruined systematically. The owners of the equity of redemption got nothing but the privilege of paying costs and fees. When I reached the court, the main contest was over some rolling stock worth half a million of dollars. They had possession but no right whatever, or title. I so decided in the circuit, three or four times. The Supreme Court affirmed these judgments once or twice, but in the face of all this the Supreme Court at the last term, decided everything in their favour.[10] When the circuit court rendered decrees for possession of property, the district judge refused to join in an order of attachment to compel obedience, and thus defeated the very decrees he had joined in making. He had not half the courage, nor is he as bad a man, as your district judge.[11] Certain members of the Supreme Court are *always* in favour of enforcing bonds, at the expense of all other rights. The men you are fighting, have personal access to certain judges, whose influence on the bench is predominant. They understand beyond all men I have ever known the *art* of influencing men. They have unlimited means for they are worth fifty millions of dollars, and they are not illiberal in the use of them. You are engaged in a protracted, and intensely exciting, and a certainly unsuccessful struggle; for all that they think worth fighting for they will win.

I wish you were out of it, unless you get well paid for your trouble.

I have written you this with two objects. 1st That if you continue the fight, you may secure some pay, outside of the *Res* for which you are fighting; 2nd that you may not be too seriously disappointed at the result. If it is consistent with honor, get something from them for self and clients, and compromise.

---

[9] Andrew G. Miller.
[10] Minnesota Co. *v.* St. Paul Co., 6 Wallace 742 (1868). The many phases of this litigation are reported *sub nom.* La Crosse and Milwaukee R. R., and Milwaukee and Minnesota R. R., in 1 Wallace to 6 Wallace, and more completely in 17 L. Ed. 347, 359, 604, 616, 725, 860, 861, 886, 900, 924; 18 L. Ed. 247, 252, 676, 678, 680, 847, 854, 856, 859, 862, 885, 887.
[11] John C. Watrous.

In regard to the rule which you suggest about security from the party at whose instance a receiver is appointed, I fear I could not induce the court if I should try, to take so very radical a step. I think you have overlooked an important difference between this case and the cases of attachment and replevin, to which you refer. In those cases the seizure of property is by a proceeding wholly *ex parte*. The plaintiff makes his affidavit, and files his bond, and the clerk issues the writ as of course.

There is no hearing before a court or judge or other officer.

But in the case of appointing a Receiver, there is a preliminary hearing before the Judge or Court. The order for his appointment is the result of judicial investigation. The same principle rules in applications for an injunction. There must be a hearing. The act of Congress requires notice to the opposite party. Now although the statutes of most of the States require a bond, where the injunction is to stay a judgment at law, there is no such rule in the federal Courts.

But in that case, as also in case of a receiver, it is undoubtedly in the discretion of the court or judge granting the order, to make it dependent upon filing a bond for the protection of defendants.

Is not this sufficient? I could hardly hope to get the Judges of the Sup. Court, to make a rule which required a bond in all cases. But I will consider of the matter, and talk with some of them about it next winter. What good would it do you now?

In 1894 the legislature of South Carolina, then under the agrarian leadership of "Pitch-fork" Ben Tillman, and particularly irritated by the difficulties experienced in attempting to collect state taxes from railroads in the hands of the federal court, presented to Congress a memorial of grievances in the matter of equity receiverships. In the course of the memorial it was said that

had all Federal judges been like Mr. Justice Miller, Mr. Circuit Judge Dillon or Mr. Circuit Judge Caldwell, the courts of equity of the United States would never have been degraded to their present position of being feared by the patriotic and avoided by the honest; nor would they have opened the door to the mismanagement, corruption and nepotism which have marked, and still mark, the administration of railroads by the courts.[12]

[12] 28 *American Law Review* 161, 189 (1894).

The experienced editors of the *American Law Review*,[13] while expressing no opinion on the merits of the particular complaint of the government of South Carolina, did say:

> This subject of Federal railway receiverships is loaded down with abuses which seriously demand the investigation of Congress. Not the least is the refusal to pay the taxes assessed by the States upon the property in the hands of the receivers, and the obstruction of the police laws of the States. As great a grievance lies in the striking down of contracts by the issuing of receivers' certificates, cutting into the oldest mortgages, and used to take up floating debts incurred by manipulators who have drained the revenues of the railroads steadily into their own pockets.[14]

Judge John F. Dillon [15] and Judge Henry C. Caldwell,[16] whose names were bracketed with that of Justice Miller in the South Carolina memorial, were among his most intimate associates on the bench of the Eighth Circuit. Judge Caldwell in particular had a prominent part in the history of the railroad receivership, of which something may be said here because of the similarity of his outlook to that of the circuit justice.[17] One of the attractive features of a foreclosure was

[13] Seymour D. Thompson of Saint Louis, author, among other writings, of *Commentaries on the Law of Private Corporations*, and Leonard A. Jones of Boston, author of *A Treatise on the Law of Railroad and other Corporate Securities* (Boston, 1879) and many other standard works.

[14] 28 *American Law Review* 283, 287 (1894).

[15] Circuit judge, Eighth Circuit, 1869–1879.

[16] District judge, Arkansas (later of the Eastern District of Arkansas), 1864–1890, circuit judge, Eighth Circuit, 1890–1903.

[17] See his lecture on "Railroad Receiverships in the Federal Courts," 30 *American Law Review* 161 (1896), and the editorial comments, in the same journal, p. 282. In accord with Justice Miller's reluctance to grant a receivership, compare the opinion of Judge Caldwell in Overton v. Memphis and Little Rock R. R., 10 Fed. 866 (1882), and that of Circuit Judge McCrary in Sage v. Memphis and Little Rock R. R., 18 Fed. 571 (1883). But their colleague, District Judge Treat, in the Circuit Court for the Eastern District of Missouri, made history when in 1884 he granted a receivership over the Wabash, St. Louis and Pacific Railway Company, not at the suit of its creditors, but on the application of the company itself. See the judge's remarks in Central Trust Co. v. Wabash, St. L. and P. Ry., 29 Fed. 618 at 623 (1886). This evidently had the approval of Circuit Judge Brewer: Central Trust Co. v. Wabash, St. L. and P. Ry., 23 Fed. 863, 865 (1885). Among the severely adverse comments on this action, see State ex rel. Merriam v. Ross, 122 Mo. 435, 457ff. (1894), and 20 *American Law Review* 586 (1886).

that it cut off accumulated debts,[18] including those for materials and labor, even where such current expenses had gone unpaid in order that income might be diverted to the benefit of bondholders and stockholders. In admiralty those who supply the means without which the adventure could not have been carried on are given a preferred standing. But the claim of a like equity in a railroad receivership was derided as "an admiralty lien on wheels." One day a woodcutter in a coonskin cap appeared before Judge Caldwell in the federal court at Little Rock, in order personally to assert his claim in respect of wood and ties supplied to a railroad.[19] The balance due amounted to over seven hundred dollars, representing several years of work and the man's entire fortune. He said that when he sold wood to steamboats on the Mississippi he had a lien on the boat ahead of all mortgages, and he had supposed that the same was true of wood sold to a railroad. When the court ruled against his claim for priority [20] the man went home and, in his despair, hanged himself. The result of Judge Caldwell's reflection upon this episode was that the Judge resolved that thereafter, in applying a remedy which lay in

---

Thompson's *Commentaries on the Law of Corporations*, v, 5399, describes Judge Caldwell as "one of the most experienced, learned, competent, firm, and just-minded judges on the Federal bench." *Cf.* also Ralph E. Clark, *A Treatise on the Law and Practice of Receivers* (2d ed., 2 vols., Cincinnati, 1929), vol i, pp. 973ff.

[18] *Cf.* 4 *Central Law Journal* 2, 73, 92, 458 (1877). Mr. George B. Rose relates that at the time when the great Ashtabula wreck occurred his father, the late U. M. Rose, conversing with the principal owner of the railroad, remarked that the accident would no doubt bankrupt the company. " 'Oh, no,' said the gentleman, 'it will not cost us much. The next time the interest falls due, we will make default on the bonds, and we will then foreclose and cut out all these claims. [The bonds and stocks were in the same hands.] It will cost us nothing but the expense of the foreclosure, some ten or twenty thousand dollars.' " (*Judge Henry C. Caldwell; An Address Delivered by George B. Rose before the Bar Association of Arkansas at Hot Springs, on the 29th of April, ·938* [n.p., n.d], p. 9.)

[19] See Judge Caldwell's remarks on "Coon-Skin Cap Law" before the Colorado Bar Association, 1898, *Report of the Organization and First Annual Meeting* (Denver, 1898), p. 43; also Edward H. Stiles, *Recollections and Sketches of Notable Lawyers and Public Men of Early Iowa* (Des Moines: Homestead Publishing Co., 1916), pp. 222ff.

[20] Following Galveston R. R. *v.* Cowdrey, 11 Wallace 459 (1871).

the sound discretion of the court, he would grant a receivership only on the terms that claims for labor and materials should be paid ahead of the mortgages.[21] Thereafter "Judge Caldwell was looked upon by the men who owned railroads and by their attorneys as a monster. They raged furiously against his ruling, but they had to submit, since otherwise the property would be torn to pieces by attachments and executions in the State courts." [22] Presently the Supreme Court, cautiously and within narrower limits, approved the position which Judge Caldwell had first taken.[23] But in 1890 Mr. Justice Brewer, who had just been elevated to the Supreme Court from the circuit judgeship for the Eighth Circuit,[24] took occasion to administer a thinly-veiled rebuke to his old associate. As illustrating how much of public policy lies secreted in judicial decision upon even such a matter as priority among creditors, the episode as narrated in a contemporary law journal is worth preserving. Brewer was as instinctively conservative in his sympathies as Caldwell was liberal.

In Kneeland v. American Loan &c. Co., 136 U. S., at p. 97, opinion by Mr. Justice Brewer, the following language occurs, the italics being ours: "Indeed, we are advised that some courts have made the appointment of a receiver conditional upon the payment of all unsecured indebtedness in preference to the mortgage liens sought to be enforced. Can anything be conceived which more thoroughly destroys the sacredness of contract obligations? One holding a mortgage debt upon a railroad has the *same right to demand and expect* of the court respect for his vested and contracted priority as a *holder of a mortgage on a farm or lot*." The bar in the Eighth Federal Circuit understood that this language was directed against the practice of Judge Caldwell above referred to. We may shrewdly suspect that it was to offset these remarks that Judge Caldwell carefully collated

---

[21] See his interesting opinions in Dow v. Memphis and Little Rock R. R., 20 Fed. 260 (1884); Farmers' Loan and Trust Co. v. Kansas City W. and N. R. R., 53 Fed. 182 (1892), with appended note by M. M. Cohn.

[22] George B. Rose, "Judge Henry C. Caldwell," *supra*. Mr. Rose often appeared before Judge Caldwell and his remarks are full of interest.

[23] Fosdick v. Schall, 99 U. S. 235 (1878); doctrine extended in Burnham v. Bowen, 111 U. S. 776 (1884).

[24] Judge Caldwell had been promoted to the circuit judgeship in his stead.

and cited in his subsequent opinion in Farmers Loan &c. Co. v. Kansas City &c. R. Co., 53 Fed. Rep. 182, all the utterances on this subject of Mr. Justice Brewer while still holding the office of United States Circuit Judge: showing that in one case, where the receivership had been granted on a bill filed by the railroad company against its creditors, receivers' certificates had been issued to take up over $3,000,000, much of it evidenced by promissory notes of the railroad corporation indorsed by certain rich men, given to raise money to keep the road in operation. The debts evidenced by these notes [had] been contracted more than six months before the receivership — some of them nearly two years before — and the case did not come within the so-called "six months rule." The idea of a railroad mortgage being the same as "a mortgage on a farm or lot," did not seem to operate here. Of course, no order was ever made by any court making *all* the unsecured indebtedness of a railroad company preferential. . . . Our courts have justified the exercise of this jurisdiction chiefly on the ground that a railroad is a public institution, and cannot, when embarrassed, be allowed to be impeded by the levying of executions upon its rolling stock or other properties. This very reason assimilates a railroad on land to a ship at sea, and calls, of course within reasonable limits, for the application of the rule of admiralty law, which requires the liens on a vessel to be discharged in the inverse order of their date.[25]

The view of social justice which held that claims for wages should have priority over the claims of mortgagees has now been widely recognized, by statute and by judicial decision.

No casebook on corporations would be complete without the leading case of *Sawyer* v. *Hoag*,[26] where Justice Miller spoke for the Supreme Court. An insurance company had been launched by means of a scheme whereby the stockholders made a simulated payment of their subscriptions and then received back as a loan 85 per cent of their apparent investment. Sawyer, such a stockholder, when the company subsequently became insolvent, bought up a depreciated claim against the company and demanded that the assignee in bankruptcy accept this claim as a set-off to the note he had given

[25] Footnote to an editorial, probably by Seymour D. Thompson, in 30 *American Law Review* 282 (1896).
[26] 17 Wallace 610 (1873).

at the time of his subscription to the stock. Justice Miller observed that the device had apparently been practiced generally by this and by other insurance companies.

It was, therefore, a regular system of operations to the injury of the creditor, beneficial alone to the stockholder and the corporation.
We do not believe we characterize it too strongly when we say that it was a fraud upon the public who were expected to deal with them.

This would have sufficed to make the stockholder liable to the extent of his purported subscription. But in the course of his opinion Justice Miller propounded the following proposition:

Though it be a doctrine of modern date, we think it now well established that the capital stock of a corporation, especially its unpaid subscriptions, is a trust fund for the benefit of the general creditors of the corporation. And when we consider the rapid development of corporations as instrumentalities of the commercial and business world in the last few years, with the corresponding necessity of adapting legal principles to the new and varying exigencies of this business, it is no solid objection to such a principle that it is modern, for the occasion for it could not sooner have arisen.[27]

As Professor E. H. Warren has observed, "this is a venerable utterance, sonorous, and of benevolent connotation. But it is not true." [28] One recognizes that Justice Miller's thought was to fix a high standard for corporate management and to protect the public from such evils as watered stock. But the rationale set forth has proved unsound and troublesome in application, as for example when a corporation has sold its stock below par for the adequate reason that that was all it would bring. Could creditors claim from the purchaser the difference between the price paid and the nominal value? [29]

[27] 17 Wallace at 620.
[28] "Safeguarding the Creditors of Corporations," 36 *Harvard Law Review* 509, 546 (1923).
[29] Handley *v.* Stutz, 139 U. S. 417 (1891).

Other judges, including Story at the circuit [30] and some of Miller's contemporaries in the Supreme Court,[31] gave expression to the same theory. But *Sawyer* v. *Hoag* became the leading case because it was there that the doctrine "was first squarely announced by that court with all the vigor and force characteristic of the great jurist who wrote the opinion." [32] Subsequently, and with Justice Miller's concurrence, it was explained that the trust fund doctrine "only means that the property must first be appropriated to the payment of the debts of the company before any portion of it can be distributed to the stockholders." [33]

Justice Miller's strength lay in the wisdom of his judgments rather than in the artistry of their doctrinal elaboration. He wrought with an eye to practical results rather than to formal elegance. His preparation for the bar had afforded no adequate study of the law against its historical and philosophical background. Neither his tastes nor the exigencies of a busy life were conducive to theoretical reflections. To a student of analytical jurisprudence his opinions would be far less instructive than, for example, those of his brother Bradley. It is therefore not surprising occasionally to find a sound decision placed upon an impermanent foundation. Even Justice Holmes — whose awareness of the logical implications of

[30] Wood *v.* Dummer, 3 Mason 308, Fed. Case No. 17,944 (1824).

[31] Strong, J., in New Albany *v.* Burke, 11 Wallace 96, 106 (1871); Swayne, J., in Sanger *v.* Upton, 91 U. S. 56, 60 (1875). Bradley, J., expressed himself with characteristic accuracy in Graham *v.* Railroad Co. (1880), when he said: "When a corporation becomes insolvent, it is so far civilly dead, that its property may be administered as a trust-fund for the benefit of its stockholders and creditors. A court of equity, at the instance of the proper parties, will then make those funds trust-funds, which, in other circumstances, are as much the absolute property of the corporation, as any man's property is his." (102 U. S. 148, 161.)

[32] Mitchell, J., in Hospes *v.* Northwestern Mfg. and Car Co., 48 Minn. 174 (1892). It is there said: "This 'trust fund' doctrine, commonly called the 'American doctrine' has given rise to much confusion of ideas as to its real meaning, and much conflict of decision in its application. To such an extent has this been the case that many have questioned the accuracy of the phrase, as well as doubted the necessity or expediency of inventing any such doctrine" — a point of view which the judge goes on to substantiate.

[33] Field, J., in Fogg *v.* Blair, 133 U. S. 534, 541 (1890). Similarly Gray, J., in Wabash, St. Louis and Pacific Ry. *v.* Ham, 114 U. S. 587, 594 (1885).

a proposition was unexcelled — sometimes said more than a prophetic foresight would have approved.[34]

[34] For example, compare his statement, following Blackstone, that the main purpose of the constitutional protection of freedom of speech was to prevent *previous* restraint, Patterson *v.* Colorado, 205 U. S. 454, 462 (1907), with his language in Schenck *v.* United States, 249 U. S. 47, 51 (1919). Again, compare the language in Moyer *v.* Peabody, 212 U. S. 78, 85 (1909), on the finality of the governor's decision as to the measures necessary to suppress an insurrection, with that of Hughes, C.J., in Sterling *v.* Constantine, 287 U. S. 378, 400 (1932).

XI

THE CHIEF JUSTICESHIP

SALMON P. CHASE died of paralysis on May 7, 1873. The chief justiceship had never satisfied his ambition and, notwithstanding occasional protestations, he had remained a most receptive presidential possibility. Plans had been laid to secure his nomination at the Democratic convention in 1868, where his admirers hailed him as "the only man who can beat Grant." His remarkable daughter, Mrs. Sprague, had been on hand as a sort of campaign manager. But the choice fell upon Governor Seymour, who had promised to support Chase. By 1870 the friends of the Chief Justice were planning another attempt in the Democratic convention of 1872. At this moment, however, he suffered a paralytic stroke which left his recovery in doubt for some time. He was unable to sit in court during the winter of 1870–71, but by the following term was so far recovered as to be able to walk to court from his home on the outskirts of Washington: "not too far for a good walk — only three miles to the Capitol — less than an hour's walk either way." [1]

The possibility of a vacancy in 1870 had led to the suggestion that Judge Miller should receive the chief justiceship, and this he discussed with his brother-in-law:

At Home
Oct 18. 1870

My Dear Brother,

. . . I appreciate very highly your remark about the Chief Justiceship. The matter has been forced upon my attention by many gentlemen who will have influence in that direction, and in a proper contingency my name will be strongly presented to the President.

---

[1] Mary M. Phelps, *Kate Chase, Dominant Daughter* (New York: T. Y. Crowell Company, 1935), p. 231.

But I confess to you that it is the first time in my life that I have felt a serious and uncomfortable distrust of my capability of properly discharging the duties of a place to which I might possibly be called. This is not affectation which would be folly between you and me.

Nor does it extend to the real and substantial duties of the place as the presiding or chief officer of this court of law. But there are ancillary matters in which a call upon me would probably make me feel painfully the original defects in my education as regards the languages, and some of the sciences.

I might also feel embarrassed by a want of familiarity with other systems of jurisprudence besides our own.

I should like to have your own unbiassed opinion on this matter. For the place I hold has this decided advantage that without being conspicuous as I would if Chief Justice, I think I may say that hereafter I shall be a leading member of the court. . . .

Affectionately your brother
Sam. F. Miller

Metropolitan Hotel
Sunday Nov 6. 1870

My Dear Brother

. . . I value very highly your advice and suggestions about the Chief Justiceship. The more recent indications are that the Chief will recover. Whether he will be able to serve efficiently may remain doubtful. But I do not think he will resign unless he is provided with something else. This is not now probable. The paralytic stroke places him out of the list of probable candidates for the Presidency, and thereby removes any inducement for Grant to propitiate him or send him to Europe which is the only alternative to his remaining a figure head to the court. His daughters, especially Mrs. Sprague will never consent to his retiring to private life. . . .

Affectionately your more than brother
Sam. F. Miller

Several years after Chase was gone Miller set down this candid appraisal of his late colleague:

Your estimate of Chase is remarkably true. Religious by training and conviction, and outward discipline, endowed by nature with a warm heart and vigorous intellect, but all these warped, perverted, shrivelled by the selfishness generated by ambition. I doubt if for years before his death, his first thought in meeting

[251]

any man of force, was not invariably how can I utilize him for my presidential aspirations.

But he was a great man and a better man than public life generally leaves one, after forty years of service.[2]

Judge Miller's family had gone abroad in 1872, and when the Court rose in the spring following he hastened to join them, with the result that he was in Europe when the chief justiceship became vacant. The lawyers in attendance on the federal circuit court at Des Moines immediately adopted a resolution endorsing Justice Miller,[3] and the bar of Kansas promptly took the same action.[4]

It is seldom indeed in connection with a vacancy on the Supreme Court that any name receives such general and spontaneous professional endorsement as was now accorded to Judge Miller. In its issue of May 24 the *Albany Law Journal* said:

We know of no one in the country whose appointment . . . would be so appropriate, or give such universal satisfaction, as would that of Mr. Justice Miller. Endowed with every moral as well as intellectual attribute which can adorn the highest judicial character, in the maturity of life, and with great experience upon the bench, he would make a worthy successor of Marshall, of Taney, and of Chase.[5]

A week later, after surveying the field, the *Journal* concluded:

Among all those whose names have been mentioned . . . we know of no one who combines all the qualities requisite for the position as completely as does Mr. Associate Justice Miller. . . . His opinions are monuments of ability, and unmistakably show him to be the ablest of the able men upon that Bench. To the great body of the legal profession his appointment would give entire satisfaction, and would be regarded as a fortunate omen.[6]

The *American Law Review* of Boston, in its issue of July, said: "Mr. Justice Miller appears to be [Chase's] probable

[2] Letter of October 15, 1876.
[3] Chicago *Inter-Ocean*, May 14, 16, 1873.
[4] The two sets of resolutions are published in 7 *Albany Law Journal* 335 (May 24, 1873).
[5] Page 324.   [6] 7:338.

successor, if promotion be the rule adopted by the President.
. . . For our own part, no name would please us as well." [7]
At Washington the *United States Jurist* of the same date said,
in its discussion of the vacancy:

We may take it for granted, in the first place, that no one will
be selected whose political opinions are at variance with those
of the present administration; and this consideration, of itself,
may serve to dispose of a number of gentlemen whose merits and
qualifications for the position of Chief Justice are of the highest
order. Next, if promotion from among the Associates who are
at present on the Supreme bench shall be in order, the indications are that the choice falls upon Mr. Justice Miller. In talent,
experience, and legal aptitude, this gentleman, it seems to us,
stands above his distinguished colleagues; and as spokesman for
that portion of the court which most harmonized with the administration in opinion on the legal-tender and other political
suits, he presents some exceptionally strong claims for promotion
which are not likely to be overlooked.

It thought, however, that there were some reasons in favor
of an appointment from outside the Court.[8] In October it
reported that of the associate justices "the voice of the bar is
still for Mr. Justice Miller." [9]

The *Legal Gazette* of Philadelphia for May 23 carried a long
unsigned letter urging the promotion of Justice Miller. It
recalled that, while he was unknown when appointed,

it very soon became apparent to the Bar that his was a master
mind, capable of grappling with the most intricate questions of
law in all its varied departments and countless ramifications.
His opinions bear evidence of his industry and ability, and are
remarkable for clearness of statement, purity of diction, and evident mastery of any subject which they touch. *Quod non tetigit,
quod non ornavit.* . . .

To those who have had the pleasure of seeing Mr. Justice
Miller on the bench, it need not be said that his manner is the
combination of the *suaviter in modo* with the *fortiter in re*; and
all those who know him in the private relations of life, will be
satisfied that, as Chief Justice, he would be exactly the right man
in the right place. . . .[10]

[7] 7:749 (1873).   [8] 3:322.   [9] 3:421.
[10] 5:164. The letter bears the initial M. [Wayne MacVeagh?] The author
is described on p. 340.

Five months later the *Legal Gazette* devoted seven columns to an editorial, perhaps the most flattering as well as discriminating of all the expressions in Miller's behalf.[11] It disposed one by one of the other contenders. Benjamin R. Curtis was failing physically: his time was passed. (Judge Curtis died the following September.) E. R. Hoar was an honest man, and of true judicial mind. "But he had been bred too *technically*, we think, for a chief justice of this *great* court. He is too purely of New England. Besides, his manners are constitutionally bad." Let him be an associate justice when Clifford retired. Evarts was described as "a very practiced advocate, a superior *nisi prius* lawyer; nay more, . . . an able and a fairly learned lawyer"; but of a reputation rather greater than his merits. To Attorney General Williams the editor conceded "a mind of parts sufficiently strong; nothing wonderful however." He did well enough in some offices; "but the chief justiceship, — 'that strain is of a higher mood.' " Senator Conkling did not stand high enough as a lawyer. As chief justice he would "encounter on the bench, as now constituted, really able men; pretty rough men some of them too. Such men as Field, Miller, Bradley, Strong and others are athletes," and Conkling would always be inferior to them.

The *Gazette* then came to Miller as the one to whom the bar of the country had spontaneously turned.

Judge Miller is at this time probably the man of the best natural abilities on the bench. He was so recognized to be from almost the hour that he came there (for Grier soon afterwards began somewhat to decline), and though Judge Strong and Judge Bradley excited and have *well* fulfilled high public expectation, they have not put Miller from that eminence which he had when they came there. All admit his very superior natural powers; strong, discriminating, steady, sound. Weight does not oppress him; variety does not confuse him. . . . His mind is not technical in form or tastes. He never puts things on technical grounds, except such grounds are the plain grounds of justice. . . .

With very able and upright men beside him on that side of the question, he has been perhaps the head of the republican

[11] 5:340–341.

portion of the court, and, in the face of the plain influence which the venerable Justice Nelson exercised over the late chief justice, it is said that before Strong and Bradley, JJ., came on, Miller kept things from drifting, as otherwise they might have gone. A pretty strong will has doubtless had something to do with all this; but in a chief justice who is right, a pretty strong will is a very requisite quality.

He is an upright man, pecuniarily, personally, politically. His domestic purity and excellence are acknowledged. He is a man, who though free and open in manner, has ever been strictly temperate in every enjoyment; not a distinction universal in the Federal metropolis. . . . He is a popular man in his manners; dignified enough, not stately; and courteous, without appearance of condescension. Everybody likes Judge Miller; and it is an affection of which respect and esteem is the basis. . . .

He is a strict man in the business of his court; he takes no holidays; he is ever punctual, steady and attentive. . . . His years and physical health are in his favor. . . . He is a thoroughly national man. . . . Whatever promise others may give, the friends of Judge Miller can point to performance.

As to the fact that Clifford and Swayne were senior in appointment, the *Gazette* pointed to their age — the one seventy-three and the other approaching sixty-nine — and said that whatever their qualities, this was a conclusive bar. "Congress has fixed the age of seventy, as that in which the members of *this* bench may reasonably yield to the claims of age and forever retire."

On hearing of the drift of events Justice Miller wrote to his brother-in-law from Brussels on July 27:

For your good wishes and exertions in regard to the C. Justiceship you have my thanks. I have nothing else to give and in that regard I am beggared by the free and unsought efforts of my friends put forth when I am so far away. I have had forwarded to me newspaper articles, and also some from the ablest Law Magazines and Journals that surprised me as much as they have gratified me. The spontaneous expression of my own circuit from every district in it is a testimonial that any man might be proud of.

Genl. Belknap [12] who is my earnest active friend writes me

[12] Secretary of War in the Grant cabinet.

that in view of the number and strength of the recommendations in my favour he thinks it quite fortunate that I was abroad when the Chief Justice died.

I believe I can sincerely say that if I am not made Chief Justice but few men would feel as little disappointment whose chances seemed so fair, and if approved there are as few who would feel the weight of the responsibilities and duties of the place as sensibly and would be as conscious of their deficiencies.

This you know well from what I have already written you long ago. I doubt if my effective influence in the court would be increased by being made its chief, while I know I should be subjected to much criticism from my associates which I now escape. The Chief Justice of our court while held responsible by the public for all its acts has but little influence over those acts by reason of the position and it is only when the character, or rather quali[fications?] of the Chief Justice are such [as?] would give him a controlling influence without the position, that he can exercise that which is justly his due.

Among the newspapers pressing Justice Miller's name upon the President was the Washington *Chronicle*, controlled by George B. Corkhill, Miller's son-in-law. On October 9 it ran an editorial as follows:

JUSTICE MILLER

This distinguished jurist returned from Europe only a day or two since. . . . He has reason to feel gratified with the complimentary manner in which his name has been mentioned by the bar and the press throughout the country during his absence for the vacant Chief Justiceship. . . . Although known to be a decided Republican this commendation has come from every section without regard to political parties.

Three days later it published an editorial on the Supreme Court, recalling that the new term would begin on the morrow and that the judges would pay their respects to the President. As he greeted them he could not fail to ask himself if these able jurists should all be ignored in the selection of a chief.

One of these is yet comparatively a young man, and has served as a justice of this court about twelve years with remarkable ability. . . . No one pretends that he is inferior in native talents, in legal learning, in judicial acumen, in power of original analysis, in tenacity for the right, in unyielding firmness, in breadth of view and depth of thought, in far-reaching forecast and purity of character, to any one named in that connection not now a member of the court. And he is a firm, outspoken Republican, tried in the fire during the long years of the recent rebellion, without being an objectionable partisan — a man who loved his profession better than place, never having accepted or been a candidate for a political office in his life. . . .

On November 9 the *Chronicle* quoted the Dubuque *Times* as favoring Miller for chief justice and reiterated its own endorsement. The *Daily Gate City* of Keokuk, May 13, 1873, had described Justice Miller as the Republican statesman of the Supreme Bench — free from demagoguerie and heedless partisanship, but imbued with the best principles of the party. Other editorials urged the appointment. The insistent support Miller's name was receiving in the Iowa press provoked an editorial from the Washington *National Republican* of November 10:

We cannot but think that Mr. Justice Miller, of the Supreme Court, is mentally crying, "Save me from my friends." It is scarcely to be doubted for a moment that the indiscreet pressure of his name for the Chief Justiceship in the dictatorial manner which has, for some months past, characterized the Iowa press, is calculated to prejudice his interests. Whilst the President is pretty sure to follow his own judgment in the matter, yet, other things being equal, voluntary outside meddling is likely to defeat the party in whose favor it is exerted.

But the *Republican* was very deferential to the sentiment of the administration.

In the mean time President Grant had made quite a different and characteristic choice, having offered the appointment to Senator Roscoe Conkling. It was pointed out in the press that while the salary of the chief justice had been increased by the last General Salary Bill, Conkling was not ineligible, inasmuch as he had entered upon a new term of office since that time. No one doubted his intelligence; his professional qualifications were a matter of controversy; his want of judicial temperament was obvious. The newspapers gave varied reactions to the rumor. The *Springfield Republican* hailed him as "this Senatorial railway attorney, this small-beer statesman, this toad-eater in ordinary to the Administration, this Snarleyow of the stump, Mr. Roscoe Conkling, of Utica, N. Y." The Chicago *Inter-Ocean*, October 6, 1873, attributed this to pique, and assured the country that Conkling was a scholar hardly inferior to any in the nation ("In legal ability he is inferior to no man in Congress"); he never descended to blackguardism or buffoonery, and assertions that he was arrogant or supercilious were said to be unjust. This encomium scarcely demonstrates Conkling's fitness for the chief justiceship. He himself is quoted as saying: "I could not take the place, for I would be forever gnawing my chains." [13]

Conkling declined the nomination in a letter of November 20,[14] though the fact was not made public for some days. By the end of November rumors were thick, and it appears that the President himself was quite undecided. On November 25 there was a report in the press that Grant had not fully determined whether to appoint from the Court, but that if he did he would select Justice Swayne.[15] Next day it was once more reported that Conkling had positively declined. A few days later one read that the name of Morrison R. Waite of Ohio was talked of, and that "the persistent and somewhat unseemly struggle among members of the bench to secure the place had placed great difficulties in the way of any of the

[13] Conkling's disregard of propriety may be gauged by the following letter found in Justice Bradley's papers. Under date of April 7, 1876, Conkling wrote to Justice Bradley:
"My dear Sir:
"I venture to ask you read the enclosed letter from Mr. Synonds [*sic*] an assignee whose interests are involved in a matter now I learn undergoing your consideration.
"I may without impropriety I trust assure you of the probity of Mr. S. and of the confidence his statements deserve."

[14] Facsimiles of offer and declination appear in A. R. Conkling's *Life and Letters of Roscoe Conkling* (New York, Charles L. Webster and Company, 1889), p. 460.

[15] Chicago *Inter-Ocean*, November 25, 1873.

present Justices." [16] On December 1, the news was that Attorney General Williams would be nominated. On December 2 this nomination was sent to the Senate.

From Professor Nevins' recent biography of Hamilton Fish [17] we learn for the first time that after Conkling's refusal Grant offered the appointment to his Secretary of State, but that Fish declined on the ground of his long absence from the bar. This was recorded in his diary entry for November 30. On December 1 he states that the President put forward a plan sprung from Ben Butler's ever-active brain: to give his friend Caleb Cushing the chief justiceship with the understanding that he would resign in time to permit Grant to make another appointment. In the face of opposition from the cabinet this plan was withdrawn. It was then that the President submitted the name of Williams to the Senate.

The nomination evoked no enthusiasm. Williams had become Attorney General shortly after the Department of Justice had been created, but had made no reputation as an administrator. The *Albany Law Journal* reviewed his career, and said:

We have taken the pains to examine the three volumes of Green[e]'s Reports, and find that nearly fifty per cent of his decisions while on the district bench of Iowa were reversed by the Supreme Court. His opinions as Chief Justice of Oregon are all contained in the first volume of Oregon Reports, and are, with scarcely an exception, on questions of trifling importance.[18]

The Bar Association of the City of New York passed a resolution that the nomination "disappoints the just expectations of the legal profession, and does not deserve the approval of the people." [19]

Williams did not receive the compliment often accorded to ex-senators of confirmation without reference to committee. Presently it was reported that opposition had developed,

[16] *Inter-Ocean*, November 28, 1873.
[17] Allan Nevins, *Hamilton Fish* (New York: Dodd, Mead and Company, 1936), pp. 659ff.
[18] 8:358; December 6, 1873.　　　　[19] 9 *Albany Law Journal* 21.

and that the President was not pleased with the reception his nomination was meeting. By the middle of December it appeared that the Judiciary Committee was engaged in investigating certain charges, and a despatch sent on December 22 announced that the committee was particularly interested in a voucher which ran as follows:

Jan. 19, 1872.

The United States to N. J. Joyce Dr.:
To one landaulet for Department of Justice, sixteen hundred (1,600) dollars.[20]

The Attorney General had one of the most elegant turnouts in Washington, — purchased out of the contingent fund of the Department. But this was the merest peccadillo compared with the activities of the beautiful and daring Mrs. Williams. From Professor Nevins' inquiry it appears she had dispensed immunity from prosecution for a consideration of $30,000 and had otherwise played an unworthy part in the affairs of the administration. Miller alluded to these rumors in a "short note written while a collision case which I cant understand is in argument":

Confidential

Supreme Court Room
Dec 10. 1873

My dear Brother.
. . . Williams nomination is received with universal disgust. It is attributed to the personal influence of his wife, and remarks are made publicly as to the nature of that influence, which are of the most discreditable or rather disgraceful character.

The nomination has brought out many stories of her interference in legislative and departmental action involving large moneyed interests which will be most humiliating to the court, for whether true or false, the supposition being once admitted that she's capable of such things, her husband's action as a judge will always be liable to such charges, however unjust or unfounded in fact.

Williams was an old friend of mine. He has been the rock on which my own fortunes were wrecked as regards to this office. But he had a right to get it if he could, and I do not know that he did

[20] Chicago *Inter-Ocean*, December 23, 1873.

or said any thing personally against me. He had the shuffling of the cards and stacked them for his own benefit. Most other men would have done the same, and I have no quarrel with him about it. I believe *him* to be honest. He will be as acceptable to me as anyone likely to be named by the President. There is fierce opposition to his confirmation and the result is doubtful. I *could* beat him but shall not interfere either way. . . .

The Senate Judiciary Committee, with the implacably honest Edmunds as its chairman, offered the President a choice between an adverse report and the withdrawal of Williams' nomination. Secretary Fish was sent to tell Williams that the President would appreciate a letter requesting that his name be withdrawn from the Senate, and this was reluctantly forthcoming under date of January 7.

Grant now returned to Butler's proposal. On the afternoon of January 9 the nomination of Caleb Cushing to be chief justice was sent to the Senate. This was indeed a surprising move. No one doubted Cushing's legal attainments. In the range of his political experience he had no superior in public life. He had recently returned from service as senior counsel with Evarts and Waite in the Alabama Arbitration. At the conclusion of that employment he had published a book, *The Treaty of Washington*, in which he dealt very unflatteringly with Lord Chief Justice Cockburn, the dissenting member of the Arbitration Tribunal. The provocation had been great, but the controversy attained notoriety and suggested doubts as to whether Cushing was preëminent in those qualities which make an effective chief on a court made up of nine very distinct personalities.[21] He

---

[21] Since the appropriateness of Cushing's nomination is in issue here, it is relevant to quote at some length the diary of Attorney General Bates for February 24, 25, 26, 1864. Bates is making notes on the argument of Fossat *v.* United States, 2 Wallace 649, the important Quicksilver Mine Case from California. Cushing and Black appeared for Fossat, Bates and A. J. Wills for the government. "Mr. Cushing opened for Fossat, and made an effort which greatly disappointed me. It was far below the standard of his reputation. I have suspected for some time, that he is a little, narrow-minded unprincipled man. No doubt, he has a good deal of *learning*, but very little *knowledge*; as indeed, no man can have much useful knowledge (which is wisdom) who is destitute of morals.

had just received the appointment as minister to Spain, which seemed a more fitting recognition for his services at Geneva. But most of all men remembered Cushing's reputation for inconstancy in politics. What was to be expected from the Attorney General of Pierce's cabinet, the defender of the principle of the Dred Scott decision, the associate of the extreme wing of the Democratic party led by Jefferson Davis and William L. Yancey, the president of the Charleston Convention of 1860? The appointment seemed highly inappropriate.

The *Nation*, which had been heaping its scorn on Williams, now turned its attention to Cushing:

In the nomination of Mr. Cushing for Chief-Justice, it may be said that the President has at last entered the small circle of eminent lawyers and then with great care has chosen the worst man in it. His entering the circle was the result of the public feeling caused by the appointment of an utterly unfit man of doubtful reputation like Williams; his selection of Mr. Cushing a consequence of his fixed policy of making public appointments on private considerations. As to Mr. Cushing, it may be said on the one hand that he is past the age [he lacked only a few days of being seventy-four] at which the law contemplated a Chief-Justice retiring, is of a crafty nature and erratic temperament, and more renowned for shrewdness and learning than respected for integrity; on the other hand, he is more active in body and mind than many a man of half his years, and, like Chief-Justice Taney, may live to be eighty-eight.

"Mr. Cushing continued for some time to day (wednesday) flowndering [*sic*] on, from one blunder to another, doing his case more harm than good. He was followed by Mr. Wills (with me for the U. S.) who spoke with great ability and effect, during the remainder of that day, and a good part of the next — thursday 25. Feb- . . .

"*Feb 26* . . . By the way, *Cushing* has sunk immeasurably. He seems to have excited the implacable disgust of the whole court — Judge Wayne (who is habitually bland, and never forgets that he, himself is a perfect gentleman) said to me privately, that Cushing's effort was a perfect failure — Swaine [Swayne] sd. that C[ushing]'s attack upon Wills (about the map) was a *brutal outrage*, and the court had determined to let W.[ills] answer as he pleased, and not allow C.[ushing] to reply! But that W.[ills] had ansd. most effectually and in good taste.

"Judge Grier said to me, in a loud whisper, that everybody in ten feet must have heard — 'Ef you speak, give that damned Yankee hell.' I need not say I was disgusted at his grossness; but Mr. Justice Grier is a natural-born vulgarian, and, by long habit, coarse and harsh." (*The Diary of Edward Bates*, pp. 339–340.)

It thought that such favor as the nomination had at first received was due to fear of some worse alternative.[22]

The Washington *National Republican* greeted the nomination of Cushing "with pleased surprise." But the *Republican* was obsequious, and had extolled Williams as a second Marshall. Now it explained that whereas in Williams the President had offered a young man who would grow up to the position, "in the nomination of Mr. Cushing the bar have the foremost lawyer of the country and the greatest experience, statesmanship, and ability." [23] It marshaled the opinions of the press, its selections being generally favorable, but only mildly so.[24]

Forney's *Sunday Chronicle* of Washington (not to be confused with the *Washington Chronicle*) discussed the nomination in a long article whose burden was, Is it necessary? Admitting Cushing's many excellent qualities, it continued: "but as to his being the safest man to trust a liberal and progressive construction of the Constitution to is a matter of grave and suggestive doubt. . . . Perhaps there never was a nomination . . . involving the same responsibility. . . ." [25]

The *Washington Chronicle* of Saturday, January 10, led off with an editorial, "Make Haste Slowly." It stated that the Democrats and Liberals of the Senate had wished to confirm at once, but that on the objection of one senator (later disclosed as Sargent of California) the nomination went over. It recalled that Cushing was credited with having induced Pierce to support the repeal of the Missouri Compromise, and that he had been in agreement with the Court in the Dred Scott Case. "Between this and the next executive session of the Senate it is expected that the question of the possibility of finding a Republican lawyer in the United States fit to be Chief Justice will be maturely considered." There was a good deal more editorial comment, all in the vein that Cushing still adhered to his ante-bellum views.

[22] January 15, 1874.
[23] January 10, 1874.
[24] January 12.
[25] January 11.

Cushing's eventual defeat is attributed by Dr. Fuess, his biographer, to the efforts of Senator A. A. Sargent and the *Chronicle*. The motive of the former is said to have been revenge for some ancient controversy; of the latter he says: "Nothing, indeed, could have been more vile than the methods of the *Chronicle*. It hesitated at no falsehood or perversion of fact." [26] It will be evident on reading the following letter that a close examination of the *Chronicle's* methods becomes necessary. For on January 18, 1874, Justice Miller wrote to Ballinger:

I am overworked in the court to the serious detriment of my health and have had no peace since my return from Europe about the Chief Justiceship. It has been nothing but a source of grievous annoyance to me since Chase's death in every aspect except the gratifying expression of public and professional confidence in my fitness for the place. I am interviewed, consulted, urged by friends in a way which I can neither repel, or avail myself of with any advantage. I was urged by leading Senators like Morton to take part in having Williams rejected. But Williams was an old Keokuk friend, without nerve, personally agreeable to me, and more likely to make my place on the bench influential and pleasant, than any other man the President will appoint.

But the manner in which his appointment was secured, his want of ability, and the fact that I believed it was he who had set the President against any appointment from the Bench, made me willing to see him defeated. I did not however lay a straw in his path, and the "Washington Chronicle" now under Corkhill's control preserved an absolute silence.

But when Cushing was nominated we both broke ground openly and vigorously, and in three days we had him beaten. I need not give my reasons for opposition to him. You have described him so well, as he is known to every man familiar with public affairs for the last thirty years, that I need only add that with his character and his years (74 yesterday) his appointment was considered an insult to the Bench by every man on it except Clifford, who is himself over 70 and a life long bitter democrat.

Who will be the next nominated no one knows. The President has said that it is only a question of which one of his *friends* is next to be sacrificed. If any one would have the courage to tell

[26] Claude M. Fuess, *The Life of Caleb Cushing* (New York: Harcourt Brace and Company, 1923), ii, 366.

him, that if he would consent to look out of the small coterie of
his personal following, to the true friends of himself and the country, he could easily find a fit man acceptable to the country, a
service would be rendered to him and to his party. For there is
the great difficulty. He is alarmed and he is obstinate. He will
not give it to any man except as a personal favor conferred on a
friend and associate. It is beginning to dawn on him that among
them he may not find a man acceptable to the public. Fitness for
the office has at no time been an element of his choice.

As to me I am satisfied that Williams and Swayne are the rocks
on which my barque was wrecked. The latter has artfully be-
slobbered the President, since Chase was stricken with paralysis
in a way that no one was aware until now. He has through
Delano [27] kept up personal intercourse on the subject from the
hour of Chase's death, and the President has been so far amenable
to his influence, that he has been persuaded that he ought not
to appoint me over his head. To this point he was also led by
Williams, who by encouraging this inclination was killing off
Swayne, Bradley and myself at the same time, each of whom had
in the cabinet an earnest advocate, namely Delano, Robeson,[28]
and Belknap. The President no doubt was willing to find in this
proposition a refuge from deciding between these friends of his
in the cabinet.

But he has gone further, and asserts that what he calls the
precedents, are founded on good reasons. That no judge once on
that court, should ever look for any other appointment or place
even the Chief Justiceship. And he has lent a ready ear to such
illustrations as the ambition of Chase and Davis. Of all this I
believe Williams to have been the man who fixed his bias for
his own ends. Many friends have talked with the President on
the subject and they all bring the same answer; that the President is firmly, some say bitterly set against any man from the
Court.

Justice Miller's statement above calls for a careful scrutiny
of the means by which Cushing's nomination was defeated.
Miller had not only wanted the honor, but felt convinced
that he was justly entitled to it. Thereafter he always thought
of himself as the spontaneous choice of the bar. But one may
be sure that self-seeking would not have brought him to wage

[27] Columbus Delano of Ohio, Secretary of the Interior.
[28] George M. Robeson of New Jersey, Secretary of the Navy.

war on any nominee had he not believed whole-heartedly that the public good would be seriously compromised by the appointment. He had held his hand in the Williams matter, evidently believing that if Williams came to the Court he would be amenable to Miller's influence and would go the right way on important questions. (Miller had no doubt that his own constitutional views were wise and statesmanlike.) But Cushing would be quite a different matter. Most assuredly he would know his own mind, and Miller had not the least doubt that his mind was bent in the wrong direction. Dr. Fuess argues persuasively that Cushing the adviser of Lincoln and Seward and Sumner entertained quite a different outlook from the Cushing of earlier years. But this friendly appraisal could hardly be expected of contemporaries who still thought of him as he had been characterized in the *Biglow Papers* — a "dreffle smart man [who had] ben on all sides that give places or pelf." To repeat that Cushing was very learned misses the point, for the great critical cases can go either way, and the determinant is something beyond the knowledge of the books. It is bootless now to speculate on what sort of chief justice he might have made. But Miller, whose consuming desire was to keep the course wisely set, had no wish to see the experiment tried. And indeed it seemed not an experiment, but a tragic certainty.

Now to the facts. The *Chronicle* for Sunday January 11 set out on its first page quotations from New York papers, the *Tribune, Herald, World, Times,* and *Sun* — all unsympathetic. The headlines were telling phrases culled from the press comments, such as "A Supporter of the Dred Scott Decision." Then on the editorial page were three articles. The first was entitled "Tiding It Over." It met the argument that Cushing would "do well enough to tide it over" by asking why not allow Justice Clifford to continue to act as chief justice if a fit appointment could not be made at once. The second was on "Republicans 'Crowning' a Democrat," and met the contention that the chief justiceship would be a fitting crown to Cushing's professional career:

He is unquestionably an accomplished and excellent gentleman and a successful lawyer. But there are many others his full equals in these respects in the Democratic as well as in the Republican party; and one would naturally suppose that Republicans would feel just as happy in witnessing this sort of coronation for one of their own political friends as for a leader in the Democratic party, if this transaction is to be regarded in the light of a mere compliment.

The last was headed "Charles Sumner and Caleb Cushing," and viewed these two gentlemen from Massachusetts the one as the antipode of the other:

Sumner has ever been on the side of the oppressed and groaning slave, and Mr. Cushing as steadily on the side of the slave-master. These clanking chains have filled the breast of a Sumner with mortal anguish and wrung his heart with deepest grief; to the ears of a Cushing the ring of the slaves' shackles has only drawn out that Roman virtue shadowed forth in the Dred Scott decision. Mr. Sumner's civil-rights bill will be as worthless as blank paper, unless its constitutionality shall be sustained by the Supreme Court of the United States. To sustain its validity, Mr. Cushing will have to go back on the record of a somewhat protracted lifetime.

It was a bid to Sumner to oppose confirmation. For some years past these two former opponents had been friends, and while Sumner would not have recommended the nomination, he came to the conclusion that, feeling sure that Cushing's views were in accord with his own, he ought to support him in the Senate.[29]

The *Chronicle* of Monday morning was of a similar character. On the front page it continued its extracts, this time from nine newspapers. They stress Cushing's age, admit his ability, regard him as out of sympathy with the recent course of the nation, mistrust his constancy, and find his consistency and integrity not so incontrovertibly established as to make him the most desirable appointee — but an excellent minister to Spain. These are headed again by a solid battalion of ad-

[29] Letter of January 15, 1874, quoted in Fuess, *Cushing*, II, 369.

verse comments, such as "We Can Not Afford to Put in Our Last Court of Appeal a Man Who Has Shown Such Alacrity in Selling His Avowed Principles; Such Shallowness of Conviction, Such Close Friendship for the Slave Power, that Struck at the Vitals of the Republic."

The editorial page had several short items in the nature of debating points. A leader on "Unjust Criticism" says that the President's action should not be regarded as captious; when the Senate demanded a better lawyer than Williams he gave them a very learned one; let the Senate do its duty and the President will send another, and so on until there is satisfaction. There is a long quotation from T. H. Benton's *Thirty Years' View*,[30] unfavorable to Cushing. The nearest to a reflection on personal character is a reference to "the statement made that Mr. Cushing has been noticed by press reporters and news gatherers on his peregrinations to the rooms of Republican Senators" since his nomination was made.

Tuesday's issue continued the same tactics. Page five quoted thirty-six newspapers opposed to Cushing's confirmation. A fair sample of the lot is this from the *Boston Transcript* of January 10:

The new appointment for Chief Justice rather strikes the nation by surprise. No one doubts the capacity of the Hon. Caleb Cushing, nor his remarkable attainments, but his infirmities of temper and advanced age are alleged as disqualifications. . . . But, in addition, does the Government feel quite sure, not on the low ground of political considerations, but for reasons of State, that Mr. Cushing is entirely sound on the question of civil rights, which will be carried to the Supreme Court? It would be extremely unfortunate to have another Dred Scott decision from a Chief Justice owing his nomination to the Republicans.

There were four editorials. "Party Abdication" argued that the nominee had done virtually nothing to show that he supported the gains made by the war, and suggested that his long silence on public questions came from a desire not to offend the government lest he lose his opportunities for professional

[30] II, 505.

employment on its behalf. "How Can Republicans Justify?" asked why a lawyer from that party was not selected, even if Cushing had all the virtues claimed for him. "Look at the Secret Record" was another quotation from Benton's book, dealing with Cushing's appointment and labors as commissioner to China. "Cushing Stamping out the Press" recalled an opinion he had rendered as Attorney General,[31] holding that a postmaster was not bound to deliver a newspaper, sent through the mail, whose design and tendency was to promote insurrection in the state where received — this in the case of the *Cincinnati Gazette*, then the organ of S. P. Chase.

So far the *Chronicle* had simply put down a pitiless barrage of adverse comment upon the nominee. It had concentrated upon this effort as probably no other newspaper in the country. But both its quotations and its own remarks had been fair comment on a matter of public interest.

On Tuesday, January 13, when confirmation hung in the balance, an incident occurred which, as Dr. Fuess says, "decided the issue." [32] Fish wrote in his diary for that day, "It looks pretty black for Cushing's chances." [33] It should be borne in mind that the damage was done on Tuesday, and that it was not until Wednesday morning that the next issue of the *Chronicle* appeared.

The Republican Senators had met on Monday morning for the purpose of agreeing upon a time for concluding debate on the salary bill. A few moments before the conclusion of the caucus an advocate of Cushing's confirmation offered a resolution that it was the sense of those present that the appointment should be made. This was not acted upon, and the caucus adjourned and met again on Tuesday morning. Speeches were made for and against, and at noon the caucus adjourned to meet at the close of the session of the Senate. At the afternoon meeting of the caucus Senator Sargent produced a letter written by Cushing to Jefferson Davis in March 1861 which had the effect of putting an end to Cushing's

---

[31] 8 Opinions of the Attorney General 489 (1857).
[32] II, 370. [33] Nevins, *Fish*, p. 665.

chances of receiving confirmation. Our concern is to follow this letter throughout this decisive Tuesday.

The letter, it seems, had been found by a clerk who was looking through certain Confederate archives.[34] Who started him upon his researches does not appear. Dr. Fuess says it was "Cushing's opponents," which seems almost certain under the circumstances. His discovery was taken to the Secretary of War, Belknap. A copy was in the Secretary's pocket when he attended the cabinet meeting on Tuesday. Senator Sargent, to quote the *National Republican*, declared

that the first information he had of its existence was communicated in an anonymous note. This note, Mr. Sargent says, was received by him on Tuesday, and that immediately upon the receipt of it he went to the War Department to obtain a copy. Gen. Belknap was not at the Department at the time, having gone to the White House to attend a meeting of the Cabinet. There Mr. Sargent obtained a copy of the letter, and hastening to the Capitol read it to the second caucus, with what result is already known.

Dr. Fuess writes that Sargent read the letter to the caucus on Wednesday morning, after having spread the information among his friends. The *Chronicle* for Wednesday morning said it was read in the second caucus of Tuesday; and its rival, the *Republican*, has just been quoted to the same effect. There is unanimity that the reading marked the end of Cushing's chance of confirmation. Cushing wrote a letter to the President asking that his nomination be withdrawn, and this, Dr. Fuess says, reached Grant about eleven o'clock Wednesday morning. He had already called a special meeting of the cabinet and had prepared a note withdrawing the nomination. During the meeting Butler was announced with Cushing's letter, a copy of which was then attached to the President's communication to the Senate.

On Wednesday morning the *Chronicle*, as on previous days,

[34] My account is based on the Washington *National Republican* (which had supported Cushing since his nomination was made) in its issue for Thursday morning, January 15; on Fuess's *Cushing*, and on Nevins' *Hamilton Fish* for the evidence of Fish's diary.

devoted one page of news and the editorial page to Cushing. The news page bears the headline "GOOD-BY, CALEB." Then there is a cut of the flag, surmounted by a liberty cap. "Our Flag is Still There." "A COMPLETE ROUT." " 'My Dear Friend, Jefferson Davis.' " It recounts Tuesday's caucus, where "a letter was produced and read, which we publish below as complete and perfect as we can decipher from the copy in our possession." It goes on to say that letters have been pouring in on the *Chronicle* commenting on its course, and furnishing testimony and facts on the political character of Cushing. It is obliged for these communications, but they arrived after the desired result had been obtained. "We print below the extracts from the press and communications which were in type before the action of the caucus was known."

Sixteen papers are quoted, a typical opinion being that of the *New York Times* of January 13:

In three respects, then, the nomination is eminently unfit to be made — character, reputation, and loyalty to the Constitution. What remains, great as it may be, weighs little against that three-fold union of essential unfitness.

On the same page the *Chronicle* prints "The Startling Letter":

Washington, March 21, 1861.

Hon. Jefferson Davis:

My dear Friend:

The bearer of this letter, Archibald Rowan, has had seven years' experience in the Ordnance Department at Washington, and has been an efficient officer. He has been a contributor to *De Bow's Review*, where he has discussed the complications and causes which have resulted in the destruction of the American Union, and now leaves here for the Southern Confederacy, through loyalty to the South. I think you will find him of special service to you.

Your friend,
Caleb Cushing

This report of the letter was a grossly inaccurate version of the original.

Another item began: "The following is a sample of numerous letters received from all parts of the country by the *Chronicle*: The First Rebel Flag." There followed a communication stating that a brig belonging to Cushing and his brothers had been anchored in Charleston Harbor when Fort Sumter was fired on, and hoisted the palmetto flag under orders of Cushing himself, then at Charleston. The truth, as Dr. Fuess states, was that the flag was raised under compulsion, that Cushing was not in Charleston, and that he disclaimed the act as soon as he heard of it. And then there was a sneering "Ballad of Dr. Faustus" with Cushing cast in the title role.

The Wednesday editorials were "Security for a Sound Conversion," saying that if Senator Sumner stood ready to go security for Cushing's views, this ought to be satisfactory on the subject — of the wonderful character of Sumner's faith. "There Has Been an Appointment from the Bench" recalled that Associate Justice William Cushing had been nominated and confirmed as Jay's successor. This was obviously an allusion to Justice Miller. "The United States Senate": this editorial said that the care with which the Senate was considering the nomination for the chief justiceship was most praiseworthy. Then the leader, entitled "A Startling Revelation," recounts the episode of the letter, with details drawn from the spurious version. It says that the letter read at the caucus on Tuesday was the original in Cushing's own hand. Nevins speaks of Sargent's securing "a copy" from Belknap. In either case it was the authentic version — not the counterfeit printed next day in the *Chronicle* — which did its work among the senators. This is no justification of the *Chronicle*, but it does put its canard out of the chain of causation leading to Cushing's defeat. The final editorial, on January 14, was entitled "The Conflict Ended," saying that it was now certain that Cushing would not receive confirmation and concluding that "the greater his talents, being wrong in principle, the more dangerous the selection" would have been.

On Thursday the *Chronicle* fired a few parting shots. But

the morning *National Republican* gave the account of Tuesday's events already quoted and continued:

> The bitter and venomous assaults made by our cotemporary, the *Chronicle*, upon the loyalty and character of Mr. Cushing have astonished all who read them. It was natural that in the disappointment at not having obtained the nomination of their pet candidate they should have used every means to blacken and defame Mr. Cushing, but that they should have been guilty of *forgery* to accomplish their purpose and bring odium upon the Administration was hardly to be expected of a journal claiming to be respectable.

In parallel columns it then produces "the forged letter" and "what Mr. Cushing did write." The latter is as follows:

Washington, March 20, 1861

Dear Sir:

Mr. Archibald Roane, for the last six or seven years a clerk in the Attorney General's office, desires from me a letter of introduction to you, and he desires it not in view of anticipation of administrative favors, but that he may have the honor of your personal intercourse. Of this, I take pleasure in assuring you, he is eminently worthy. A Southern man by birth, family, and affection, he has carefully studied and ably discussed in Mr. De Bow's *Review* and other Southern works the lamentable events which have been gradually undermining and have at length overthrown the American Union. Whilst a practical man, he is also a ripe and accomplished scholar, with predominating literary tastes and habits. In the discharge of his official duties he has combined in a singular degree the purest integrity and most enlightened intelligence with modest contentment in his lot. Having more than once declined offices of more conspicuous employment in the public service, he now resigns his present office from sentiments of devotion to that which alone he can feel to be his country, the Confederate States, from one of which (Texas) he was appointed. I most heartily commend him as a gentleman and a man of confidence and esteem, and I am, with the highest consideration,

Your obedient servant,
C. Cushing

Hon. Jefferson Davis,
    President of the Confederate States.

The salutation and conclusion are more formal than in the false version, and the name of the person in question is different.[35] But by whatever name, the man was only a law clerk, and not an ordnance officer.

Friday's *Chronicle* printed a "true" version, substantially as given above, putting the passages it considered most damaging in bold type, and pronouncing the whole much worse than the one it printed on Wednesday. It offered an explanation which is no excuse for its inaccuracy. But feeling no inclination to make out a case for the *Chronicle* on this point, we leave it to its own showing:

LET JUSTICE BE DONE

The night after the Senatorial caucus, which resulted in the withdrawal of Mr. Cushing's name for Chief Justice, we received what purported to be a copy of a letter written on the 21st of March, 1861, by Caleb Cushing, addressed to Jefferson Davis, and which had been read in the caucus, creating consternation among his two or three Republican friends, and causing the unanimous rejection of the pending resolution favoring his confirmation. This copy, being in shorthand, was written out, and means adopted to ascertain its authenticity. By a late hour at night we had been able to trace the original from its former hiding place to the War Department, thence to the President's, and, between 12 and 1 oclock at night, to a Senator, who refused to give a copy on account of honorable obligations, although told that our copy would be printed on the conviction that it was substantially correct, if means of a verification with the original were not afforded. It was printed with a preface stating it to be a copy, which we published as complete and perfect as we could decipher from the copy in our possession. We are told by a warm and intimate personal friend of Mr. Cushing that he feels aggrieved on account of verbal inaccuracies, which, he thinks, subjects

[35] The man's true name was Roane. He had served as a clerk in the office of the Attorney General from 1854 to 1861. (Homer Cummings and Carl McFarland, *Federal Justice*, New York: The Macmillan Company, 1937, p. 156; *cf.* the *Diary of Edward Bates*.) The point is inconsequential, but it adds to the complications, for Dr. Fuess states that "the man's name was 'Rowan'" as shown by comparison with the retained copy in Cushing's own files. He chides the *Chronicle* for spelling it "Roane." In fact the spurious version in Wednesday's *Chronicle* had it "Rowan," while the form printed in the *National Republican* of Thursday and in the *Chronicle* for Friday (confessing previous error) was "Roane."

him to a degree of censure by the public which an accurate copy would not warrant. As we have set down naught in malice and entertain none other than the kindest feelings for him personally, we will take pleasure in correcting any possibly incorrect statement if any has been made, in anything we have printed. We have carefully excluded everything from our columns which called in question his personal honor, other than that which, in our opinion, is so aptly described by Governor Andrew, of his own State, who thought that, having been so intimately associated in opinion and sympathy with the rebel leaders, made it unfit, if not unsafe, to intrust him with high official station. It was this feature of the case which we endeavored to impress on the Senate. If, in this discussion, anything has been inadvertently printed which does him injustice, our columns are open to him for any explanation or correction which he may choose to make. This offer is made in the utmost good faith, as it would be a cause of regret to believe that we had done any person the least wrong without putting forth an effort to rectify it.

With this we take leave of the episode. It was the true version of the letter to Jefferson Davis which was the proximate cause of Cushing's defeat. Whether his nomination would otherwise have been confirmed none can say. It seems somewhat irrational that so small a matter should have been so decisive. Cushing is not the only nominee to the Court whose defeat was in part attributable to some objection not going to the merits of the question of fitness. Which always leaves unanswered the important issue, Should he have been confirmed? The *Chronicle's* explanation of the spurious version seems to be truthful, however inadequate as a justification. What had been printed down to Wednesday, it is submitted, was rough, but not "vile" or otherwise censurable. And no one, it is supposed, will imagine that Justice Miller would have been party to the publication of a false statement.

Cushing never forgot who it was that led the hue and cry. Among his papers in the Library of Congress is a dossier containing clippings critical of his opponents in this and other connections. There are three on Judge Miller, apropos of a canard in the press just prior to his participation in the Electoral Commission three years later. This will be dealt with in its proper place.

At long last the President nominated Morrison R. Waite of Toledo, Ohio, and a grateful Senate gave its confirmation by a vote of sixty-three to six. When the nomination was made, somebody started a rumor that he had voted for McClellan in 1864, but this was promptly denied before the quest for a chief justice was rendered more ridiculous than it had already become. Waite was the son of a chief justice of Connecticut and graduated from Yale in 1837. He began practice in the Maumee Valley in Ohio, and enjoyed an excellent local reputation. Diligent in his profession, he had never hungered for public employment, but had been in the legislature for one term and had held municipal office. At the desire of Secretary Delano he was retained as counsel in the Alabama Claims Arbitration, and at the moment of his nomination he was presiding over the Ohio constitutional convention. To the country at large he was relatively unknown. If one chose a single word to describe him, it would be, not brilliance of mind, nor erudition, nor experience in large affairs, but character. From the perils of Grant's ineptitude the country had had a safe deliverance.

Justice Miller wrote one more letter dealing with the chief justiceship — on July 1, 1874. It should be premised that Justice Bradley, for his first eleven years on the bench, had the southern circuit, which included the State of Texas. Thus Ballinger had had frequent occasion to appear before him. Justice Miller wrote:

I note with interest what you write about Bradley's expressions concerning myself with pleasure but without surprise. I think I have endeavored to convey to you before this, a sense of antagonism on Bradley's part toward me ever since he came on the bench. It was perceptible rather in the fact that I never could get into confidential relations with him, or feel that I had established any relation with him whatever. I became satisfied during the term of the court which preceded the death of Chase, that he had from the hour he entered the court entertained the hope that he might succeed Chase as C. Justice. Nor was he without

foundation for such hope. One member of the cabinet, a great
favorite with Grant was his devoted personal and political
friend.[36] And Bradley himself had both the learning in and out
of his profession, and the native ability which justified his ambition. He knew that when a vacancy occurred I would be strongly
urged for the place, and hence his unwillingness to embarrass
himself with any close relation with me. This also led to what
I was well aware of during the term before the last as was also
clear to all the balance of the judges, that there was a special
bond [of] union between Bradley and Swayne, and I did not
doubt it was a common feeling of the necessity of combining
against me as a person in the way prominently of both of them.
I felt the effect of this sensibiy as soon as I reached home from
Europe last fall.

But with the settlement of that question against the Bench,
which these efforts of Bradley and Swayne largely brought about,
Bradley['s] antagonism to me ceased, and I was quite conscious
of the change during the latter part of the last term. I am also
convinced that Bradley had come to prefer that I should be appointed after he found the untoward results of his machinations
with Swayne. I was glad of it, for with some allowance for eccentricity he is a useful and valuable man on the bench.

Without quoting from Justice Bradley's letters at length
it may be said that they show, however, that in May 1873 he
expected that Miller would be promoted to the chief justiceship, and that he expressed no resentment. One may catch
between the lines an awareness that he, too, was well qualified — but Justice Bradley would have been a stranger to
himself if he had thought otherwise. And when the chief
justiceship again became vacant, in 1888, he wished to see it
filled by an appointment from the Court, and would have
been content to see the honor go to Miller as the senior associate justice.

A few other matters should be mentioned in conclusion.
In January 1874 Justice Miller counted General Belknap as
a friend. But the Secretary's dishonesty was then unknown.
Miller had reposed faith in his fellow townsman, and in 1869
had written: "He is quite equal to the place and I am happy
in having been one of the first to telegraph Grant to appoint

him." [37] His chagrin over Belknap's subsequent dishonesty is disclosed in the concluding paragraph of the following letter commenting on Grant's administration:

I am not much interested in politics these times. I confess I dread democratic ascendancy in all the branches of the government. The House shows that the democratic leaders are still what they always were superior in demagoguery to any party that ever lived unless it was the party of Julius Caesar at Rome.

I am quite disgusted with Grant and his surroundings, and heartily agree with you that he has done as much to lower the standard of that high office as any man who ever held it unless it was Genl. Jackson. They are much of a sort obstinate, small men, with low standard of morals and no proper estimate of the high functions they have been called on to discharge. Both of them looked upon the offices they were called on to fill as personal perquisites of the office which they held. Both were fond of low company.

But I do believe Grant is the first man who has prostrated that great place to exhibiting its holder as a weak adorer of moneyed men and moneyed influences. I do not charge or believe that he has ever received a bribe either in money or in property. But he has habitually bowed himself down and submitted himself to the control and sought the society of men whose only recommendation was their wealth and their readiness to attach themselves to his fortunes.

He has a great fondness for money and has placed his kin and his pets in positions to make it. But I do not so much mind this as the fact obvious to all, that it is in his nature to bow the great office he holds in a kind of disgusting worship at the feet of all the coarse rich men he meets without regard to the means by which their wealth has been acquired. . . .

I feel a personal chagrin when some man in whom I have placed confidence as Genl Belknap shows of what poor clay he was made.[38]

Since the newspaper attack upon Cushing has necessarily bulked large in this chapter, it may be of interest to quote Justice Miller on the press. He characterizes as "a damned fool and coward" a certain district judge who had taken notice of criticism in the press,[39] and says further:

[37] Letter of October 31, 1869.   [38] Letter of March 29, 1875.
[39] Judge Morrill, of the federal district court at Galveston, had called on the proprietors of the Galveston *News* to show cause why they should not be at-

The newspaper tyranny is the most oppressive now in existence, and the gravest problem of the age is to determine where relief shall come from. They have invaded everything sacred to human nature. Private character, domestic relations, and everything. They have respected the Courts longer than anything else, and lately they have combined to bring the Courts and the administration of justice under their control, by their appeals to popular prejudice, accompanied by the usual amount of lying.[40]

There may be some who will feel disposed to censure Justice Miller for taking any part in the Cushing affair. In the forum of his own conscience he suffered no condemnation. Some years later he set down this revealing judgment of himself:

It is a source of no little consolation to me in advanced life, that while I have had strong passions, an excitable temperament, ardent desires and powerful antipathies, and while I feel sometimes that I have not been as forgiving and as lenient to the errors of others as a more perfect character would have been, I have in all emergencies done my duty, to the extent of my skill in ascertaining what it was, and my ability to perform what it required. But this is egotism.[41]

It was not egotism at all. Justice Miller found himself on occasion in a position where to act on his own view of what was right would subject him to misconstruction and criticism. A man of delicate and introspective sensibility might have denied the promptings of his own conscience lest he do, or appear to do, injustice. It was Miller's way to continue to march breast forward, firm in the right as he understood it. True of the Cushing episode, this is even more true of Miller's part in the disputed election of 1876.

---

tached for contempt of court by the publication of an article on "Law and Higher Law," critical of the Judge. Ballinger represented the respondents. He moved to quash, demurred, and read an answer. The Judge, declaring that the answer had been sufficient, refused to allow him to argue the question of the Court's jurisdiction over constructive contempts. (Ballinger's Diary, June 6 to 8, 1875; also 11 *Albany Law Journal* 373, 390, 1875.)

[40] Letter of June 23, 1875.
[41] Letter of October 3, 1879.

XII

THE ELECTORAL COMMISSION

WHILE THE EPISODE of the disputed election of 1876 forms properly no part of the history of the Supreme Court, the participation of five of the justices in the proceedings of the Electoral Commission was an unwelcome experience which requires some mention. The judicial members were forced to the very center of an unprecedented political contest. And when, on every crucial question, the division coincided with party affiliation, the public image of judicial impartiality was affected in a way from which the Court did not at once recover. The Court's ordinary work of adjudication presents burning issues enough without calling the justices to any extra-judicial functions, but in the distracted condition prevailing in January 1877 there was no other element in the State in which the requisite confidence could be reposed.

It will be recalled that in the Republican Convention, which met on June 14, James G. Blaine, Speaker of the House, had been the leading candidate, followed by Senator Morton, Senator Conkling, and Benjamin H. Bristow of Kentucky, one of the few able members of the Grant cabinet. The outcome was that Blaine's opponents finally united in support of Governor Hayes of Ohio, a respectable but hardly a dashing candidate. The Democratic nomination went to Governor Tilden of New York, a railroad lawyer who had manifested a belated interest in "reform." The runner-up, Governor Hendricks of Indiana, was nominated for the vice-presidency.

In late July Justice Miller was spending part of his vacation at Saratoga Springs, where he wrote Ballinger a long letter on the political situation:

Your remarks about Blaine and Tilden are somewhat provoking and still more amusing. I do not wonder that after having

[*280*]

expressed the opinion that "Providence" (vague phrase) has furnished the American public with Tilden to fill the mission of a second Moses, you should precede that declaration with a statement that you "don't set up to be free from prejudices." A smaller "trickster" as you call him, a man of more selfish aims and purposes hardly ever had a place in our public life. Prominently concerned in all the corruption and frauds of N. York democratic politics for forty years. Intimately cooperating with Tweed, Hoffman, Connally & Co during the whole term of their stealing and theft; writing himself the well known circular by which the vote of the rural districts of the State were in 1868 to be furnished to him, in time for the city vote to be counted so as to give the vote to Seymour,[1] and the head of the device by which 25.000 votes were fraudulently manufactured for that purpose, it is indeed strange to hear one of the purest men I know in the world, speak of him as a man raised up by Providence to reform the corrupt practices of our government. If he is the instrument of "Providence" then that word has a different meaning from any I have usually attached to it.

As to Blaine he is the only man worthy to be President of the United States who has come so near to receiving a party nomination for that office, since the plan of placing Candidates before the people by national conventions was adopted fifty years ago, except Mr. Clay. I might except Mr. Lincoln who afterward justified his nomination, but who was nominated on the prevailing rule of availability, because so little known as to have made no enemies.

There is in Blaine's history and character, more of that courage, statesmanship, ability, and scorn of small truckling ways for popular support, than any man since Mr. Clay; and like his great prototype he has fallen the victim of the malignity of partizan persecution from his political enemies, aided by the little men who were his rivals in his own party.

I admire him more than any man now in public life, and if he had been nominated he would have inspired an enthusiasm unknown to the present day in the hearts of his supporters.

There! I have said my say, whether it be prejudice or not. It is the opinion of one personally familiar with Blaine, and his rivals in his own party. Of Tilden I know nothing that is not open to all men. But a man who never argued half a dozen cases in his life in court, who has made $5.000.000 by being Trustee and

---

[1] The letter is quoted in full in D. T. Lynch's *"Boss" Tweed* (New York: Boni and Liveright, 1927), p. 293.

Director of rotten rail roads, who was Tweeds intimate friend and associate during all his rascalities, and who only came in to assist at the destruction after there was no doubt that he would be destroyed, and who had to choose between going down with him, or saving himself by his friends ruin, you may get all the purifying reform out of him you expect. I shall most certainly get all I expect.

I think the result of the election is more uncertain than I have felt it to be for twelve years. There is enough of opposition to the *Administration*, perhaps enough to the Republican party, to defeat the latter if it could be combined. But the folly of the opposition has saved us before and will probably do it again. The Hamburg murders [2] are good for thousands of votes, and may turn the scale in close states like Indiana or N. York. If your friends will kill negroes, I am glad they select the Presidential year for that amusement.

The essential defects of a Kangaroo ticket, in which the strength is in the hind legs, is working well for the good of the country; as is seen in the fact that Tilden and Hendricks after a long personal conference at this place, were unable to agree on their letter of acceptance. And the personal hatred of Tilden among his party leaders in this State, growing out of his duplicity and corrupt character, his profuse use of his own money for his own election, — a mode of electioneering now witnessed for the first time — will probably lose him his own state, and with it the election. The unanimity of the rebel states, and the manner in which that unanimity is produced, are having its effect in the north, and on the whole I am hopeful, that no such misfortune as Tilden's *providential election* will befall us in the centennial year. I hope you will excuse all this, as you know I seldom allude to politics in my letters to you. But your remarks justify me in this. They are to me to speak mildly a *great surprise*.[3]

It will be evident that the Judge was not devoid of political feeling. Nor was he in this respect unique among the members of the Court.

The outcome of the election was that Tilden was certain of 184 electoral votes, Hayes of 165. Twenty votes, coming respectively from Florida, Louisiana, Oregon, and South Carolina, were in dispute. Since 185 votes constituted a majority

[2] Race riot in South Carolina on July 8, in which several Negroes were killed.
[3] Letter of July 26, 1876.

in the electoral college, if Tilden received a single one of the contested votes he would be elected. Hayes conversely must secure the entire lot.

We need not set out all the *tu quoque* contentions concerning the disputed returns from Florida and Louisiana.[4] Negro Republicans had certainly been intimidated on a large scale. On the other hand, the state canvassing boards had exercised the discretionary powers which the law vested in them so as to exclude certain returns and thus to certify a majority of popular votes for Hayes. Republican electors thus certified proceeded to cast their votes, while the Democratic candidates for elector met and prepared returns for Tilden. In South Carolina, it should be remembered, the Hayes electors received a majority of votes without the need of any rejections by the canvassing board. Here the Democratic contention was that there had been no legal election in that the legislature had failed to carry out a provision of the state constitution to the effect that "it shall be the duty of the general assembly to provide from time to time for the registration of all electors." Also that there was no republican form of government in South Carolina; and that because of the presence of United States forces no fair election had been held there.

The controversy over Oregon had to do with an ineligible elector. There was no question that a majority of popular votes had been cast for the three Republican candidates for elector. But one of them was at the time of election a postmaster, and hence constitutionally ineligible. After the election he resigned his postmastership. The secretary of state, who was by law the canvassing authority, certified that the three Republican candidates had received the "highest number of votes." But the Governor, a Democrat, assumed jurisdiction to hear a protest, and thereupon decided that two Republicans and one Democratic elector had been chosen, on the view that the election of the postmaster was a complete

---

[4] One may consult P. L. Haworth, *The Hayes-Tilden Election* (Indianapolis: Bobbs-Merrill Company, 1927) on the whole subject.

nullity, and that the highest Democratic candidate had thus been elected. The two Republican electors, however, acted upon the view that there was a vacancy (the ineligible elector had presented his resignation from the electoral college); the state law provided that vacancies should be filled by the other electors; therefore they chose the man who at the time of the election had been ineligible. The Governor's lone Democrat acted under the same law to choose two other electors, choosing Republicans. The result was rival returns: one by the three Republicans who had the canvassing authority's certificate of election, the other by the Democrat and his coöpted colleagues, whose title consisted in the Governor's certificate.

Each case, it should be added, was complicated by its own particular difficulties which need not be considered here.

The Constitution does not speak directly to the question who shall choose between two or more returns from a given state. It provides that the electoral votes shall be sent to the seat of government of the United States, directed to the president of the Senate; "the President of the Senate shall, in the presence of the Senate and House of Representatives, open all the certificates and the votes shall then be counted." By whom? The Senate was Republican, and had a Republican presiding officer. The House was Democratic. If both Houses must agree upon which were the valid votes, an impasse seemed inevitable.

In a letter of November 19 Miller turned to the impending controversy in Congress:

I am distressed and fearful at the aspect of the presidential canvas [sic]. I dread the scene in the Hall of Representatives when the vote comes to be counted there. I would prefer that Tilden should be the President to some possible results that may happen, even if Hayes be declared and lawfully declared elected.

I have expressed the conviction often, in regard to other matters, that the House is gradually absorbing all the powers of the government. The emergency if the three states [5] now in dispute

---

[5] The possibilities of the situation in Oregon were not realized at first.

certify Hayes electors, presents a terrible temptation to action in that line of conduct, and the House as now constituted is not one likely to resist such temptation or to be very considerate in the mere manner of exercising its functions. . . .

And again in a letter written at Christmas:

If I was gloomy and uncomfortable over the political prospect, your letter has not tended in any manner to dispel the cloud. I have generally believed that you were a reasonably cool and dispassionate thinker but I have seen occasional hints of passion, and an indisposition or incapacity to see more than one side, which surprises me to say the least, very much.

I think I am unprejudiced enough to admit frankly that the returning board of Louisiana is not what it should be, in fact that it is governed if not by corrupt, certainly by partizan influence. On the other hand is it possible that you cannot see and admit that by reason of violence, and the absolute fear of death thus produced, there was no honest vote in that State? And that the laws which governed the returning board were made as the negroes when in power had a right to make them, to protect themselves against this very danger?

Suppose I admit the republican party to be more or less corrupt, I am of opinion that it is purity itself compared to the one which you call your friend.

It is not that you and I differ, that your remarks have such a significance, but it is that you should look at the matter now with the same one sided spirit and speak of it with the same bitterness you did when in 1857 you told me, that if the South could not get their negroes into the Territories any other way you could whip us in a fight and would do it.

Where am I to look for any spirit of judicial fairness, if *you* are actuated by such thoughts and feelings.

After there had been a good deal of menacing speech-making, committees of the two Houses got down to evolving some plan for the peaceful settlement of the issue. The outcome was the Act of January 29, 1877. It provided that where more than one return was received from any state the same should be referred to a commission to consist of five members chosen from each house and five associate justices. The Act designated the justices from the first, third, eighth, and ninth circuits, and a fifth to be chosen by them. Clifford and Field were Democrats, Swayne and Miller of course Republicans. It was expected that they would choose Judge Davis, whose political sympathies at the moment were supposed to be in a state of equipoise. It so happened that just before the bill was passed the Democrats of the Illinois legislature had chosen Davis for United States senator. The result was that Justice Bradley was chosen to be the odd member of the tribunal. Of the five senators, three were Republicans; of the commissioners from the House, three were Democrats. The result was a bare majority of Republican members, and while on procedural matters Judge Bradley often voted with the Democrats, the decisive votes went to Hayes, eight to seven.

Now that Miller was drawn into the electoral contest he was considerably embarrassed by a newspaper interview attributed to him. On December 11 the Chicago *Times* published what was alleged to be a conversation which took place between Justice Miller and the *Times's* Washington representative. The substance of the views attributed to the Judge was that there was "grave danger to be apprehended" from "the evident tendency of the Democrats to make mischief." They would accomplish their end by bribing an elector not to vote: Tilden's "past career indicates that he would resort to anything to carry his point and attain his ambition." The purported conversation contained fifteen exchanges of question and answer, said to have taken place as the parties walked along the street — which in itself shows that the correspondent could not have taken down the specific replies made to his queries. A briefer account of the remarks appeared in the Washington *Republican* on the same day.

On December 12 the Washington *Chronicle* published an editorial, "That 'Interview' with Judge Miller," saying, "We have authority for stating that much of this conversation is unfounded in fact, and that that part of it which has any foundation is so colored and exaggerated as to convey impressions by no means correct as to what really was said." On December 13 the entire article in the *Times* was reprinted in the Washington *National Republican*.

Then on February 1 the *New York Herald* carried a report from its New Orleans correspondent representing that from a letter Miller had written to Ballinger it appeared that Miller regarded reconstruction in the South as well-nigh intolerable, that the people had chosen Tilden and that there was evidently a plot on foot to thwart the popular will. What purported to be a corroboratory statement by another newspaper man appeared in the *Herald* for February 3.

Miller was of opinion that this report in the *Herald* originated in some conversation in which Ballinger had repeated what he had written to Miller, and that these sentiments had erroneously been attributed to Miller. Ballinger's diary [6] shows that this is precisely what had happened. While the report in the Chicago *Times* had some foundation, the *Herald's* account was wholly erroneous. Miller writes of his troubles in a letter of February 2:

> Ever since my name was first mentioned as one of the Judges likely to constitute a new and anomalous tribunal I have been the subject of newspaper comment not personally unfavorable, but from correspondence professing to give statements of my views as coming from myself on the condition of the present presidential contest.
>
> A few weeks ago, a young man, formerly belonging to Corkhill's Chronicle corps, who had been recently discharged, met me in the Street and after exciting my sympathy for his discharge made a few observations as to the condition of the electoral vote. I was quite cautious, declined to express my opinion of the Oregon difficulty, and said that a reference of the difficulty to the Sup. Court was impracticable.
>
> I also expressed some apprehension that the democratic majority in Congress might not be as amenable to moderate influences as it ought to be. He was poor and out of employment, and stimulated by his necessities he made an article of a column for the "Chicago Times" in which I was said to have expressed a belief that the democratic majority intended mischief, and would without regard to right or wrong seek to inaugurate Tilden by violence if necessary &c &c &c
>
> I enclose you herewith extracts from the New York Herald of yesterday in which the opinions imputed to me on your authority

[6] January 28 to February 7, 1877.

are exactly the reverse of those above mentioned. This last thing has been held over me for several days *in terrorem*.

Several friends have come to me and said such a story was in existence and they would prevent its publication if I desired, and day before yesterday the bureau of the Herald sent me a note to know what I had to say about it. I simply repeated that I had written no such thing.

Last night one of the Herald men called on me and I hunted up your last letter and showed him that the sentiments and in some cases the words his correspondent attributed to *me* were those which *you* had written to me. I also suggested that his New York editor telegraph to you on the subject and gave your address. . . .

I am not very thin skinned about newspaper stories, and there is nothing in the language used which is disrespectful, but as bearing on the very weighty duties I am now performing, and as an attempt to forestall my official action it is annoying.

Two days later he wrote again about the *Herald* article:

I saw Whitelaw Reid, the Managing Editor of the New York Tribune at an evening party last night and he told me that the thing had been offered to him for $100 and refused.

The meanness of the Herald men in publishing it after they knew through Thrasher that you denied it, and from their bureau here that I denied is too plain for discussion. But as it refers to a man now exercising before the face of the whole nation a public function which intensely interests everybody it is used as an evidence of journalistic enterprise.

Objections to each contested return were presented to the Commission by spokesmen from Congress, while the principles involved were argued by counsel. On the Republican side were William M. Evarts and E. W. Stoughton of New York, Stanley Matthews and Samuel Shellabarger of Ohio. The Democrats were represented by advocates certainly not less distinguished, including Charles O'Conor, Judge Black, Judge Campbell, Lyman Trumbull, Matt Carpenter, and George Hoadly.

As was to be expected, Justice Miller took a prominent part in the proceedings. Just as he did on the bench, he kept insisting, "We must get along and discharge this business." [7] He was active in the consultations and in drafting the reports returned to Congress, and his opinions, prepared to support his votes, are cogent arguments for the soundness of the position he had taken.

The decisive question in the Florida and Louisiana cases was whether Congress (and the Commission in its stead) could "go behind the returns" to inquire what results the canvassing boards should have certified. The Constitution provides that "each State shall appoint, in such Manner as the Legislature thereof may direct, a number of Electors. . . ." The electors are to cast their votes and send them to the seat of government, etc.; "and the votes shall then be counted." The Democratic contention was that "if the Constitution has devolved upon the two Houses of Congress the duty of counting the votes, the true votes, and the necessary power of determining what are the true votes," the Congress (and the Commission) must have power to consider any evidence relative to the question what were true votes.[8]

This view was rejected by the majority. From the constitutional provision that "each State shall appoint," etc., Miller concludes: "The legislature of Florida has vested in her board of canvassers the authority to determine who are elected electors. It has conferred no power on any tribunal to revise that decision. The board in this respect represents the State." The refusal to consider evidence *aliunde* the certificates and papers virtually ended the Florida case in favor of Hayes.

In the Louisiana case there were very serious charges of fraud against the canvassing board. The Republican position was that the power of a state over the choice of its electors was "one of the original conditions, . . . one of the original distributions of power," by which the government under the Constitution was created. It was one of the reserved rights of the states, whose exercise was not subject to federal control.[9]

---

[7] *Proceedings of the Electoral Commission*, p. 40.
[8] Argument of Mr. Merrick, *Proceedings*, p. 23.
[9] Mr. Evarts, *Proceedings*, p. 103.

Judge Campbell on the other hand insisted it was a power derived directly from the people of the United States and exercised in trust for the whole nation.[10] One will note that here, just as in the Slaughter-House Case, Judge Campbell was arguing in the language of high-toned nationalism. It is interesting, though not surprising, to observe how convincingly Northern Republicans and Southern Democrats could debate from their reversed positions.

The Democrats had contended that if the commission refused to go behind the face of the returns from the South, then it must by parity of reasoning accept the votes certified by the governor of Oregon, and so let in one vote for Tilden. Stanley Matthews had referred to Evarts, his leader, as the Palinurus who had guided the argument between Scylla and Charybdis, an unhappy metaphor which suggested that a course which got the Republicans past Florida might bring them to grief on Oregon. But they escaped both hazards. And indeed the Democratic argument on the Oregon question was plausible rather than substantial. The state law made the secretary of state the canvassing authority. He had certified the election of the three Republicans. To be sure, the governor had withheld his signature from the certificate of election. But this failure on the part of the governor to carry out a duty prescribed by Congress did not defeat the vote of the electors found to have been duly chosen. As Matthews had said in his argument on the returns from Oregon, "we undertook to draw a line . . . between things and proofs, between the thing to be certified and the certificate which certified it." [11] This was the view on which the majority justified their decision. The action of the canvassing authority was held to be the voice of the state; it was the substantial thing.

In the result, all contests were decided in favor of the returns for Hayes.

On March 4 Miller heaved a sigh of relief and set down some of his thoughts in a letter:

[10] At p. 110.   [11] *Proceedings*, p. 160.

I am just returned from the inauguration ceremonies and the cannon are peacefully playing the last part in that drama. It is to me a great relief. . . .

The events of the last ten days have demonstrated how well founded were my fears. If it was with the utmost difficulty the House of Representatives could be induced to proceed with counting the vote after the decision of a tribunal which the majority in that house had created, and which had been favored and supported by every democrat in the Senate but one, how far would its count have proceeded without such a tribunal? It is now too clear for disputation, that the Senate and House would have separated without completing the count. That each body would have declared a different man President and no human wisdom can now tell what evils would have followed.

The peaceful inauguration of Hayes as President is due largely, very largely, to the discretion, forbearance, good sense and patriotism of the southern leaders of the democratic party. To Lamar,[12] Ben Hill,[13] Brown,[14] and Hancock [15] of your state too much credit cannot be awarded. The conduct of the latter is a striking contrast to his colleague Mills [16] who ought to have leave to retire from the public service at the earliest occasion.

Years later Miller was led to talk of the disputed election and one of his listeners made a memorandum of the remarks. He reiterated the view that the law of Louisiana made the determination of the canvassing board final; there was no power in the federal government to go behind it. "To permit Congress to determine the vote would have resulted in the destruction of the Government. That body never acts judicially. It would be like their determination upon the rights to seats which are invariably decided in favor of those in sympathy

[12] L. Q. C. Lamar, senator from Mississippi; later Secretary of the Interior, and justice of the Supreme Court.
[13] Representative from Georgia. He secured the pledges of forty-two ex-Confederates in the House to oppose all attempts to frustrate the counting of the electoral votes.
[14] John Y. Brown, Representative from Kentucky. He participated in arranging an understanding that if conciliatory Southern Democrats would continue to oppose filibustering, Hayes would withdraw federal support from the carpetbag governments.
[15] Representative John Hancock, a Unionist who during the War had moved North. He returned to Texas in 1865 and endeavored to mediate between conservatives and radicals.
[16] Roger Q. Mills.

with the majority." [17] While this last statement is too sweeping, there is a considerable measure of truth in it. And Congress had notoriously abused its power just prior to the election of 1876.

Of the very broad equities of the contest it is well to speak with diffidence. Neither side came to it with clean hands. On the construction of the law the majority seem to have had a very strong position. But one hesitates to say that it was because of the strength of that view that all eight voted as they did — or that it was any weakness in the legal position which caused the seven to dissent.

[17] Pennypacker, *Autobiography of a Pennsylvanian*, p. 132.

XIII

PRESIDENTIAL ASPIRATIONS

SOMETHING SHOULD BE SAID of the political avocations of certain of the justices throughout the post-war years. Chase, Davis, and Field were in turn candidates for a presidential nomination, and while Justice Miller received nothing more tangible than two stray votes cast in the Republican National Convention of 1888,[1] he was generally regarded as a presidential possibility and had a certain amount of latent support.

Chief Justice Chase's efforts to secure the Democratic nomination in 1868, and his disappointment when Governor Seymour was selected, have already been mentioned. Judge Davis, who had managed Lincoln's pre-convention campaign, was always preoccupied with political developments and was moving toward the Democratic party. In a letter which he wrote to Justice Clifford in November 1868 Davis discussed the Chief Justice's unsuccessful candidacy and the Seymour-Blair ticket:

> The Democratic party in ancient days had wisdom — Lately it has none — The Country was ripe for a change, When the Convention met in N Y. but it was plain on account of the quasi hostility of the Democratic party to the War, that one who had acted with the Republicans during that War must be the Standard bearer — and the Chief Justice, through the Events of last winter, was properly disciplined for the race — There was great anxiety out here. that he shd be nominated. by conservative men — His nomination wd have split the [Republican] party in pieces — Chase & [Charles Francis] Adams should have been the ticket, or Chase & Hendricks [2] — Gov Seymour wanted Chase nominated, &

---

[1] On the third ballot he received two votes from the Kansas delegation.

[2] Thomas A. Hendricks, then senator from Indiana. He was elected governor in 1872, was unsuccessful candidate for the vice-presidency in 1876, and was elected vice-president in 1884.

a man who could not say *no* when pressed to take a nomination — Knowing that Chase was the available man — is now the *man* for the crisis.

As if the very Devil was in it — Frank Blair,[3] a common Loafer, with no moral character, with his revolutionary letter to Broadhead, is nominated by Southern men, who go home & make speeches to infuriate Northern people — People — plenty of them — are voting agt the Democratic party getting power as they fear some evil, & they are not voting because they approve of what the Republican party has done, & yet the election will be considered as an endorsement in full of everything, & the Leaders — the progressive men, will press extreme measures to the bitter end —

Some people are going to be disappointed, for Grant must be either a radical or conservative — If the Democratic party would disband *now* the Republican party wd have the greatest row during even next winter that we have heard of for years — But I will forbear — I have a little hope left — [4]

About the same time Judge Nelson was writing to Brother Clifford, and it seems that he too had been thought of in some quarters as a Democratic presidential candidate for 1868:

I agree with you that the democracy seem to be doomed. I have great regard for Seymour: and would rejoice to see him President: but he has hard to carry weight [*sic*]: and I have feared the result, ever since I heard Blair was his associate. [*Several words undecipherable.*] Some of my friends were offended in N. Y. because I would not consent to be a candidate, but I had no desire for it; and, no confidence in the leaders. Indeed, was not in the particular confidence of those who would control the policy of the party in the campaign and had no feeling I could influence it. Did you ever see such folly as there is in some of them in the City. The World for instance.[5]

---

[3] Francis P. Blair, Jr., Democratic nominee for the vice-presidency, was a brother of Montgomery Blair of Lincoln's cabinet. He had supported President Johnson, and wished to have the Southern states restored on the simple conditions of accepting emancipation and supporting the Constitution. His letter to J. O. Brodhead said that if the Democratic nominee should be elected it would be his duty to abolish the Reconstruction governments.

[4] Letter of November 2, 1868; Clifford Papers.

[5] Letter of October 22, 1868; Clifford Papers.

Four years later, when Grant's political incapacity had been clearly demonstrated, it seemed as though the country might respond to a respectable opponent. Justice Davis and his friends hoped that he himself might be the candidate of both the Liberal Republicans and the Democrats in the election of 1872. The Democratic party had so many Confederate associations that, as Davis had said, their only hope was to accept some one who had acted with the Republicans during the war. For a time it appeared very probable that Davis would be that man. Among those enlisted in his support was Philip Phillips, already mentioned as a leader at the Supreme Court bar. In a letter of November 22, 1871, Phillips wrote to John Forsyth of Mobile, one of the foremost Democratic editors, suggesting Davis as a nominee, and on February 25 he assured his friend on points which seemed vital to a Southerner:

Judge D's chances for the Presidency a[re] looming up very considerably — I gave him your editorial. You are mistaken in supposing he was in early times a democrat; he was born a Federalist and was a member of the Whig party — He is an honest man and will deal fairly and liberally with the South. I do not know what his views are as to Tariff &c and dont think it very material to the Southern people. Carpet bag rule will find no favor at his hands, and if he succeed the rule of corruption will in a great measure come to an end. Much will depend upon the action of the Cincinnati liberal Rep. Convention. I think that the greater the assurance that Grant will be nominated, the greater the chances of D's success. In other words the nomination of some [one] other than Grant might tend to heal the breach which now exists and unite at least in some degree the present divided parts.[6]

On February 22, 1872, the National Labor Reform Convention, at Columbus, nominated Judge Davis for the presidency.[7] He replied sagely that "the Chief Magistracy of the Republic should neither be sought nor declined by any American citizen," and refrained from committing himself

[6] Phillips' Letterbook, 1871–72, pp. 210, 331–332.
[7] H. E. Pratt, "David Davis 1815–1886," in *Publication Thirty-seven of the Illinois State Historical Library* (1930), pp. 157, 175–176.

to its program, a combination of the radicalism and reform of the seventies. The nomination was valueless of course, unless Davis could secure the support of one or more major political groups. When the Liberal Republicans met at Cincinnati in April, Davis' friends rather overdid themselves by their noisy and expensive display. His prospects declined sharply even before the opening ballot, where he stood in the fifth place. The nomination went to Horace Greeley, who was thereupon adopted by the Democratic party as well. After this failure, Davis withdrew from his candidacy on the Labor ticket.

During the latter months of 1871 and the following spring, when members of the Republican party thought of setting their house in order by the choice of some more able candidate than President Grant, Justice Miller was mentioned as a possible nominee. That his own hopes for the future took a different direction is shown by the following memorandum in Ballinger's dairy for October 14, 1871, at a time when he was a guest in Miller's home:

I believe Judge Miller's attachment to me is ardent & sincere, and I know mine is to him. He is a very able & a very noble man. He thinks his chances good to be C. J. if there shd be a vacancy during Grant's term — Sd that he had [been] talked about as a strong man to unite the disaffected Republicans upon Pr Grant but he at once repudiated any such use of his name.

The movement against Grant collapsed, of course, within the party. If any of Miller's friends in Iowa were actively urging him as a candidate, their efforts must have been underground. When the Republican State Convention met at Des Moines on March 27, 1872, a vote endorsing the Grant administration was passed with cheers — "there being not over six or eight votes in the negative," according to the Republican *Gate City* of Keokuk.[8] The vote to instruct the delegation was unanimous.[9] At this moment there appeared in the

---

[8] March 29, 1872. The *Gate City* had been supporting Grant for renomination, but without enthusiasm.

[9] *New York Times*, March 28, 1872.

HARPER'S WEEKLY.
A
JOURNAL OF CIVILIZATION.

Vol. XVI.—No. 797.]   NEW YORK, SATURDAY, APRIL 6, 1872.   [SINGLE COPIES TEN CENTS.
$4.00 PER YEAR IN ADVANCE.

THE PRESIDENTIAL FEVER ON THE SUPREME BENCH.

Chief Justice. "Mark but my fall, and that that ruin'd me.
Judge Davis, I charge thee, fling away ambition;
By that sin fell the angels; how can man, then,
The image of his Maker, hope to win by't?"—*Shakspeare.*

Cartoon by Nast, appearing in *Harper's Weekly*, April 6, 1872

New York Times [10] a dispatch from Washington, running as follows:

> The friends of Judge Miller, of the Supreme Court, authorize the emphatic contradiction of the report circulating in the West that that gentleman has permitted the use of his name as a candidate for the Presidency. From first to last Judge Miller has uniformly and positively declined to permit any one to make any such use of his name, declaring that a position on the Bench required the subordination of all political aspirations.

Justice Field was a candidate for a Democratic nomination to the Presidency both in 1880 and in 1884.[11] While maintaining a proper appearance of aloofness, he really cherished expectations greater than the event warranted. In the Convention of 1880 he stood fifth on the opening ballot, and was soon forgotten in the landslide to General Hancock. The preparation of an indulgent biography is a usual part of the business of constructing a presidential candidacy. In 1877 Field had dictated his *Personal Reminiscences of Early Days in California*, and in 1880 his political agents, Chauncey F. Black and Samuel B. Smith, made a compilation of articles suitable for campaign purposes. This was not published at that time, but in 1881 Field's friend, John Norton Pomeroy, prepared an "Introductory Sketch" which, with the other material, was privately printed under the title *Some Account of the Work of Stephen J. Field as a Legislator, State Judge, and Judge of the Supreme Court of the United States*. Correspondence between Justice Field and Mr. Pomeroy [12] discloses the personal supervision Field gave to this production. He found Pomeroy's manuscript "so strong in its award of commendation that I should hardly dare show it to my friends." [13] Conquering this modesty, however, he did show it to many of them and discovered a unanimous desire that

---

[10] March 29, 1872.

[11] Carl B. Swisher, *Stephen J. Field* (Washington: The Brookings Institution, 1930), chaps. XI and XII, gives the story in detail.

[12] "Four Letters of Mr. Justice Field," edited by Howard Jay Graham, 47 *Yale Law Journal* 1100 (1938).

[13] Letter of June 21, 1881.

it should be published. "But your sketch has been altered in several particulars," he continued. "Much of its strong language of commendation has been omitted, and some of it has been modified, and in these respects I think the sketch will be more acceptable to others as it is to myself."

In a sanguine frame of mind Judge Field awaited the Democratic National Convention of 1884. His friends were persistent in their efforts. But in California the state convention of June 10, 1884, resenting what it regarded as Field's favoritism toward the railroads and toward coolie labor, overwhelmingly adopted a resolution repudiating "the presidential aspirations of Stephen J. Field" and pledging earnest efforts to assure his defeat. Notwithstanding this decisive setback, Field still entertained some hope that the course of the National Convention might take a fortuitous turn in his direction. After Grover Cleveland had been nominated, Field wrote to Pomeroy in California:

I shall have much to say to you when we meet; particularly of the very strange action in California. Had I received the cordial support, instead of opposition of that State my candidacy, according to the judgment of my friends, would have stood great chances of success; and even without that support, had the forces of Mr. Cleveland ever given way my name would have been presented at Chicago with reasonable prospect of success. At least, so all my friends say. But I am content where I am. There at least I have no caprices to consult and no clamors to fret me.[14]

Field was an ill-tempered person with a long memory for grudges. Professor Williston, who was secretary to Mr. Justice Gray in 1888–89, recalls an occasion when Field was conversing at large with Gray. Field said that he had made just one request of Cleveland when he became president: that he would not give federal appointments to certain persons in California with whom Field had had hostile relations. Cleveland had nevertheless appointed some of them; and consequently, Field concluded with emphasis, he would not set foot inside the White House so long as Cleveland remained president.[15]

[14] 47 *Yale Law Journal* 1100, 1107 (1938).
[15] Conversation with Professor Samuel Williston, August 6, 1938.

At times Justice Miller, returning from a day at court, would observe, somewhat wearily but without bitterness, that Brother Field had proved rather trying.[16] Miller, too, was a man of strong feeling and was convinced that his own law and politics were right, but those with whom he differed could never complain that he had been perverse or petty.

Justice Miller was also a presidential possibility in 1880 and again in 1884, but in most particulars his situation differed from that of his brother Field. The two men appealed to quite different elements in their respective parties. Miller's strength lay in his popularity among the people of Iowa and indeed throughout the Northwest, and while Field's political philosophy was strongly conservative, Miller's views tended toward agrarian radicalism. An early indication that Justice Miller was thinking seriously about the presidency is noted in an entry in Ballinger's diary on May 5, 1878:

> Long letter from Judge Miller — also a paper from him the 'National Republican' which speaks of a strong sentiment in his favor for the Presidency in the Northwest — [17] His letter is mainly

[16] Conversation with Mrs. Coker Clarkson.

[17] As was pointed out in the discussion of Miller's aspirations for the chief justiceship, the *National Republican* was one of the leading Republican newspapers at the capital. The clipping which Miller sent to Ballinger was evidently the editorial of April 23, 1870, on "The Next Republican Candidate." It opened with the remark: "Whoever he may be he must represent the straightforward, stalwart element of the Republican party. . . . At the same time due regard must be had for the possibility of winning votes from the Opposition — a possibility that can be realized without difficulty if the nominee possesses elements of character and public record to command respect and invite confidence." After elaborating this theme the *National Republican* quoted as follows from a recent editorial in the Keokuk *Gate City*:
"If Justice Samuel F. Miller, of the United States Supreme Court, were known by the nation at large as those who know him best do, the warm public heart, constraining to wise conclusion the public judgment, would break down the barriers of sentiment that will not let a President be taken from the Supreme Court, and would make him the Chief Executive of the country. Justice Miller is one of the very few men born in any generation fit to be President. Great as he is as a jurist, and he is the greatest and strongest judge on the Supreme bench, his supremest qualities are executive. He would be a President worth the name and the place. We don't know what fateful law governs government so that by luck a wise ruler is born under the monarchical rule of heredity just about as often as a people with a ballot in their hand choose a great President with a chance to profit by their experience once in every four years. Washington and Jackson, Lincoln and Grant, only four great

political — against the capacity of the Bond-holding class — who are subverting the govt to their purposes — I infer from the co-incidence of the letter & article that it is somewhat of a serious matter with him and he intends to vindicate his platform to me —

The letter to which Ballinger referred had opened with the indictment of the new capitalism, already quoted.[18] Justice Miller continued:

I suppose that in all countries there [is] such a class larger or smaller in its relation to others. These dividends however have to be paid in every instance by a tax or burden of some kind on the wealth of the country. The class I have mentioned are [a] keensighted well organized class, and do not intend that any of this tax or burden shall fall on their shoulders. The success of the quiet but intelligent effort by which they have successfully imposed all this tax on the manufacturer and the producer from the soil is amazing. The cry that to tax capital, that is bonds or mortgages, is to drain capital from the country has been reechoed from a thousand subsidized presses. And Mr David A Wells having propounded the doctrine that real estate alone should be taxed in every community, has by this influence secured a place on a commission created by the legislature of New York to consider and report on the best system of taxation. His idea, put forth in every magazine or newspaper in the East is, that as the style and value of the house in which every man resides is the best indication of his ability to pay taxes, and as every man who lives in a house must in the end pay the

---

Presidents in a hundred years, and the weak points of those four would, if considered alone, be equal to two weak Presidents. Let us have done with 'dark horses' and incompetents. Miller is fit to be President; so is Blaine; so is Conkling; so was Morton. We will not prolong the list. Let us take a man of this stature for President, or let the Opposition take the office and its responsibilities. At times, it is said, brusque, even on the bench, although it has never happened to us to see him so at any time or place, Justice Miller has a heart as gentle and tender as a girl's, and pulsating with the warmest sympathies and affections. Inflexible in will, imperious and imperial in intellect, of lofty purity and uprightness in character, of a positiveness that drives invincibly and without apologies to ends when he thinks those ends right. We know Judge Miller in his qualities of head and heart well enough to know the tribute that this great man and jurist deserves at the hands of those who know him best, and that tribute we give him with admiration and affection. He is the peer of the highest office or the greatest of American citizens."

[18] *Supra,* p. 67.

taxes on it, whether he own it or not, and as every man must live in some house, why tax the house and you need tax nothing else.

But this class is not satisfied with making the landowner pay them dividends but they are steadily at work to make that dividend of more value when paid, and so that much harder to pay, than it was when the debt was contracted.

I suppose I hazard nothing in saying that half the public securities now held by this class, were paid for in currency when that currency was worth only two thirds of what it is now, and a still larger proportion of these bonds were issued when silver dollars were a legal tender for their payment.

Yet these men have fought with the bitterness of a death struggle the restoration of the right of the debtor to pay in that same coin. In other words having their debts increased one third in value by the gradual appreciation of the currency, they wish it still further enhanced by limiting the payment to gold coin alone which was lawful in gold and silver when the contract was made. And they have subsidized every paper east of the Rocky Mountains whose circulation made it worth paying for, to cry out in this as if it were an act of dishonesty.

As to the press, there are no more newspapers owned and published by their editors. They all are owned by joint stock corporations, and the first great duty of the managers as in all corporations is to declare large dividends. Honor, religion, morals, political principles are only to be referred to and thought of as cards in [the] game for dividends. It follows therefore that while the fear of losing subscribers exercises some restraint in the matter of *partizan politics,* the columns of the paper are open to purchase, and the weight of influence can be bought for any other purpose if enough money can be raised to buy it.

I don't know why I have started off in this way except as a suggestion of the main reason why prosperity is so long delayed. There is no mode of creating wealth but by manufactures, or by the productions of the soil. If they are to be forever crippled both by the diversion of capital to these public securities, and by having all the taxes which support government and pay the interest on the capital invested adversely, it is hard to see when prosperity will return.

Do not imagine I am greenbacker. I belong to a class a very large one, the dominant one in the Northwest, who believe in a return to specie payments, but who do not believe that either honesty or sound policy require silver to be excluded from the term specie.

I believe in the payment of debts, compulsory payment if necessary, but I do not believe in legislation which adds to the value of the bond at the expense of those who have to pay it. I have a profound contempt for Tom Ewing [19] and his sort, and but little [respect] whatever for the selfish, cunning, organization of bond holders whose only object in life seems to be [to] have their golden egg, shell meat and all though they destroy the goose from which they know it must come if it come at all.[20]

When the Republican National Convention opened on June 2, 1880, the preference of the delegates was hopelessly divided between James G. Blaine and Grant, whose candidacy for a third term was supported by Conkling and the Stalwarts. It seemed quite likely that the struggle would end in a draw and the nomination of some less conspicuous candidate. Miller's friends among the delegates from Iowa thought he might be brought forward in that event. A deadlock did occur, Grant's 306 votes being checkmated by Blaine's 280-odd. But when the break came it was in favor of Garfield, who had appeared to nominate John Sherman, and in doing so had proved more attractive than the uninspiring man for whom he spoke.

Two days after the convention Miller wrote from Keokuk:

The nomination of Garfield is not wholly a surprise, though I had believed up to the last moment that Blaine would be the man.

It was quite evident in the first preliminary vote on rules, credentials &c, that the Convention primarily divided into Grant and anti Grant parties and that *he* could not *be* nominated. But I had thought there was no such hostility to Blaine that would prevent accessions enough to his support to give him the majority.

The Iowa delegation was prepared to offer my name at any time they could honorably abandon Blaine, but that time never came until they were compelled to choose between Grant and Garfield on the last ballot. They acted wisely and I am more than satisfied with the result. Garfield will make a better President than any man voted for in Convention unless it be John Sherman and he will run a better race than Sherman. I do not

[19] Thomas Ewing the younger (1829–1896), then member of Congress from Ohio, and leader of the Greenback wing of the Democratic party.
[20] Letter of April 28, 1878.

believe the democrats can find a man to beat him. If I were a democrat I would nominate Bayard and win a victory worth having or accept a defeat which would be an honorable one, and leave the party in good order for future operations.[21]

After President Garfield's death the next year Miller wrote of him that "he was the *best fitted* man in my opinion for that place since John Quincy Adams filled it. He was the only man since then who has been a man [of] scholarly attainment with a special direction to statesmanship. . . ." [22]

The next mention of the Presidency in Miller's letters to Ballinger is under date of May 9, 1883:

I have wished for sometime that I had a little leisure to write you on a subject which has been pressed on me from many quarters lately.

It will be sufficiently indicated when I tell you that knowing I was about to leave Blaine sought an interview with me this week and said to me that the inevitable result of the necessary negotiations of all the active leaders of the party was to make me the candidate of the Republican Party in the next race for President because no man will be so strong with all wings of the party.

The first leisure moment I can obtain I will write you fully on this matter.

It is serious.

Ballinger's diary for May 14 sketches the substance of his response:

Replied to him to-day — and told him he ought not to be championed by the Blaine party — but they shd if possible have him designated by the other party — in other words he had to be agreed on by all — or if brought out in advance he wd be sacrificed — Cautioned him also against all appearances of solicitude for the office — Told him he had the weight of character for the voice of the party to designate him, without reliance on managemt of any kind — Don't know how he will take my letter —

Justice Miller acknowledged this prudent counsel in a letter of May 27, 1883, written at St. Joseph, Missouri, while he was on his circuit:

[21] Letter of June 10, 1880.   [22] Letter of September 25, 1881.

I read with much interest your comments on the use of my name for President and they concur precisely with my own judgment as regards the course to be pursued by my friends. I find as far as I can trust my own judgment a rather ardent readiness in Iowa and Nebraska among active and influential men to take hold at once, and my hardest task has been to restrain them from present action. But I have told them to make no demonstration for me as yet, and at no time even when the convention for nominating delegates to the National Convention comes to seek to commit the delegates to me by instructions but to prevent such committal to any one else.

I was surprised and not a little gratified when Woodson declared that he should without hesitation vote for me if I were nominated and I think he would go to work earnestly. He said he had already been requested by the editor of a newspaper here to write an article (editorial) on my name &c, and he had been looking up my judicial decisions. But he readily concurred with me that the time had not come.

The matter crops out every once in a while in a newspaper interview of some man of public notoriety; and the remarks always the same that Miller is the safest man with the required ability who can unite the party.

Blaine I am sure from a conversation with me is marshalling his personal following which is larger and more devoted than that of any man in the United States, and holding them well in hand for use when the move will be judicious.

In August 1883 Ballinger attended the meeting of the American Bar Association at Saratoga, where he met and conversed with George B. Corkhill, Judge Miller's son-in-law. He learned that Corkhill was "very much opposed" to the presidential candidacy; "but he says Miller's heart is fixed on it — tho' he is as prudent as possibly he can be — He [Corkhill] thinks Miller can be nominated — " and, but for Garfield, might have had the nomination in 1880.[23]

It seems clear that during 1882 and 1883 Blaine gave his friends to understand that he was not a candidate for the presidency at the election of 1884.[24] At the same time he professed a desire to become Secretary of State once more. What-

[23] Ballinger Diary, August 25, 1883.
[24] D. S. Muzzey, *James G. Blaine* (New York: Dodd, Mead and Company, 1934), pp. 271ff., sets out the evidence.

ever may have been his inmost thoughts, he did nothing to preclude the former while he did precisely what was useful to realize the latter possibility. For Miller was not the only recipient of his blandishments. In April 1883 Judge Walter Q. Gresham became Postmaster General in the Arthur administration. Blaine, one recalls, was determined that "that man in the White House" should not have an election in his own right. In her biography of her husband Mrs. Gresham writes:

After Mr. Blaine's return [to Washington] for the winter [1883–84] we saw much of the Blaine family, until one day Mr. Blaine said to my husband, "I can be nominated, but I cannot be elected. Arthur cannot be nominated. Why do you stay with him? You can be elected. If you will make me Secretary of State, you cán be nominated at Chicago." My husband told him that he could not talk about that matter so long as he was in the President's cabinet.[25]

General Sherman had presidential potentialities, if not capacities, far greater than his brother John, and in the spring of 1884 it seemed quite possible that if Blaine failed to secure the nomination there would be a spontaneous demand for the General. Blaine did not fail to consider that eventuality. On May 25 he wrote Sherman a letter, "confidential and strictly and absolutely so," to tell him that

at the approaching convention at Chicago it is more than possible . . . that you may be nominated for the Presidency. If so you must stand your hand, accept the responsibility and assume the duties of the place to which you will surely be chosen if a candidate. . . . Do not say a word in advance of the convention, no matter who may ask you. You are with your friends, who will jealously guard your honor. Do not answer this.[26]

When the convention assembled in June 1884 the Blaine forces were well organized. Notwithstanding the levies which the Arthur administration had mustered, and the group of Independents supporting Senator Edmunds, Blaine received

[25] Matilda Gresham, *Life of Walter Quintin Gresham* (Chicago: Rand McNally and Company, 1919), II, 495.
[26] In 1888 General Sherman published the letter in the *North American Review*, CLVII, 616, 621.

the nomination after four ballots. Judge Miller was right in saying he had a larger personal following than any other man in the United States. But Blaine had never, it seems, intended to make a donation of his strength to Miller or to any other minor candidate. He had merely been taking out several policies of reinsurance.

Miller waited until the convention had done its work before he referred again to the presidency. On June 15, 1884, he wrote to Ballinger:

Perhaps you would like to know what became of my presidential Boom. Well as I wrote you last spring I never permitted it to rise to the dignity of a boom. It was however the nicest and quietest little scheme and well arranged that you ever.

The Iowa delegation was uninstructed, and when they got to Chicago, they had a conference and agreed unanimously that if at any time it became apparent that Blaine could not be nominated they would present my name and push it. There were men (leading men) in every delegation from my circuit and from Kentucky and several territories who would have joined the movement.

I have thought ever since the reassembling of Congress last winter that Blaine would be nominated. I do not think this was very much due to active exertion of his own. But effort to elect Arthur, and Edmunds necessarily brought Blaine's name to the front. The overthrow of the Cameron dynasty in Pennsylvania gave him that state. The northwest remained true to him and his nomination came spontaneously.

I had no reason to be dissatisfied with his course toward me. If he had failed he would have been for me and I should have been nominated, though my name was not put before the convention at all. This was my express instructions to many men who were there for that purpose. My name had but that one chance and it was not to be frittered away. No one can say now that I have ever sought the place or brought reproach or folly to the judicial ermine. I am fully content. I believe Blaine will be elected and I feel sure he ought to be. He is a friend and admirer of mine as I am of him.

He is the only man of first class ability who has been even a candidate since Mr. Lincoln. He has the courage, and much of the character of Mr Clay and like him has suffered much unmerited reproach.

XIV

SOME LEADING OPINIONS

SCIRE LEGES *non hoc est verba earum tenere, sed vim et potestatem:* thus Celsus, sometime leader of the Proculian school among the Roman jurisconsults. But Justice Miller needed no tuition from the *veteres* to learn that breadth of principle which is the mark of a great jurist.

A good example of the bold method of treatment where Miller was most himself is offered by *In re Neagle*.[1] The petitioner, a United States deputy marshal, was in the custody of the State of California, charged with the murder of one Terry. The killing had taken place when Terry assaulted Justice Field, whom Neagle had been detailed to guard during his progress through his circuit. Under the statute the writ of habeas corpus was to issue where the petitioner was "in custody for an act done or omitted in pursuance of a law of the United States." Was Neagle within the statute? In an opinion which marches confidently to its conclusion, Miller says:

In the view we take of the Constitution of the United States, any obligation fairly and properly inferable from that instrument, or any duty of the marshal to be derived from the general scope of his duties under the laws of the United States, is "a law" within the meaning of this phrase.

Having deduced from general reasoning [2] the power to grant the writ, Miller goes on to show how the same result may be reached on the basis of positive law.[3]

[1] 135 U. S. 1 (1890).

[2] It is not without significance that several of the cases where he finds support for his broad view of national authority prove to be decisions where he himself had spoken: United States *v.* Gleason, 1 Woolworth 128, Fed. Case No. 15,216 (1867); Wells *v.* Nickles, 104 U. S. 444 (1882); United States *v.* San Jacinto Tin Co., 125 U. S. 273 (1888).

[3] Of course Justice Field did not participate in the consideration and decision of *In re* Neagle. But Justice Gray told Mr. Williston (who had been his

His opinion in *Ex parte Yarbrough* [4] was cast in the same mold. The petitioners had been convicted of conspiring to intimidate a citizen of African descent in the exercise of his right to vote for a member of Congress, and, to that end, of going disguised upon the highway and beating him. The question was whether there was power in Congress to penalize such conduct.

The proposition that it has no such power is supported by the old argument often heard, often repeated, and in this court never assented to, that when a question of the power of Congress arises the advocate of the power must be able to place his finger on the words which expressly grant it.

From the constitutional provision authorizing Congress to alter the regulations which each state may make for the election of senators and representatives, and from other provisions, a power is deduced to insure free and pure elections.

If the recurrence of such acts as these prisoners stand convicted of are [*sic*] too common in one quarter of the country, and give omen of danger from lawless violence, the free use of money in elections, arising from the vast growth of recent wealth in other quarters, presents equal cause for anxiety.

The case of *United States* v. *Kagama* [5] presented the question whether the federal government had exclusive jurisdiction to punish crimes committed on an Indian reservation within the limits of one of the states. While there was no specific grant of power, Miller, speaking for the Court, said:

It seems to us that this is within the competency of Congress. These Indian tribes *are* the wards of the nation. They are communities *dependent* on the United States. Dependent largely for their daily food. Dependent for their political rights. They owe no allegiance to the States, and receive from them no protection. Because of the local ill feeling, the people of the States where they are found are often their deadliest enemies. From their very weakness and helplessness, so largely due to the course of dealing of the Federal Government with them and the treaties

secretary, 1888–89) that Field's attitude while the case was under advisement left his brethren in no doubt as to his deep concern in the outcome (conversation with Professor Williston, August 6, 1938).

[4] 110 U. S. 651 (1884).　　　　　　　　　[5] 118 U. S. 375 (1886).

in which it has been promised, there arises the duty of protection, and with it the power. This has always been recognized by the Executive and by Congress, and by this court, whenever the question has arisen.

The language of these cases is fairly illustrative of the bent of Judge Miller's mind toward upholding the authority of the federal government. Sitting in the circuit court he expressed the opinion, anticipating the decision in *Kohl* v. *United States*,[6] that the general government has power, for national purposes, to take land by eminent domain. It seemed improbable, he said, that the Constitution had left such acquisition subject to the volition of the state legislature.[7] In cases involving the question whether a state might require, as a condition to the admission of a foreign corporation, a waiver of the right to resort to a federal court — or, with intent to reach the same result, revoke its permission to enter whenever the right should be exercised — Miller was always on the side denying such power.[8] This doctrine of unconstitutional conditions has now become the law of the Court.[9] Dissenting from first to last, Justice Miller supported the view that federal bonds owned by a domestic corporation may not be included in the measure of a state tax on the corporate franchise.[10] While for a late brief moment that view seemed persuasive to a majority of the Court,[11] it has now been established that the dignity and the credit of the federal government do not require any such boon for the taxpayer.[12] Justice Miller's interpretation of the commerce clause

[6] 91 U. S. 367 (1876).

[7] United States v. Stahl, 1 Woolworth 192, Fed. Case No. 16,373 (1868).

[8] Home Insurance Co. v. Morse, 20 Wallace 445 (1874); dissenting in Doyle v. Continental Insurance Co., 94 U. S. 535 (1877), and Barron v. Burnside, 121 U. S. 186 (1887).

[9] Terral v. Burke Construction Co., 257 U. S. 529 (1922).

[10] Dissenting in Society for Savings v. Coite, 6 Wallace 594 (1867), Provident Institution v. Massachusetts, 6 Wallace 611 (1867), and Home Insurance Co. v. New York, 134 U. S. 594 (1890).

[11] Macallen Co. v. Massachusetts, 279 U. S. 620 (1929). Justice Stone (Holmes and Brandeis, JJ., concurring with him) wrote a dissenting opinion.

[12] Educational Films Co. v. Ward, 282 U. S. 379 (1931); Pacific Co. v. Johnson, 285 U. S. 480 (1932). In each case Stone, J., spoke for the Court, and Sutherland, Van Devanter, and Butler, JJ., dissented.

merits special attention. To suggest the obscurity of principle which characterized forensic and legislative discussion of commerce questions during his early years on the bench a few illustrations will suffice. During the Civil War the New Jersey Court of Chancery had enjoined a railroad, actively employed in forwarding troops to the front, from invading the monopoly over transportation between New York City and Philadelphia which the legislature had granted to a rival road.[13] The Thirty-seventh and Thirty-eighth Congresses considered a number of proposals aimed at crushing this and other state-created monopolies along the channels of interstate commerce — culminating in the attenuated enactment of the Thirty-ninth Congress to the effect that existing railroads might carry passengers and freight from one state to another, and connect with roads of other states to form continuous lines, though Congress did not presume to authorize any new construction unless the permission of the state should be obtained.[14] Strict constructionists such as Senator Reverdy Johnson [15] (protector of the mutually advantageous monopoly which Maryland had granted to the Baltimore and Ohio Railroad) found insuperable constitutional objections to such legislation. Latitudinarians, on the other hand, suggested that Congress might even regulate interstate rates, though this was hardly asserted with conviction.[16] It was argued that Marshall's bold language in the Steamboat Monopoly Case [17] was inapplicable to railroads, whose rights were held by franchise from the state, and for some years thereafter the dissimilarity between land-borne and water-borne commerce was dwelt upon in Supreme Court decisions.[18]

[13] Delaware and Raritan Canal and Camden and Amboy Railroad and Transportation Cos. v. Camden and Atlantic R. R., 16 N. J. Eq. 320 (1863), 18 N. J. Eq. 546 (1867).

[14] Act of June 15, 1866, 14 Statutes at Large 66.

[15] E.g., in Congressional Globe, 38 Cong., 2 Sess., p. 328, January 19, 1865.

[16] Senator Howard (Republican) of Michigan, Congressional Globe, 39 Cong., 1 Sess., p. 2358, May 3, 1866; Senator Howe (Republican) of Wisconsin, ibid., p. 2361.

[17] Gibbons v. Ogden, 9 Wheaton 1 (1824).

[18] E.g., The Daniel Ball, 10 Wallace 557, 566 (1871), per Field, J.; Railroad Co. v. Maryland, 21 Wallace 456, 470 (1875), per Bradley, J.

Such was the prevalent uncertainty when Judge Miller, on the circuit, framed his opinion in the case of the Clinton Bridge.[19] The situation resembled that in the Wheeling Bridge Case.[20] Under authority derived from legislation of Illinois and Iowa, a railroad drawbridge was erected over the Mississippi. After a bill in chancery had been filed asking its abatement as a nuisance, Congress enacted that it should be a lawful structure. Thereupon a motion was made to dismiss the bill, and the plaintiff, opposing, contended that Congress was without power to authorize or regulate bridges over navigable streams. Judge Miller responded that, in the circuit court, it would suffice to say that the power to pass such a law had been affirmed in the Wheeling Bridge Case.

But I will not rest on the authority of that case alone. I think that the proposition declared in it is well founded in principle. The power to regulate commerce is one of the most useful confided to the federal government; and its exercise has done as much as that of any other to create and foster that strongest bond of nationality — a community of interests among the States. The want of it was one of the most pressing necessities which led to the formation of the Constitution. The clause has always received, at the hands of the courts and of Congress, a construction tending liberally to promote its beneficent object.

This bridge, he observed, was a part of the unbroken iron track from the Atlantic to the Missouri.

It seems to me that when these roads become parts of the great highways of our Union, acting an important part in a commerce which embraces many States, and destined, as some of these roads are, to become the channels through which the nations of Europe and Asia shall interchange their commodities, there can be no reason to doubt that to regulate them is to regulate commerce both with foreign nations and among the States, and that to refuse to do this is a refusal to discharge one of the most important duties of the federal government. . . .

For myself, I must say that I have no doubt of the right of Congress to prescribe all needful and proper regulations for the

[19] 1 Woolworth 150, Fed. Case No. 2900 (1867); affirmed, 10 Wallace 454 (1870).
[20] 18 Howard 421 (1856).

[*311*]

conduct of this immense traffic, over any railroad which has voluntarily become part of any of those lines of inter-state communication, or to authorize the creation of such roads, when
the purposes of inter-state transportation of persons and property
justify or require it.

The Supreme Court at the ensuing term had to decide, in
Crandall v. *Nevada*,[21] whether a state may impose a tax on
persons leaving its borders. Miller, speaking for the Court,
answered in the negative; but the decision was not placed on
the ground that it was a regulation of interstate commerce.[22]
On former occasions the Court had spoken with a very uncertain voice on the subject of state laws relating to passengers,
and in the instant case it evaded this issue, partly, perhaps,
because there had been neither brief nor argument for the
plaintiff in error. "The people of the United States constitute
one nation," runs the opinion. "They have a government in
which all of them are deeply interested." This government
has a capital to which every citizen may resort, whilst the
government may summon any or all of its citizens to aid its
services, as well as march armies through any state. To this
general principle of freedom of movement the tax was held
obnoxious. This is reminiscent of Miller's address to the
voters in 1856, expressing his indignation that the Pierce administration allowed a body of men to arrest trade along the
Missouri River and to forbid peaceable citizens to travel or
settle in Kansas. Justice Clifford and the Chief Justice would
have hung the decision on the commerce clause.

Nine years later, after a full discussion at the bar in *Henderson* v. *Mayor of New York* [23] and other cases argued with it,
the Court through Justice Miller reviewed the problem "with
the hope of attaining a unanimity not found in the opinions
of our predecessors." The Court went on to assert the exclusive control of Congress over immigration from foreign

[21] 6 Wallace 35 (1868).
[22] Cf. Miller's reference to the case in Hinson v. Lott, 8 Wallace 148, 152 (1869).
[23] 92 U. S. 259 (1876). *Cf.* People v. Co. Gen. Transatlantique, 107 U. S. 59 (1883), per Miller, J., where the state statute as amended was held invalid.

countries. At the same time it struck down a California statute requiring a bond of certain categories of undesirable aliens.[24] Presently Congress passed a statute to assert its control over immigration, and this was upheld in a well-known opinion by Justice Miller in the Head Money Cases,[25] which is also a leading authority on the relation between statutes and treaties in municipal law.

Protracted controversy whether the regulation of interstate commerce belonged exclusively to Congress or admitted of a concurrent power in the states had at last been stilled by the statesmanlike decision in *Cooley* v. *Board of Wardens*[26] in 1851. Justice Curtis there pointed out that the commerce clause embraced a variety of subjects, some of such a nature as to require a uniform rule throughout the nation, others admitting of local control until such time as Congress should occupy the field. If a particular matter seemed to belong in this lower branch of the commerce power, it would be subject to state regulation in the silence of Congress. Justice Miller defended the wisdom of this solution in his opinion in *Pound* v. *Turck*[27] — a case closely resembling *Willson* v. *Blackbird Creek Marsh Co.*[28] — where state legislation authorizing dams on a small though navigable tributary was upheld. "To the legislature of the State," he said, "may be most appropriately confided the authority to authorize these structures where their use will do more good than harm, and to impose such regulations and limitations in their construction and use as will best reconcile and accommodate the interest of all concerned in the matter."[29]

The Cooley Case provided only an analysis, not a mechan-

---

[24] Chy Lung v. Freeman, 92 U. S. 275 (1876).
[25] 112 U. S. 580 (1884).
[26] 12 Howard 299.
[27] 95 U. S. 459 (1878).
[28] 2 Peters 245 (1829).
[29] Similarly, speaking for the Court in Packet Co. v. Catlettsburg, 105 U. S. 559 (1882), he upheld a local regulation of steamboat wharfage, and the collection of reasonable charges for the use of a public wharf, along the Ohio River. Morgan's Steamship Co. v. Louisiana Board of Health, 118 U. S. 455 (1886), upheld as a reasonable measure of police the Louisiana quarantine law as applied to vessels coming to New Orleans — Congress not having at that time undertaken to control this subject.

ical formula for reaching inerrant results. Where state legislation had responded to emerging need, the justices must decide whether under the circumstances to sustain local regulation until Congress should have exercised its paramount authority. The great case of *Wabash, St. L. and P. Ry.* v. *Illinois* [30] presented such a question. The Illinois legislature, seeking to curb a great abuse of economic power, had forbidden unjust discrimination between long and short hauls in commerce. The majority of the Court, speaking through Justice Miller, held that in respect of interstate shipments this was a matter which required exclusive national regulation. It was only a few months later that Congress, in the light of this decision, passed the Interstate Commerce Act of 1887, setting up an administrative control over the subject. [31]

The rule that a state may not tax the federal right to engage in interstate commerce is one of the most salutary of our constitutional axioms, but its application to concrete situations imposes an exacting test upon judicial wisdom. While a tax on the doing of interstate business is bad, the state may apply its general property tax to property employed in interstate commerce, may lay a tax on local business, and may set a price on the grant of corporate charters and on the privilege of being admitted to do a local business in corporate form. All of these taxes may have some effect upon interstate commerce. A judge's conclusion as to their validity often turns upon whether he looks to names and forms, or thinks in terms of economic consequences. Justice Miller's approach was pragmatic, inspired by the view expressed in *Crandall* v. *Nevada*: No state may lay a tribute on the nation. He would have

[30] 118 U. S. 557 (1886). Waite, C. J., and Bradley and Gray, JJ., dissented. Not doubting for a moment the authority of Congress over the subject, they would have sustained state regulation of interstate rates until it had exerted its power.

[31] In a letter of February 13, 1887, Miller refers to the decision in "Wabash Ry. Co. v. Illinois on the interstate commerce question which it is said contributed very much to passage of the Interstate Commerce bill, a subject in regard to which I have been a pioneer, and an authority, ever since the opinion in the Clinton Bridge Case, Woolworth 150."

agreed with Justice Holmes that "we are to look for a practical rather than a logical or philosophical distinction." [32]
Miller held state taxes on gross receipts unconstitutional in
so far as they fell upon receipts from interstate commerce.[33]
At first the majority had sustained a Pennsylvania tax on railway gross receipts, including receipts from interstate shipments carried over the state, considering that there was a
substantial difference between a tax on freight and a tax on
the receipts from freight. Miller, dissenting, said they came
to the same thing:

> I lay down the broad proposition that by no device or evasion,
> by no form of statutory words, can a State compel citizens of
> other States to pay to it a tax, contribution, or toll, for the privi-
> lege of having their goods transported through that State by the
> ordinary channels of commerce.[34]

Fourteen years later the reasoning of the majority was admitted to have been erroneous.[35]

The plea that a tax should be judged by the subject upon
which it was nominally imposed, rather than by its practical
result, Miller found unpersuasive. Thus he dissented in *Railroad Company* v. *Maryland*,[36] where the state was pocketing
one fifth of the gross receipts of the Baltimore and Ohio Railroad between Baltimore and Washington, and the Court sustained the levy on the ground that it had been stipulated, not
as a regulation of commerce, but as the price of a charter.
Miller replied that the effect was identical with that of the
tax in *Crandall* v. *Nevada*. In *Railroad Company* v. *Pen-*

---

[32] Galveston, H. and S. A. Ry. *v.* Texas, 210 U. S. 217, 227 (1908).

[33] Dissenting in State Tax on Railway Gross Receipts, 15 Wallace 284 (1873);
Fargo *v.* Michigan, 121 U. S. 230 (1887), where Miller, J., spoke for a unanimous Court; Philadelphia and Southern SS. Co. *v.* Pennsylvania, 122 U. S. 326
(1887), where the Court, per Bradley, J., confessed error in the Railway Gross
Receipts Case; Ratterman *v.* Western Union Tel. Co., 127 U. S. 411 (1888) and
Western Union Tel. Co. *v.* Alabama, 132 U. S. 472 (1889), where Miller, J.,
for a unanimous Court struck down gross receipts taxes on interstate
telegraphy.

[34] 15 Wallace at 299.

[35] Philadelphia and Southern SS. Co. *v.* Pennsylvania, 122 U. S. 326 (1887).

[36] 21 Wallace 456 (1875).

iston [37] he concurred in the dominant opinion that it would be extravagant to hold that the Union Pacific Railroad was immune to the state property tax merely because it derived its charter from Congress instead of from a state legislature. He spoke for the Court in *Western Union Telegraph Co.* v. *Massachusetts,* [38] one of the early cases upholding state taxation of property employed in interstate commerce, measured by the "unit rule." The tax, nominally upon that portion of the capital stock represented by the ratio of the length of line in Massachusetts to the entire length throughout the country, was sustained as being in effect a tax on property within the state. [39] In this characteristic of looking through forms to the substance of taxation Miller's mental processes stood in notable contrast to those of his brother Field, whose syllogistic mind would push general propositions to absolute extremes, even though they led to results which, otherwise achieved, he would have regarded as unconstitutional. [40]

[37] 18 Wallace 5 (1873). [38] 125 U. S. 530 (1888).

[39] It is to be noted that Miller, J., did not mention the case of the Delaware Railroad Tax, 18 Wallace 206 (1874), where a similar tax on a Delaware corporation had been upheld, per Field, J., emphatically *not* as a tax on the property (for if such it would have been invalid as falling on extraterritorial value), but as a tax "upon the corporation as an entity existing under its laws." Miller had silently assented to that decision.

[40] Field treated the state's power to attach conditions to the grant of a corporate charter, or (in the case of foreign corporations) to the privilege of being admitted to do a local business, as complete and unqualified. Thus in his view it followed:

(1) That while a gross receipts tax was bad in so far as it fell on foreign and interstate business (dissenting in State Tax on Railway Gross Receipts, *supra*; with the Court in Philadelphia and Southern SS. Co. *v.* Pennsylvania, *supra*), yet the same tax would be good if exacted as the price of corporate existence (with the majority in Railroad Co. *v.* Maryland, *supra*) or as an "annual excise tax for the privilege of exercising its franchises" (Maine *v.* Grand Trunk Ry., 142 U. S. 217, 1891).

(2) That while a capital stock tax was bad in so far as it fell on a corporation which came into the state to do an interstate business (Gloucester Ferry Co. *v.* Pennsylvania, 114 U. S. 196, 1885, per Field, J.; dissenting in Pullman's Palace Car Co. *v.* Pennsylvania, 141 U. S. 18, 1891; dissenting in Adams Express Co. *v.* Ohio, 165 U. S. 194, 1897), yet if the legislature dubbed it a tax "on the corporation itself," measured by capital stock, the Constitution was satisfied. "The State may impose taxes upon the corporation as an entity existing under its laws, as well as upon the capital stock of the corporation or its separate corporate property. And the manner in which its value shall be assessed and the rate of taxation, however arbitrary or capricious, are mere

Some of Justice Miller's most powerful reasoning is to be found in opinions construing the constitutional provision that "no State shall, without the consent of Congress, lay any imposts or duties on imports or exports. . . ." Chief Justice Marshall, who sometimes seized an occasion to decide as much as he could rather than as little as the case in hand required, had laid it down, in *Brown* v. *Maryland*,[41] not only that a state was forbidden to tax the business of importing from abroad, but that the goods imported, so long as they remained unsold and in unbroken packages, were exempt from a general prop-

---

matters of legislative discretion." (Field, J., in the Delaware Railroad Tax, 18 Wallace 206, 231, 1874.)

(3) Coming from interstate commerce to the field of intergovernmental relations: while "the power of taxation of every State is necessarily confined to subjects within its jurisdiction" (Field, J., 18 Wallace at 229), yet a tax "upon the corporate franchise" might be measured by values not themselves within the taxing state (Pembina Mining Co. *v.* Pennsylvania, 125 U. S. 181, 1888, per Field, J.; Horn Silver Mining Co. *v.* New York, 143 U. S. 305, 1892, per Field, J.).

(4) A corporate excise tax might be measured by assets including tax-exempt securities (Home Insurance Co. *v.* New York, 134 U. S. 594, 1890, per Field, J., Miller and Harlan, JJ., dissenting).

(5) Though Justice Field sought to extend the protection of the federal judiciary (as indicated by his dissent in the Slaughter-House Cases, 16 Wallace 36, 1873), yet he would not interfere if a state revoked the privilege of a foreign corporation to enter for the reason that the corporation had exercised its right to sue in a federal court (Doyle *v.* Continental Insurance Co., 94 U. S. 535, 1877; *cf.* Field's language in Paul *v.* Virginia, 8 Wallace 168, 181, 1869).

Much has been said, and rightly, of Field as the judicial patron of property rights and of corporate enterprise. Yet it should be noted that the above propositions, to which he adhered tenaciously, tended to increase the subjection of corporations to the discretion of state legislatures. Again, the doctrine of Swift *v.* Tyson, 16 Peters 1 (1842), was often invoked to give foreign corporations a more favorable law than the common law of the state into which they had come. Such a case was Baltimore and Ohio R. R. *v.* Baugh, 149 U. S. 368 (1893), where Field's lone dissent constitutes one of the leading indictments of the doctrine. He concluded: "I regret that the tendency of the decision of the majority of the court in this case is in favor of the largest exemptions of corporations from liability." *Cf.* Erie R. R. *v.* Tompkins, 304 U. S. 64 (1938), where Swift *v.* Tyson was finally overthrown.

In the municipal bond cases already discussed, Justice Miller, whose outlook tended to favor the agrarian taxpayer rather than the bondholder and the railroad promoter, regarded Justice Field as the most sympathetic of his brethren. *Cf.* also the uncompromising deductions of Field's opinion in Norton *v.* Shelby County, 118 U. S. 425 (1886): an unconstitutional statute creates no office; there can be no *de facto* incumbent of a non-existent office; therefore bonds issued by a legally non-existent board are unenforceable.

[41] 12 Wheaton 419 (1827).

erty tax. In *Woodruff* v. *Parham* [42] the taxpayer contended that original packages brought from a sister state were also "imports" and immune to even non-discriminatory taxation. Such a rule would have been both unnecessary to the protection of commerce and a serious clog on local taxation. Justice Miller rejected the contention in a masterly opinion. In common usage, "import" signified something from abroad. Construing the clause in its context, the same result was reached. Arguing from the evils which the Constitution was intended to prevent, the conclusion was confirmed. And finally, what perhaps counted most with Miller, the result he had reached was satisfying to the mind, as appeared from considering the consequences of the contrary view:

The merchant in Chicago who buys his goods in New York and sells at wholesale in original packages, may have his millions employed in trade for half a lifetime and escape all State, county, and city taxes; for all that he is worth is invested in goods which he claims to be protected as imports from New York. Neither the State nor the city which protects his life and property can make him contribute a dollar to the support of its government, improve its thoroughfares or educate its children. The merchant in a town in Massachusetts, who deals only in wholesale, if he purchase his goods in New York, is exempt from taxation. If his neighbor purchase in Boston, he must pay all the taxes which Massachusetts levies with equal justice on the property of all the citizens.

Thus self-assured, Justice Miller went on to brush aside opinions by Marshall and Taney which seemed to bear toward the opposite conclusion. [43] Nine years later Justice Miller had to consider the same clause in *Cook* v. *Pennsylvania*, [44] a case of a tax on sales at auction as applied to foreign imports. In fact the duty was discriminatory against non-American goods, but the opinion held broadly that no tax whatever could be imposed on an original package from abroad. Viewed in the light of the mischief at which they were aimed, the commer-

[42] 8 Wallace 123 (1869). With it was decided Hinson v. Lott, 8 Wallace 148, per Miller, J.; Nelson, J., dissented in both.

[43] Marshall, C.J., in Brown v. Maryland, *supra*, at 449; Taney, C.J., in Almy v. California, 24 Howard 169 (1861).   [44] 97 U. S. 566 (1878).

cial provisions of the Constitution disclosed a purpose to promote "the freest interchange of commodities among the people of the different States and by the people of the States with citizens and subjects of foreign governments." A tax on the sale of imports, at the discretion of a seaboard state, would, the Court believed, be inimical to that great object.

While there is, perhaps, no special obligation on this court [said Justice Miller] to defend the wisdom of the Constitution of the United States, there is the duty to ascertain the purpose of its provisions, and to give them full effect when called on by a proper case to do so.

That Justice Miller, impelled by his sense of right, sometimes jumped to a conclusion without stopping for precision of analysis, is illustrated by an episode in the decision of *Shotwell* v. *Moore*.[45] Securities of the United States, including greenbacks, were by law exempt from state taxation. To escape the Ohio property tax, Shotwell made it a practice, just before each assessment day, momentarily to convert his bank balance into greenbacks. In order to circumvent such evasion, the legislature enacted that one holding tax-exempt securities on assessment day must nonetheless pay a tax on the monthly average of his funds not so invested. The county treasurer recovered a judgment for this tax, and Shotwell carried his case to the Supreme Court. It was decided in conference that the judgment should be sustained, and the opinion was assigned to Judge Miller. The case, as he saw it, presented two aspects. First, Shotwell was a bad citizen who ought not to be permitted to impose a fraud on the treasury. An earlier case [46] had decided that so unmeritorious a litigant was not entitled to the extraordinary equitable aid of an injunction, but would be left to his remedy, if any, in a court of law. In the instant case, where Shotwell set up a claim of federal right in answer to an action at law, Justice Miller seems to have vaulted to the conclusion that he could be turned out of court

[45] 129 U. S. 590 (1889).
[46] Mitchell *v.* Commissioners of Leavenworth County, 91 U. S. 206 (1876), per Waite, C. J.

simply because his motive had been impure. In a second aspect of the case, involving closer reasoning, it was apparent that the state might have made assessments, not annually, but once a month, and that a tax on the monthly average of taxable funds did not fall on tax-exempt securities. Judge Miller's draft opinion evidently rested so heavily on the former of these points — involving the untenable position that federal securities might lose their tax-exemption by reason of the state of mind of their owner — as to evoke the following letter from his more cautious brother Gray:[47]

1601 I STREET
WASHINGTON, D. C.

Feby. 16/89.

Dear Judge Miller,

After a careful reading of your opinion in *Shotwell* v. *Moore*, I am very sorry to be compelled to say that the first part of it (especially in the passage which I have marked in the margin) is so contrary to my convictions, that I fear, unless it can be a good deal tempered, I shall have to deliver a separate opinion on the lines of the enclosed memorandum.

I am particularly troubled about this, because, if my scruples are not removed, and Justices Field, Bradley and Lamar adhere to their dissent, your opinion will represent only four judges, half of those who took part in the case.[48]

I am a little under the weather this morning, or you would have had a visit, instead of this note, from

Yours very truly,
H. Gray

Mr. Justice Miller.

Memo of opinion of Gray, J.

The Constitution and laws of the United States having exempted all treasury notes and obligations of the United States

---

[47] I inquired of Professor Williston (who was secretary to Justice Gray, 1888–89) what Gray thought of Miller. He responded that he understood that Miller and Gray used to have energetic arguments in conference; that Miller would propound some sweeping proposition on some point of common law, to which Gray would take exception. Gray used to regret that Miller's training had been so unsystematic and deficient. He said that if Miller had been properly grounded he would have been second only to Marshall among the justices of the Supreme Court. (Conversation with Professor Williston on August 6, 1938.)

[48] Justice Matthews had been absent from the Court.

from taxation under State or municipal authority, I am unable
to see how the motive with which the legal owner of such obligations has invested his money in them can enable the State to tax
them, although, as was decided in *Mitchell* v. *Leavenworth Commissioners* 91 U. S. 206, the investment may be made under such
circumstances as not to entitle him to invoke the extraordinary
interposition of a court of equity to release him from the unlawful taxation. I therefore concur in the judgment of affirmance, solely upon the last ground stated in the opinion delivered
by Mr. Justice Miller.[49]

Justice Miller revised his opinion to meet this valid objection. After dwelling on the indefensible nature of Shotwell's
transaction, he avoided any conclusion by saying,

Waiving the question whether these equitable considerations
would constitute a defence in an action at law to collect the tax
in suit, we proceed to inquire whether the statute of Ohio [can
be sustained].

Thus modified, the opinion won the assent of all but one of
the justices.

It is related that Justice Miller, "when asked what had been
the chief factor in the development of the law in the pioneer
jurisdictions of the West after the Civil War, answered 'Ignorance; the judges often did not know enough to do the wrong
thing, so they did the right thing.' " [50] But transitory beliefs
and imperfect understanding often yield poor fruit, of which
Justice Miller's dictum in *Nichols* v. *Eaton* [51] is a striking example. A testatrix had settled a trust for her children, with
a provision for forfeiture on alienation. A son became bankrupt, and the Court held that there was no interest under the
trust which the assignee could reach. Now as Lord Eldon had
said in a leading case, "there is an obvious distinction between
a disposition to a man, until he becomes bankrupt, and then
over, and an attempt to give him property, and to prevent

[49] A file copy, in Justice Gray's handwriting, was preserved in his copy of
the Record and Briefs in Shotwell *v.* Moore, and is now in the Harvard Law
Library.

[50] Roscoe Pound, "New Possibilities of Old Materials of American Legal
History," 40 *West Virginia Law Quarterly* 205, 209 (1934).

[51] 91 U. S. 716 (1875).

his creditors from obtaining any interest in it, though it is his." [52] Having shown that this trust was of the former kind, Judge Miller had no occasion to pronounce upon a different and hypothetical situation. But traveling outside of the record, and ignoring the well-established policy of the state wherein the cause arose,[53] he went on to deliver this momentous dictum:

> But, while we have thus attempted to show that Mrs. Eaton's will is valid in all its parts upon the extremest doctrine of the English Chancery Court, we do not wish to have it understood that we accept the limitations which that court has placed upon the power of testamentary disposition of property by its owner. . . . the doctrine, that the owner of property, in the free exercise of his will in disposing of it, cannot so dispose of it, but that the object of his bounty, who parts with nothing in return, must hold it subject to the debts due his creditors, though that may soon deprive him of all the benefits sought to be conferred by the testator's affection or generosity, is one which we are not prepared to announce as the doctrine of this court. . . . Why a parent, or one who loves another, and wishes to use his own property in securing the object of his affection, as far as property can do it, from the ills of life, the vicissitudes of fortune, and even his own improvidence, or incapacity for self-protection, should not be permitted to do so, is not readily perceived.

Professor Griswold considers this dictum to have been "the greatest single factor in the development of spendthrift trusts." [54] While it was prompted by the idea, then dominant in legal thought, of giving effect to the intention of the donor,

[52] Brandon v. Robinson, 18 Vesey Jr. 429, 432 (1811).

[53] The case had arisen in Rhode Island, and was brought in the federal circuit court there by reason of the diverse citizenship of the parties. Circuit Justice Clifford — who disliked judicial legislation — had decided merely that the bankrupt's estate had determined at his bankruptcy (3 Clifford 595, Fed. Case No. 10,241, 1873).

The policy of Rhode Island on the subject of spendthrift trusts had been declared succinctly: "Certainly, no man *should* have an estate to live on, but not an estate to pay his debts with. Certainly, property available for the purposes of pleasure and profit, should also be amenable to the demands of justice." (Tillinghast v. Bradford, 5 R. I. 205, 212, 1858.) Cf. Ryder v. Sisson, 7 R. I. 341, 344 (1862).

[54] Erwin N. Griswold, *Spendthrift Trusts* (Albany: Matthew Bender and Company, 1936), p. 25.

still it is surprising that Judge Miller should have gone out of his way to encourage a contrivance for the protection of wastrels.

Justice Miller's construction of the Bankrupt Act of 1867 was more favorable to debtors than to creditors. Many of the district judges had held that for an insolvent debtor to suffer one creditor to recover judgment against him necessarily amounted to an act of bankruptcy. In a case in the circuit court where the facts negatived any actual intent of fraud, Miller held otherwise, saying, "I cannot satisfy myself that mere honest inaction in a poor man, when his creditor seeks by law to make a just debt, is itself an act of bankruptcy, and if Congress means that, they must so far as I am concerned, say it in plainer terms·than are to be found in the present law." [55] Shortly afterward he was able to announce this as the judgment of the Supreme Court.[56] He shows that a man, technically insolvent, may be putting up an honest struggle to save his business, and ought not to be compelled to give up the fight whenever suit is brought on a just debt. A subsequent evaluation of the interests involved, however, led Congress and the Court to a different conclusion.[57]

There is no more sacred duty of a court [wrote Justice Miller] than, in a case properly before it, to maintain unimpaired those securities for the personal rights of the individual which have received for ages the sanction of the jurist and the statesman; and in such cases no narrow or illiberal construction should be given to the words of the fundamental law in which they are embodied.[58]

Since Miller's time, however, criminal justice has come to be regarded as only an element of the larger problem of social control. Legal values protected by the Bill of Rights have been reconsidered, and greater weight accorded to the security of the community. Thus some decisions which to Miller seemed "liberal" would now be regarded as somewhat rigid and technical. In *Ex parte Lange*, from which the above

---

[55] Wright *v.* Filley, 1 Dillon 171, Fed. Case No. 18,077 (1871).
[56] Wilson *v.* City Bank, 17 Wallace 473 (1873).
[57] Bankrupt Act of 1898, construed in Wilson Bros. *v.* Nelson, 183 U. S. 191 (1901).   [58] *Ex parte* Lange, 18 Wallace 163, 178 (1874).

quotation is taken, the statute made the theft of mail bags punishable by fine of $200 *or* imprisonment for one year. The trial judge inadvertently imposed *both* punishments. A few days later, and after the fine had been paid, the court vacated its erroneous judgment and sentenced the prisoner to one year's imprisonment. But the Supreme Court, per Miller, J. (Clifford and Strong, JJ., dissenting), held that this violated the constitutional provision that no person should be twice placed in jeopardy of life or limb for the same offense. The petitioner was therefore released.

Justice Miller did not believe in capital punishment,[59] and, like many judges of his day, was very willing to find constitutional grounds for setting aside a sentence of death. His judgments in the Kring and Medley cases [60] set two mur-

[59] United States *v.* Gleason, 1 Woolworth 128, 140; Fed. Case No. 15,216 (1867).

[60] Kring *v.* Missouri, 107 U. S. 221 (1883), Waite, C.J., Bradley, Matthews, and Gray, JJ., dissenting; *Ex parte* Medley, 134 U. S. 160 (1890), Bradley and Brewer, JJ., dissenting. Kring, indicted for murder in the first degree, had, with the consent of the prosecuting attorney and the court, withdrawn a plea of not guilty, and pleaded guilty of murder in the second degree. Not liking the sentence imposed, he moved to have his plea of guilty withdrawn, and his plea of not guilty restored. On appeal this motion was granted. At the next trial Kring was convicted of murder in the first degree, and sentenced to death. At the time of the homicide with which Kring was charged, it was the law of Missouri that a conviction for murder in the second degree, though set aside, was thereafter a bar to trial for first degree murder. A new constitution abrogated this rule. *Held:* that, as applied to Kring, the new constitutional provision was an *ex post facto* law.

Medley had been sentenced under a statute passed after the commission of the offence, which changed in various details the mode in which the sentence of death was to be executed. *Held:* that as applied to him the new statute was *ex post facto*. Brewer, J., dissenting, accurately described the differences between the two statutes: "By the old law, execution must be within twenty-five days from the day of sentence. By the new, within twenty-eight. By the old, confinement prior to execution was in the county jail. By the new, in the penitentiary. By the old, the sheriff was the hangman. By the new, the warden. Under the old, no one had a right of access to the condemned except his counsel, though the sheriff might, in his discretion, permit any one to see him. By the new, his attendants, counsel, physician, spiritual adviser and members of his family have a right of access, and no one else is permitted to see him. Under the old, his confinement might be absolutely solitary, at the discretion of the sheriff, with but a single interruption. Under the new, access is given to him as a matter of right, to all who ought to be permitted to see him. . . . Again, by the old law, the sheriff fixes the hour within a prescribed day. By the new, the warden fixes the hour and day within a named week."

derers at liberty because, subsequent to their offenses, the criminal law had been amended in particulars which, as we should now think, infringed upon no just interest of the accused. These decisions have been severely criticized.[61]

On the law of extradition, where the international and the criminal law come together, Justice Miller's opinion in *United States* v. *Rauscher* [62] is a familiar authority. Under the provisions of the Ashburton treaty of 1842, Rauscher had been surrendered by the British government on a charge of murder on the high seas. He was brought to trial for the offense of inflicting cruel and unusual punishment. On a motion in arrest of judgment he raised the question whether he could lawfully be tried for a crime different from that for which he had been extradited. It was held, on a construction of the treaty and the relevant Act of Congress, that he was exempt from trial for any other offense until he had had an opportunity to return to the country from which he had been taken.

If upon the face of this treaty it could be seen that its sole object was to secure the transfer of an individual from the jurisdiction of one sovereignty to that of another, the argument might be sound; but as this right of transfer, the right to demand it, the obligation to grant it, the proceedings under which it takes place, all show that it is for a limited and defined purpose that the transfer is made, it is impossible to conceive of the exercise of jurisdiction in such a case for any other purpose than that mentioned in the treaty, and ascertained by the proceedings under which the party is extradited, without an implication of fraud upon the rights of the party extradited, and of bad faith to the country which permitted his extradition. No such view of solemn public treaties between the great nations of the earth can be sustained by a tribunal called upon to give judicial construction to them.

[61] It may be noted, however, that in Boyd v. United States, 116 U. S. 616 (1886), Miller, J., dissented from that portion of the judgment which held that the compulsory production of a party's papers in a criminal proceeding amounted to an "unreasonable search or seizure," though he agreed that the constitutional provision against compulsory self-incrimination had been infringed.

[62] 119 U. S. 407 (1886). Gray, J., concurred specially, and Waite, C. J., dissented.

This was the position which the British government had taken in a diplomatic controversy with Secretary of State Fish ten years earlier.[63] Mr. Fish, who sometimes wrote slightly sardonic comments to his old junior, J. C. Bancroft Davis, now reporter to the Supreme Court, dashed off the following:

I see in the morning papers another decision of the Supreme Court, all wrong — but after the decision that 'rags & lamp black' may discharge an obligation to repay a debt contracted in real money,[64] one is not surprised at any opinion this Court may give — Gen. Butler ('glorious Ben') once said to me, that what that Court wanted, was not so much, large legal knowledge (& they have none to[o] much of that) but practical political knowledge, & experience in public affairs, & strong Americanism — I believe he was right — I am glad to see the C. J. dissented — [65]

What Miller thought of the two opinions is disclosed in a letter of December 20:

The Chief Justice dissented rather feebly I think in the Rauscher Case. It is an unusually long opinion for me, but the matter having been much controverted in the last ten or twelve years before the general public and in the courts and being sure that the opinion would attract the attention of statesmen and diplomats of both nations, I felt called upon to show that we had considered all that was entitled to be called authority, and that it was not a case for economy of space. . . .

The objections of Mr. Fish and Judge Waite notwithstanding, the opinion has been accepted as right and has stood the test of time, being followed in the practice of governments and in the writings of publicists.[66]

[63] Winslow's Case; see J. B. Moore, *Digest of International Law* (Washington: 1906–), IV, 306ff.

[64] A fling at the last Legal Tender Case, Juilliard *v.* Greenman, 110 U. S. 444 (1884).

[65] Letter of December 7, 1887, J. C. B. Davis Papers, Library of Congress, vol. XL.

In preparing his dissenting opinion a few days after that of the Court had been announced, Chief Justice Waite had written to Mr. Davis: "Will you please look over my dissent in the extradition case and tell me if it is in accord with what I understand to have been the position of Mr. Fish in the discussion he had with the English government in the Winslow matter? I don't care to argue the question, but I want to state the position accurately." (Letter of December 11, J. C. B. Davis Papers, vol. XL.)

[66] Harvard Research in International Law, Draft Convention on Extradition, Article 23.

On the rare occasions when the loser in an ecclesiastical dispute asks the civil courts to overhaul the action of the church authorities, Miller's opinion in *Watson* v. *Jones* [67] is cited as the *locus classicus*. At the close of the Civil War the Walnut Street Presbyterian Church of Louisville was divided between anti-slavery and pro-slavery factions. The opposing groups of elders carried their dispute before the Court of Appeals of Kentucky, whose decision was in favor of the Southern sympathizers.[68] The losers then resorted to protracted interlocutory skirmishing to prevent the mandate of the court from being executed.[69]

In the meantime the Northern elders admitted to church membership Jones and others, citizens of Indiana. This laid the basis for transferring the fight to the federal court on the ground of diversity of citizenship. In the meantime, too, the General Assembly of the Presbyterian Church exscinded the Southern group and recognized the Northern elders. Jones now resorted to the United States Circuit Court for Kentucky, asking an injunction against the elders who had won in the state court. From a decree in his favor an appeal was taken to the Supreme Court.[70]

One surmises that the justices were not averse to giving victory to the Union sympathizers. When, after holding the case under advisement for a year, no reconciliation had taken place, the Court, speaking through Justice Miller, gave judgment for the appellees. The first question to be met was whether the circuit court had had jurisdiction, notwithstanding the suit pending in the state court. The two suits, said the Court, were not identical: the one had been to determine whether the Northern elders were entitled to participate in the church session, while the latter arose after the Southerners had been exscinded by the General Assembly, and was to

---

[67] 13 Wallace 679 (1872).
[68] Watson *v.* Avery, 2 Bush 332 (1867). The Republican judge dissented.
[69] Watson *v.* Avery, 3 Bush 635 (1868); Fulton *v.* Farley, 9 *American Law Register*, n.s., 401.
[70] Jeremiah S. Black and Thomas W. Bullitt were of counsel for the appellants, Benjamin H. Bristow and John M. Harlan for the appellees.

determine which of two bodies was entitled to use the church building. The federal circuit court had had jurisdiction, therefore, to decree that when the Southern elders were put in possession of the property by the state court they should hold it in trust for the Northern sympathizers. Judges Clifford and Davis dissented on the question of jurisdiction, and the holding was criticized by state judges, who felt that the Supreme Court had sanctioned a violent intrusion upon the jurisdiction of a state court.[71]

This aspect of the case was accentuated in that part of the opinion where Justice Miller treated the substantive issues. For after discussing the rationale of the subject he concluded:

We think the rule of action which should govern the civil courts . . . is, that, whenever the questions of discipline or of faith, or ecclesiastical rule, custom or law have been decided by the highest of these church judicatories to which the matter has been carried, the legal tribunals must accept such decisions as final, and as binding on them, in their application to the case before them.

Now it was well known that the highest court of Kentucky had taken a very different view of the rule to be applied to this Presbyterian schism.[72] It had recently held that it was

[71] Judge Redfield reviewed the case in a long note, making the following points: (1) he disagreed with the view which the Court of Appeals of Kentucky took of the law of religious societies; but (2) he thought the federal court was without jurisdiction; and (3) since the Kentucky court, right or wrong, should settle the law for Kentucky, the Supreme Court should have conformed to its view (11 *American Law Register*, n.s., 452).

On September 24, 1872, five months after judgment had been rendered, Justice Davis wrote from Illinois to his dissenting colleague: "Did you see in one of the numbers of the American Law Register Judge Redfield's comments on Miller's church case?

"I dined with the judges of our Supreme Court the other day, & the unanimous opinion was that on the question of jurisdiction the court had got itself into trouble —" (Clifford Papers).

There was a like schism in the Presbyterian Church in Missouri, and the Supreme Court of that state followed the Kentucky court. It criticized the Supreme Court of the United States for upholding federal jurisdiction, and then for refusing to follow the doctrine of the Kentucky court. (Watson *v.* Garvin, 54 Mo. 353, 383, 1873, one judge dissenting.)

[72] Gartin *v.* Penick, 5 Bush 110 (1869), one judge dissenting. The state judges were evidently not without emotion.

the duty of the civil court to decide for itself whether the General Assembly had been acting according to church law, and had concluded that its act in cutting off its pro-slavery members was void. If the Louisville church had not had a member resident on the other bank of the river, its case would have remained in the Kentucky courts and have been decided the other way.

So we may say that by asserting the authority of the federal courts at the expense of the state courts Justice Miller was able to establish a large measure of independence for ecclesiastical tribunals in their relation to the civil. If he slighted the comity between federal and state courts, it was to affirm a principle of judicial self-restraint in ecclesiastical affairs — and also to protect the anti-slavery group in the Louisville schism.

The doctrine that so long as church tribunals stay within the realm called ecclesiastical the civil courts will not overhaul their decisions has been criticized on the ground that it enables church tribunals to abuse their authority with impunity. Miller recognized the objection, but replied that justice would not be promoted by subjecting ecclesiastical decisions to civil review: "It would . . . be an appeal from the more learned tribunal in the law which should decide the case, to one which is less so." His successors have cited his opinion with respect. Thus when the "persisting Cumberlands" challenged the authority of their Church Assembly to unite with the Presbyterian Church, and brought suits in a dozen jurisdictions, the Supreme Court dismissed their complaint in a short memorandum opinion, because "the doctrines by which the case is controlled [had] been so affirmatively and conclusively settled" by *Watson* v. *Jones* that it was unnecessary to restate them.[73]

Justice Miller sought to bring the law to the test of reason, as his opinion in *Lovejoy* v. *Murray* [74] serves to illustrate.

[73] Shepard *v.* Barkley, 247 U. S. 1 (1918), per White, C.J. *Cf.* also the remarks of Brandeis, J., in Gonzalez *v.* Archbishop, 280 U. S. 1, 16 (1929).

[74] 3 Wallace 1 (1865).

Plaintiff's property had been converted by two joint tres-
passers. Judgment had been recovered in an action against
the one, but remained largely unsatisfied. Could suit now
be brought to recover the balance from the other? The lay-
man would suppose the answer was obvious. Yet the English
precedents were in the negative, the result being explained
on the ground that the claim *transit in rem judicatum*. But
Miller was never impressed by dogmatism dressed in Latin.
The American decisions were found to be generally the other
way. He concluded:

> If we turn from the examination of adjudged cases, which
> largely preponderate in favor of the doctrine that a judgment,
> without satisfaction, is no bar, to look at the question in the
> light of reason, that doctrine commends itself to us still more
> strongly. The whole theory of the opposite view is based upon
> technical, artificial, and unsatisfactory reasoning.[75]

A solicitude that the agencies of government be allowed
to function pervades Judge Miller's opinions. Though he
was expressing the judgment of the whole Court, he managed
to impart to an opinion his own particular concern that the
administration of justice should not prevent government from
being carried on. For example, in the matter of taxation he
felt it imperative to maintain the general principle that the
proper way to test the validity of a tax is for the claimant
first to pay the exaction and then pursue his remedies by
administrative appeal and at law, rather than by enjoining
the collection of the tax while its validity is being litigated.
Thus in a letter to Justice Clifford he writes:

> You say that Judge Nelson has taken jurisdiction in equity
> of a case arising under the internal revenue law, and I take it for
> granted that you mean that he has done this by way of in-
> junction.[76]

[75] In Brinsmead *v.* Harrison, L. R. 7 C. P. 547 (1872), Blackburn, J., cited
this decision with respect, but the weight of English precedent was found too
heavy to be overthrown. On the recommendation of the Law Revision Committee set up by Lord Sankey (Third Interim Report, 1934, Cmd. 4637) this
illogicality was finally removed by legislation (25 & 26 Geo. V, c. 30).

[76] *Cf.* Clark *v.* Gilbert, 5 Blatchford 330, Fed. Case No. 2822 (1866), per
Nelson, J. The date given for that judgment, however, is July 14, whereas

If this be so I concur with you now as I did last winter that Judge Nelson is in error. I think we have no jurisdiction to *prevent* the collection of the tax by that process; or any other.

I place my objections to such a proceeding on two grounds.

1. That the act of Congress provides if not expressly, by very clear implication, for relief in such cases by suit against the officer or officers who have done the injury, and enacts that the commissioner of internal revenue shall pay the judgments recovered in such cases and I think that this remedy is exclusive.

2. Upon the still stronger ground of public policy; namely, that no government could long exist, which depended upon taxes for its maintenance; if in any individual case the courts had jurisdiction, first to injoin the collection, and *then* inquire into the legality of the proceedings under which the tax was assessed or was about to be collected.

Acting upon these views I overruled an application to the circuit court of Missouri last fall, which was argued in open court, in which I had the concurrence of the two district Judges who sat with me in the Court.

I feel also quite sure that the majority of the judges last winter expressed the same views which you and I entertain, although the question was waived; and the decision placed upon other grounds in the case which was under consideration.[77]

Years later he was to express this view as the organ of the Supreme Court, employing language of characteristic vigor:

If there existed in the courts, State or National, any general power of impeding or controlling the collection of taxes, or relieving the hardship ˙incident to taxation, the very existence of the government might be placed in the power of a hostile judiciary.[78]

And again:

It is a wise policy. It is founded on the simple philosophy derived from the experience of ages, that the payment of taxes

Miller's reply was dated June 1. *Cf.* Cutting *v.* Gilbert, 5 Blatchford 259, Fed. Case No. 3519 (1865); United States *v.* Cutting, 3 Wallace 441 (1866); United States *v.* Fisk, 3 Wallace 445 (1866).

[77] Letter of June 1, 1866; Clifford Papers.

[78] Cheatham *v.* United States, 92 U. S. 85, 89 (1876). *Cf.* the specially concurring opinion of Reed, J. (Stone and Black, JJ., concurring) in Allen *v.* Regents of the University System of Georgia, 304 U. S. 439, 456 (1938), where the reasoning of Cheatham *v.* United States is cited with approval.

has to be enforced by summary and stringent means against a reluctant and often adverse sentiment; and to do this successfully, other instrumentalities and other modes of procedure are necessary, than those which belong to courts of justice.[79]

In spite of what has just been said, the fact is that Justice Miller was the author of an opinion which went far toward denying Congress a power essential to its effective action. It will be recalled that the headlong pace at which Congress during the Reconstruction period was carrying along the whole governmental system had filled him with apprehension. In November 1876, when intransigence in Congress bade fair to prevent the regular inauguration of a president, he had expressed the belief "that the House is gradually absorbing all the powers of the government." [80] That apprehension dominates the opinion he delivered for the Court in *Kilbourn v. Thompson*.[81] The case holds that the House of Representatives was without power to punish a recusant witness whose testimony had been sought in an investigation of a real-estate pool in which a bankrupt debtor of the United States was believed to be interested. The parliamentary precedents were rejected as irrelevant on the ground that Parliament was historically a court and thus derived its power to punish for contempt. One of the chief merits of the American system of government was the separation of powers. A "general power of making inquiry into the private affairs of the citizen" does not pertain to either House of Congress: the power to inquire is limited to matters of which the House "has jurisdiction." Though the opinion stops short of denying a power to inquire as a preliminary to legislation, "there are expressions . . . which, separately considered, might bear such an interpretation." [82]

[79] State Railroad Tax Cases, 92 U. S. 575, 613 (1876). These two passages were quoted with approval by White, J., in his dissenting opinion in Pollock *v.* Farmers' Loan and Trust Co., 157 U. S. 429, 610 (1895).

[80] Letter of November 19, 1876. *Cf.* his address at the celebration of the hundredth anniversary of the promulgation of the Constitution.

[81] 103 U. S. 168 (1880).

[82] Van Devanter, J., in McGrain *v.* Daugherty, 273 U. S. 135, 171 (1927).

The opinion has been criticized on several grounds, and cannot be said to have given lasting satisfaction. Justice Miller's remarks on the historical relation between the judicial powers of the Houses of Parliament and the punishment for contempt were very probably wrong. His sharp differentiation of judicial from legislative power seems doctrinaire and unrealistic. He shows himself zealous to resolve any doubt against the good faith of the House. One may share his regret at the low standard of legislative performance without concluding that public policy requires a narrow construction of inquisitorial powers. Perhaps intellectual muscularity cannot be developed in a constitutional strait-jacket.

It is interesting to learn from Miller's correspondence that a majority of the Court was prepared to go so far as to deny a power to punish as an aid to the legislative function, and to find a more specific statement of the Justice's dislike for legislative fishing expeditions:

I think if you had had the opinion [in Kilbourn v. Thompson] before you so as to examine it again you would have seen that there was a careful and avowed avoidance of the ground which you have discussed, namely, the power of one house to compel by punishment witnesses to appear and answer questions which may throw light on the legislative duties of those bodies. The reason of this was that on that point the court was not united, and dealing as we were with the asserted privileges of one of the most important coordinate branches of the government, it was very desirable to have unanimity in the court, as well as to decide no more than what was necessary. It was partly due to my conservative habit of deciding no more than is necessary in any case, that I was selected to write the opinion.

The majority of the court however was prepared to decide that no power to punish a witness for contempt in any other case than those which I specifically enumerate in the opinion exists in either house separately. It is explicitly decided in the Privy Council cases which I cited, that such a power is not incidental or necessary to the discharge of duties exclusively legislative, and higher authority cannot be found. This was my own opinion. This however is wholly apart from the power of Congress to pass statutes giving such power, and providing for such punishment, and it is much more conformable to our notions of personal rights that such a power should rest on a law enacted by the legislative authority, than on the loose notions [of] one branch of the legislative and irresponsible power in the matter.

I might and perhaps ought to rest what I have to say on that part of your letter here. But I am free to say that I hold no such opinion as you suggest as to legislative power of investigation. Not even as to state legislatures, whose powers are to be construed on a much more liberal principle than those of Congress. I think the public has been much abused, the time of legislative bodies uselessly consumed and rights of the citizen ruthlessly invaded under the now familiar pretext of legislative investigation and that it is time that it was understood that courts and grand juries are the only inquisitions, into crime in this country. I do not recognize the doctrine that Congress is *the grand inquest* of the nation, or has any such function to perform, nor that it can by the name of a report slander the citizen so as to protect the newspaper which publishes such slander.[83] If the whole body cannot do this much less can one house do it. . . .

As regards needed information on subjects purely legislative no doubt committees can be raised to inquire and report, money can be used to pay for such information and laws may be made to compel reluctant witnesses to give it under proper guaranty of their personal rights. This is sufficient, without subjecting a witness to the unlimited power of a legislative committee or a single branch of the legislative body.[84]

Justice Miller's remarks in favor of the tripartite division of governmental power are continually being quoted by his successors. We know that he had been shocked by the failure of the congressional committees on elections to put aside purely partisan considerations when hearing contested cases,[85] and this was doubtless a factor in his opinion. The experience of congressional reconstruction had caused him to think of the legislature as the least rational branch of government. And it will appear presently that when Miller had approached

[83] Cf. Stockdale *v.* Hansard, 9 A. & E. 1 (1839); 3 Vict. c. 9.

[84] Letter of March 20, 1881.

[85] It is not without significance that McCrary, Miller's close friend, when chairman of the House Committee on Privileges and Elections in the Forty-second Congress, "struggled hard to introduce the principle that an election contest . . . should be treated as a judicial question" (24 *American Law Review* 660, 1890). McCrary published in 1875 the first edition of his *Treatise on the American Law of Elections,* which he dedicated to Miller, "my teacher in the law."

the committees on the judiciary in an effort to secure effective coöperation in judicial reform he had not found a very sympathetic understanding on the part of members of Congress. He had often expressed the view that state legislatures were allowing themselves to be prostituted to the service of special interests, as in granting bonds and tax-exemptions. It is not surprising that he developed a certain rigidity in his attitude toward the legislative process. And yet it appears from his letters that there had been a time when his thinking on the doctrine of the separation of powers was quite fluid. At least he was aware that popular election was not an apt mode of choosing administrative officers. Whether his thought went so far as to approve continuous legislative control over administration, or only the selection by the legislature of officers who, thereafter, would exercise the "executive power" during their term of office, one cannot say. In 1866, apropos of the question whether Negro suffrage should be imposed upon the South as a condition of reconstruction, he wrote:

If I had it in my power to make any modification on this subject it would be in another direction. While I would allow every person (perhaps women about which I am not clear) to vote for members of the State legislatures and for members of the House of Rep in Congress, I would take every other office in the government from the range of popular elections.

I would have no municipal officers, of cities, counties, or towns thus elected. I would have no person whose duty it is to enforce or administer the law dependent for his office on popular elections. Thus I would remove Presidents, Governor, Judges, Sheriffs Clerks &c &c from the class of persons elected by the general voice. It seems reasonable that in making laws which are to govern the whole people, the whole people should have some voice in their adoption, for which no better plan offers than the representative system. But when those laws are to be put in execution, it is unsafe to confide to the people upon whom they are to be enforced the selection of the persons on whom the duty of enforcement is to be devolved.

But I have no time to elaborate this abstraction, which is never likely to become a practical question in my time.[86]

[86] Letter of February 6, 1866.

[*335*]

By 1878 he had come to the conclusion that "of all the depositories of political power . . . the legislative bodies . . . are the most unfit to be trusted with appointments to office." [87]

What Justice Miller regarded as his greatest opinion — *United States* v. *Lee* [88] — has been reserved for the last. The Court has always experienced great difficulty in dealing with controversies wherein the power of the judiciary was challenged on the ground that the action was an attempt to implead a sovereign — either one of the states, or the United States. In seeking to protect the citizen from official injustice it has been found hard to keep on firm ground, and the reasoning has often been subtle. Dissent has been frequent. One situation is that where an officer is sued for some act injurious to the person or property of another, to which his defense is that he acted under the orders of the government. The theory on which the courts proceed in such a case is that "he is not sued as, or because he is, an officer, but as an individual, and the court is not ousted of jurisdiction because he *asserts* authority as such officer. To make out his defence he must show that his authority was sufficient in law to protect him."[89] Under this head five of the justices held the case of *United States* v. *Lee* to fall. Specifically, the judgment holds that an action of ejectment can be maintained against an officer in possession under claim of title in the United States, where the United States is not a party and has not consented to suit. As Miller elsewhere related the facts which gave the case its peculiar human interest, it "was a suit by Lee, a grandson of Martha Washington to recover the Arlington estate which had been seized by order of the President during the war, and part of it converted into a cemetery for the dead of our side. The officers of the army set up the President's order as a sufficient defense of their possession." [90] After hold-

---

[87] *New York State Bar Association Reports*, II, 34.

[88] 106 U. S. 196 (1882).

[89] Miller, J., in Cunningham v. Macon & Brunswick R. R. Co., 109 U. S. 446 (1883).

[90] Inclosure in letter of February 22, 1888, to Charles Aldrich, then curator of the Historical Department of Iowa. It is in the collection of autographs there.

ing the English cases on the immunity of the sovereign to be inapplicable to our form of constitutional government, and the American precedents to uphold the maintenance of the action, Justice Miller examined the question "upon principle, and apart from the authority of adjudged cases," and concluded:

No man in this country is so high that he is above the law. No officer of the law may set that law at defiance with impunity. All the officers of the government, from the highest to the lowest, are creatures of the law, and are bound to obey it.

It is the only supreme power in our system of government, and every man who by accepting office participates in its functions is only the more strongly bound to submit to that supremacy, and to observe the limitations which it imposes upon the exercise of the authority which it gives.[91]

Where the moral issue was clear, Miller was a bold and courageous magistrate, and the researches of Justice Gray, dissenting, into the extent of the royal prerogative since the middle ages left Justice Miller unmoved.

[91] In response to a request from the curator of the Historical Department of Iowa Judge Miller copied out the above passage, and sent it with the observation, "It has been much admired and is I think one of the best things ever uttered by me in the court" (letter of February 22, 1888). He quoted it in his oration at the celebration of the hundredth anniversary of the promulgation of the Constitution, introduced by the phrase, "I but repeat the language of the Supreme Court of the United States when I say . . ." He sent the same quotation to Ellery S. Ayer, who was compiling a "National Album of Favorite Mottoes of Eminent Men."

XV

SECTIONAL POLITICS AND JUDICIAL APPOINTMENTS

IT WILL BE recalled that in 1863 Congress raised the membership of the Court to ten; that in order to deprive President Johnson of the power to appoint a successor to Justice Catron, or to fill any other vacancy which might occur during his term of office, it had provided in 1866 that the Court should be allowed to fall to seven; that on the death of Justice Wayne in July 1867 its actual membership was reduced to eight; and that as soon as Grant became president the number was raised to nine, where it had stood from 1837 to 1863. This last Act, of April 10, 1869, in addition to providing for the appointment of one new associate justice, authorized the payment of salary for life to any justice who should resign after having reached the age of seventy and after having held his commission for as long as ten years. It also created the office of circuit judge for each of the nine circuits. The Act was to become effective on the first Monday in December following. These facts form the background of the correspondence which follows.

There was a good deal of talk to the effect that the new associate justiceship should be filled from the South. The difficulty was that Southern lawyers of the requisite ability had not remained loyal to the Union, and the party which had won the war had no intention of placing an unfriendly judge on the Supreme Court. The outstanding Southern Unionists, Thomas J. Durant of New Orleans and George W. Paschal of Texas, entertained ambitions greater than their professional attainments. Doubtless the two most distinguished Southern lawyers in active practice at the Supreme Court bar were John A. Campbell, who had resigned from the Court in 1861, and Philip Phillips. On April 13 Phillips wrote from Washington to his friend Campbell at New Orleans:

The new Court Bill has for some time been the subject of much interest and discussion. The additional judge it is conceded *ought* to be from the South. Your name as well as my own have been frequently mentioned. It is supposed the Judges will be consulted. My own opinion is that the political current is too strong and swift to permit anything to arrest its onward course. So I told Judge Grier who spoke to me that the contingency was so remote that I did not permit myself to think of it. I understand that Durant is looking in that direction, and that even Paschal who has rejuvenated himself by a young wife has his eyes upturned. The appointments are not to be made until next winter — a wise move to prevent log rolling with the political appointments now being made.

The appointment and confirmation of Longstreet [1] is the only ray of light yet seen. The movement of Morton on the 15 Amendt. shows that the wheels of Revolution are still going forward. The South is the mere shuttlecock of those who play the battledore.[2]

Justice Miller's brother-in-law, William Pitt Ballinger, had a large practice in the federal courts at Galveston, and was therefore particularly concerned with the choice to be made of a circuit judge for the Fifth, or Southern, Circuit. He was coming to Washington during the summer of 1869, and Miller, writing from Keokuk, explains what may be done to promote a good appointment. At the same time he discloses his desire that Judge Caldwell of the federal district court for Arkansas should be appointed to the new associate justice-ship, and enlists Ballinger's interest in that behalf.

Henry Clay Caldwell had practiced law in Iowa, in a county adjacent to that where Miller lived, from 1852 until the outbreak of the war. He had distinguished himself as colonel of a cavalry regiment, and then almost literally swung out of the

---

[1] The Confederate General, James Longstreet, who had turned Republican at the close of the war, was nominated for surveyor of customs for the port of New Orleans by President Grant on March 11, 1869; on April 3 the Senate granted confirmation by a vote of twenty-five to ten (*Journal of the Executive Proceedings of the Senate*, XVII, 5, 81).

[2] Phillips' Letterbook, 1867–69, p. 197.

saddle to take his seat on the bench of the district court in June 1864. He remained a district judge until 1890, being promoted to the circuit judgeship when Judge Brewer went on the Supreme Court. He retired in 1903. Caldwell was a man after Miller's own heart, and one of the great judges of his time. If appointment to judicial office in the South had been reserved for men approaching him in honesty and wisdom, the history of the federal courts during Reconstruction would have been very different. Like Miller, Caldwell was impatient of technicalities and sought to liberalize the administration of justice. In the period of the receiverships, as has been pointed out,[3] he stood with Miller in his unwillingness to put his court into the railroad business. An example of his transparent honesty is the fact that, departing from a well-nigh universal practice, he declined to accept passes from the railroads, and paid his fare out of his own pocket as he traveled about his circuit. In the tense months of 1894 Caldwell was one federal judge in whose impartiality working people had confidence.[4] He is reckoned among the outstanding humane and liberal figures in the annals of the federal courts.[5]

Now to Justice Miller's letter:

I am satisfied that both he [Attorney General Hoar] and the President [Grant] desire to make *good* appointments on the Bench under the new law, and Hoar assured me that they wished very much to get the honest sentiment of the Bar, as distinguished from the recommendations of the members of Congress. In fact it is very well known both to the President and Judge Hoar, that the provision in that bill postponing its operation until next December was inserted by the Senate, because it was believed that the various Congressional delegations in the House, had the Circuit Judges all arranged; and it was to break up this arrangement, and to give the President an opportunity to make his selections for those offices in the absence of the members of Congress that it was done.

[3] *Supra*, p. 243ff.
[4] These two sentences are based on correspondence in the Library of the Historical Department of Iowa, at Des Moines.
[5] George B. Rose, "Judge Henry C. Caldwell," address before the Bar Association of Arkansas, April 29, 1938.

I have also written as you will see such a letter to Hoar, as will incline him to listen with consideration to any thing you may have to say.

In reference to the Circuit Judge of your circuit, I have given to Judge Jeffords, one of the present Judges of the Court of Errors and Appeals of Mississippi, a letter recommending him for the office. He is an honest man and a good lawyer, and will be a better Judge than you are likely to get; for I do not think the chances are good for any very *good* man in your circuit. I recommended him because I know this, and because he is an old friend having resided several years in Keokuk. But I have no special interest in this matter, and do not write this to have you take any interest in his behalf — though if appointed you may be sure of a fair hearing and of a personal friend on the bench. That he knows nothing of the civil codes of Texas and Louisiana is I admit an objection to him.

But I have recommended earnestly, and shall make a vigorous effort to have Judge H. C. Caldwell of the District Court for Arkansas, appointed to the vacant seat in the Supreme Court Bench.

In giving you my reasons for desiring his appointment, and for some slight hope which I indulge that it may be made I shall also put you in possession of the views which I think ought, and to a large extent I believe will, govern in making the appointments, for these new judicial offices.

In the first place as there are now eight Judges of the Sup. Court whose residences are all north of the old free and slave State line, I think it is both justice and good policy to take the new Judge from the south of that line, and from some of the States engaged in the rebellion. It would also for the same considerations be desirable if the right man could be had, to appoint a lawyer of the [sic] established reputation, and of a citizenship south, antecedent to the rebellion.

But there are two objections to this in my judgment and I think in that of the appointing power not easily to be overcome.

1st All the lawyers now of sufficient years, educated in the South, whether of whig or democratic politics, are more or less imbued with the strict construction principles as regards the Constitution. The more honest they are as men, therefore the greater danger that when in future, great questions shall arise before them, affecting the validity of the various legislative steps involved in the reconstruction policy, intended to give peace and stability to the government and the country, they may feel bound to hold those acts unconstitutional. I think the mere possibility of this to any general extent, would be a calamity hardly second to the rebellion itself. And no statesman in making an appointment to the Sup. Court would disregard this consideration. This implies no reflection on the patriotism, or devotion of the party under consideration, to the Union now or during the rebellion, for it excludes such suffering friends of the north, as Durant and Paschal and many others perhaps not so well known to me.

The mention of these names suggests the second of the objections I refer to.

It must be admitted that the rebellion included within its ranks nearly every name among the lawyers of the South, which represented enough of ability and integrity to be worthy a seat in the Federal Court[s] either Supreme or inferior. Of the lawyers who did *not* join the rebellion, or who have not fiercely opposed reconstruction, the two whose names I mentioned are perhaps among the best. Yet it would be a calamity if either of them should be made a judge either of the Supreme or Circuit Court.

I consider that the Judge of the Sup Court ought to come from your circuit. I admit that it is desirable that he should be familiar with Codes of Louisiana and Texas, so much alike in many things, in which they both differ from the laws of the other States. But where is the man? I must say that with a knowledge of the Lawyers of that circuit, much larger than is possessed as I think by the President or Judge Hoar, I do not know one who ought to be appointed Judge of the Supreme Court.

Judge Caldwell is the ablest District Judge that is in my circuit, and equal to any I believe in the United States. He is about forty years old.[6] Was raised in Iowa, and attained distinction as a lawyer and politician before the war. Was colonel of an Iowa Regiment which led the advance when Little Rock was taken in 1862, by our forces. Was appointed soon after Judge of that District by Mr. Lincoln.

He immediately removed his family to Little Rock, bought a homestead there, and has only been to Iowa twice since.

He has given himself wholly to his office, and to legal studies since then, though well known to be in accord with the republican party in all his sympathy.

He is however popular with the bar of Arkansas, and will receive the recommendation of all the lawyers of Little Rock rebel and loyal. The Arkansas delegation will also urge his name, and the Iowa delegation will do the same.

---

[6] He was not quite thirty-seven, having been born on September 4, 1832.

The Senate would undoubtedly confirm his nomination without hesitation; while they would be very cautious in confirming any old citizen of a rebel State. He has been longer in the South and is less obnoxious than any northern lawyer settling there since the rebellion began. He has all the elements of an able Judge, and will be if appointed as pure, and as impartial as it is in the nature of man to be.

Now if you have views of your own do not hesitate to follow them out for I am by no means sanguine of Caldwell's chances. He is besides without your circuit, and you may have personal friends whom you hope to see appointed.

But if you have no strong reasons to the contrary, I believe that your best chance to get rid of some such a man as Paschal, or Durant who is no lawyer, is to help me have Caldwell appointed by recommending him yourself and by getting him a fair share of recommendations from the Texas Bar.

If appointed, Caldwell will feel that he owes it mainly to me, and he will be very pleasant to me on the bench, and I assure you that you can find no more pleasant Judge on the bench, or more industrious and upright one.

But I repeat again do not take any part in the matter out of mere defference [sic] to my wishes which is not according to your best sense of what is right, and of what concerns your own interest.[7]

At the close of the year 1869 the situation was as follows. To the newly created associate justiceship Grant had on December 15 nominated Attorney General Hoar. A week later the Senate Judiciary Committee reported adversely, and the nomination was laid on the table.[8] On December 15 also the President had received Justice Grier's resignation to take effect on February 1.[9] To fill this vacancy he named Edwin M. Stanton. The nomination was received by the Senate on December 20, and promptly confirmed without reference to committee. Four days later Stanton died. It was evident that two new nominations were in order, and it appeared that the new justices would be assigned to the Third and Fifth

[7] Letter of July 30, 1869.
[8] *Journal of the Executive Proceedings of the Senate*, XVII, 314, 316, 328, 329, 330. On February 3 the nomination was rejected by a vote of twenty-four to thirty-three (p. 357).
[9] 8 Wallace vii.

circuits. On December 31 Justice Miller wrote to his brother-in-law:

I am making a strenuous effort for a circuit composed of Texas Arkansas Louisiana and Mississippi for which I hope to have my friend Caldwell appointed.

The case of Hoar is hopeless. There is no chance of his confirmation.

The Pennsylvania Circuit has not for the last ten years had as much business as any single State in the circuit above mentioned, or any average State in the Union. I go in for distributing that circuit among the adjoining ones and giving you two circuits South. The one I have given the other is S. Carolina, Georgia, Florida Alabama, Tennessee. Bills for this purpose will be introduced as soon as Congress meets.

This letter gives the clue to impending developments, and for the rest one consults the daily press and compares the record of legislative proceedings with the journal of the executive sessions of the Senate. For during the ensuing months Southern senators and such allies as their colleagues from Iowa were engaged in an effort to forestall the President's nominations until they could secure legislation to rearrange the circuits. It will be recalled that the Southern senators at this time were Republicans, so that the contest over the judicial appointments was within the party.

On January 1 the press announced that a bill would shortly be introduced for this purpose, outlining a scheme which would break up the Third Circuit by separating New Jersey from Pennsylvania and assigning them to adjacent circuits, and divide the Southern states into two groups. The Southwestern circuit was to consist of Texas, Arkansas, Louisiana, and Mississippi. On January 13 Senator Rice of Arkansas brought in such a bill,[10] as did Representative Loughridge of the House Judiciary Committee a few days later.[11] When Senator Rice's bill came from committee on February 9 certain amendments were proposed, in particular one of dubious constitutionality providing "that the Justices of the Supreme Court of the United States shall be residents of

<hr/>

[10] S. No. 387, 41 Cong., 1 Sess.   [11] H. R. No. 1005.

their respective circuits, and vacancies now or hereafter existing in said court shall, in every case, be filled by a resident of the circuit" — provided however that the chief justice might preside in any circuit to which he was allotted without change of residence.[12] It was about the Senate bill that the struggle occurred.

On February 3 the Senate finally rejected Attorney General Hoar, one of the objections — sincere or ostensible — being that no New Englander should be chosen to preside over Justice Wayne's old circuit. A number of candidates were brought to the President's attention, including, according to the press, Senator Drake of Missouri; D. K. Cartter of Ohio, then chief justice of the Supreme Court of the District of Columbia; Judge Advocate General Holt of Kentucky; T. J. Durant of Louisiana; District Judge Erskine of Georgia; and "Colwell [sic], late of Iowa and now district Judge of Arkansas." [13] Early in January the President was said to have made a careful canvass of the South and to have found no one whom he could fully trust.[14] A dispatch of February 5 said that the President and the Attorney General were decidedly opposed to any appointment from the South.[15]

When the Senate went into executive session on February 8 it had before it two nominations for associate justice: William Strong of Pennsylvania and Joseph P. Bradley of New Jersey, both from the circuit which the Southern senators proposed to distribute. On February 9 the Judiciary Committee brought in a report favoring the passage of Senator Rice's bill with amendments. On the 14th the same committee reported favorably on the nominations of Strong and Bradley, though it was evident that the enactment of the Rice bill would be fatal to at least one of the nominations. Thereafter the Southern Republicans obstructed all proceedings on Strong and Bradley. On February 18 Cameron of Pennsylvania secured a vote confirming the nomination of the former, but

[12] *Congressional Globe*, 41 Cong., 2 Sess., p. 1651.
[13] *Boston Daily Advertiser*, February 7, 1870.
[14] *New York Tribune*, January 8, 1870.
[15] *Boston Transcript*, February 7.

Rice of Arkansas at once moved to reconsider. Next day it was reported that "Southern Senators have given notice that they intend to talk against time to defeat action in Bradley's case until the bill fixing the Judicial Circuits is disposed of." [16] Finally, on March 1, the motion to reconsider was withdrawn, so that the confirmation of Justice Strong became definitive.

The opposition then concentrated upon Bradley. On March 3, according to a press dispatch,

Bradley's friends called upon the President . . . and asked him whether he had informed Southern Senators that he would withdraw Bradley if he was not acceptable to them. He denied having made such a remark. He said that he told them that if the Senate passed a bill requiring the Associate Justice to live in the district where the court was held, he would carry out the law and appoint a Southern man. The question now is whether they can pass a bill.[17]

An effort was at once made in the Senate to secure an amendment which merely required a justice to reside in his circuit after he was appointed, and Mr. Bradley was reported in the newspapers to have expressed his willingness to make his residence in South Carolina or Georgia if his nomination should be confirmed.[18] Senator Rice secured a postponement in Bradley's case until March 21, while his bill was being debated. When that day arrived a further effort to postpone failed; Justice Bradley was then confirmed by a vote of forty-six to nine.

While the plans to promote Judge Caldwell thus collapsed, the effort to rearrange the circuits went on. Senator Trumbull of Illinois, in charge of the bill, explained that out of a total of 378 cases from the circuits pending in the Supreme Court, only five came up from the Third Circuit. Scott of Pennsylvania sought to explain this away by recalling that

it was well known that in consequence of Judge Grier's physical inability to travel and sit upon the bench during any long period he was not to be expected at the circuit courts, and consequently

[16] *Boston Transcript,* February 21.
[17] *Boston Transcript,* March 4.
[18] *Boston Daily Advertiser,* February 9 and March 2; *Boston Transcript,* March 14.

members of the bar preferred going into the State courts where they could have their cases tried in some reasonable time.

He added that since Circuit Judge McKennan's appointment litigants were crowding into the courts.[19] Senator Hamilton, from the recently readmitted State of Texas, was seated in time to speak in favor of a separate circuit for the Southwest, stressing the particular importance of strengthening the federal courts in an area where the law to be administered was distasteful to the ruling class, and where the district judges ought not to be holding the circuit courts alone.[20] On June 1 the Senate passed Rice's bill with the amendments proposed by the Judiciary Committee, but the movement was arrested in the House, where the bill was laid on the table. Justice Bradley was assigned to the Fifth Circuit, extending from Georgia to the Rio Grande. He was not, however, required to take up his residence within his circuit.

In January 1874 Governor Coke appointed Ballinger an associate justice of the Supreme Court of Texas, but he resigned without entering upon his office. One may infer the reason for his action from the fact that a year later, when serving as a member of the state constitutional convention, he opposed, unsuccessfully, an elective judiciary and sought to obtain a provision making the judges independent and secure in their tenure. In a letter of March 21, 1874, Miller discloses his hope that Ballinger may presently be appointed to the federal Supreme Court:

I think you acted very wisely in declining the judgeship. Yet I fully appreciate your desire for the highest honour of the profession. I was myself willing to have accepted the same position in the Iowa courts.

I know now how very unwise it would have been to do so. For I should have been struggling through old age with very limited means for the demands of my family. I am well satisfied that there is as much honor, as much respect and esteem of the kind which you and I both value in being recognized as the first, or among the few that are first in the profession in a State as to

[19] *Congressional Globe*, 41 Cong., 2 Sess., p. 3973.
[20] At that time there were two federal courts of first instance — the district and the circuit court. The latter had much larger jurisdiction, but in practice was very often held by the district judge alone.

be a judge of its highest court. And the terms on which such a place is held are far more satisfactory. It is one's own by right of conquest. It is rarely contested after it is once attained and is never lost but by the laches or other fault of the party.

I hope yet to see you in our Court. If ever the republican party is overthrown or divided, events which are far from improbable, those who succeed to power must recognise the right of the South to representation on our bench. The first requisite for such a place is the knowledge of that peculiar system of local law of which Louisiana and Texas are the principal examples.

A man of moderation, but at the same time of the South and sharing their feelings to some extent, though not responsible for their extravagance and occasional outrages will be in request. I think the chances are that the republican party cannot hold together three years longer. The elements of discord are powerful among them. The issues of the past on which they agree are dead. They are not agreed and don't seem to have the courage to meet the new and living questions of currency, transportation of freight, government of rail roads &c &c. No party can live long on issues that are past when they shut their ears to those that touch the people in the present. Grant is recklessly assisting this by his appointments to office, in which he gives himself up to Butler and men of that class. He has no aid from a Cabinet which is without talent influence or character, each member of which knows that he owes his place to Grant's personal favour and his own insignificance. They *dare not* advise him against his inclination on any subject. There is but one man in the Cabinet who has any independence and that is Fish, and he has great influence with Grant for that very reason. He is rich, is tired of his place, and ready to go when things don't suit him.

In short there is every chance of a disruption of the party if it is not kept together by the folly of the old democracy. If the dash [?] and open defiance which Thurman [21] marshalled so successfully in Ohio last fall, shall mislead the democracy to the belief that its old leaders can again come to the front, no one can tell the result. For just as soon as this is apparent, and the probable accession of the Southern electoral vote to the party thus led is made known, the people of the North will shrink from the combination, and endure anything rather than that. If that old party organization would consent to die, it looks to me as if the republican party would also perish.

[21] Allen G. Thurman was senator from Ohio. Under his leadership the Democrats had elected a governor and a majority in both houses of the legislature in October 1873.

We have had our new Chief Justice [Waite] with us now three weeks, twice in conference. He is pleasant, a good presiding officer, *mediocre*, with fair amount of professional learning.

The hope which Miller had expressed in 1874 that his brother-in-law might join him on the bench seemed a possibility three years later. Justice Davis entered the Senate at the beginning of Hayes's term of office, creating a vacancy in the Court. The demand for an appointment from the South was reiterated. But the political situation had evolved so that there were now Democratic as well as Republican spokesmen; representation for the South thus had more than one connotation. The circumstances of Hayes's election gave some reason to think that a moderate Southern Democrat might be chosen. Miller was determined to use all the means at his disposal to bring the President to the conclusion that his kinsman was peculiarly fitted for the place.

It should be explained that Ballinger had in another brother-in-law, Guy M. Bryan, an advocate who stood in close personal relation to the President. Bryan came of a distinguished Texas family, being a nephew of Stephen F. Austin. He had attended Kenyon College, where he and Hayes were classmates. Hayes's *Diary and Letters* shows abundantly that their affection was deep and lasting: the Civil War worked no estrangement, and down to his death Hayes referred to Bryan as "my best friend." After leaving college Bryan read law with William H. Jack of Brazoria, Texas, and subsequently married his youngest daughter. When Hayes spent the winter of 1848–49 as Bryan's guest he was taken to visit the Jack family, and thereafter remembered the older sister as "the belle of the Brazos," "such a vision of loveliness." This lady became Mrs. Ballinger. Hayes also heard Ballinger make a political speech. When Mrs. Bryan died in 1872 her husband and children went to live in her sister's home. It will thus be evident that when Ballinger was urged as a candidate for the Supreme Court the name was not that of a stranger to President Hayes.

Ballinger's diary entry for March 1, 1877, records that

[Colonel Bryan said] that he expected to use his influence with Hayes to appoint me to the Supreme Court of the U. S. . . . I told him I appreciated his kind feeling of this; but that I didn't want that idea to exert the slightest influence upon him. That I wd not be willing for him to ask Hayes to appoint me, or to say to any one he intended asking him — I would be supposed to favor & be privy to it — & I felt it wd be considered great presumption on my part — that I no more thought of myself in connexion with the Supreme Bench than with the Roman papacy — and didn't want my friends or not friends to attribute it to me — He sd he wd not put me in a position objectionable to me; but he believed I could be appointed — that Miller's influence & his with Hayes' disposition could control the matter — I told him that I considered this an utter delusion — that I didn't believe Miller wd attempt it — & I should certainly not ask him & I felt it was incongruous and out of place. . . .

I was free to say I oughtn't to be appointed — that there were men in the South of far higher qualifications — conspicuously John A Campbell and if I assented to accept if tendered — I wd act selfishly & wrong —

A few days later Ballinger received a letter from Justice Miller, eager to put his hopes to the test. In his diary Ballinger set down the substance of his reply:

I told him that John A Campbell was the right man to appoint & begged him to try to get the Republican members of the Court to go in a body & ask the Prest. to put Campbell back on the bench — Told him it would electrify the South — that nothing in history would be handsomer — Told him if a Republican from the Southern Bench was to be appointed Woods [22] wd meet with strong approval here.[23]

---

[22] William B. Woods, then federal circuit judge for the Fifth Circuit. Hayes subsequently appointed him to the Supreme Court, vice Justice Strong, who resigned in 1880. Woods was originally an Ohioan, but on leaving the army at the close of the war had settled in Alabama.

Ballinger thought highly of Woods, as a number of his diary entries testify. E.g., when he first held court at Galveston: "Judge Woods seems prompt, businesslike & sensible" (entry for May 19, 1871). "He is a pleasant gentleman & a good judge — and I like him" (February 16, 1872). "Judge Woods left to-day. The bar all esteem him; but I believe none have paid him any social civilities but myself — It is a shame." (February 19, 1872.)

[23] Entry for March 12, 1877.

On March 18, 1877, Justice Miller made an emphatic and very interesting rejoinder:

My dear Brother

Your letter of the 11th instant came to hand yesterday morning and was read. Last night I read it over again and I must say that I find it very unsatisfactory. It is only less quixotic and wanting in common sense than the one I received last night from Col Bryan, forbidding me to mention his name to President Hayes in any connection with appointment to office.

There is no man on the bench of the Supreme Court more interested in the character and efficiency of its personel [sic] than I am. If I live so long, it will still be nine years before I can retire with the salary. I have already been there longer than any man but two both of whom are over seventy.

Within five years from this time three other of the present Judges will be over seventy. Strong is now in his sixty ninth, Hunt in his sixty eighth, and broken down with gout, and Bradley in feeble health and in his sixty sixth year.

In the name of God what do I and Waite and Field all men in our sixty first year want with another old, old man on the Bench. Paschal[']s Constitution [24] makes Campbell seventy five some time this year, and Judge Clifford thinks that when they served together they were about the same age and he is near seventy four. Campbell looks five years the older. I have already told the Attorney General that if an old man was appointed we should have within five years a majority of old imbeciles on the bench, for the hard work we have to do no man ought to be there after he is seventy. But they will not resign. Neither Swayne nor Clifford whose mental failure is obvious to all the Court, who have come to do nothing but write garrulous opinions and clamor for more of that work have any thought of resigning.

I am of opinion that Judge Campbell was the most capable efficient and useful man on the bench when he resigned. He made by far the ablest argument before the Electoral Commission on his side and I am not sure but it was the ablest of all. His argument and his conduct as counsel were more lawyerlike and manly than any of his associates. He had and has my respect and my sympathy. But I do not want him on the bench and if

[24] George W. Paschal, *The Constitution of the United States Defined and Carefully Annotated* (Washington, 1868). At p. 193 he prints a list of those who have been associate justices, including "James A. Campbell," born in 1802. In fact, John A. Campbell was born June 24, 1811.

he were a much younger man I do not think his appointment would be justifiable. I think his course in resigning and giving to the rebellion the full influence and support of his name and character and services should forbid it. I could forgive him much sooner if like To[o]mbs [25] and that class of men the confederate cause had commanded his convictions. But they did not. It was well known that he violated them to aid in overthrowing a government he had sworn to support and in whose service he held one of the highest posts of honor his country had to give. Beside all this I have neither seen nor heard of any action of Judge Campbell's since the rebellion which was aimed at healing the breach he contributed so much to make. He has made himself an active leader of the worst branch of the New Orleans democracy. Writing their pronunciamentos, arguing their cases in our Court, and showing all the evidences of a discontented and embittered old man, filled with the disappointments of an unsuccessful partizan politician. If the south can only be conciliated by the replacing such a man on our bench they must wait so far as I am concerned until the democracy pure and simple come into power to do it for them.

The Senate adjourned *sine die* yesterday. It remains in doubt whether an extra session will be called. The vacancy on our bench will not be filled until the Senate is in session again. I am well posted as to the Presidents feeling without having said a word to him. Caldwell and Wood[s] have been pressed on his consideration by more men of influence than any other nominees. Judge Bruce of Alabama who is graduate of my law office had an interview three days ago with the President as I suppose to favour Wood[s]; but of that I am not sure. He told me however, that the President was hesitating between Harlan of Kentucky or possibly Bristow their interest being one, and a *real* Southern man, and in this latter sense he did not consider Wood[s] or Caldwell to meet the requirement. Now the difficulty of selecting a real Southern man is that all the men who before the rebellion had made high reputation as lawyers are either dead or too old for the place.

If a proper man can be found the place ought to be filled with a lawyer familiar with civil code system of Louisiana and Texas. He ought also to come from that circuit. Where can a man be found more suitable under all the circumstances than yourself?

---

[25] Robert Toombs of Georgia. Democratic representative and senator before the War; congressman, Secretary of State, and brigadier general under the Confederacy.

You are about the right age [26] with I thank God a fair hope of such health and vigor as gives promise of good service.

You are from the right geographical quarter and familiar with the civil codes I have named.

You have not been an active politician and did nothing to promote secession. You have shown no disposition to foster the animosities of the late war.

Permit me to say that your fear of want of capacity for the place is a little nonsensical. You have been nothing but a hard working lawyer all your life. With the best library, constant practice in courts of remarkably varied jurisdiction, to suppose you have not become a sound and a learned lawyer is a reflection on your native capacity not justified by the facts or by your success in your profession. I take the liberty of saying that you would be the peer of your brothers if you had a place on our bench and in usefulness the superior of many.

I shall so far obey Col Bryan's request as to say nothing to the President about him in connection with office until it is made too clear for doubt with me that you cannot be appointed.[27] In saying this I repeat that I do not propose unless under very peculiar circumstances to ask your appointment unsupported by local influence, but I will do nothing to destroy the little hope I have in a matter that would give me so much happiness in my remaining years.

The thing is within possible reach if you or your friends will do what is necessary and what I take the liberty of saying is in these times not indelicate, or improper. I was requested to recommend Judge Caldwell who is supported by the Iowa delegation. I would prefer him to any one but yourself. I explained to Judge Wright [28] (his kinsman) that though your name might never be presented, I would do nothing that would embarrass or cripple my action if it should be. That is the precise position I occupy now; and it applies to Col Bryan for it is clear you and he cannot both receive important appointments at the hands of the President

A place in the Supreme Court is so much more important, besides being a life office, than anything Col Bryan could possibly get that I see no reason why one should stand in the way of the other.

I will send you my remarks in the electoral commission in a

[26] Ballinger was then fifty-one years old.

[27] Bryan hoped that Hayes would appoint him minister to Mexico.

[28] George G. Wright, formerly of the Supreme Court of Iowa; he had just completed a single term as senator.

few days, notwithstanding the partizan and dogmatic manner in which you speak of the excellent Mr Tilden being 'counted out.' But *unless you desire it* I shall not trouble you with the full report of the proceedings before the commission including the arguments in secret conference, of which Congress has ordered me forty copies.

A month later Bryan came to visit his classmate in the White House. On April 23 Judge Miller informed Ballinger what progress was being made with his candidacy:

I learned last Tuesday from the President himself that Col Bryan was at the Mansion and I called on him immediately. He called that evening at my house and passed the evening with us. I called on him again on Saturday and he came yesterday and took a Sunday dinner with the family and with Judge & Mrs Adams [29] — He expects to leave to night for Ellicott City on his way home.

I have been very much interested in him finding him to be a man of much information and cultivation, of sound judgment, and reasonably free from prejudices —

He is very fond of the President, has faith in his policy and full confidence in his purity of purpose.

He has had a very free conversation with him in regard to the vacancy on our Bench and filling it by appointing you. Bryan himself is in high courage in the matter and he desires me to give you the substance of his conversation with the President, because he feared to write you fully as his letter to you would probably be treated as a family affair, a thing he does not think altogether prudent.

He says that the President gave him to understand that his present purpose was to appoint a real Southern man. That he did not consider Judge Wood[s] who [*sic*] he believed to be otherwise capable, as filling the requirement in that respect.

Bryan then suggested you as the proper man. Gave him your political history so far as you had one and placed in prominence your conservatism and ancient affection for the whig party. The President said he had heard you make a public speech on Wilmot Proviso in Galveston many years ago [and] was much impressed by it. Seemed to have thought of you in regard to the selection and Bryan said left the impression that he had mainly in his

[29] Green Adams, formerly of Barbourville; chief clerk of the House of Representatives at this time. He was an uncle of Ballinger's and of Miller's first wife.

mind your name and that of a lawyer in New Orleans whose name Bryan either did not know or could not recall.

He asked the President if recommendations were desired. The reply was that general or numerous recommendations were not desirable. That after he had made up his mind he might wish something in that way as a support or justification for his action.

I feel bound to say as a countershading to this picture that in conversation with the Attorney General he gave me to understand that he thought it unsafe to place any man in the position who had not been always a Union man, but he said he had no conversation at all with the President in regard to the appointment.

In a very short talk which I [had] with the President in which no name was mentioned he said he should be in no haste to make the appointment and turning to a Mississippian present he said it seemed wrong that so large a part of the Union should be without a representative in that Court.

I have said nothing about you in connection with the appointment this far, but I shall leave here in about two or three weeks for my circuit. Before I go I shall endeavor to enlist McCrary and Bradley in the cause. I shall have a conversation with the President about your appointment and if I can put in operation any other agency to that effect I will do it.

We drank the health of our Galveston friends in good Champaign [sic] at dinner last evening with great energy.

On May 6 Miller sent another long report on operations:

I fear you will think I have been careless or inattentive in the matter of which I expressed so much interest because I have delayed so long to reply to your letter of the 18 of April. But it would be quite a mistake if you did. . . . I received a few days later a letter from Gov. Coke [30] enclosing a letter to the President written by Senator Maxey.[31] recommending your appointment, also one couched in very handsome terms signed by all the Judges of your Supreme Court and of the Court of Appeals with Senator Coke's own indorsement. He is evidently in earnest and says he shall get the recommendation of the entire Texas delegation as he thinks and also the present Governor.

With the papers sent by Gov. Coke I determined to have an interview with the President, but as an uninterrupted interview

[30] Richard Coke, Governor of Texas and recently elected to the Senate. It was he who had appointed Ballinger to the Supreme Court of Texas in 1874.
[31] S. B. Maxey, then Democratic Senator from Texas.

of half an hour is very hard to secure and as I was very busy with the closing up of the business of our Court, I did not see the President until Friday morning, the day before yesterday.

Before I proceed to detail that conversation I will say that we had our last consultation of the Court yesterday and we read our opinions and adjourn tomorrow. I shall leave in about three or four days for my circuit in the West and do not expect to be back until about the first of October. Any letters, memorials or recommendations intended for the President or to be filed in the department had better be addressed to your uncle Green Adams whether forwarded by you or your friends.

I shall be at Des Moines May 14 to June 1. At Leavenworth June 4 to 14. At St Paul June 18 to 28th. At Denver July 3 to 15. Communications will reach me at those dates. My Dear brother you see since the ball is in motion I make a regular business matter of it, as it must be if successful.

When I saw the President I told him I had called because I was going to leave in a few days and might not return to Washington before he would feel himself called on to fill the vacancy in our court and I desired to say something to him in that matter especially if he intended to send in a nomination to the approaching session of the Senate this Summer. He said at once that it was very doubtful if such a session would be held but that if it was he had fully decided that he would not nominate for that office at that time.

He said however as he would certainly be thinking the matter over he would like to hear what I had to say and to ask me some questions himself. I then made the suggestion that we ought not to have an old man, that the South whatever might be meant by that term ought to have a man on our bench, that to satisfy that requirement a true Southern man was wanted, and that our Court very much needed one who was familiar with civil law or civil code system which entered so largely into the jurisprudence of Louisiana and Texas. I then told him of the correspondence which Senator Coke had voluntarily opened up with you and with me, of the recommendations which I then had in my hand including one from myself. As to this I remarked that since I had come to ask him to appoint you it was due both to him and my-self that I should place my recommendation in the files in a formal manner.

I then gave him your history so far as it had any bearing on the matter and my view of your peculiar fitness for the place generally and at this particular time. He listened with great interest and then took up the conversation. He said that in reference to my views his attention had been turned to Mr. Wm Hunt [32] of New Orleans, asked if I knew him and what I thought of him in that relation. I replied that Mr Hunt had argued two cases before our court in person and several others by printed argument. That he was I thought a man of ability and a fair lawyer. That how far he would fill any policy of a political character which might influence the appointment he was better qualified to judge than I was but that he probably knew that Hunt was a fierce partizan in politics though probably on what he and I would call the right side, but that his nomination would be very distasteful to all but extreme republicans and might meet serious opposition in the Senate.

He then mentioned Bristow and Harlan of Kentucky, said he had been thinking of both of them, and wished to know what I thought of them individually and relatively. I said I knew them both well. That both were fully up to the standard required both by native ability and professional attainments. That of the two Harlan was probably a man of the most vigorous intellect, while Bristow was believed to be if any different of the soundest judgment. He said that Bristow's presidential aspirations were to be feared, in which I concurred and made some very forcible remarks on the evils of presidential hopes in our court and especially how the present members of it had felt the annoyance and misfortune of the thing in the case of Judge Davis and the late Chief Justice Chase.

Bringing the conversation back to you he said he had been very favorably impressed in regard to you, was a little distrustful that his judgment might be unduly influenced by his great friendship for Bryan, and that if he nominated you it would be attributed to that motive by the public. I replied that I did not believe that any name that had been mentioned would command a stronger vote on confirmation in the Senate than yours, to which he responded at once that he believed that was true. I added, that before he came to act in the matter I thought that such papers would be laid before him and such public urgings of your name for the place, that he would feel relieved of any charge that his action was governed by mere personal considerations of friendship or favoritism.

This ended the interview and I left him holding in his hands

[32] William H. Hunt of New Orleans. He had studied at Yale; had been a Whig, and was a Unionist during the war. He was appointed to the Court of Claims in 1878, and became Secretary of the Navy in the Garfield cabinet.

the letters forwarded by Coke and my own letter with same subject.

Before I saw the President I had two conversations with Bradley. He said that you had the requisite learning and ability, and while he could not say you were either the ablest lawyer of the South or the fittest man for the place, he authorized me to tell the President that your appointment would be a good one and acceptable to him. In the second interview I suggested that I would like him to join me in requesting your appointment if he felt inclined, but that if it interfered with his own wishes, or if he felt any hesitation I did not ask him to do so under any feeling of hesitation. He said he thought the President ought to ask his advice, that he thought he would do so, and he did not care to speak until that time came. He spoke of his relation to Wood[s], whom he liked very much, and my own opinion is that if he finds it of any avail he will indicate Wood[s] as his choice. But I think he will do you justice in the matter. He said he had received a letter from Judge Campbell on the subject, who strangely enough deprecated the idea of a lawyer for the place trained exclusively in the civil code system, on the ground that he would be unfit for the states whose laws were based on the common law. Bradley said he thought this was meant for Hunt whom Campbell dislikes.

I had a casual conversation yesterday with the Chief Justice and told him frankly of my wishes for your appointment and what the President said of Hunt, of Bristow and Harlan. He is decidedly opposed to all three of them. Thinks Hunt not up to the mark in ability; Bristow to[o] much aspiring and that it would be very unpolitic to fill the place from a circuit which now has two members of the court,[33] and that this would give Davis' circuit just ground of complaint. I think if it is narrowed down to the men named by the President the C. Justice will say what he may properly say in your favour.

I have yet to see McCrary, the Secretary of War. He has undoubtedly committed himself with the Iowa delegation for Judge Caldwell. But he owes me much and I think I can secure his action and for you when he becomes satisfied that Caldwell is not among those from whom the President intends to select, and I am satisfied that at present he does not look much either to Caldwell or Woods. In this event also I have some hope of aid from Bradley. . . .

[33] Waite and Swayne being from Ohio, which lay in the same circuit as Kentucky.

You will see from the President's remark to me that all the aid in the way of recommendations from suitable quarters will be very useful and that my first suggestion to you was sound notwithstanding the apparent intimation of the President to the contrary to Col Bryan.

There is now ample time for all this and the campaign is opened. When it becomes known that Hunt is the New Orleans favorite of the President, I should think a judicious friend of yours might get valuable aid from his opponents of whom no doubt there are many. Campbell himself might be useful under proper circumstances.

I shall make a point of seeing Gov. Woodson while in his region this summer and get a letter from him if nothing more.

I have done some service here for John White late member from Kentucky and shall ask him for a letter. I have spoken casually to Mr Evarts [34] who is next door neighbor, but one, to me now. What else I shall do I know not. It is proper to add that my mention of your name was in response to Evarts' suggestion that he thought the place ought to be filled by a southern lawyer, but that the difficulty lay in finding the right man, as no man since the war had been able to make sufficient reputation, and those of a prior date who were well known had grown too old. His suggestion was too good for the opportunity of giving him a sketch of you to pass —

I am not sanguine. I never am where my interest is deep. I have hope enough and I believe it has foundation enough to justify all the thought and effort which can be judiciously given to the matter.

Miller had set his heart on securing Ballinger's appointment, and threw himself into the enterprise with all his indomitable energy. Neither the aspirations of Judge Caldwell, whom he had supported in 1870, nor those of his other close friend, Circuit Judge Dillon, deflected him from his course. While on his circuit he made a point of recruiting Silas Woodson, who had known Ballinger in the Barbourville days:

When I mentioned the fact, that you were talked of for the vacant judgeship he expressed a warm interest in the matter and a desire to contribute to your success. He said he would write a letter himself and would make a point of obtaining other letters.

I am quite sure he will do all that he can.

[34] Secretary of State in the Hayes cabinet.

He brought to me on Monday Genl Willard A. Hall perhaps the leading lawyer of North West Missouri who seemed anxious to aid in the matter, but said letters had been written from Missouri recommending Dillon in which I think he had taken part. He seemed to wish me to say that Dillon stood no chance, but I said at once that I did not wish any one's action to rest on any thing said by me on that point and that I had nothing to say. Woodson thought he could secure some aid from St Louis and also from Kentucky.

I have not said one word to Dillon on the subject because the Albany Law Journal, the Central Law Journal of St Louis, and no doubt other persons have suggested his name. I thought it the better course to say nothing nor elicit any thing from him on the subject.

I find there is a very prevalent impression that the new Judge ought to come and will come from the South. I do not believe that the President will think of taking any Northern man outside of the 7th Circuit, and I doubt if the nomination would be confirmed if any such were made. The three great States of Illinois Indiana and Wisconsin would resent actively such a reflection on the bar of those States.

I note your remark that you scarcely hope for the place. In the sense of expectation, or a preponderance of belief that your chances are better than that of all *others* I do not hope for it myself. But I believe they are equal to that of any other one person, and they are worth cultivating. I certainly shall not feel like I have lost any thing in which I had a vested right if some one else is appointed, but I shall not I hope have to reproach myself that I lost it, through inactivity or inattention or want of any honorable effort.

I think your friends in Texas are moving very judiciously and especially Col Bryan.

I am staying at Judge Nelson's [35] here, and last night he gave a reception to some fifty gentlemen on my account.

I have had a regular ovation wherever I have been this spring. I have hardly passed a day, except in travel without being invited to a dinner or supper or something of the kind. I do not feel that the abuse heaped upon me by the Democratic press has injured my popularity or impaired my usefulness as a judge. . . .

I am writing this while an argument to a jury is going on before me. You must consider this in reading.[36]

[35] Rensselaer R. Nelson, district judge for Minnesota; son of Justice Nelson of the Supreme Court.
[36] Letter of June 22, 1877, written from Saint Paul, Minn.

From Chicago he wrote on August 11:

I have made no effort at getting recommendations in my circuit except through Woodson and some members of the bar at Keokuk. If I had thought it prudent to do so otherwise, I would have been deterred by the fact that a serious effort on behalf of Dillon has been made by his friends in this circuit; and I do not wish to embarrass the members of the bar who practice before him and like him by asking them to do what he might consider an interference with his prospects.

Back in Washington in the autumn, Justice Miller lost no time in getting the situation in hand. On October 8 he wrote:

We have just made our official call on the President and to-morrow we commence the treadmill which we must continue to turn for about seven months. I called to see the President last Saturday, intending to talk with him about the judgeship. He was not at the mansion. . . . I had a long and confidential conversation with Mr Rogers [37] his private secretary who I think was frank with me.

He said that Harlan and Wood[s] were pressed very much. That he did not think the President was much inclined to Hunt. That he believed the President's personal preferences lay between Harlan and yourself.

I suggested that as to Harlan his locality was a serious objection. That his appointment would make three Judges of our Court from one circuit. That the appointment would be no concession to the Southern men and would be a marked offence to Judge Davis' circuit as Harlan lived out of the circuit and in a State which never seceded. That it would embarrass the President in the probable event of Judge Swayne's retirement during his administration.

He said that these considerations had been in the President's mind, who felt the force of them.

McCrary the Secretary of War is also of the impression that the President is hesitating between you and Harlan with a personal inclination to appoint Harlan. He said if any one not a republican was appointed he believed it would be you, but he gave me to understand that the Cabinet did not favour the appointment of a democrat.

McCrary was one of my main reliances. He told me last spring that if Caldwell stood no chance he would favour your nomina-

[37] W. K. Rogers, formerly Hayes's law partner.

tion. He says now that he sees no hope for Caldwell; but I am satisfied that he has advised the President to appoint no one but a republican. He owes me a great deal and his promise last spring was very clear. I had some very plain talk with him last week and if he does not actively support your nomination I shall feel very badly and shall make him feel so too. . . .

I have still strong hopes of success. I shall have another talk with McCrary. I do not see how the President can appoint Harlan, though I think he wishes to do so. If not Harlan then there is much hope for you. His action thus far in making appointments shows the strong perhaps too strong influence of his personal wishes. Next to Harlan I think his wishes are in your favour.

Mr Rodgers [sic] says that Judge Bradley spoke in high terms of you to the President. I had supposed that he would favour Wood[s], but I learn now that with his usual eccentricity he has earnestly recommended some man from Mobile whose name is Hamilton. He [Justice Bradley] is a queer man. As Judge Strong said the other day, 'If there is a principle on which a case can be decided that no one else has thought of it has for that reason a charm for him.' And so I suppose he is in other matters of life.

There are at least two aspirants in St Louis — Breckenridge [38] and Hitchcock.[39] Dillon has also had his friends and his hopes in my circuit. And I have lost the assistance of some of my most influential friends on this account and that of Judge Caldwell —

We shall make a good fight. We may succeed. If we do not we shall have so presented your name that it will be one to be considered on some future occasion.

That the contest was being lost appears from his report five days later. One will note the severe judgment passed upon John A. Campbell. It seems that Miller's objection to him on political grounds went at least as deep as that based on age.

I agree with all you say about Johnson [40] and about the principle which would lead to such an appointment. But I am quite

[38] Samuel Miller Breckenridge. He had studied at Union, Princeton, and Transylvania, and settled in Saint Louis in 1849. He was circuit judge from 1859 to 1863.

[39] Henry Hitchcock, prominent Saint Louis lawyer; president of the American Bar Association 1889-90.

[40] Herschel V. Johnson of Georgia. A moderate Democrat before the war, he opposed the division of the party, was candidate for vice president on the

satisfied Bryan has been mistaken and that the President has never seriously thought of Johnson. I believe that if at any time he had made up his mind to appoint a Democrat he would have taken you.

I think you are infatuated about old Campbell. I think no man that has survived the rebellion is more saturated today with its spirit than he unless it be old To[o]mbs. While I admit his pluck and energy, admit his ability and purity, he deserves all the punishment he has received or can receive, not so much for joining in the rebellion as for the persistency with which he continues the fight when all good men ought to seek to forget it as much as possible.

If he wants to keep up that contest he shall get no vantage ground with my consent to fight to better advantage.

I had an interview with Gov Coke and Mr. Giddings [41] yesterday. I put them in full possession of the situation as I understand it. They are correct and active in your behalf. After I saw them I went last night to see McCrary. I think he felt the force of what I said to him at our previous interview. He had certainly talked the matter over since then with the President. He is convinced that since the Ohio election [42] the President will not have the courage to appoint any one but a recognized Republican to the place and he believes that Harlan's name will be sent in early next week. This concurs with what I have learned from other sources. It is quite certain that the correspondents of newspapers here, (who though great liars do learn a wonderful deal of truth if they would only use it) all feel sure Harlan is the man. I think it prudent to say no more to the President myself. From what Col. Bryan told your Uncle Green and from something that fell from McCrary I am satisfied that the President is either truly or as a sham suggesting the idea that the fact that you are my brother in law is an embarrassment to him.

While I would smother the natural indignation which arises on such a suggestion if a talk with him would do any good, I am sure that with such a feeling on his part an interview which must be generally known would be more likely to do harm.

On October 16, 1877, John Marshall Harlan of Kentucky was nominated for the vacancy on the Court. Miller nursed

---

ticket with Douglas in 1860, and struggled to delay secession. He displayed self-control during the years of Reconstruction.

[41] Doubtless De Witt C. Giddings, then representative from Texas.

[42] At the election of October 9, 1877, Democrats were elected to all the state offices then to be filled.

his thoughts for some time before setting them out on paper. He was a very human person. It will be remembered that after Grant had broken his hopes of the chief justiceship, his opinion of the President — which had never been high — declined rapidly. Again, and this time with much less reason, he turned against the author of his disappointment. On October 28 he wrote:

I thought of writing to you immediately upon Harlan's nomination. But I expected every day that the Senate would act upon it and really the whole subject has left with me such a feeling of deep regret, I can hardly say disappointment[,] that I wished to make but one more letter about it to you, and felt it wise to postpone that on my own account. Though the judiciary committee still holds the nomination in its hands, my information is that it is from no unfavorable disposition towards him. But is part of a plan by which the leading republican Senators who have control of all the committees to whom all nominations are referred desire to impress the President with their power to defeat his nominations and by this means to bring him to terms. How long it will last I do not know, nor what effect it will have on the President. If he is firm and they are persistent it will probably lead to a complete rupture, in which event the President by the aid of the Democratic Senators and two or three republican Senators who will adhere to him will be master of the situation, but will by this course fall more under the influence of the democrats than he has intended. I feel pretty sure that Harlan will be confirmed in any event and probably without a division.

As for the President and his policy, and the fight it may get up in the party I think I never felt as indifferent about any political movement since I shouted as a little boy in the streets of Richmond for Adams and Clay, sometimes varying it by a "hurrah for the Administration," with no idea in the world what that word of many syllables meant. While my judgment approves of what the President *wishes to do*, I am disgusted with the *method* he adopts to accomplish those purposes. In reference to his civil service, it is quite clear that the main features of that policy, in fact the only ones of any real importance are 1 Permanent tenure of office and 2, To break down the control of Congressmen in appointments.

This last any statesman could have seen was by far the most important, for success in the other would follow this very largely if not entirely.

[*364*]

Now long before he has reached this last struggle he has crippled himself by a series of silly skirmishes in which victory would amount to nothing, but which has really destroyed for no practicable good half the influence which the confidence of his party gave him when he was inaugurated. By this I mean his silly order that all men in office must disconnect themselves from active politics or go out. The effect of this on the eve of the fall elections on the results of those elections I do not consider. But upon the men themselves who had been long accustomed to the management of the local organizations on which all parties depend for means was very hard. They could only serve their personal or party friends by secret aid, and were compelled to keep out of the county and State conventions and see everything go wrong without power to correct the errors of the party which they had faithfully served and on whose domination their offices depended.

The purpose to be accomplished might much more effectually have been accomplished by a quiet understanding with the heads of departments to discourage the thing, with little or no general offence to strong men in the party.

But the worst mistake of all is this; that while diffusively and ostentatiously proclaiming civil service reform as the corner stone of the Administration policy, and as one republican administration succeeding another leaves little excuse for removals from office, there have been more causeless removals by this administration than for years.

Mr Evarts for instance causes it to be understood that eight years service abroad is long enough to justify a change in the diplomatic corps whether of higher or lower grade. As this covers the precise period of the Grant administration it opens to Mr. Evarts the entire patronage of the State department. In direct antagonism to the real principle of the civil service, the very men who by length of time spent in that service, have become best qualified for it must now all give way to new ones. Of the qualifications of these as far as appointments have been made, but two are required. 1. That they must be the personal friends or adherents of the President or of Mr Evarts, and 2. have been personally hostile to President Grant.

Again. Congress several years ago inserted in an appropriation a provision that the offices of the various departments should be distributed among the States and Territories in proportion to their population.

Bristow who was the first man called to administer this law held as I think very wisely, that this equality was to [be] obtained, by observing the rule in future appointments. But Sherman notwithstanding this precedent and the civil service policy, holds that it [is] his duty to enter at once upon the execution of that law, by turning out of office those from any state who are in excess of the proper share of that State and appointing others to fill their place. It is needless to say that when he wants to serve a friend, both the necessary residence of that friend in a State entitled to the office, and the man in excess in some other State can easily be arranged, while to all unacceptable applications for office the rigid rule is ostentatiously pleaded as a bar. It is a sickening fact that all appointments to office thus far, which are worth considering can be traced to personal friendship or obligation of the President, of Evarts or of Schurz; or to the President's desire to conciliate the South. But the former will ruin the administration inside of a year if it is kept up as it has [been]. The source of the President's misfortune is, that the three men in his Cabinet and out of it who exercise most influence over him are the three last men whom he ought to trust. These are Evarts, Schurz and Sherman. The two former are selfish, visionary doctrinaires, eminently fitted to lead a minority in opposition and peculiarly fitted to reduce any majority to the condition in which their talents can have fair play. As to Mr. Sherman, he is a heartless soulless party hack. A man who has succeeded with a very moderate amount of brains by the use of all the worst appliances of party machinery, in keeping himself and friends long in office, and in making a deal of money. He belongs heart and soul to the moneyed, bond-holding interest of the country, who no doubt in some shape or other pay him well for his many services to them, and who has no more interest in the President's civil service than its worst enemy, and who fully recognizes and intends to permit the exercise of all the rights claimed by members of Congress in the appointments of his department.

On the other hand Conkling Blaine Edmunds et cet would prefer to take the chances of what would come from a democratic administration after the next election, to yielding any of their ancient rights of controlling public patronage and submit[ting] to Evarts, Schurz & Co. They profess to dislike the policy. They really want the offices.

Why should I take any more interest in these matters. It is probable, — I dont know — It is best to say possible, that the Democratic party may fall under the control of such men as

Lamar,[43] and Gordon [44] and Hill [45] instead of the murdering Butler of S.C.[46] or the thieving Fernando Wood of N. York, and may after much suffering be wiser and better than it has been. But I confess it is but a faint hope.

Why then should I vex my declining years in a matter in regard to which my official position disables me from exercising any active influence. As I said before I feel an unaffected indifference as to existing or future politics.

I have fairly paid the party to whom I owe my place by honest and conscientious service to the country for that place. I know I stand with that party as with the country as the best appointment to the bench which has been made since the party came into power, and I have rendered fifteen years of faithful irreproachable service. We are quits. I shall hereafter feel myself at perfect liberty to oppose or disapprove of any man or any measure as my judgment may dictate. And have but little care as I really have which *party* has possession of the government.

I find myself thus withdrawing active interest, one by one from much that used to absorb me wholly. I think I have already written to you of my failing interest in the Court. The work there now is merely a matter of duty, often irksome duty — rarely of any interest. I would gladly accept my salary, or even part of it and retire, before I get too old to seek an interest in something else.

The failure to secure your appointment weighs on me more than I expected, for I never really believed in success though I had come to hope for it. I feel myself responsible *to you* for the effort that has been made for I think without my urging it on you it would never have been made. But it has done you no harm unless it be that a hope was inspired to be disappointed and for that I think Col Bryan is more responsible than I am. But you have been brought prominently before the country in a most creditable manner. Neither you or your friends have done anything but what was strictly honorable to you and to them. If additional circuit judges are made under the Davis bill,[47] I see no

[43] L. Q. C. Lamar, then senator from Mississippi; subsequently a member of Cleveland's first cabinet, and associate justice of the Supreme Court. He practiced sweet reasonableness in a troubled period. *Cf.* Wirt A. Cate, *Lucius Q. C. Lamar* (Chapel Hill: University of North Carolina Press, 1935).
[44] John B. Gordon, former Confederate general, then senator from Georgia.
[45] Benjamin H. Hill, formerly representative, then senator from Georgia. Gordon and Hill had acted with Lamar in the period of the disputed election.
[46] Matthew C. Butler, senator from South Carolina. The adjective doubtless referred to his relation to the then recent "Hamburg Massacre."
[47] On entering the Senate David Davis assumed the leadership in urging a reform of the judicial system. His bill called for the appointment of addi-

one now who can rival you for one of the places. If the bill passes as I think it will, it will be on some honorable assurance that the President will deal fairly with the democracy in filling the new offices. Make no resolutions or declarations of what you will or will not do. None are asked or called for. Bryan will probably be at home before this reaches you. I presented Bryan's case to the President. It was a delicate matter and I think I did it judiciously. I made no application for any office. I told him I acted without any request from Bryan but I knew he needed and would accept a fitting office. He said he had had it in mind. That he must have time. Asked me if I had thought of any office, saying first that there were charges against the present Collector and he had thought of Bryan in that connection, but he could not tell what the charges would come to. I said that office or the Marshalship would probably suit Bryan. He can tell you all of this and much more. I have come to like him very much and have a real hope that the President will in time do something for him.

My dear brother I feel relieved by thus opening my heart to you. I hope it will not bore you. . . .

P. S. *In confidence.* Your case No 38, Radich v. Hutchins [48] was affirmed in conference yesterday unanimously. Judge Field is to write the opinion. Dont let any one know this until it is publicly announced. I wish you had come on to argue it.

It will be noted that while Miller had made the most of the geographical objection against Harlan, he held him in high regard. He took no satisfaction in efforts of members of the Judiciary Committee, inspired in part by personal disappointment, to play politics with the confirmation. On November 21, 1877, he wrote:

I have not heard from you since I wrote you my long lugubrious letter. I fear its sad tone made a reply of any thing appropriate impracticable. I have observed more than once when I have poured my griefs into your ear, that you have done very much as I do under similar circumstances, leave your correspondent to the benefit of his own religion, philosophy or capacity of endurance, for they really amount to about the same thing. . . .

tional circuit judges and created an intermediate appellate court in each circuit. Had this been enacted it would have relieved the pressure on the Supreme Court.
[48] 95 U. S. 210. Argued October 25, decided November 12, 1877. Philip Phillips (Ballinger with him on the brief) represented the defendants in error.

The Senate Judiciary Committee are making great trouble about Harlan's nomination. Edmunds the Chairman and Christiancy [49] have both called on me about it. As far as I can learn Edmunds, Conkling and Howe [50] are disposed to make protracted inquiry into his fidelity to the constitutional amendments and the reconstruction acts of Congress. Also to inquire into charges made to the effect that he and other members of the committee who went to New Orleans at the request of the President, aided and abetted or at least connived at a system of intimidation and bribery by which a sufficient number of the Packard legislature was induced to join the Nicholls body to give it a quorum.[51] I think this both unwise and unjust. Harlan is as true a man I have no doubt to the constitutional amendments as any man from a Southern State, who may have doubted the wisdom of some of them when they passed. And no one who knows him, or Judge Lawrence of Illinois or Hawley of Conn. would believe for a moment that they would countenance either bribery or intimidation in the other matter.

I told Judge Christiancy who holds the balance probably in Committee that, and I also told him that if the Republican party in Congress was going to have a rupture with the President they could not afford to inaugurate the fight by refusing to confirm such a man as Harlan. I hardly think it will come to a fight and if it does he will be confirmed.

They (the men I have mentioned) have selected Harlan because two members of the Committee, namely Howe and Davis [52] are from the circuit which is vacant and both are mortified that a name outside of the district has been presented. Howe no doubt is inclined to resent this as well as to join Edmunds and Conkling on general principles. But Davis is personally friendly to Harlan and will not I feel sure join to defeat him on the grounds assumed by the three gentlemen at the head of the committee. If

[49] Isaac P. Christiancy, Republican senator from Michigan. He had been on the Supreme Court of that state from 1857 to 1875; his name had been put forward for the vacancy to which Harlan was now nominated.

[50] Timothy O. Howe, Republican senator from Wisconsin. He had been a judge of the state Supreme Court. "He was an eager candidate for judge of the Supreme Court in the place of David Davis of Illinois. The appointment of General Harlan of Kentucky soured him." (*Diary and Letters of Rutherford B. Hayes*, III, 471.)

[51] Harlan had been a member of the commission sent to Louisiana to report on the situation resulting from the existence of two rival governments at New Orleans. They reported in favor of the recognition of the Nicholls government. The result was the end of carpetbag rule in Louisiana.

[52] David Davis, whose resignation from the Court in 1877 created the vacancy now to be filled.

however the Committee should report against him I think he would still be confirmed.

As things stand I think the President is willing to yield to the Senate so far as to nominate no more democrats, and thus I fear would end Col Bryan's chances. But if the rupture should become pronounced, the President would then have to rely on the democratic Senators for confirmation of his nominations and would be in honor and policy bound to give them some share of the patronage.

On November 26, 1877, the Senate confirmed Harlan's nomination. He lived to serve almost thirty-four years on the Court, and became one of its most remarkable members.

Shortly after these events Miller was "twice approached to know if [Ballinger] would accept a place on the bench of the Court of Claims. . . . It is thought important to have a Southern man on the Bench. The gentlemen who spoke to me about it are the C. J. Waite and Mr Phillips." [53] Ballinger wrote that he was not interested,[54] to which Justice Miller replied: "You have done what I supposed you would do in regard to the Court of Claims matter. Of all the judicial positions under the federal Government it is in my eyes the least desirable." [55]

At the close of the Hayes administration, Justice Strong resigned from the Court, and it seemed evident that a Southerner would be nominated in his place, especially as Justice Bradley wished to be assigned to the Third Circuit. Judge Miller's hopes for Ballinger were slightly revived, but the appointment was given to Circuit Judge Woods. Then Miller sought the circuit judgeship for his kinsman, and enlisted the aid of Justice Harlan, "who has secured more favours at the hands of the President than any man I know, and who is skilled in such matters." [56] But word came back that while the President would prefer Ballinger if he appointed any one

[53] Letter of January 20, 1878.

[54] "Salary $4500 — too little to support my family — a judge of all men ought to be independent pecuniarily —" wrote Ballinger in his diary on January 23, 1878.

[55] Letter of February 3, 1878.

[56] Letter of December 25, 1880.

not a distinct Republican, he seemed unwilling to go outside the party.

This agrees with a conversation between the President and Garfield since the election reported to me authoritatively in which he told·Garfield as the one piece of advice he had to offer about appointments, justified by his experience, to appoint no democrat to office nor to be misled by the hope of securing their support to his administration in that way.

Harlan advised Miller not to call personally on the President in the matter.[57]

In 1883 the federal district judge at Galveston expressed his intention of resigning, though he proceeded very deliberately, evidently in the hope of controlling the choice of a successor. Miller asked that this office be given to Ballinger, and quotes President Arthur as replying that "he had found so much difficulty in getting an acceptable republican among the names presented that he did not know but he would have to appoint you."[58] Miller appealed to Justice Woods for aid, but found he had previously given his recommendation to a Republican.

He said however that when [District Judge] Morrill resigned he would see the President and say to him, that if it was open to him to consider the nomination of any other than a pronounced republican, there was no man in the State equally fitted for the place as yourself, or whose nomination would be so well received universally.[59]

Justice Bradley also gave his endorsement. But the President was then mustering Southern support for the approaching national convention, and this seemed a serious impediment to the appointment.[60] For a last time Miller's hopes came to nought.

After the lapse of half a century we find no diminution in the political element in judicial appointment. Sectional considerations, however, seem to be less important in determining selections for the Supreme Court. This is due in part to the

[57] Letter of January 2, 1881.
[58] Letter of January 6, 1883.
[59] Letter of April 17, 1883.
[60] Letter of May 2, 1883.

fact that since the justices have been excused from sitting in their circuits, their official duties are only slightly related to locality. The notion of sectional representation has broken down before the growing consciousness that state boundaries are not significant lines of social cleavage. Certainly the plea of locality ought never to be permitted to defeat the claims of superior fitness wherever found. The entire nation would have been the poorer if Justice Brandeis had not been chosen to sit beside Justice Holmes, or if the late Justice Cardozo had been passed over because there were already two citizens of New York on the Court.

XVI

THE PERSONNEL OF THE COURT

IT IS CLEAR that Judge Miller suffered deeply from a sense of injustice when his claims to the chief justiceship were passed over in favor of Waite. He was continually aware of the contrast between his own vigor in insisting upon what seemed wise and the less masterful ways of his colleague. It is only fair to say that his estimate may need some correction. For though Waite was less forceful, his unaffected kindliness was a most useful lubricant in a Court which included some very strong personalities, and in other ways he proved to be a more considerable person than his associates at first recognized. Miller knew himself well enough to admit that perhaps his disappointment had entered into his judgment.

Certainly he remained dissatisfied for several years. At the close of 1875 his thoughts ran as follows:

I confess that much as I like the law as a science, its practice as a pursuit, and the office of Judge as filling my ambition, I find its monotony begins to pall upon my taste and feelings.

I have for thirteen years given all my energies and my intellect to the duties of my office, and to the effort to make and to keep our court what it should be. If I had been made Chief Justice I think I should never have tired in this effort. And I may be more affected by the fact that I was not than I am conscious of. But I certainly strove very hard last term to have things go right and to get all the good out of our Chief and my brethren that could be had.

But I feel like taking it easy now. I can't make a silk purse out of a sow's ear. I can't make a great Chief Justice out of a small man. I can't make Clifford and Swayne, who are too old resign, nor keep the Chief Justice from giving them cases to write opinions in which their garrulity is often mixed with mischief. I can't hinder Davis from governing every act of his life by his hope of the Presidency, though I admit him to be as honest a

[*373*]

man as I ever knew. But the best of us cannot prevent ardent wishes from coloring and warping our inner judgment.

It is vain to contend with judges who have been at the bar the advocates for forty years of rail road companies, and all the forms of associated capital, when they are called upon to decide cases where such interests are in contest. All their training, all their feelings are from the start in favor of those who need no such influence.

I am losing interest in these matters. I will do my duty but will *fight* no more. I am perhaps beginning to experience that loss of interest in many things which is the natural result of years, and which wise men have felt the necessity of guarding against as age approaches.[1]

A few months later came another letter in the same vein:

I worked very hard last summer [2] and more so this winter. You are aware that I am now since April 5 sixty years old. The 60th anniversary came amidst the severest labours of the closing days of the term and I felt sensibly that I could not stand what I could years ago. If I could work as some of my brother Judges do, it would not be so hard. The two oldest Judges on the bench have written the most opinions and more than they ever wrote before. I mean Clifford and Swayne, who are seventy one and seventy three years old. And they boast of it, and always vote for the longest term and the shortest recess.

If I could content myself with *such opinions* as they write, and such investigation as they give to cases, and put no more solid mental product in them than they do, I could sit from one year to another without much source of fatigue, beyond the confinement to place and routine.[3]

Next autumn, after Judge Miller had made his exhausting round of circuit courts and then undergone a brief but painful illness, he wrote to Judge Treat of the federal district court at Saint Louis to caution him against overwork, adding by way of example:

I myself have for several years taken matters much easier than formerly. I am however blessed with much more vigorous associates than when I came to the bench, and in my judgment much

---

[1] Letter to Ballinger, December 5, 1875.

[2] Judge Dillon was in Europe, and Miller therefore had additional circuit work.

[3] Letter of May 27, 1876.

abler men in their profession. But at all events I no longer act on the idea that the responsibility of every decision rests on me. It is a divided responsibility and I feel liable only for my fair proportion.[4]

From time to time Ballinger's practice would take him to Washington, and so give occasion for brief notes in his diary characterizing the justices and lawyers whom he met. Thus on a visit in October 1871 he wrote: "Called to see Judge Clifford & admired him much more than I had done at a distance — He is a stately gentle old fellow." "Swaine seems artificial — tho' entertaining." And of Justice Strong: "Like his face & manner very much." [5] The important municipal bond case of *Hitchcock* v. *Galveston* [6] was set for argument before the Supreme Court during December 1877, and Ballinger came north to represent the city. At York, Pennsylvania, Jeremiah S. Black boarded the train. The two men had been acquainted for years, and engaged in conversation. Black is quoted as saying that Miller was "the most honest man on the Bench," but that he thought it "God's service to keep out Democrats." [7] Considering how Black had ranted against the majority members of the Electoral Commission nine months earlier, this was indeed a testimonial of character. The following day Ballinger attended court:

Opinion day in the Supreme Ct. Judge Miller introduced me to all the Judges (except Swayne who didn't come in) in their consultation Room — all very kind. Judge Hunt sd. he had hoped to have seen me on the Bench — quite singular —

Spent the day in the court room mostly — Nearly all the judges read opinions — Clifford's very prosy and not audible [8] — Brad-

[4] Letter of November 16, 1876; Treat Collection, Missouri Historical Society. Of himself he said: "It is the first time in twenty years that I have on account of illness, been compelled to go to bed and send for a doctor." He admonished Judge Treat: "Do not let your sense of duty induce you to overwork yourself. The duty which $3500 requires at your hand should not hazard your health."

[5] Ballinger Diary, October 11 and 14, 1871; Library, University of Texas.

[6] 96 U. S. 341.

[7] Ballinger Diary, December 2, 1877.

[8] *Fabbri* v. *Murphy*, 95 U. S. 191 (1877), and Lycoming Fire Insurance Co. v. Haven, 95 U. S. 242 (1877).

ley's long [9] — C. J. Waite has solid face — not unamiable — but it is not a handsome one —

[Dexter G.] Hitchcock [plaintiff in error in Hitchcock v. Galveston] is here — very active & friendly — Don't know whether he can organize for his case efficiently —

On December 5 he set down this unfavorable observation:

The court gave them [counsel] little attention — The chief & the other Judges send for, examn books, & give attention evidently to other matters — Unavoidable, I suppose, but not right in the chief especially — I think he ought to affect at least to give the speaker good attention.

Two days later he had an opportunity to observe J. S. Black and Matt Carpenter in typical performances:

S. C. U. S. — 12:15 — McGaraghan case [10] before the court — Mr. [Charles P.] Shaw of Cal. just concluded — Montgomery Blair follows — Sensible & forcible but not very impressive —
Then Judge Black — said good things but in a very loose rambling way, not a lawyerlike argument at all — Most of it a kind of badinage towds Carpenter who seemed to encourage the old fellow's antics —
Carpenter concluded, occupying about an hour and a half in a most lawyerlike speech delivered in most admirable manner — He struggled on the wrong side apparently and against the strong prepossession of the court but did it to the best advantage — I admire him extremely — Looks to be full of liquor though — [11]

The personnel of the Court figures prominently in Miller's letters for several years prior to 1882. This was a period when the failing powers of some of the justices produced a rather critical situation, presently to be relieved by a season of renewal. Justice Hunt, who had come on in Nelson's place, held office from December 1872 to February 1882, but his health failed not long after his appointment, and his participation in the work of the Court came to a complete stop in December 1878. On January 5, 1879, he was struck speechless with

[9] Thompson v. Maxwell Land-Grant and Ry. Co., 95 U. S. 391 (1877).
[10] McGarrahan v. New Idria Mining Co., 96 U. S. 316 (1878).
[11] Ballinger Diary.

paralysis.[12] Justice Miller refers to him in a letter of January 12, 1879:

Judge Hunt whether he shall die within the next ten days, or within the year will never return to the court. This is a great grief to me. He is not a very strong man in intellect, but he is a cultivated lawyer and gentleman. A warm hearted courteous man. Having no family with him but his wife, and of a sociable nature, he has made himself one of the most agreeable men on the bench.

Last winter he had three attacks of gout which is with him inherited. It enfeebled him so much that when we all adjourned it was much doubted if he would live to return. Such was also the feeling with regard to myself.[13] He and I sympathised with each other and talked it over very freely, and I came to have a warmer affection for him than I can at my years get up for many men.

At the end of the year Miller returned to the subject, disclosing the reason why Justice Hunt's resignation was not forthcoming:

It is quite certain that if Hunt were to resign or die soon that Edmunds of Vermont [14] would be his successor. He is probably the only republican thought of for the place who could be confirmed by the Senate.

Judge Hunt would resign at once if Conkling would express his willingness. But he owed his appointment to Conkling and the latter is selfish enough to wish the chance of dictating his successor under a new administration.

This last sentence is confidential. I care very little about it myself. I would prefer Stoughton [15] to Edmunds, and Stoughton might be Conkling's choice. But Edmunds is able and honest, though I fear dogmatical and contentious. My interest in the court as I have told you is largely on the wane and I shall give myself but little trouble about future accessions to it.[16]

Impending alterations in the Court are foreshadowed in a long letter written November 28, 1880:

[12] Justice Bradley's diary for that day.
[13] In the summer of 1878 Miller underwent a dangerous operation for stones in the bladder.
[14] Then a member of the Senate. He frequently appeared before the Court.
[15] E. W. Stoughton, prominent New York lawyer. He had appeared before the Electoral Commission.   [16] Letter of December 14, 1879.

Matters have taken a turn very suddenly in regard to changes of the court which I will make the subject of the remainder of this letter.

Judge Hunt came to Washington ten days ago with no improvement in his condition and it is quite certain now that he will never go on the bench again. He will not resign while Hayes is President because Conklin[g] does not want Hayes to appoint his successor. It was well ascertained last winter that if Hunt had resigned Edmunds whose state is in the circuit would have been nominated and confirmed, and Conklin[g] kept Hunt from resigning after he had made up his mind to do so.

Miller then writes of the collapse of Justice Clifford's mind. This is not a congenial subject upon which to dwell, yet the public significance seems to warrant a complete quotation. For it will be remembered that the process of mental decay had been going on for several years during which the Justice had participated actively in the decision of cases, and as a matter of law he remained a member of the Court until his death on July 25, 1881, nine months later.

Judge Clifford reached Washington on the 8th October. . . . I saw him within three hours after his arrival, and he did not know me or any thing, and though his tongue framed words there was no sense in them.

An effort was made . . . to call it paralysis because he was taken suddenly between Boston and Washington, but there was no paralysis in the case. He remains yet about in the same condition. His general health good as usual. Able to ride out and walk about the house, but his mind is a wreck and no one believes that he will ever try another case, though the one idea which he seems to have is a desire to get to his seat in the capitol. I have seen him twice and other judges have also. It is doubtful if he knew any of us. His wife thought I could do more to persuade him to return home than any one else and sent for me. But when I saw him I saw also that it was no use to try it for he introduced me to his wife twice in ten minutes, though I have known her for eighteen years quite intimately. His work is ended though he may live for several years.

Justice Clifford had been eligible to resign with full salary since August 1873. While it would perhaps be too much to say that his decision to remain on the bench was determined by his desire to hold on until there should be a Democratic president to choose his successor, this seems to have been a considerable factor. His biographer points out that he was the sole remaining appointee of a Democratic administration, and says that he felt he held a sacred trust "to use what power he had to keep alive the flickering flame of the faith to which his first and abiding allegiance had been sworn. . . . His long life drew to its close; while he, refusing to resign . . . , fought on, but died too soon to see the accomplishment of the hope of his later years, the return to power of the party whose standard he had always followed." [17]

Justice Miller had recently been giving some thought to the problem of judicial tenure. In an address before the New York State Bar Association in 1878 he said:

Whether it is wiser to make the office one for life, or of a period so long that reasonable stability in the court, and security in the office is guaranteed to the judge, I will not undertake to say. But it is a fair subject for consideration in future legislation, and there can be no doubt that such advances can be made and ought to be made, as will secure ample compensation, and stable tenure in office.

On the other hand it must be confessed that the means provided by the system of organic law in America for removing a judge, who for any reason is found to be unfit for his office, is very unsatisfactory. With the exception of a few States which have retained the old-fashioned mode of removing an officer by an address to the Governor of two-thirds of each house in the Legislature, impeachment is the only remedy.

This latter he finds quite inappropriate:

There are many matters which ought to be causes of removal that are neither treason, bribery, nor high crimes or misdemeanors. Physical infirmities for which a man is not to blame, but which may wholly unfit him for judicial duty, are of this class. Deafness, loss of sight, the decay of the faculties by reason of age, insanity, prostration by disease from which there is no hope of recovery — these should all be reasons for removal, rather than that the administration of justice should be obstructed or indefinitely postponed.

[17] P. G. Clifford, *Nathan Clifford, Democrat*, 275–276.

. . . A vile and overbearing temper becomes sometimes in one long accustomed to the exercise of power unendurable to those who are subjected to its humors.

While he found it difficult to propose a proper remedy, Justice Miller offered two suggestions as worth considering in an effort at constitutional amendment. The causes for which a judge might be removed should be described with precision, and the facts should be found by a jury or some similar tribunal. But "in view of the resentments of disappointed suitors the providing for removal should not be made too easy." [18]

Passing from the cases of Judges Hunt and Clifford, Miller's letter of November 28, 1880, went on to other matters of personnel:

In this condition of affairs Judges Swayne and Strong both announced to their brethren a short time since their purpose of resigning. They had agreed it seems to resign simultaneously but with Clifford and Hunt disabled, they would leave us without a quorum. And as the Senate might not confirm other nominations these gentlemen have hesitated. Swayne has never wished to resign, but I think that influences have been brought to bear which have induced him to agree to let Hay[e]s have an opportunity to appoint Stanley Matthews. But as the old fox don't want to go he readily seizes on the objection, that the business of the court might be suspended to delay action.

Things were in this condition when Judge Strong with whom I have always been on terms of great friendship and confidence told me yesterday at conference, that without reference to Swayne's action he should send in his resignation during the second week of the approaching session of Congress. Thus far what I have said is based on satisfactory evidence. I now enter the region of conjecture.

It is said that the President is anxious to secure Matthews confirmation at the hands of the Senate, by filling Strong's place with a Southern man. As Bradley really belongs to Strong's circuit, and wants to have it when Strong resigns it is thought to be a good occasion to appoint a Judge from the South. Whether Swayne will resign at once, or will await until some one fills Strong's place no one can tell for he is both selfish and unreliable. But that Strong will resign I have no doubt and that there is

[18] *Proceedings of the New York State Bar Association*, II (1878), 31, 39, 40.

serious thought of nominating his successor from Bradley's circuit is I think very probable.

I have been told that the President favors Wood[s], and that Swayne who is for some reason fond of Wood[s] is trying to make his own resignation (desired by the President for Matthews' sake) dependent on the nomination of Wood[s]. This is a nice little plan but complex and may fail of carrying out. I do not like to make suggestions again about your name, but cannot forbear to remark that the matter is one in which there is a chance. Your papers are all before the President. He has thought of you and favorably. He may find himself compelled to give up Wood[s] either by the Senate, or by friends who will tell him that Wood[s] and Matthews will both be regarded as Ohio appointments and that Chase and Wait[e] and Swayne and Wood[s] and Matthews are too many Judges from Ohio in a few years with Harlan from the same circuit.

If Garfield had the nomination, as he may yet, I would be willing to make another personal effort with him for I know I stand well with him. But there are reasons which make me believe, known I think to you and Col Bryan that such an effort with Hay[e]s would probably do no good.

But there is no reason why your other friends should not be on the alert and why you should not call their attention to the matter. I shall see Governor Coke when he comes and put him in possession of the whole case.

He added that he understood that Attorney General Devens wished to succeed to Justice Clifford's place on the bench.

The statutory provision for resignation at seventy after ten years' service has seemed to imply a judgment that one older than sixty ought not to be nominated for the Court. Justice Strong, who was as conscientious a man as ever sat on the bench, felt the force of this at the time he was nominated, being then almost sixty-two.[19] He resigned after eleven years' service, and the high sense of public duty which prompted his action is recorded in the memoirs of a kinsman:

Mr. Justice Strong gave me the following story of his retirement. . . . Having reached the age of seventy-three years, and although remarkably well preserved physically and mentally and quite as capable of efficient service as any of the other justices,

[19] Conversation with his daughter, the late Julia D. Strong.

he became convinced that it would be for the interest of the court
if one or two of the justices who had become enfeebled by age
were to retire and their places be filled by more vigorous men.
He enjoyed the position and its duties, and would not have retired at that time if the retirement of other justices could have
been effected without his setting an example. This conviction
led him to say to Mr. Justice Swayne, who had been on the bench
a long time and was quite enfeebled, that he had had in mind
the strengthening of the bench by resigning, and as they had both
reached the period in life when they could retire with the continuance of their salaries during life, he would offer his resignation if Mr. Justice Swayne would follow him in so doing. Justice
Swayne assented to this. . . .[20]

This account was corroborated by Justice Strong's last surviv-
ing daughter, who added as another consideration that he had
thought it preferable to resign while people would exclaim
"Why does he?" than to delay until they asked, "Why doesn't
he?"

Justice Miller's view was that "the loss of Judge Strong is
a heavy one to the court, while the men occupying the other
places could well be spared." [21] Precisely coinciding with this
is the opinion which John W. Wallace, formerly the Reporter
of the Court, had expressed in a letter written a month before:

The 'shorter handed' the Court is — while the observation
comes from the absence of such judges as Clifford & Swayne, the
more business it will do, and the better. I often used to wonder
whether in the history of the whole world there ever was such
a man as the first named one, in *such a place.* . . . Swayne was
no worse than some other cases, but bad enough no doubt. But
unless Strong has lost a good deal since I came away, his departure would, I think, be to be regretted. In the department of
Patent Cases he was of great value on that particular bench.[22]

[20] Theron G. Strong, *Landmarks of a Lawyer's Lifetime* (New York: Dodd,
Mead and Company, 1914), p. 28.
[21] Letter of December 25, 1880.
[22] Letter of November 9, 1880, to William A. Maury of Washington, D. C.,
a prominent member of the bar of the Supreme Court. The letter is attached
to one of nine bound volumes of legal articles and briefs prepared by Maury,
now in the possession of J. Spalding Flannery, Esq., of Washington, D. C., to
whom I am indebted for permission to use this material.

As successor to Justice Strong, President Hayes nominated William B. Woods, the Senate giving its confirmation on December 21, 1880. The new justice was originally an Ohio man, a War Democrat and brevet major general, who at the close of hostilities had settled in Alabama and been elected a chancellor in the state courts. On the creation of the federal circuit judgeships in 1869 he had received the appointment for the Southern circuit.

Justice Swayne resigned on January 24, 1881, and professed to find so many interesting things to do in this final holiday that he hastened to commend it to his brethren. In a letter of March 16, 1882, he wrote to Justice Bradley (who had just turned sixty-nine):

I have no doubt you will resign at the close of your seventieth year or very soon afterwards & I think you ought to. You need have no apprehension that you will not find enough to do — constantly and agreeably to employ you — nor that a moment of your time will necessarily be attended with a sense of tedium or *ennui*. You will be brighter & happier than you have been for the last five years or will be in the future while you remain on the bench.[23]

To fill the vacancy thus created President Hayes promptly sent the nomination of Stanley Matthews to the Senate. Opposition developed and his name was not acted upon while Hayes was in office. But President Garfield renewed the nomination, which was confirmed by a bare majority after a delay of two months. One of Justice Matthews' fine qualities was a certain breadth and urbanity, shown, for example, in his opinion for the Court in *Hurtado* v. *California*,[24] where he rejects the contention that the Fourteenth Amendment forbids the legislature to alter the procedural methods sanctioned by the common law. This, he said, "would be to deny every quality of the law but its age, and render it incapable of progress or improvement." One will also recall his opinion in *Yick Wo* v. *Hopkins*,[25] releasing a Chinese laundryman

---

[23] Letter in Bradley Papers.
[24] 110 U. S. 516 (1884).
[25] 118 U. S. 356 (1886).

who stood convicted under a California statute which had been enforced only to oppress Orientals: "Though the law itself be fair on its face and impartial in appearance, yet, if it is applied and administered by public authority with an evil eye and an unequal hand, so as practically to make unjust and illegal discriminations . . . , the denial of equal justice is still within the prohibition of the Constitution."

Early in the autumn of 1881 Justice Miller wrote:

> Our court resumes its session in a few days Oct. 10. There is one actual vacancy and one in effect on account of Judge Hunt's condition. It is my impression that Chief Justice Grey [sic] of Massachusetts will be appointed to fill Judge Clifford's place. I told the President yesterday in a call I made on him that I thought Gray was the man for the place, in which Harlan joined me. He is the choice of our Court and of the Massachusetts delegation.[26]

On December 19 President Arthur nominated Horace Gray to be an associate justice, and the Senate promptly confirmed the nomination. Gray had spent virtually his entire professional life in the court room, first as reporter of the Supreme Judicial Court of Massachusetts, then from 1864 as justice, and from 1873 as chief justice, of that court. He sat on the Supreme Court of the United States for twenty years, being succeeded by another chief justice of Massachusetts, Oliver Wendell Holmes. Gray was a very learned lawyer whose opinions often begin with an exhaustive treatment of the historical background of the subject. He never forgot that he had once been a reporter; all that pertained to the style and form in which the work of the Court was published he made a matter of close personal interest.[27]

In January 1882 Congress enacted a measure introduced by Senator David Davis specially authorizing Justice Hunt to resign with salary, notwithstanding the fact that he had held office less than ten years.[28] There was considerable opposition,

[26] Letter of September 25, 1881.

[27] As may be seen from his many notes on this subject to J. C. B. Davis, the Reporter (Davis Papers, Library of Congress).

[28] *Congressional Record.* 47 Cong., 1 Sess., pp. 505, 512–518.

particularly on the part of Southern Democrats, who took this opportunity to voice their general unfriendliness to the federal judiciary. Representative Robinson, Democrat, of New York, thought that the bill should be recommitted so that the Judiciary Committee "can in its wisdom recommend a plan by which Judge Swayne, who is still able, still in the full vigor of his glorious intellect, could be restored to the court, to take the position which would be assigned to the new judge. That would be better than establishing any precedent like that proposed in this bill." [29] Congress, however, did not find it necessary to call Justice Swayne back to fill the breach. The bill became a law on January 27, and was conditioned upon Judge Hunt's resignation being submitted within thirty days. He acted upon it, and thus permitted the Court to be restored to its full strength. President Arthur nominated his old mentor, Roscoe Conkling, to fill the vacancy. After confirmation had been voted Conkling declined, and the appointment was then given to Samuel Blatchford of New York.

The personnel of the Supreme Court is variously recruited. Some appointees come from active practice at the bar, others are chosen in recognition of their political activities. (Since the business of the Court is, in large part, statesmanship, there is an advantage in including some members who have had experience in legislation or in administrative office.) Some, again, are appointed from the highest state courts, while others have come up through the federal judiciary. Judge Blatchford was of this last-named class. After an apprenticeship as William H. Seward's secretary and then his law partner, he subsequently served five years as district judge, and ten years as circuit judge for the second circuit. As Joseph H. Choate later recalled,

on May 3, 1867, he was appointed United States District Judge for the Southern District of New York, in place of Judge Samuel R. Betts. Judge Betts had been a great admiralty judge in his day, but had become superannuated and it severely taxed his powers to deal with the great questions of prize and public law,

[29] *Ibid.*, pp. 613–614.

of vast importance to the community, which flooded the Federal courts, and especially his court, in the years of the war and reconstruction. It was hardly a well-kept secret that for some years he had received most able assistance from Mr. Blatchford, so that when his resignation and the appointment of Mr. Blatchford in his place were announced, the advent of so well-equipped a judge to fill a place of such transcendent importance was received with great satisfaction, both by the profession and the community.[30]

In his service from 1882 to 1893 Judge Blatchford proved to be an adequate, though not a particularly strong or colorful, member of the Court. His avocation was to collect almanacs, which seemed quite in keeping with the steadiness and unvarying routine of his life. In a statement [31] which he drew up for the Court under date of October 19, 1891, it appears that he had written only two dissenting opinions, and had differed from the *maior et senior pars* only eight times in nine years. He was thus far less disposed to disagree than any of his contemporaries.

Justice Blatchford's compilation of statistics will repay examination. The reader should, however, be careful to note that the final percentage is of total dissents (whether the justice in question filed an opinion or not) compared to the total number of opinions he had written for the Court. The ratio between the number of times any particular justice dissented and the total number of cases in which he had participated would, of course, be very much smaller, roughly one ninth of the percentage given, assuming that cases were assigned to the several justices with substantial equality. There is a fair correlation between these final percentages and the intellectual vigor which the various justices are supposed to have displayed. The figures for Justice Miller (who had died a year earlier) would show 616 opinions for the Court, and dissents in 160 cases; the percentage would therefore be 26. It would not do to say that these percentages are an index of the wisdom of the several justices, for wisdom cannot be computed statistically; and if it could one would not be justified

[30] Clipping from unidentified periodical.
[31] Found among Justice Bradley's papers.

Statement by Judge Blatchford, October 19, 1891

	Fuller [1888–]	Field [1863–]	Bradley [1870–]	Harlan [1877–]	Gray [1882–]	Blatchford [1882–]	Lamar [1888–]	Brewer [1890–]	Brown [1891–]
Opinions of the Court delivered	165	504	405	349	237	359	87	62	32
Dissenting opinions delivered	3	70	66	37	4	2	1	9	4
Dissents merely	8	108	69	57	40	6	7	9	9
Total dissenting opinions and dissents	11	178	135	94	44	8	8	18	13
Percentage of dissenting opinions and dissents to opinions of the Court, by each Judge	6.69	35.31	33.33	26.93	18.69	2.22	9.19	29.03	40.62

in saying that it is always to be measured by the frequency with which the judge disagrees with the majority.

The Court as it was constituted from 1882 until the death of Judge Woods in 1887 stood at a remarkably high level of distinction. Five or six of its members would find places in any respectable list of the outstanding justices in the entire annals of the Court. This was Judge Miller's contemporary view. Writing on May 16, 1886, he said:

I believe that the Court is as strong mentally and physically as it ever was and is as capable of usefulness as it has ever been. . . .

The reporter and some of the Judges say that more important and well written opinions have been delivered at this term than at any previous one.[32] I doubt this as affirming both propositions. But I think it is true that it has been a successful term and many questions of importance have been decided.

Justice Blatchford remained the junior member of the Court until the appointment of Lucius Quintus Cincinnatus Lamar in 1888. Their respective qualifications form a striking contrast. The one had behind him years spent in the diligent application of the details of federal jurisprudence. The other had practiced for a brief period, and then been a member of Congress in years before the war; a colonel and later a diplomat in the Confederate service; professor of political economy and then of law; a Senator preëminent in counsels of moderation; and finally Secretary of the Interior in the Cleveland cabinet. Lamar's age — he was sixty-two — and his lack of experience at the bar were urged against him, and the question of confirmation was made a partisan issue. After a month of delay the Senate gave its consent by a vote of thirty-two to twenty-eight. Lamar entered upon his unfamiliar duties with great diffidence; and his solicitude to test his own views by submitting them to the consideration of his brethren is attributable to something more than a naturally

[32] The cases, to be found in 116, 117, and 118 U. S. Reports, include Boyd v. United States, Coe v. Errol, the Express Cases, Norton v. Shelby County, Presser v. Illinois, the Railroad Commission Cases, United States v. Kagama, Van Brocklin v. Tennessee, Walling v. Michigan, and Yick Wo v. Hopkins.

THE SUPREME COURT ABOUT 1882

Standing: JUSTICES WOODS, BRADLEY, MATTHEWS, BLATCHFORD
Seated: JUSTICES GRAY, MILLER, WAITE, C.J., FIELD, HARLAN

sensitive disposition. So while he cannot be said to have brought tremendous strength to a court of law, yet his experience in public affairs, his contemplative temperament, his "faculty of expressing himself in nervous English," [33] and withal a unique delicacy of character, entitled his name to a grateful remembrance.

This and the two succeeding appointments came so late in Justice Miller's career as to have a small place in the story of his life. On the death of Chief Justice Waite in 1888 the President appointed Melville W. Fuller of Chicago. Under the particular circumstances, Cleveland was doubtless wise in selecting a relatively young chief justice rather than making a promotion from the bench — though, sitting in court with Miller and Bradley on the one hand and Field and Harlan on the other, Fuller was quite aware, as he put it, that "no rising sun prevails with these . . . luminaries blazing away with all their ancient fires." [34] On Judge Matthews' death in 1889 the President appointed David J. Brewer, sometime judge of the Supreme Court of Kansas, and for the past five years circuit judge in the Eighth (Miller's) Circuit. Brewer was a nephew of Justice Field, and did much to perpetuate Field's conservative influence on the Court.

When Justice Miller was so emphatically in favor of retirement for some of his brethren one will wonder what he thought of his own case, and how it came about that he remained on the bench until his death at the age of seventy-four. Even before he was sixty he had begun to look forward to retirement. In 1875 Ballinger had been writing of the active part he was taking in the Texas constitutional convention, and Miller in reply confessed to

a secret desire, hardly formed, that some similar diversion of my own thoughts could come opportunely into my own life. I was lecturing to a law class for two or three years, but it fell through. . . . I have completed four volumes after the manner of Curtis including the last seven of Howard and the two of Blacks Reports.

[33] Resolutions of the bar, 148 U. S. 709.
[34] Letter of January 18, 1890, to J. C. B. Davis; Davis Papers, vol. LXIV.

[389]

But these activities had not satisfied his craving. He continued:

> I have bought me a house. I am settled down for life. I am for the first time ennui and not hopeful.
>
> While I appreciate the honours of my place, they have lost their novelty. I doubt if much remains to be added to my judicial reputation and not much therefore for the future is before me.
>
> Do not understand me as disappointed, or unhappy. I am only saying that if without ceasing to be a judge some thing to do, should fall in my way which would vary my pursuit and in which I could take the interest that you have in the convention it would not be unacceptable.
>
> I have the same capacity for work. I think I do it as well as ever, but without that healthful zest, that absorbing interest which heretofore has made my judicial work sufficient for my mental and moral food.[35]

The circuit work which the justices were then required to do after the Supreme Court rose each spring proved very fatiguing, especially where distance and climate added to the burden. On June 10, 1880, Miller wrote from Keokuk:

> I find myself more affected by the hot weather last summer and this than ever before and my experience of the benefit of sea bathing the two last summers has fixed my purpose of spending as much of each summer by the sea shore as I can. If I live out my six years, necessary to enable me to resign with my salary, I shall do but very little on the circuit during that time. I am feeling sensibly the need of more rest, and have earned the right to have it. In Judge McCrary I have a fresh hard working safe and acceptable Judge and can leave the business of the circuit to him and to the District Judges.

A letter of November 21, 1881, when Miller had reached the age of sixty-five, renewed this theme:

> I am getting tired very tired of the labour and indifferent to the honors. Not to the honors I have won. I am proud of them, perhaps vain. But the harvest has been gathered and there remains but the gleanings and the labour. If it were not that for most of the questions which arise I am able to decide without great research, and that habit has enabled me to write with ease

[35] Letter of December 5, 1875.

I should feel the duties of the place very irksome, for I feel no vivid interest in them.

After eleven years in office Judge Waite had something of a breakdown, and during his absence from the Court his duties fell upon Miller as the senior associate justice. On January 18, 1885, he wrote:

In consequence of the illness of the Chief Justice I have had to be acting Chief Justice in his place. I always knew that he did a great deal more work than I, and had many apparently unimportant matters to look after to which the other judges gave no time and very little attention. I find now that what I had suspected hardly came up to the draft on his time as he performed these duties. Disposition of practice cases, motions to dismiss for want of jurisdiction, reading carefully and [*word illegible*] and answering letters or telling the Clerk how to answer them constituted in his way of doing it a heavy load on his time and on his mind.

It is this which caused his illness. He is much broken down and if [he] does not diminish his excessive labours, he will not be capable of any work in a year or two more.

He leaves tomorrow for Florida to be gone a month for recuperation.

As Justice Miller neared the age of seventy he evidently shrank from the prospect of a sudden cessation of labor. He knew that from the first he had been pulling a wheel-horse's load, and would have welcomed some lightening of the labor. At the beginning of what, had he so wished, might have been his last term, he wrote:

Our Court had its formal opening yesterday, and when I have finished this letter I shall start to begin anew the labors of the court for nine months with such slight intermissions as are necessary for the useful performance of that work itself. I believe I have told you that I do not feel the interest in it that I once did, and which my conscience tells me I ought to feel now. I am well resolved that I will not do my own and other men's work in future, and yet I have been so resolved before and have done it. I do not believe a healthy man of seventy years accustomed to any kind of work, mental or physical, ought to quit it suddenly. But I do believe that when that time comes he will be the better for a moderation in the severity and uninterrupted continuousness of that labor.[36]

And in 1887, speaking of *Wabash Railroad Co.* v. *Illinois* and other cases which had been assigned to him, he wrote:

The Chief Justice recognizes no claims of old age in me to abatement of service, for he has given me quite a full share of opinions to write both as to number and importance.[37]

It so happened that Ballinger was a guest in Miller's home on April 4, 1886 — exactly two days before the Justice's seventieth birthday, when he would become eligible to resign with salary for life. His diary contained this record of their conversation:

Spent most of the day with the Judge in his Library — Talked over old times & our acquaintances & kin — He is most warmhearted — Few people have as strong attachments — . . . The Judge will not resign at present — Says his wife is strongly opposed to it, that it wd weaken their social position influence &c —

Miller's correspondence with his brother-in-law came to a close in 1887, as Ballinger died on January 20, 1888. There remains to mention only one other reference to the subject of retirement. Writing in the summer of 1886, Miller says:

I did not perceive while on the circuit any overt symptoms of a design to have me resign, though there are doubtless men who think they could fill the place and [that] as democrats they ought to have a chance.[38]

In 1887 Miller's old colleague at the circuit, District Judge Treat of Saint Louis, resigned his office. On learning of this Miller dashed off the following note:

My dear old friend.
So you have done it at last — Well, I don't blame you. The work is so hard and the pay so inadequate, and you have so well earned your right to the little salary for the remaining years.
I almost wish I had the courage to follow your example.

[36] Letter of October 13, 1885.
[37] Letter of February 13, 1887.
[38] Letter of July 18, 1886.

In a letter to [John W.] Noble who speaks of how much you will be missed I replied, that by no one more than by me, unless you carried out an intimation once made to me of coming to Washington. How that would rejoice me.[39]

While Justice Miller never acted upon his earlier view that no man should remain on the Court after seventy, there should be no doubt that his mind retained its full vigor to the last. And the same may be said of his colleague Justice Bradley, who stayed at his place until his death at the age of seventy-eight. Neither one knew any time when his opinion was not held in high regard by his brethren.

That the problem of overdue resignations [40] has here been given prominence is attributable, not to the selective faculties of the author, but to the fact that it bulks large in Justice Miller's letters. The difficulty has been recurrent. Much that was said on the occasion of President Roosevelt's proposal for renewing the Supreme Court was anticipated in congressional debates in 1869. When Senator Trumbull introduced his bill [41] to amend the judicial system, it increased the membership of the Court and created the office of circuit judge, but made no provision for retirement. Passed in this form by the Senate, the measure came before the House, where Bingham of Ohio, on behalf of the Judiciary Committee, moved the adoption of a substitute. The substantial difference lay in the addition of two new sections. It was provided that any judge of any court of the United States who attained the age of seventy and had held his commission at least ten years, "may, upon his filing with the President a certificate of that fact, be excused and retired from active service as such judge; and thereafter he shall, during the time he shall continue to hold said office, be entitled to receive" his salary. It added that "if any judge who shall have attained the aforesaid age shall be incompetent, by reason of disease or infirmity, to make and file such certificate, the facts of his age and in-

[39] Letter of February 27, 1887, Treat Collection, Missouri Historical Society.
[40] Cf. my article on "The Retirement of Federal Judges," 51 Harvard Law Review 397 (1938).   [41] S. No. 44.

competency may be proved by satisfactory evidence before any judge of the Supreme Court; and upon such justice filing his certificate of such facts with the President the said judge shall thereupon be excused and retired with like effect as upon his own certificate." [42]

The committe's substitute proposal added another section to the effect that within six months after such a certificate was filed, or if a judge failed to make the certificate within one year after attaining the age of seventy,

it shall in either of such cases be the duty of the President to nominate and appoint, by and with the advice and consent of the Senate, an additional judge for the said court, who shall have the same power and perform the same duties and receive the same compensation as the judge then acting in such court, or who shall be retired and excused from so acting . . . ; and upon the decease of said senior, associate, or retired judge, or upon his ceasing for any cause to hold said office, the said additional judge appointed under the provisions of said act shall be and become the judge of such court.

Kerr, Democrat, of Indiana, strove without success to secure an amendment to raise the age from seventy to seventy-five. The substitute motion was then adopted by a vote of ninety-nine to fifty, forty-seven not voting. The division was along party lines, though several Republicans opposed the measure. The bill so amended was carried and returned to the Senate.

The House Committee had drafted its proposal with an eye to constitutional difficulties. It did not remove any judge

[42] Compare the measure, S. No. 20, introduced by Senator Harlan of Iowa on December 17, 1863. It authorized a justice of the Supreme Court who had attained the age of seventy to be retired at his own request on account of physical infirmity. Compensation was to vary from two-thirds to full salary, according to length of service. On January 25, 1864, the Judiciary Committee reported adversely.

Attorney General Bates made this comment: "The principle is right, but the details all wrong. 70 years is no proper time; for a Judge may be much younger than that, yet, mentally or physically incapable of his duties, and still too poor to give up his salary. There ought to be no *retired list* of *Judges*; but worn out Judges ought to be respectably provided for, by allowing them to *resign*, upon a competent pension." (*Diary of Edward Bates*, p. 322.)

from his office, even in the event of paralysis or insanity: "It is clear . . . that the retired judges remain members of the court, although they are not acting judges, nor their presence required to constitute a quorum. . . ." [43] The Committee had in mind particularly Justices Grier and Nelson. Evidently it was the former who was alluded to as "one of the most eminent members . . . who is not able to-day to reach the bench without being borne to it by the hands of others."

Back in the upper house Bingham's amendment proved unacceptable, though not on the ground that it was unduly radical. As Senator Trumbull explained, "it would continue the persons upon the bench as judges still although they were retired. There would be nothing to prevent their coming back in an emergency and sitting on the bench, and we might have twenty judges of the Supreme Court." [44] On the proposal of its committee, the Senate amended the bill to authorize the payment of salary for life to any judge who should resign having attained the age of seventy. The care of the president and of the Senate was relied upon to prevent abuse by the appointment of a judge who was already too near that age. The House preferred to be definite and added a requirement that the commission must have been held for at least ten years. In this form the bill became the law of April 10, 1869.

In his first term President Grant appointed four members of the Court; in his second, none. Had the Bingham proposal been adopted, he would have appointed an additional justice in respect of Judge Clifford in 1873 and of Judge Swayne in 1874, and his selection of a successor to Judge Nelson would have been accelerated. Whether the effective size of the Court would have been thereby increased would, of course, have depended upon the action of those justices.

In 1890 the *American Law Review* proposed what was, wittingly or not, a revival of the Bingham amendment.[45] It

[43] Remarks of Representative Bingham, *Congressional Globe*, 41 Cong., 1 Sess., p. 337.
[44] *Ibid.*, 574.   [45] 24: 321, 462.

quoted the London *Times*, apropos of the death of Justice Manisty at the age of eighty-two, as saying that the public service would be strengthened by having a younger judge in his place. The *Review* continued:

There ought to be some provision for the compulsory retirement of superannuated judges, as there is of superannuated officers of the army, or else for the appointment of supplementary judges when existing judges become superannuated, after the example of coadjutant bishops in the Catholic church, — leaving the superannuated judge to jog along and do what work he may choose, and give the courts the benefit of his learning and experience, without being under the obligation of burdening himself with labor.

Returning later to the theme, it said that

in the case of a judge of the Supreme Court of the United States, such a scheme . . . would . . . increase the number of the judges from nine to twelve. It would be optional with the pensioned judges, so to speak, to continue to meet and consult with the court, as they should see fit, and to take upon themselves the full labor of a judge of the court, or merely to do such limited portion of the work which would otherwise be assigned to them, as they might judge suitable to their health and strength. The learning and experience of the aged judges of such a court are of such great and unquestioned value, that they ought not to be dispensed with as long as they can be retained consistently with the public interests. But their services cannot be retained consistently with the public interests, when they become so far disabled, by advancing years, from capacity to work, that their continued presence upon the bench prevents its being recruited by the strength of younger men.

It will be noted that neither the House Judiciary Committee of 1869 nor the editors of the *American Law Review* proposed a permanent increase in the size of the Court. In this respect their proposal differed from the draft bill attached to President Roosevelt's message to Congress on February 5, 1937. The latter would have permanently augmented the Court by such number of additional judges, not exceeding six, as might be appointed in respect of then existing justices over the age of seventy. If all the justices already over that age should have retired, the Court would have remained at nine. It will appear in the next chapter that Justice Miller was strongly opposed to increasing the membership of the Court to any such number as fifteen.

There are in fact two distinct reasons for urging some scheme for renewing the personnel of the Supreme Court, though they often converge in the case of particular justices. There is, first, the actual impairment of mental or physical powers. What has been set out above leaves no doubt that at times this has been a very real problem. Mr. Hughes, in the interval between his two appointments to the Supreme Court, expressed the view that "under present conditions of living, and in view of the increased facility of maintaining health and vigor, the age of seventy may well be thought too early for compulsory retirement"; seventy-five, he thought, "could more easily be defended." [46] An arbitrary figure takes no account of exceptional strength of mind and carefully husbanded vitality. It may prove too low, or too high, or now the one and now the other. The justice's own colleagues are the ones best situated to know, and in two very clear cases — Justice Grier and Justice Field — Mr. Hughes recalled that the Court found a way to bring its opinion home.

The public interest has not been served when judges have taken advantage of tenure for good behavior to establish an endurance record, as when Justice Field hung on until he had surpassed Marshall by three months — (by way of compensation for his failure to attain the presidency or the chief justiceship?). Far better the spirit of Justice Strong in the incident already recounted: or of Justice Clarke at sixty-five and while still possessing "strength sufficient to take up other duties": [47]

For a long time I have promised what I think is my better self that at that age I would free myself as much as possible from imperative duties that I may have time to read many books which

[46] Hughes, *The Supreme Court of the United States*, pp. 73ff., esp. at 76.
[47] 260 U. S. vi.

I have not had time to read in a busy life; to travel and to serve my neighbors and some public causes. . . .[48]

Justice Clarke was followed in the next few months by Justice Day at seventy-three and Justice Pitney at just under sixty-five. In their stead President Harding appointed Justices Sutherland at the age of sixty, Butler at fifty-six, and Sanford at fifty-seven.

A second ground for insuring renewal of the Court involves considerations of a different order. The course of political development in America has not followed a straight line pointed out by the men of 1787. Our path has been along a curve which tends generally to keep swinging toward the political left. The broadening of the suffrage, which to Justice Samuel Chase meant the beginning of the end, has necessarily been followed by a demand for the widening of economic advantage. Government control has grown more pervasive as every man's life has become more implicated in the lives of others. But if the course of social movement has been along a curve, the tendency of the Court has been to go along a tangent. A justice will often keep his face set in the direction on which the course was set at the time of his appointment, or earlier. All the world knows of individual cases where this has not been true — instances where by intelligence if not also by sympathy the judge has kept responsive to contemporary impulses. But, speaking broadly, the thought of the Court on the one hand and the view of public policy entertained by the political branches of the government on the other tend continually to part company. As the membership of the Court is renewed, the disparity is reduced. It is not suggested that a justice ought to take leave of conscience and join the procession. That he think as greatly as he can is the measure of his duty so long as he continues on the bench. The question remains whether it would not be wise to reduce the variance by a system of compulsory retirement.

[48] *New York Times*, September 5, 1922.

If we had an absolute standard we should know where the error lay. It is an idle fancy to suppose that the Constitution as judicially construed furnishes any such mechanical standard. Nor on the other hand would any thoughtful man assert that wisdom is always found on the side of the popular majorities. One can only affirm a faith that no safer guide for the long run has been found. Its promise lies in the possibility that public action may increasingly be informed with reason. The Supreme Court can make a unique contribution to that end: but only if its application of constitutional restraints can be respected as a rational process. The spirit in which the Court might acceptably apply limits to legislative and administrative action has never been put more persuasively than by Mr. Justice Brandeis in the concluding pages of his dissent in *New State Ice Co.* v. *Liebmann*: "In the exercise of this high power, we must be ever on our guard, lest we erect our prejudices into legal principles. If we would guide by the light of reason, we must let our minds be bold." [49]

Perhaps it is too much to expect that a justice should relinquish office when he finds himself wholly out of sympathy with the course of events. When he sees "not much to hope for" he may yet convince himself that it is his public duty to restrain his "inclinations to seek freedom from the incessant demands on [his] time and strength" — to quote Mr. Justice McReynolds.[50] Yet history does not lend support to the hope that by lamentations from the bench will a deluded public be brought to its senses. A century ago Mr. Justice Story was quoted to the effect that

all sensible men at Washington, in private conversation, admit that the government is deplorable weak, factious, and corrupt. That every thing is sinking down into despotism, under the dis-

---

[49] 285 U. S. 262 (1932), at 306ff. The economic consequences of the decision by the majority of the Court have been found good (Parker, "Control of Production under the Ice Code," *Harvard Business Review*, XIII, 483), but it is not always wise to assert judicial power, even though the Court is wiser than the legislature or administrative body whose action is challenged.

[50] As quoted in the *New York Times*, April 3, 1937.

guise of a democratic Government. He says the Sup. Court is sinking, and so is the Judicial in every State. . . . The senate of the U.S. are discouraged. There are 20 men in that Senate who are as wise and patriotic as any Sages of the Roman Senate, and last year they sustained the Constitution against the President and his collared House of Representatives, and yet *public opinion* remains unmoved, and not shaken and equally devoted to Tyranny and Corruption." [51]

Does one believe today that the pessimism of Story's later years reflected a more sane and wholesome view than that implicit in Jackson's administration? When a judge's instinctive reaction to all the legislation of his day is to condemn it out of hand, the intellectual operation involved in applying constitutional tests commands no respect.

It would be fraught with the greatest danger to have the courts of justice new-minted to bear the image of each succeeding administration. It is quite a different matter to adopt such means as will assure some continuity to the process of renewal.

[51] A memorandum by Chancellor Kent of a conversation with Justice Story, March 18, 1835, written on the fly-leaf of Kent's copy of Story on the Constitution (5 *American Law Review* 368).

XVII

THE BUSINESS OF THE COURTS

T O DELAY JUSTICE is to deny justice. Miller was quick to see that if the federal courts were to function effectively there must be some improvement in the judicial system. In the press of business after the Civil War the Supreme Court could not keep up with its docket, while the requirement of going on circuit prevented lengthening the term at Washington. In 1865 Senator Trumbull of Illinois, and then Senator Harris of New York, brought forward a plan to fuse the district and circuit courts — both courts of first instance; to create an intermediate appellate court to be held by the circuit justice and the district judges, thus interposing a barrier between the lowest and the highest court; and to prevent resort to the Supreme Court except in limited categories of important cases. The Harris bill passed the Senate on April 4, 1866, and went to the House.

The following June Chief Justice Chase sent Miller a letter suggesting that the bill might be improved. The latter was alarmed lest any attempt to modify should jeopardize the much-needed reform. He replied to Chase in this characteristically frank language:

I fear our judiciary bill will fail. The session draws near its close. The bill had full consideration in the Senate. Judge Harris submitted it repeatedly to the Judges, and it was approved by all except Clifford.

If it is attempted to remodel it now, at the close of the session, with no opportunity to consult with the Judges of the Supreme or district courts, it may be doubted if it will succeed or if it will be generally satisfactory.

The bill as it passed the Senate had the approval of all the district judges, of all the Judges of the Sup Court but one — Clifford. Can it be hoped that serious changes can now be introduced in the house, without dissatisfaction and danger of defeat. Besides the Senate as a body, is much more inclined to respect the views of the members of our court than the House, and it was there you could have exerted yourself to perfect the bill with more success. If this fails I shall trouble myself no more with efforts to procure legislation. I have suggested to Mr. Wilson,[1] that he should call on you on the subject, and have also made mention of the matter of salaries in connection with a reduction of the number of the judges. I have done this with some reluctance, as I have a great indisposition to seem to ask for legislation for mere personal advantage to myself.

But in reference to the January bill I have been painfully conscious of the delay of justice in the Sup. Court. I commenced agitating the subject before you came on the bench, in a long communication to the chairmen of the judiciary com. of both houses. I thought when I left Washington there was strong prospect of fair fruit for [?] these exertions, in the passage of the Senate bill. I am of course aware that no bill can embody all that every person may desire. But as none of the court expressed dissatisfaction with that bill, except Clifford, as it passed the Senate with nearly unanimity I had some ground to hope it would be accepted by the house, and pass. I know not what modifications you wish to make. From your sound sense I infer they must be wise ones. If they result in defeating the bill, either by delay or by the contests they provoke I shall doubt if they are worth that sacrifice.

You will excuse this frankness as that quality is one of the great pleasures of our intercourse. I am so deeply interested in the passage of the bill I could not say less.[2]

The Harris bill was never taken up in the House, and attention was turned to some more modest measure. Justices Miller and Field — whose circuits covered almost all the states west of the Mississippi River — then prepared what became a part of the Act of April 10, 1869, creating the office of circuit judge and authorizing one for each circuit, thus giving some relief to the circuit justice. At the same time the latter was required to cover his circuit only once in two years.

Miller urged further legislation to curtail the jurisdiction

---

[1] Senator Henry Wilson of Massachusetts, later vice president; interested in judiciary legislation.

[2] Letter of June 27, 1866, written from Keokuk; Chase Papers.

of the Supreme Court: resort from the Territories and the District of Columbia should be limited as in cases from the state courts; appeals in admiralty should be restricted and there should be no review on questions of fact in equity cases; the *ad damnum* should be raised from $2000 to $5000.[3]

This time it was the Senate that denied relief. On April 23, 1872, Miller surveyed the situation in the Court and in Congress:

Our Court has decided one third more cases since it met in October last than it ever did and our docket is left with about 450 cases. This is at least 150 more than we ever left before.

My bill which passed the House hangs fire in the Senate Committee which is a Committee of all the talents and all the politicians and all the elements of discord, and is the greatest nuisance of its kind in either House of Congress.

At this moment Southern lawyers were somewhat alarmed at the proposal to restrict appeal to the Supreme Court just as they were concerned about inferior judicial appointments, for a reason which appears in a letter from John A. Campbell to Philip Phillips:

My letter was written to Justice Nelson & its subject was to secure good Circuit Court Judges for the Southern Circuits. The District Judges at all points are in bad odour for common honesty.

My statement was to the effect that I hardly supposed that a man in any relation to the rebellion would be appointed to the Sup Court & that I know of no man in the Circuit who was qualified belonging to the republican party & not many of the other, who had any possibility of attaining the office. That under those conditions I preferred an honorable upright able man from another section to one that was thus selected.[4]

Ballinger evidently expressed a similar apprehension, for Justice Miller wrote in reply:

I note what you say . . . about the effect of my bill in leaving the people of the Southern States at the mercy of their district judges in finding of facts which is made conclusive. The same

---

[3] 2 *U. S. Jurist* 1; 6 *Western Jurist* 49.
[4] Letter of January 4, 1870; Phillips Papers, Library of Congress.

objection is urged here by Mr. Phillips and other lawyers interested in cases coming from that region. But I do not see how to avoid the difficulty. The one important feature on which all our court is agreed, and the only one which seems to be without objection in Congress is to relieve this court from that business. It is a necessity. The bill passed the House six weeks ago without material amendment. . . . It has hung fire in the Senate Judiciary Committee, a committee which is the damnedest nuisance the Congress presents. Every man on it thinks himself the embodiment of constitutional wisdom and statesmanship, and each is jealous of the other. The only way they can ever report a bill is to permit some one to report with the understanding that each member shall vote and talk as he pleases when it comes up for action. I hardly hope for the passage of the bill in any shape satisfactory to me.

Nor do I now care much if it should fail. The docket of the present term has already reached 615 cases, and before it ends it will probably number near 800. For such a docket as this and such a vast increase as it indicates for the future, my bill is a very imperfect remedy. When the evil becomes of such a magnitude as to demand instant and efficient remedy, it will probably compel the adoption of the plan which has always had my preference, an intermediate appellate court in each circuit, or such a number of intermediate courts of appeal as may be found useful.[5]

The Court returned in the autumn of 1872 to a condition which Miller thus described:

We commence next Monday with our adjourned term and we shall have for the new term in December a docket of over 600 cases.

It is frightful, but I feel less anxiety about it than I ever did. I have introduced and carried rules to curtail argument, as far as it can be wisely done. I have prepared and carried through the House a bill curtailing our jurisdiction and facilitating its exercise. I can do no more, and shall leave the responsibility where it belongs.[6]

Some of his proposals were realized by the Act of February 16, 1875. But adequate relief for the Court, through the creation of intermediate appellate tribunals, was not achieved

[5] Letter of March 9, 1872.
[6] Letter of October 24, 1872.

until after Miller's death, by the Circuit Courts of Appeals Act of 1891. So he went about his circuit to the last. As he grew older this summer work became very fatiguing, and indeed the collapse from which his death ensued was attributed to this labor.

While Justice Miller looked at the problem of strengthening the federal judicial system from the angle of a justice of the Supreme Court, Ballinger's concern was that of a practitioner in the courts of first instance. The latter's correspondence was filled with comments on local inadequacies, and evidently he was urging the propriety of making the State of Texas a separate judicial circuit with sufficient personnel of its own. In a letter of December 8, 1870, Miller explains why he thinks it would be unfortunate at that moment to expand the federal courts in the South:

I think the fewer permanent offices made and filled just now in the South the better for the people of that region. There is not material among the republican party out of which to fill such offices in the rebel States, or if there is, the class of men who have the present control of appointments are not likely to have them appointed. The time will come when the intelligence and wealth of the South will have its natural influence, and whether this be through the democratic party as I fear it will, or by some reform in the leadership of the republicans, its effect must be to give you better officers. I do not stop to inquire here who is to blame, but you are in a transition state easy to account for, and you are at the worst of it. It is not advisable that such appointments as your system contemplates should be made now for life. I would rather suffer a little while and take no chances. Even if Grant shall be elected for a second term, as I think probable, the carpet bag element of the South *must* subside as leaders, and though but few good men seem willing to accept the place of republican leaders, still things must improve.

Justice Miller made a visit to Texas during an adjournment of the Supreme Court in February 1879 — "one of the few periods of unalloyed pleasure which comes to a man of my years" — where he evidently learned at first hand how the federal courts were functioning. Ballinger had revived the subject of making Texas a circuit by itself and enlisted Miller's support. After his return to Washington, Miller reviewed the prospect of securing legislation to energize the judicial system. It had long been the conviction of the justices that a series of intermediate courts was the only adequate solution. McCrary and then David Davis had tried to carry such a measure through Congress. The inclination of the Democrats, however, especially those from the South, was to go at the problem from the other end, by cutting down the jurisdiction of the federal courts to fit the existing establishment. Their party had controlled the House since 1875, and had captured the Senate in March 1879. So there was no likelihood that new judgeships would be created for President Hayes to fill. Such is the background of Justice Miller's letter of April 30, 1879:

When I attempt to recall your observations on . . . the judicial condition of the federal courts in the State of Texas and the business of those courts and the remedies suggested by you, I cannot repress the question *Cui bono* as regards myself. It is not that I do not feel a deep interest in the general subject, and on your account especially as it regards Texas. But it is useless [?]. I am myself so little able to do you any good.

I have not only felt a deep anxiety about the business in our own Court for years, but this has been shared by all the Judges. We have also had substantial unanimity as to the remedy. There has also been no objection of any weight or which any body has relied on to its enactment.

In spite of all this it has been impossible to get it enacted into a law, or even in the senate to get the proper Committee to report on it. This has been for a time the fault of my own political party or rather of one or two members of it. If I could exercise no influence in a matter where I had a right to speak and with persons who ought to have listened, backed as I was by the whole Court, what can I hope to do for a State to which I do not belong, with a political party in the flush of newly acquired power who would look upon suggestions from me of such a plan as yours as a device to get one or two more Republican Judges before our party dies fixed on the bench for life.

The present condition of party feeling is as bitter as it has been since the rebellion broke out. There is no disposition to concede on either side. As things stand I would not ask the President to appoint a Democrat to a life office for I would not do it myself under existing circumstances.

The thing you suggest is simply hopeless as matters stand. Mr. Hayes thinks his effort to conciliate the South, to do it justice if you please, has been met by a very poor return and is little like to risk for a second time a rupture with his party by making democratic nominations. At least that is the inference I draw from his recent nominations for judicial offices in your state.

But if I am powerless to aid you, I may serve you by giving you information. I am satisfied that the leading democratic lawyers in Congress, have a program built on a theory directly the opposite of what you desire, namely, to contract the jurisdiction of all the federal courts, so that half of the business now done in them will be done if at all in the State courts.

The policy is a part of the State Rights doctrine. In what particular mode, or in how many shapes it will be attempted I cannot tell. But I had a conversation the other day with McDonald of Indiana who is the leading Democrat in the Senate Judiciary Committee in which he suggested $2000, or $2500 as the lowest sum to give the circuit court jurisdiction and $10.000 for our court, and in this I agreed with him. Of course since the war broke out many statutes for removing causes from the State courts have been passed which might also be well repealed. I am of opinion that after appearance of defendant no cause should be removable.

I am well assured from other sources that such is the policy rather than an increase of judicial force and if it were once thoroughly carried out I should be well content.

If however any effort shall be made in the direction of your plan I would advise that in view of any hope of success, Louisiana should be included with Texas. The similarity of your laws in many respects suggests this, which is supported by locality.

It would also seem less exceptional and selfish if some other State is included in yours — and it might be the beginning of a policy in which the number of circuits and circuit Judges should have no relation to the number of the Judges of the Supreme Court, which I think is wise.

In the protracted discussion of what to do to relieve the Court an alternative was continually proposed of increasing its membership and then either providing that it sit in divisions, or sending some of the Justices out to hold the circuit courts. When these schemes were first broached, Justice

Davis for one became very much alarmed. On November 2, 1868, he wrote from his home in Illinois to Justice Clifford:

If this Congress passes off without any more outrageous things being done, I have hopes in Decr 1869. when the next Congress meets, that the Capital of the Country will be arroused [*sic*] at the danger to *it*, of destroying the Supreme Court — I wd not give one fig for Corporate rights in this Country; unless the Supreme Court is preserved, pretty much as it is now — But for us there is but one course to pursue — do our duty. faithfully & conscientiously — leaving the consequences which we cannot control to God — [7]

Miller regarded the proposal to increase and divide the Court as part of a plan "to break down its conservative influence," and added:

As the court now stands, it has the confidence of the people of all political parties more than any branch of the government. But this plan would convert it into a large debating club, with hostile subdivisions, enfeeble its decisions, and soon destroy the esteem and veneration with which it is now regarded.[8]

Justice Miller was aware that some reforms lay within the power of the Court itself. Among these was the matter of the writing and reporting of opinions. Ever since the days of the Barbourville Debating Society Miller had set a high value on concise statement. He believed that opinions should be brief. In this respect he was sorely tried by some of his brothers. Justice Clifford especially, in his later years, found himself dissenting frequently and copiously. He would quote from this court and that, winding up on the eighteenth or twentieth page with the conclusion that "viewed in the light of these considerations" the judgment should have been so and so. In a letter written October 29, 1879, Miller discusses the growing need for brevity:

I have also been on a committee of our court appointed at the close of our last term to consider the subject of Reporting. The main object is to secure more condensed reporting. We have thus

[7] Clifford Papers.
[8] Letter of March 7, 1875.

far been unable to agree on any thing useful, because the main objection is the length of the opinions themselves.

While perfectly conscious as the committee is, of whom the C. Justice and Swayne are the other members, and as also are most of the judges, that the opinions are far too long we have not been able to suggest any satisfactory remedy.

The truth is that the one man [9] of our court who ought to take the lead and without whose firmness and courage nothing can be done is sadly wanting in both those qualities. He is much more anxious to be popular as an amiable, kind hearted man (which he is) than as the dignified and capable head of the greatest court the world ever knew. Of what is due to that court, and what is becoming its character, he has no conception. It is probably the last effort I shall ever make for any serious reform in the body. My interest in it fades rapidly and if I could leave it tomorrow I would gladly do so.

The extent of Justice Miller's thought on the subject of improvement in the administration of justice is apt to be underestimated. For he never sat in a legislature, his efforts to secure relief for the Court met small response, and he was never invited to lend the aid of his experience to any effort at law reform. Yet the range of his interest was wide, and several of his ideas are as useful today as when he broached them. They are to be found in his address before the New York State Bar Association in 1878 [10] and in an article on "The System of Trial by Jury." [11] While Miller recognized the need for some provision against decrepitude on the bench, he was opposed to any form of tenure, such as by popular election for short terms, which exposed the judge to the influence of great corporations or of sudden popular impulse. On the common-law jury system his thought underwent an evolution:

I must confess that my practice . . . , before I came to the bench, left upon my mind the impression that as regards . . . civil suits, the jury system was one of doubtful utility; and if I had been called upon, as a legislator, to provide for a system of trial in that class of actions, I should have preferred a court constituted of three or more judges. . . .

[9] Chief Justice Waite.
[10] *Reports*, II, 31ff.   [11] 21 *American Law Review* 859ff. (1887).

This impression . . . I have since come to think, however, was largely due to the fact that owing to popular and frequent elections of the State judges, and insufficient salaries, the judges of those courts in which I mainly practiced were neither very competent as to their learning, nor sufficiently assured of their position, to exercise that control over the proceedings in a jury case, and especially in instructing the jury upon the law applicable to it, which is essential to a right result in a jury trial. It may as well be stated here that a case submitted to the unregulated discretion of a jury, without that careful discrimination between matters of fact and matters of law which it is the duty of the court to lay before them, it but little better than a popular trial before a town meeting.[12]

It is evident that the procedure which Justice Miller carried on in his own court was very different from that trial of skill in the corruption of intelligence, with the judge a mere umpire between contesting counsel, which sometimes passes as trial by jury.

In civil cases Judge Miller thought that a verdict of nine jurors, or even of eight, should suffice.

The common law of evidence he pronounced "a very artificial system, and probably more restrictive in the rules which admitted testimony than any civilized code of laws." [13] It remained "an inviting field for the jurist and the legislator." He commended the then recent works of Judge Appleton and James Fitzjames Stephen, while "an examination of Mr. Bentham's labors on the subject would well repay the time so expended." What Miller would think of the practical operation of our system of criminal justice today, with the third degree as its logical counterpart, may be imagined from the following remark:

Without enlarging on the subject, I am of opinion that in criminal causes the French system of repeated and very free preliminary examination of the prisoner, in the presence of a judicial officer, in which questions are put and answered with great freedom, as the facts are developed, in which the accused has the fullest opportunity of prompt and early explanation, and is held

[12] 21 *American Law Review* 861, 862.
[13] *Reports of the New York State Bar Association*, II, 42.

responsible for its absence, . . . is much more likely to relieve the party, if innocent, of the disgrace and trouble of a formal trial, and to produce conviction in case of guilt, than our artificial strait-laced law of evidence permits. It is the boast of the common law that it protects the innocent at all hazards, and that it is better that many guilty should escape than that one innocent man should be punished. Yet I entertain a very strong conviction that, leaving out of the account prosecutions for offenses purely political, fewer men are wrongfully punished, and fewer guilty ones escape, under the French, than under our system of criminal procedure.

He welcomed legislation to admit the testimony of parties in interest. In criminal cases it had, he recalled, been thought proper to instruct the jury that the silence of the accused raised no presumption against him: "It may be doubted, however, if the charge of the court in such cases will be very effectual."

There was a clear gain, he thought, in fusing the administration of law and equity. It has already been pointed out that his experience at the bar in Iowa confirmed what would in any case have been a natural preference for the simplified system of code pleading. His address to the New York bar ended with a plea to rise above traditional habits of thought: "In the work of your profession, unless you sink into the merest routinist, you will be the first to discern the imperfections of the rules by which your action is governed, and to make wise suggestions for remedy."

Justice Miller's life on the circuit calls for some attention. There he reigned supreme, was known at close range by the bar, and left a reputation which was quite unique. To preside over a great western circuit in those days called for robustness of character, as the following letter will illustrate. In June 1879 he held court in Denver, hearing among others "a contest for the possession of a rail road and a rail road route through narrow mountain gorges, where violence has already disgraced the State and resulted in homicide." [14] Back in Washington that autumn he wrote:

[14] Letter of June 29, 1879.

I came very near breaking down at the close of the circuit at Denver this summer. I sat six weeks in very hot weather of June and July. I had heavy mining and rail road cases in which every move of the court involved millions of dollars, and the personal feelings of clients invaded the court room too visibly in the ill concealed temper of their lawyers. It was a trial of my temper and a draft on my mind that I have never met on the bench. It resulted in a shaky hand, an interrupted pulse, and strong evidences of heart trouble, which caused me to leave the court suddenly and seek the sea shore at Block Island. Though I have not held the court at St Louis for two years and Treat [15] is in Europe, and there is no circuit Judge [16] I have resisted all entreaties to go there this fall feeling quite sure that duty to my own health and to the Supreme Court which assembles within ten days justified me in seeking repose until that time. A month at Block Island and a week or two at Saratoga have apparently restored me to my usual health. But with seven long months of such work as our court requires before a man it is essential that he should enter upon it in good condition.[17]

Justice Miller's letters to Judge Treat are indicative of the affection and good feeling which prevailed among the judges of the Eighth Circuit. In May 1876, Miller wrote urging Treat to leave Saint Louis for the summer and come to visit the Centennial Exposition at Philadelphia:

My Dear Judge.

I have not felt easy in my mind about you since I sat in court with you last October. There is a current belief that having escaped death from consumption some twenty five years ago, you were turned into a pine knot of which your sallow complexion was the evidence and your capacity for unlimited labour a result. This inference has been strengthened by the great fondness for work which you have shown, doing the business of three or four Judges,[18] and by your exhaustive researches doing also the work of the lawyers to such an extent that they have almost ceased to make any preparation in their cases.

[15] District judge, Eastern District of Missouri.

[16] Judge Dillon had resigned, and McCrary was appointed later in the year. "It is not known that a single vote was cast against his nomination in the Senate. It is certain that the Judiciary Committee were unanimous." (Letter of December 14, 1879.)

[17] Letter of October 3, 1879.

[18] On the congestion of business in the circuit courts of the Eighth Circuit, cf. 3 *Central Law Journal* 68 (1876).

Now my dear friend the day for all this is past, and I saw very clearly last fall that you were vulnerable and susceptible of fatigue, and was not surprised that you had a serious time for ten or twelve days after the Babcock trial.[19]

Now I insist, and with as much of friendly authority as you will permit, I use it, to order you away from St. Louis for the entire Summer commencing June 1.

---

[19] Judge Treat had just been conducting the trials growing out of the exposure of the Whiskey Ring, one of the major scandals of the Grant Administration. It will suffice to explain the following letter to recall some rhymes from "The Whiskey Ring Alphabet":

> "A — stands for Avery, clerk of the ring;
> B — for Babcock, who had a big thing;
> . . . .
> S — stands for St. Louis, where the ring came to grief;
> T — is for Treat, of all judges the chief."

On the occasion of these trials Miller had sent the following letter of advice to Judge Treat:

"Washington
"Dec 24. 1875

"My Dear Judge

"I have received your two letters written during the trials of the whiskey cases, and can very easily see how much you must be worn out, with all your capacity for enduring the labour of the bench. The truth is — a truth which I have some reluctance to acknowledge to myself — that years begin to exert their influence on me, and I suppose also on you; for while I find myself thus far able to do my full share of the duties of my own office or rather offices, I do find that I approach these duties with less relish, some times even with distaste, and that a sense of weariness comes over me oftener and sooner, than in days that are past.

"I take it for granted that Dillon will be with you on the 10th proximo and will remain with you while those cases or any of them are in the circuit court.

"I have read your charges to the jury in these cases, and read that in the Avery case with special interest.

"I received the impression from reading it that whatever might be your private opinion as to Avery's guilt, you had strong doubt as to the sufficiency of the legal evidence for his conviction, and had fears that the jury might not give him the just benefit of reasonable doubts.

"I think you were quite right in this. There is undoubtedly a strong popular feeling, a current if I may so express it in favour of punishing all parties concerned in those frauds. Such a feeling does not always distinguish with care between the innocent and the guilty, and as it is apt to invade the jury box in cases which excite the public interest, it is in our form of government the especial duty of the bench to guard and protect the prisoner's rights in such an emergency.

"I should myself have no hesitation in awarding a new trial in such a case if I believed the verdict was not supported by sufficient testimony, or was largely influenced by a public sentiment however just, which demanded more victims than were lawfully liable to be offered up.

"Of the guilt of McDonald, Joyce and others there seems to be no doubt

I have written to Dillon telling him that however hard it may seem, it is the duty of the district Judges to submit to some equalization of labour where they are serving the same master, and receiving the same compensation, and the law provides for it.

He informs me that he has ordered Caldwell to St. Louis.

Justice Miller goes on to give his impression of the Centennial Exposition:

. . . I say to you after four days examination of it when far from complete, that the world has known nothing equal to it.

I am not fond of shows. I was not much in favour of this special enterprize. The ceremonies in which I took a formal part officially were a bore. But the exposition exceeds in interest all my ideas of such a thing.

I passed the better part of three days in the art gallery, and did not begin to get through or to lose my interest in it.

The letter ends on a note of friendly admonition:

Now don't be misled by your conscience. Conscience is a very good thing when it is enlightened. I can better afford — the courts can better afford to have you do less work *now* and last *longer*, than to have you break down and linger along in permanent ill health.

I can't spare you, so with love to Mrs. Treat and my warmest and most affectionate wishes for your real good I am yours

Sam. F. Miller [20]

The quality of Judge Miller's work at *nisi prius* is particularly to be noted. That he felt a keen pride in his ability to dispatch cases in the circuit court is evident from this letter of July 1, 1874:

I doubt whether as much important business was ever done in the same length of time by a court, or courts. The weather was

---

in any quarter, but I have heard several candid men who have paid attention to the course of the trials, express serious doubts of Avery's guilt, at least of his having any corrupt motive in this matter, which is of the essence of his legal guilt.

"I shall write to Judge Dillon to say that in my judgment he should exercise the power given him by the statute, to give you some relief. He ought to give his personal attention as far as possible to the business of the circuit court there this winter. I hope he will." (Treat Collection, Missouri Historical Society.)

[20] Letter of May 29, 1876; Treat Collection, Missouri Historical Society.

excessively warm and the terms succeeded each other with short intervals of time and I availed myself of the provisions of the statute to have both Circuit and District Judges employed in different rooms, while I held the principal court myself. But beside this I think I have a very rare faculty of inducing the bar to dispense with Rhetoric, with mere forms and to come directly and speedily to the points on which their cases rest if they have any merits at all and for a case which is all sham I have a quick eye and no toleration. In this manner I am able to dispatch business more rapidly than any judge I ever saw, and by making the pressure on the lawyers very gentle, but firm I find that what ever feeling of reluctance they have at the time, they are more than satisfied at the end of the term. I make it a point with whatever of rapidity we go over the case as a whole, to make them see, that as to the main points, the controlling questions, they have had a fair and full hearing and careful consideration by the Court, while I have but little patience with motions, points and questions which do not affect the merits of the case. I always get verdicts when I preside at a jury trial. In two very important cases in which juries had failed to agree one under Dillon and the other under Nelson [21] I had verdicts in less than two hours. I never leave the jury in doubt as [to] what the law of the case is; and I have never had any trouble with lawyers about my bills of exception. If I decide the case as I generally do by instructions and rulings, I am consistently careful to give a bill of exceptions which shows what I have done, and oftener err in making it too favorable to the losing party than the other.

I take pleasure in the fact that while it is well known that I am a judge who takes responsibility boldly I have never in twelve years service had the least trouble or ill feeling with a member of the bar so far as I know.

That in pronouncing this encomium the Judge was not unduly complacent is evident from the comment of two legal periodicals published at Saint Louis, where acquaintance with his methods was at first hand. The *Central Law Journal* of July 1877 [22] — just three years after the above letter — published an engraving of Justice Miller accompanied by a note of appreciation. Coming to his work as a trial judge it ex-

[21] Rensselaer R. Nelson, district judge in Minnesota, son of Justice Nelson of the Supreme Court.
[22] 5:vii.

pressed precisely the estimate which Miller had made of himself:

His extraordinary quickness of perception, and the rapidity of his mental movements, combined with his industry and large experience, enable him to dispose of the business of a term with a dispatch that is really extraordinary. He wastes no time and allows the bar to waste none. No judge is more patient until he has been put in full possession of all of the facts and considerations pertaining to the case in hand, but when he is *sure* he has these, and when his own mind sees its way clearly to a satisfactory judgment, he does not allow time of the court to be consumed in useless and immaterial discussions. . . .

Hung juries are almost unknown when he presides at a trial; for he extracts the turning point of the case and then lays down the law so plainly as to preclude such a miscarriage. . . . And no losing party complains, for he knows he will get a fair bill of exceptions. . . . [Judge Miller] is popular with his bar — a popularity which is based upon their respect for his character, admiration for his abilities, and attachment for his personal and social qualities. No other word will express the sentiments of his associates on the Bench of the Circuit except to say, *they love him.*

And the *American Law Review* of 1889, at the conclusion of a note in deprecation of technicality in the administration of justice, said:

There is one judge whom we regard as the most eminent of our time. He carries into his circuit work what we have often thought was too great a freedom from strict legal rules; but his *nisi prius* work is distinguished by a most animated sense of justice, — we refer to Mr. Justice Miller. . . .[23]

In supposing that he had never aroused resentment on the part of the bar Miller was certainly mistaken. There were many who approached his circuit court room in the spirit of the lawyer who said he was "going up to be stamped all over by that damned old Hippopotamus."[24] "A perfect terror on the trial bench" was the comment of a lawyer who appeared before him both at *nisi prius* and in the Supreme Court, and

[23] 23:425. [24] Gregory, *Miller*, p. 60.

who still remembers him with affection.[25] Two years after Miller's death there appeared a sketch of his days on the circuit, entitled "He Frightened the Lawyers." [26] The writer was evidently familiar with Miller's court room, and other evidence tends to corroborate his story:

To those who did not know the real kindliness and goodness of heart that lay behind his gruff judicial demeanor, his abrupt and apparently tyrannical behavior to the members of the bar made him almost obnoxious. He was the terror of the younger members, and indeed of many of the older and more seasoned ones, when he came upon the circuit. . . . In the free-and-easy atmosphere of the circuit court room . . . he occasionally gave vent to startling interjections.

He tells of Miller holding court in Saint Louis one sultry day, collar and cravat loosened, working a palm-leaf fan, and shifting uneasily in his seat. Finally —

"Damn it, Brown, come to the point!"

"What point, your Honor?"

"I don't know; any point; some point."

At Des Moines there was a young attorney who was to argue a case before Miller. Older lawyers fed him on stories of the Judge's rugged manner, with the result that when Miller hurled some remark at him the man fainted. When the truth of the affair came to Miller's attention he was greatly displeased, and sending for the young man put matters right in such a way that he was thereafter the Judge's ardent admirer.[27]

There was an occasion when a lawyer in Iowa felt so incensed at the way he was treated that at the conclusion of his case he said he would never appear before Judge Miller again. At the hotel that night some members of the bar talked the matter over, recalling that the Judge had not meant to offend and would wish to make the matter right if he realized what

[25] Conversation with Mr. James C. Davis of Des Moines, Iowa, September 6, 1935.

[26] By "C. H." (Clark Howell?), New York *Sun*, September 26, 1892; 25 *Chicago Legal News* 52 (1892).

[27] From the article by "C. H.," cited above. Mr. Davis knew of the incident and mentioned the lawyer's name.

he had done. They sent a committee to call on the district judge, Love, requesting him to bring the situation to Miller's attention. To which that gentle and kindly man replied that "he wasn't going to beard the lion in his den." [28]

"A keen mind to determine and simplify intricate issues," commented one who knew Judge Miller, going on to recall a case of the foreclosure of a mortgage on a railroad running from Keokuk to Saint Louis. Earlier stages had already consumed much of the circuit judge's time, and Miller wanted to dispose of the case without more delay.

"Who represents the plaintiff in this case?" he asked. A lawyer rose and began to read a long petition. Miller cut him short: "Don't read me that!" He "wouldn't give a cent for a lawyer who couldn't make a better oral statement." Miller got the counsel for all the parties on their feet, and disposed of the matter within two hours.

There was a case of a company in Keokuk which had failed after borrowing money from a bank. The letter requesting the loan asked for it "under the same terms and conditions as heretofore," or with some similar expression. Other debts were paid without satisfying the note, and the bank contended that there had been fraud, the company being insolvent when they sought the loan. To the consternation of counsel for the plaintiff, the case came before Judge Miller. Prominent citizens were involved, and the suit aroused a good deal of local interest. At the end of the sitting on the first day Miller asked if *that* was all the evidence, and was informed that the rest would be merely corroboratory. He observed that it would be difficult to convince *him* there had been fraud, and adjourned Court. That night the lawyer worked diligently. He found a paragraph on concealed fraud in Kerr on Fraud and Mistake which he thought was precisely in point. Judge Miller often talked about "common fairness," "fairness be-

[28] Told by Judge Love to Professor Wambaugh. The latter recalls seeing Justice Miller hold court in Saint Louis about 1880. He speaks of the Judge's great severity, adding two comments: that he bore down on old and young counsel alike; and that when he did they deserved it. (Conversations on August 6, 1935, and November 11, 1936.)

tween man and man," and if he could only be made to see the
case in the true light it should be won. On resuming next
morning, counsel asked a personal favor: that the Judge would
listen to him for five minutes without interrupting. "Go on,"
Miller responded somewhat gruffly. The lawyer did, and was
rewarded presently with the remark: "Young man, you're
right this morning, and I was wrong yesterday." At dinner
that night — the Judge's friends had a round of dinners when
he came to town — Judge Miller referred to the incident in
very agreeable terms.[29]

Judge Miller thoroughly enjoyed trying a criminal case
with a jury, and it is said that if there was a prosecution on
the docket the clerk of the circuit court at Omaha would try
to steer it into a July term so that Mr. Justice Miller could
preside. On one of these occasions the Judge charged the jury
so furiously that a conviction seemed almost certain. Counsel
for the defendant, wishing to break the force of the charge,
asked Judge Miller to explain to the jury that they must dismiss from their minds the circumstance that his client had
not taken the stand in his own defense. Miller's face contracted until his eyebrows seemed to come down and hang
over his nose — his expression when annoyed. Then his countenance changed. He turned to the jury and in his blandest
manner, which could be very bland indeed, said to them:
"Mr. ———— is quite right. I have not charged you as I
should have done that the circumstance that this accused person did not take the stand on his own behalf, as he might have
done, and did not explain the matters in evidence against
him, as he might have done, is something that you are not to
consider at all. Now, gentlemen, the law says you must entirely dismiss this from your mind, give it no consideration,
forget it completely, but", — and then he looked up reflec-
tively at the roof of the court room, and added in a distinctly
audible stage whisper — "it is a mighty strange rule of law,
isn't it?" [30]

[29] Mr. Davis, in the conversation already quoted.
[30] For this anecdote I am indebted to Professor Roscoe Pound, who knew

It is of a piece with what has been said that in the Supreme Court Justice Miller, Jove-like, would occasionally hurl a devastating bolt at counsel, as for example announcing that the Court "was not with him and never would be." [31] A lawyer who during a terrifying thunder storm had continued his argument without apparent distraction, explained when complimented on his performance that it had really been not nearly so disconcerting as Justice Miller's questions from the bench. (This is not to imply that he interposed from any disposition to hector counsel.) "We allow but one to talk here at a time," the Justice is quoted as announcing sternly when his reading of an opinion was disturbed by whispering in the chamber. Shortly afterward the offenders retired. They proved to be the Emperor Dom Pedro and the Brazilian Minister.[32]

Justice Miller realized that one aid in expediting the work of the Court was a rigorous insistence upon the rules of practice. At the time he came to the bench there seems to have been considerable laxity in this regard. Attorney General Bates wrote in his diary in 1864:

The great, and now c[h]ronic, error which has well nigh destroyed the dignity and is impairing the usefulness of the court, is the extreme looseness and irregularity of practice in the courts below, allowed and encouraged here; and this has gone to such a pitch that no man — not the Ch Justice — knows what is the *true record* from the Court below, it is so hidden and smothered with the *hotch potch* matter, thrust into the miscellaneous collection miscalled the record of the case.[33]

In 1868 we find Miller writing to Ballinger, who had considerable practice before the Court:

By the way let me suggest to you that questions concerning jurisdiction, and questions concerning practice in the federal courts, have much increased of late years, and no lawyer is safe

---

Justice Miller. He recalls it as having been told by lawyers at the bar of the Eighth Circuit.

[31] *Harper's Weekly*, October 18, 1890.

[32] Clipping from the Baltimore *Sun*, date not ascertained.

[33] Entry for April 10, 1864; *Diary of Edward Bates*, p. 356.

on those subjects who does not examine the Supreme Court reports of which there is no digest, namely since 17 Howard.

But my experience as a judge shows me that many careful lawyers omit cases directly in point in these volumes.[34]

He goes on to say that when Abbott's Digest [35] is published it will in a measure serve to remedy this condition, and to express a poor opinion of the chief work then available, Judge Conkling's *Treatise on the Organization, Jurisdiction and Practice of the Courts of the United States.* A few years later Philip Phillips' useful book, *Statutory Jurisdiction and Practice of the Supreme Court of the United States,* was published, and Miller hailed it with the observation that "if every practitioner in our Court had a copy, and would consult it, the Court would be spared the waste of much time, and its labors greatly facilitated." [36] Miller's zeal for the effective administration of justice caused him to bear down heavily upon all ineptitude, and his opinions are studded with pointed rebukes to counsel, clerks, and inferior judges who imposed needless burdens upon the Court.[37]

Justice Miller was loath to construe statutory language so as to bring to the Supreme Court questions which he believed should be determined in the state courts. In *Murdock* v. *Memphis* [38] the Court had to determine the meaning of a statute revising the original Judiciary Act as to the removal of causes from state courts. In the Act of 1789 there had been a clause to the effect that "no other error shall be assigned or regarded as a ground of reversal . . . than such as . . . immediately respects the before mentioned questions of validity or construction of the said [federal] constitution, treaties, statutes, commissions, or authorities in dispute." This was omitted from the revised Act of 1867. Did it follow that the Supreme Court was now to pass, not only on the federal ques-

[34] Letter of March 22, 1868.

[35] *Enactments Relative to the Federal Courts* (1869), with the rules of practice.

[36] Quoted in an advertisement in the 4th edition, 1878.

[37] 2 Black at 581; 2 Wallace at 339; 5 Wallace 419; 11 Wallace at 652; 12 Wallace at 261; 91 U. S. at 603; 20 Fed. 712.

[38] 20 Wallace 590 (1875), Clifford, Swayne, and Bradley, JJ., dissenting.

tion involved, but upon all the questions which had been before the state court? Justice Miller, for the Court, points out how tremendously this would widen the scope of its review, and concludes that

it requires a very bold reach of thought, and a readiness to impute to Congress a radical and hazardous change of a policy vital in its essential nature to the independence of the State courts, to believe that that body contemplated, or intended, what is claimed, by the mere omission of a clause in the substituted statute which may well be held to have been superfluous, or nearly so, in the old one.

In the same spirit he dissented in the Pacific Railroad Removal Cases,[39] where the Court held that a corporation created under an Act of Congress was entitled to remove any suit brought against it to the federal courts, as a suit "arising under the laws of the United States." The result was to bring a mass of litigation concerning the Pacific railroads — actions for negligence and the like — into the federal courts. This proved very inconvenient, and was gradually cut away by subsequent legislation.

The Act of Congress of March 3, 1875, just referred to as authorizing the removal from a state to a federal court of "any suit . . . arising under the Constitution or laws of the United States," was construed by the Supreme Court to support removal wherever a law of the United States was relied upon, not only as the basis of the cause of action, but also as a defense thereto.[40] Justice Miller dissented:

It is always a matter of delicacy when a cause of which a court has undoubted jurisdiction is transferred, at the instance of one party, to another court of concurrent jurisdiction. It is especially so when the transfer is made to a Federal from a State court, without regard to the consent of the latter, and against the objection of the other party.

In such a case the right of removal should be made very clear on the application for that purpose. . . .

I do not think such a case is presented here.

[39] 115 U. S. 1 (1885). Miller concurred in a dissent by Waite, C.J.
[40] Railroad Co. v. Mississippi, 102 U. S. 135.

Legislation of 1887 and 1888 expressed the purpose of Congress to contract the jurisdiction which had been conferred in the post-war years. The Act of August 13, 1888, amended the provision just quoted above, and the Court came around to the view that to permit removal from the state court the question of federal law must appear on the plaintiff's statement of his own claim. In reaching this conclusion Justice Gray said:

Congress, in making this change, may well have had in mind the reasons which so eminent a judge as Mr. Justice Miller invoked in support of his dissent from the original decision. . . . "Looking," said he, "to the reasons which may have influenced Congress, it may well be supposed that while that body intended to allow the removal of a suit where the very foundation and support thereof was a law of the United States, it did not intend to authorize a removal where the cause of action depended solely on the law of the State, and when the act of Congress only came in question incidentally as part (it might be a very small part) of the defendant's plea of avoidance. In support of this view, it may be added, that he in such a case is not without remedy in a Federal court; for if he has pleaded and relied on such defence in the state court, and that court has decided against him in regard to it, he can remove the case into this court by writ of error, and have the question decided here." [41]

Section 5 of the Act of March 3, 1875, directed that if a cause had been improperly brought in or removed to a federal court it should be dismissed or remanded. Ballinger had raised some question as to the construction of this section, and Miller, knowing how prone litigants were to smuggle their cases into a federal court, states in reply the rigor with which he enforces the statute:

The only difficulty about the law is whether after a case has proceeded to hearing or decree, or to trial before a jury, the court on discovering at this late stage of the case its want of jurisdiction, or rather the falsity of the statement on which its jurisdiction has been invoked it must then remand the case as if nothing had been done. That it is the duty of the court to be vigilant in this matter and to remand without hesitation in a proper case I have no

[41] In Tennessee *v.* Union and Planters' Bank, 152 U. S. 454 (1894).

[*423*]

doubt, for my experience on the circuit presents me with too many cases in which both parties prefer that court.[42]

A word should be set down in conclusion lest what has been said of Justice Miller's severity leave too strong an impression. In the memorial proceedings of the bar of the Court, former Attorney General Garland recalled the Judge's first court in Arkansas at the close of the War:

> The means sometimes that he used to discipline us in these new ways were not entirely agreeable to us at the time, and to some extent we flinched under his affectionate chastisement, but when he left Little Rock, at the close of that term, there was not a member of that Bar who did not esteem and admire him, and he has had their unbroken affection ever since.

"I love Miller; he has so much backbone!" said his brother Field,[43] a judge whose will was no less strong, nor always guided, as was Miller's, by a great fundamental kindliness. To the attendants of the Court Miller remained a hero. When the annual dinner was given to the pages, he was the one invited as the honored guest.[44] And among the personnel of the Court's staff, whose memory is longer than that of any other branch of the government, the name of Justice Miller is still happily recalled.

In October 1890 the Judge held his last circuit court at Saint Louis, and came on to Washington for the fall term. He went to visit the rooms of the Court and, returning, was seized with paralysis and collapsed in Thomas Circle, within sight of his home. Three days later, on October 13, he died. A few days more and Major Wright, the Marshal, recorded in a note to Judge Davis, the Reporter: "The Court has settled down to work with the judges in their new places, but though his place is not vacant, the strong and fine old man I liked so well is sadly missed. I don't know where there is another like him." [45]

[42] Letter of January 5, 1880.
[43] To William A. Maury; quoted in Maury's manuscript "Recollections."
[44] Conversation with Mrs. Clarkson.
[45] Letter of October 23, 1890; J. C. B. Davis Papers.

XVIII

THE REWARDS OF A LIFETIME

WE SEEK to remake the world after our own mental images. When a man is confident of his intellectual processes and ambitious to see his conclusions materialized he is impatient with narrow-visioned opposition. Such a man was Justice Miller. To bring about a right ordering of affairs amounted with him to a creative passion. The pattern he sought to establish has now been set out. He opposed that great extension of federal judicial protection to adventurers which made possible the "era of acquisition and enjoyment." He sought to perfect the administration of justice, and lost patience with the paucity of achievement. He set his face against making the Fourteenth Amendment the basis for a *Naturrecht*, but it was upon the dissenting opinions of Justice Field that their successors built. Miller had few of the philosophical resources of Justice Holmes, and found difficulty in adapting himself to frustration. His judgment was not wholly unaffected by disappointment, but the generosity and sanity of his nature saved him from crabbed pettiness.

Miller greatly desired that power of directing the work of the Court which would have come to him if Grant had appointed him to the chief justiceship. He was conscious that, to quote the contemporary opinion of a law journal, while "he had not the nominal honor . . . , it is probably the general opinion of the legal profession that he would have been the real chief in any court in which he might have sat." [1] Judge Dillon hailed him as "easily . . . the master of us all. His frame, features and majestic port duly put in marble

[1] 42 *Albany Law Journal* 321 (1890).

might stand for those of a Roman Caesar in Rome's best days; and Rome, so distinguished for its legal genius, never produced a jurisconsult more worthy of perpetual honor than . . . Justice Miller." "If during his twenty-eight years of service he had been the chief justice of the Supreme Court I verily believe his fame would have been second only to that of Marshall." [2]

When Justice Miller died it was generally remarked that the Court had lost the ablest of its members and the greatest figure in constitutional law since Marshall. "When the history of constitutional interpretation for the quarter of a century succeeding the rebellion comes to be written," said the *Springfield Republican,* "the most influential of all the minds engaged will probably be regarded as that of Samuel F. Miller." The reader can judge if, indeed, this is not so.

"It may perhaps be not too much to say that his strength of will gave him an undue influence in the deliberations of the court, and sometimes led the court into undoubted errors," ran the measured comment of the editor of the *American Law Review.*[3] "He would have had less influence in its deliberations if his strong will had not been accompanied with absolute and undoubted honesty. He was entirely frank and truthful. He hated all sham and subterfuge. He had nothing to conceal, either in public or private character. He acted according to his convictions without reference to how others thought or acted." Other law journals were less reserved in their acclaim.

In a day when public virtue was no commonplace, Miller remained poor, honest, unwarped in sympathy or intellect. He lived well as befitted his office, but his personal tastes were of the simplest. Congress, he felt, was generous in compensating the justices at $6000, presently $10,000, per annum.[4]

---

[2] These sentences are found in two typewritten addresses by Judge Dillon, in the archives of the Historical Department of Iowa. One, dated October 16, 1891, was to be read at memorial proceedings for Judge Love. The other was a response to be given at the annual dinner of the Iowa Society of New York, April 28, 1906, to the sentiment, "Early Iowa Lawyers and Judges."

[3] 24:997 (1890). *Cf.* 23:976 (1889).   [4] 18 *Albany Law Journal* 405.

In this he was speaking for himself. For when he had lost Judge Dillon as a colleague on the circuit, and then Judge McCrary, both of whom became counsel to railroad companies, he expressed his regret "that by a niggardly policy and insufficient salaries, the best offices of the country, especially its judicial offices, are abandoned for the pursuits of private life." [5] One Sunday morning Roscoe Conkling called by appointment on Judge Miller. At lunch the latter remarked that Conkling had brought him offers of four retainers at $25,000 each, to act as consulting attorney for certain New York firms, the employment leaving him free to represent any other interests not competing with his clients. The question instantly was, "Well, what did you say?" Mrs. Miller would have been well content to have so much larger an income. Miller's reply was that he had told Conkling that he supposed he must still be worth $10,000 to the government. He would not consent to Mrs. Miller's investing in property along Sixteenth Street lest it appreciate greatly and he be accused of speculation.[6] Whatever he had in his purse was available to all who had claims upon him.[7]

Miller felt disdain for some of the rich Westerners who came to Washington with nothing but money to commend them, showering expensive gifts on their friends and taking place only by virtue of wealth. He never liked to hear money praised.

In the personal relations of life he got on easily and with no false sense of dignity. He was "as ready to talk to a hod-carrier as to a cardinal." Full of reminiscence and an excellent raconteur, he was as welcome at an official dinner as he was at home at a frolic of the Gridiron Club. "Nor has there

---

[5] *Harper's Magazine*, July 1889.

[6] Conversation with Mrs. Clarkson, who spoke from personal recollection, September 19, 1935.

[7] He educated some of his nieces (conversation with Mrs. N. L. McBroom, a niece) and had two of his nephews living at his home, securing them positions in the government service while they attended law school. (*Cf.* letter in Gregory, *Miller*, p. 51.)

ever been a public man in Washington of a more cosmopolitan acquaintance or a more democratic disposition. The hack-drivers and street-car conductors all knew him as well as the Senators and members of the diplomatic corps, and he was able to greet many of them by name." [8]

For the greater part of his life after moving to Washington Miller's home was at 1415 Massachusetts Avenue, a large and shaded brick house, still standing, on the north side of the street, just west of Thomas Circle. There was an entrance on the ground floor where Miller had his office and library. The room was furnished with comfortable leather chairs and inviting sofas. On two sides of the room walnut bookcases rose to the ceiling. In the center stood Miller's large desk, covered with a disorderly mass of books and papers. Here he worked in the morning before court, and again in the evening. "When he gets at it he works like a well-fed, well-contented steam engine," wrote a reporter in a magazine article.[8a] "He works very rapidly and, as his opinions show, very clearly. He will often sit at his desk for four hours without rising, and when he is tired out he rests himself with a novel. Judge Miller has no fixed time for anything but his dinner. . . ." When he broke off at the end of the day he would go upstairs to spend some time with his family, playing a game of whist (of which he was extremely fond), or conversing while he had his evening refreshment of a glass of whisky and a plate of soda crackers. The Judge "dunked."

One of Miller's jests was that some day he was going to retire and write a novel about life in Washington. What transformations he had witnessed in the nation's life are suggested by the reflection that he was the first Supreme Court justice born west of the Appalachians as well as the first to be appointed from beyond the Mississippi. His own conscience free from self-reproach, he could recall complacently the varied scenes of his career: Richmond, where as a boy

[8] *Gate City*, October 12, 1890, quoting other papers.
[8a] *The Republic* (Washington), July 18, 1880, p. 341, one of a series of articles on "Celebrities at Home."

he had gone about crying "Hurrah for Henry Clay," a sentiment he supported throughout his life; Barbourville and the debating society, of whose active contributors there was "only [one] man who did not attain high distinction in public life"; [9] Keokuk and the people from about there who had become national figures — honest men like Caldwell and McCrary, others like Belknap, and the fabulous Mrs. George H. Williams — Kate Hughes of Keokuk, who at fourteen had run away to the first of her three marriages, and who was to end life in a religious fast, the priestess of a new sect.[10] Miller's memory was full of incident and color.

He retained his faith in the Republican Party and bore with its excesses long after it had ceased to be entirely worthy of his early characterization, a party "of national and patriotic aims, in which good men are combining without hope of office or pecuniary reward." [11] He was never devoid of political feeling. Blaine he regarded as the most like Henry Clay of any of the contemporary figures, and when the election of 1884 went to Grover Cleveland, Miller greeted the change with no enthusiasm, writing to Ballinger:

I have no interest in politics or in the change of administration. There is a dull feeling that I shall be relieved of the importunity of office seeking friends, and a belief that the country will not go to the dogs altogether, but no belief in the democratic party or a democratic administration as capable of governing the country well. It is not to be expected that a party composed of three fourths southern politicians who have learned nothing by misfortune will be impressed with the best feeling for a country of which they constitute so small a part, in numbers, in wealth, in energy as in experience in government.

If they will put you on our Bench I will forgive many shortcomings. We shall see.[12]

[9] "Under all the circumstances of its locality and the limited opportunity for acquiring information, and the little assistance any of us had from pecuniary fortune or personal aid from others I think the result is very remarkable" (Letter of May 30, 1885).

[10] The *Gate City*, April 20, 1894, gives her remarkable story.

[11] *Gate City*, June 17, 1856.

[12] Letter of January 18, 1885.

In December 1886 there appeared in the New York *World* a long interview in which Judge Miller talked somewhat freely of the political retrospect and remarked:

> I should like to have seen in my lifetime the election of a great political leader to the office of the presidency. I am sick and tired to death of the taking of characterless Tom Noddys simply because the politicians hate the leaders and cannot consent to see them win the great prize of politics.[13]

Looking back after fifty years Cleveland does not seem a Tom Noddy, while Blaine's attractiveness has pretty well evaporated.

Eventually the forces that had brought Justice Miller to power ran their course. Toward the end of his life new social problems were emerging on which he had no mandate. He regarded with mistrust the growth of a foreign-born population not accustomed to Anglo-Saxon traditions of government.[14] Nor did he have the basis of a sympathetic awareness of the needs and incidents of an urban civilization. In 1886 occurred the Haymarket riots, and manifestations such as these alarmed even the sturdiest minds on the Supreme Court. When Justice Bradley went on his circuit that September "he gave a forcible denunciation of anarchy and communism." [15] Miller too was affected, and when two years later he was invited to deliver the commencement address at Iowa City he chose as his subject "The Conflict in this Country between Socialism and Organized Society." [16] After some solid talk to the effect that what the sanguine call "progress" is not an inevitable cosmic trend, and a reference to the necessity of reckoning with the desire for personal distinction in any scheme of social organization, he launched into an alarming discourse wherein anarchists, nihilists, socialists,

---

[13] Sunday, December 12, 1886. Miller refers to the interview in a letter of February 13, 1887, evidently content with the way in which he had been quoted.

[14] New York *World*, as cited.

[15] At Scranton, September 6 (*New York Herald*, September 7, and *Newark Evening News*, September 16, 1886).

[16] Printed in Gregory, *Miller*, Appendix C.

communists, and single-taxers are banded together in indiscriminate condemnation. He warned the "virtuous population" of the Northwest against the foreign agitators who meet "at night and in secluded places" to plot the overthrow of the system of private property. He thought man essentially selfish: even the artist and the parson work for their monetary reward. One wonders how he would have reacted to legislation expressing the social aspirations of a new industrial order.

If one turns to the probate records of the District Court for the District of Columbia [17] he will find that Justice Miller died intestate; that his cash assets consisted of the proceeds from the sale of his law books and the balance due on his salary; that when current bills were met there was no balance remaining.[18] This is called to mind as a pointed refutation of the pessimism of his commencement address and of the thesis that only by unlimited monetary rewards can society get its work done. One recalls his twenty-eight years of unremitting toil, and his belief that "the few days left to me by nature are not worth coddling at the expense of public duty." [19] It serves as a datum to recall that wisdom and integrity may be joined to public power on terms of the highest advantage to society.

[17] No. 4135.
[18] It should be added that Miller's series of law-school lectures on the Constitution (which J. C. B. Davis was good enough to refurbish) brought $2000 from the publisher (Davis Papers, vol. XLVI). H. R. No. 12,469, a bill to pay one year's salary to the widow, never emerged from committee.
[19] Letter of June 29, 1879.

TABLE OF CASES CITED OR REFERRED TO
IN TEXT AND NOTES

(Page numbers in italics indicate a somewhat extended discussion)

[*433*]

TABLE OF CASES CITED

[434]

TABLE OF CASES CITED

TABLE OF CASES CITED

TABLE OF CASES CITED

[*437*]

TABLE OF CASES CITED

TABLE OF CASES CITED

[439]

TABLE OF CASES CITED

TABLE OF CASES CITED

INDEX

INDEX

INDEX

Diary and Letters of Rutherford Birchard Hayes, quoted, 101, 349, 369

Diary of Edward Bates 1859–1866, Howard K. Beale, ed., quoted, 44, 70, 87, 89, 99, 164, 177, 261, 394, 420; cited, 85, 115, 274

Diary of Gideon Welles, cited, 99; quoted, 100, 104, 177

Diary of James K. Polk, cited, 107

Diary of Orville Hickman Browning, quoted, 34, 94, 102, 112, 119, 131; referred to, 57, 134

Dickens, Charles, quoted, 234

Dickinson, John, Administrative Justice and the Supremacy of Law, cited, 204

Dillon, Judge John F., on railroad-aid bonds, 210–12; on Judge Wright, 216; and railroad receiverships, 238, 242, 243; urged for appointment to Supreme Court, 359–62; on the circuit with Miller, 374, 412, 413, 414, 415; on Miller, 425–26; leaves the bench, 427

Dillon, John F., The Law of Municipal Bonds, quoted, 211

Dillon, John F., Treatise on the Law of Municipal Corporations, quoted, 212

Dixon, Senator James, 192

Dixon, Chief Justice Luther S., in Kemp Case, 86; in bond cases, 216, 221

Dom Pedro, Emperor, 420

Doolittle, Senator James R., aspirant for judicial appointment, 44, 48

Douglas, Stephen A., 27, 35, 44, 54

Douglass, Frederick, 31

Dow, General Neal, sued for military seizure, 147

Drake, Senator Charles D., possible appointee to the Court, 345

Drummond, Judge Thomas, possible appointee to the Court, 44, 53, 54; in municipal bond case, 221

Durant, Thomas J., possible appointee to the Court, 338, 339, 342, 345

Dyer, Brainerd, Public Career of William M. Evarts, cited, 100

Eames, Charles, argues the Prize Cases, 89

Edmunds, Senator George F., opposed to confirming Williams, 261; presidential possibility, 305, 306; mentioned, 366; and Harlan's confirmation, 369; possible successor to Hunt, 377, 378

Eldon, Lord, on spendthrift trusts, 321

Electoral Commission, proceedings discussed, 280–92

Emancipation Proclamation, 58

Embry, James H., quoted, 63

Enster, T. F., Miller's partner, 21

Erskine, Judge John, possible appointee to the Court, 345

Evarts, Sherman, ed., Arguments and Speeches of William Maxwell Evarts, cited, 100

Evarts, William M., argues Prize Cases, 79; candidate for chief justiceship, 100; appointed Attorney General, 119; counsel before Electoral Commission, 288, 290; on selection of successor to Davis, 359; and the patronage, 365

Eve, Joseph, 7, 10

Ewing, Thomas, opposes appointment of Chase, 102; on Speed and Stanbery, 118

Ewing, Thomas, Jr., Miller on, 302

Fairman, Charles, The Law of Martial Rule, cited, 77, 96

Fessenden, William Pitt, 102

Field, David Dudley, labors for law reform, 23; argues Milligan Case, 94; described, 115; argues Cummings v. Missouri, 130, 134; argues McCardle Case, 141

Field, Justice Stephen J., appointment, 60; authority on mining law, 65; described, 110; referred to, 115, 141, 170, 174, 176, 200, 227, 230, 248, 254, 320, 351; discusses Test Oath Cases, 131; denies making disclosure, 133; delivers opinions in those cases, 135; on Confiscation Act, 146; opinion in Dow v. Johnson, 147; in Legal Tender Cases, 160, 173, 175; dissents in Slaughter-House Cases, 181, 185; opinion on railroad rate regulation, 202; his individualistic philosophy, 206; re-